If you have a home computer with internet access you may:
- -request an item be placed on hold
- -renew an item that is overdue
- -view titles and due dates checked out on your card
- -view your own outstanding fines

To view your patron record from your home computer:
Click on the NSPL homepage:
http://nspl.suffolk.lib.ny.us

North Shore Public Library

Barack Obama,
The Aloha Zen President

Barack Obama, The Aloha Zen President

HOW A SON OF THE 50TH STATE MAY REVITALIZE AMERICA BASED ON 12 MULTICULTURAL PRINCIPLES

Michael Haas, Editor

Foreword by Michael Dukakis

with the kōkua of Ibrahim Aoudé, Edward D. Beechert, Dan Boylan,
Nina K. Buchanan, A. Didrick Castberg, Helen Geracimos Chapin,
Robert A. Fox, Yasumasa Kuroda, Lāpaki, Rodney Morales,
and Anthony J. Palmer

 PRAEGER

AN IMPRINT OF ABC-CLIO, LLC
Santa Barbara, California • Denver, Colorado • Oxford, England

Copyright 2011 by ABC-CLIO, LLC

Library of Congress Cataloging-in-Publication Data

Barack Obama, the aloha zen president : how a son of the 50th state may revitalize America
based on 12 multicultural principles / Michael Haas, editor.
    p. cm.
  Includes bibliographical references and index.
  ISBN 978-0-313-39402-7 (hard copy : alk. paper)—ISBN 978-0-313-39403-4 (e-book)
1. Multiculturalism—United States. 2. Cultural pluralism—United States. 3. Obama, Barack.
I. Haas, Michael, 1938–

  HN90.M84B37   2011
  305.800973—dc22   2010035771

ISBN: 978-0-313-39402-7
EISBN: 978-0-313-39403-4

15 14 13 12 11   1 2 3 4 5

This book is also available on the World Wide Web as an eBook.
Visit www.abc-clio.com for details.

Praeger
An Imprint of ABC-CLIO, LLC

ABC-CLIO, LLC
130 Cremona Drive, P.O. Box 1911
Santa Barbara, California 93116-1911

This book is printed on acid-free paper ∞

Manufactured in the United States of America

Dedicated to

Ponciano S. Amodo
Henry Y. T. Au
Stanley Mark Castillo
Mel Cummings
Johnny Fung
Reginald K. Holbron
Toney James
Miguel Mattos
David Nonesa
Peter Patrick Resurrection
Young Eun So
Julius Yamamura
and
Doo Sun Yoo

President Obama has brought a more relaxed sensibility to his public appearances, an Aloha Zen, a comfortable calm that reflects a man who seems easy going, not so full of himself.
—Professor David Gergen, Harvard University

When you come from Hawaii, you start understanding that what's on the surface, what people look like, that doesn't determine who they are. And that the power and strength of diversity, the ability of people from everywhere, whether they're black or white, whether they're Japanese-American or Korean-American or Filipino-American or whatever they are, they are just Americans, that all of us can work together and all of us can join together to create a better country. It's that spirit, that I'm absolutely convinced, is what America is looking for right now.
—Barack Obama

If you really want to understand who Barack Obama is, you have to understand the culture of inclusivity. You need to go to Hawaii.
—Kathleen Hall Jamieson, University of Pennsylvania

You do not understand Barack Obama until you understand Hawaii.
—Michelle Obama

Contents

List of Tables

Foreword

Back in the winter of 1991 my wife Kitty and I had the rare good fortune to spend most of the spring semester at the University of Hawai'i.

Both of us had been there only a few times before—she campaigning for me for the presidency, and both of us when I spoke to the Hawai'i chapter of the American Civil Liberties annual meeting the previous year. But I saw something as we approached the hotel for the ACLU event that I had never seen before in my then 57 years—one after another interracial couple arriving for a senior high school prom at the hotel.

And nobody was making a fuss about it. These kids, attired in their prom best, were going to their prom with people of other ethnic and racial backgrounds, and they were doing it as if it was the most natural thing in the world. Needless to say, in the rest of the continental United States it was not the most natural thing in the world. Quite the contrary. It would have provoked a lot of comments and at least some not-so-quiet disapproval.

I've never forgotten it.

So it was not a surprise when I arrived at the UH campus in early March to teach public policy to undergraduates and to co-teach a seminar on health policy to graduate students that included six public events in and around Honolulu on the subject of national health care reform and the development of a plan for national and universal health care that was based on what Hawai'i, alone among the states, had been doing for the previous 15 years.

I might add, parenthetically, that that plan could have been the model for a national health care reform bill in the Clinton administration, but although I discussed it at length with President and Mrs. Clinton, I could never persuade them that a simple national version of Hawai'i's health plan was the way to go. Their plan proved to be far more complex and, ultimately, unable to command a Congressional majority despite their impressive efforts to win support for their proposed legislation. I have often wondered if a much-less-complicated plan for universal health care anchored in Hawai'i's experience might not have fared better in the 1993–1994 Congress and given us truly universal health care long before the Obama administration, but it wasn't to be.

Both of these experiences, in addition to all the other things that we did in Hawai'i in the spring of 1991, left an indelible impression on me about a state and a culture that, in many ways, differs significantly from what we have on the Mainland and, as this book so clearly points out, had an indelible impression on another American politician—Barack Obama.

Why is it that Hawai'i is so unique among the American states in accepting diversity as a matter of course and celebrating it? Why was it that those kids in Hawai'i seemed so unselfconscious about the fact that they were going to their senior prom with a group of young people who reflected an extraordinary array of ethnic and racial backgrounds— and, by the way, were beautiful? And how is it that long before my own state, inspired by the Hawai'i's example, passed legislation creating a near-universal health plan, Hawai'i had done so on its own even though Congress had failed in the early 1970s to do what Richard Nixon, of all people, was urging it to do in extending the guarantee of comprehensive health care to all Americans?

As this book makes clear, there is something very different about the Fiftieth State, and it undoubtedly had a profound impact on our president. That doesn't mean that racial bias is nonexistent in Hawai'i or that he didn't encounter some of it. But I have no doubt that growing up in Hawai'i had much to do with his remarkable ability to think, to listen, and to then build consensus among a lot of folks who often don't agree with each other.

Even the Aloha spirit, however, appears to be incapable of building consensus in the current Congress, especially as the minority party has effectively turned the Senate filibuster into a virtually unbreakable super majority. There is no warrant for any such supermajority in the Constitution. That document is very explicit about when and where supermajorities are required, and they number just five: impeaching the president; removing a Congressional member; approving a Constitutional amendment; ratifying a treaty; and overriding a presidential veto.

Unless, therefore, the president and fair-minded people on both sides of the aisle take on the filibuster and modify it so that, after reasonable debate, a simple majority can pass a bill, no amount of the Aloha Spirit is going to end a system in which consensus is virtually impossible because a mere 41 Senators can stop 59 from acting.

And yet despite his difficulties, the president has brought a very different approach to the White House from what we observed under his predecessor. It involves a lot of listening, much deliberation, bringing together a wide range of people and constituencies, respecting your opponents—at least until they make it clear that they have no interest in working with you—and trying to make decisions that make sense for the American people. And that is true of the way he tries to conduct foreign as well as domestic policy.

Time will tell if the American people will support the president's leadership style. Foreign wars, economic crises, Gulf oil spills, and 24/7 cable news are not the kinds of things that have contributed to the evolution of the Aloha Spirit. And yet, deep down, I think most Americans would prefer that kind of leadership to what we experienced during the eight years preceding Mr. Obama's presidency.

Enjoy this book. It is a window on a culture and political environment that most Americans have never experienced. Fortunately, our president has, and he—and we—are the better for it.

Michael Dukakis

Preface

Much has changed in Hawai'i during the 21st century. Perhaps the most significant change is the political rise of Honolulu-born Barack Obama from Illinois State Senator to United States Senator to President of the United States. The impact of his experiences outside the United States Mainland during the first 18 years of his life needs to be better understood in order to fathom his unique approach to governance. His presidential style has baffled many observers because they are unaware that the Aloha State, where he grew up, has a culture so different from the other 49 states that they would experience culture shock if they moved to the Islands.

Insofar as Obama brings the values of Hawai'i to the country and the world, he can effect a cultural transformation from conflictual to cooperative modes of human interaction, from hyperindividualism to communitarianism. But without a broader understanding of the multicultural realities of the Aloha State, he may not succeed in that transformation. As his spouse, Michelle, has said, "You can't really understand Barack until you understand Hawai'i."

Although the connection between Barack Obama's life in Hawai'i and his demeanor and philosophy seem obvious to those who live and have lived in the Aloha State, the rest of the country has no idea what those experiences and values are because he has never stated them clearly enough for journalists and pundits to grasp. Those who write in this book recognize them, but most Mainland Americans see Hawai'i only

as a tourist destination and are rarely interested in the multiculturalism
that pervades the Fiftieth State.

Indeed, comparisons in Mainland publications between cities, states,
and universities about ethnic diversity seldom include statistics about
Hawai'i, Honolulu, or the University of Hawai'i. I have written several
letters to the editor of the *Los Angeles Times* and other publications
when such omissions have occurred in their pages, but their editorial
offices have consistently responded by failing to print information deliberately left out, and reporters have continued as before. That neglect
perhaps will end now that Barack Obama has put the Fiftieth State on
the map.

Accordingly, a new edition of my edited book *Multicultural Hawai'i*,
which was published more than a decade ago, seems essential and timely.
Instead of a quotidian second edition, my contributors and I have herein
condensed what was written previously, focused more on the 1960s and
1970s when Obama lived in the Aloha State, provided updates, rewrote
many passages, and minimized arcane technical matters. The biography
is unauthorized, as in vain I tried to route questions through several persons close to the president.

There is another special need. Pundits, commenting on the rise of
Barack Obama's candidacy as a sign that America may have entered
a "post-racial" era, clearly were trying to find a way to explain why a
Black politician appealed to so many White voters. Some Black observers
even hesitated to call him authentically "African American." Few op-eds
written on the Mainland have referred to his multicultural background
in Hawai'i. Clearly, they lack relevant experience and knowledge. From
the time of the first mention of the term "post-racial", I began to write
op-ed essays for publication in various periodicals, and transmit e-mails
to various television programs' websites and commentators, pointing
out in some specificity that Barack Obama's demeanor, philosophy, and
temperament are rooted in values that were ingrained in him before he
decided to try his luck on the American Mainland. My efforts, univer-
sally received without acknowledgment, further underscore the need for
this book because they profoundly testify to the smug self-confidence
among the punditocracy that there is nothing special that anyone from
Hawai'i can bring to American politics despite the resonance of his message of Aloha with millions of voters who hope for a profound change
in the political culture of the country, if not the world.

The unwillingness of his biographers to discuss Obama's philosophy
and values in depth may be understandable, as his *Dreams from My*

Father has said so quite eloquently. But the utter poverty of interest in Obama's political theory in the chattering class is a silent repudiation of his main purpose in running for office, a rejection of the reason why millions supported him, thereby enabling irresponsible critics to hurl inappropriate epithets without fear that they will be called out. This volume, in contrast, is a book about ideas, possibilities, and a reality in the Fiftieth State that challenges the broken political system that has prevailed in Washington for far too long.

For the present volume, I have solicited new chapter authors for fresh perspectives. I consider all contributors to be, in effect, coauthors for their kōkua (assistance). The term "multicultural" was left largely undefined in *Multicultural Hawai'i* so that readers would grasp multicultural Hawai'i empirically without polemical labels. In light of Barack Obama's arrival in Washington as president, this book positions the culture of the Islands within the context of an ongoing debate about the pros and cons of multiculturalism.

As before, I am the principal author of Chapter 1, which provides a minibiography of Barack Obama and then identifies 12 principles of the multicultural ethos that I discovered while living most of my adult life in the Aloha State. When I arrived in Honolulu during 1964 at the age of 26, I conducted myself as perhaps a typical young American college professor. I was judged by values from Native Hawaiian and Japanese cultural traditions, an unexpected if ultimately pleasant culture shock. Barack Obama was only three when I arrived, and I never met him by the time he left for college in 1979. Had he attended the University of Hawai'i, he would certainly have taken my political science course "Race & Politics." If he read the newspapers carefully during the 1970s, he would have known that I was raising issues of civil rights for Filipinos that were embarrassing to the political establishment.

In the 1990s, I began to formulate principles of Hawai'i's multicultural ethos and presented them at academic conferences to some acclaim, but they did not appear in the first edition of *Multicultural Hawai'i*. I developed the 12 principles independently of Pilahi Paki, whose fivefold definition of Aloha was presented at the Governor's Conference on the Year 2000 and was later embedded in the Aloha Spirit Law (see Appendix).

I became more convinced of my formulation after retiring to Los Angeles in 1998, when I again experienced culture shock, finding the Mainland to be much less hospitable than before. I now have had a special responsibility—to spread Aloha. In part because my father's remains are at Punchbowl Cemetery, my heart will always remain in Hawai'i.

I am again the author of Chapter 2, which I have updated with particular attention to the sovereignty movement of Native Hawaiians. Most readers unacquainted with the history of Hawai'i will be shocked on learning how the indigenous people have been mistreated for over a century. Although recent developments suggest that Native Hawaiians are closer to receiving some sort of reparations, I hope to convey admiration for their patience amid the seemingly endless wrangling over details, a testament to the Spirit of Aloha.

Yas Kuroda remains the principal author of Chapter 3. The pseudonymous Lāpaki is responsible for Chapter 4, working from the earlier version by Derek Bickerton. Due to her unfortunate health situation, I revised Helen Chapin's Chapter 5, since there have been changes in the media over the past decade. In Chapter 6, talented fiction writer Rodney Morales extends his previous essay with customary fascinating prose, adding commentary about Obama. Tony Palmer's Chapter 7 has become more chronological. Dan Boylan corrects and provides color to Chapter 8, improving upon what I wrote previously. Ed Beechert solidly updates his Chapter 9. I have entirely rewritten Chapter 10, including census data for the year 2000. Nina K. Buchanan and Robert A. Fox make important new contributions to Chapter 11, which are incorporated into the previous text. In revising my essay in Chapter 12, I incorporate insightful paragraphs by Dan Boylan. Rick Castberg's new research augments his Chapter 13. Ibrahim Aoudé's Chapter 14 provides an important new context for mobilization movements. Chapter 15, which I wrote, is entirely new.

I am following several unusual editorial conventions. One is to capitalize certain words. Usually terms referring to skin pigmentation are identified as "black" or "white." However, they also can refer to ethnicity or race. Accordingly, I capitalize "Black" and "White" to make clear when I am referring to ethnicity or race and not just color. To employ some literary variety, I will sometimes refer to African Americans as Blacks, and Caucasians will be referred to as Whites or as "Haoles."

In keeping with the convention of Bernhard Hormann, I capitalize the Hawaiian word "Haole." Lexically, the word means foreigner, outsider, or more literally "without breath," and was applied to Caucasians because they were the first non-Hawaiian ethnic group to settle in the Islands. But descendants of the original settlers in the present day are hardly foreigners. A second meaning, popularized by Native Hawaiians objecting to their mistreatment since the Kingdom of Hawai'i was deposed, is that Haoles are the historic bad guys. Accordingly, I distinguish between

Haoles who dominated politics and tried to monoculturalize the Islands from Caucasians or Whites who came later, many of whom have accepted the multicultural reality in the Islands.

I do not italicize Hawaiian words because they are part of the everyday vocabulary in the Islands. Newspapers do not italicize Hawaiian words, so I follow suit.

Another term is spelled unusually. There are many mainlands throughout the world, but I refer to "the Mainland" as the contiguous continental 48 states of the United States plus Alaska, just as I sometimes refer to Hawai'i as "the Islands."

In addition, I have elevated the Hawaiian word "Aloha" to a proper noun. Why? Because the word means something more than just "hello" but rather incorporates a variety of ideas, if not a philosophy. Those who have not lived in Hawai'i might find my editorial orthography a bit eccentric, but residents of the Aloha State fully understand the need to convey special meaning, even if subliminally.

Finally, italics are used to highlight quotes from Barack Obama.

Special acknowledgment should be given to several University of Hawai'i colleagues who have been helpful in preparing the manuscript—professors Alice Dewey, Susan Hippensteele, Neil Milner, Karl Minke, Kent Sakoda, and Jon Van Dyke; Lesbian, Gay, Bisexual, Transgender, and Intersex Student Services Coordinator Camaron Miyamoto; former ethnic studies professor Kathryn Takara; affirmative action officer Mie Watanabe; and Joan Hori and Dore Minatodani, reference librarians at Hamilton Library's Hawaiian Collection.

Among government agency officials, I have received data and documents thanks to Marcella Jones of the Bureau of the Census, Kris Kasianovitz of the UCLA Library, Shirley Oliver of the U.S. Department of Education's Office for Civil Rights, Angelica Trevino of the Los Angeles office for the U.S. Commission on Civil Rights, librarians at the Hawai'i State Library and the Legislative Reference Library in Honolulu, Bryan Mick of Honolulu's Neighborhood Commission Office, as well as David Grinberg and Linda Reed of the U.S. Equal Employment Opportunity Commission. The Hawai'i Department of Health also provided useful information.

In addition, I have received kōkua from my former students Keiko Hirata and the late Vincent Pollard, actress Nichelle Nichols, my good friend Reverend Jack Isbell, and the health benefits office of Bank of Hawaii. Biographers, who have provided corroborating information, should be congratulated as well, particularly Jonathan Alter and David

Remnick. I am also grateful to David Gergen, adviser to many presidents and now of Harvard University, who graciously agreed to allow me to use his phrase "Aloha Zen" in the title of the book.

For Chapter 5, I want to thank several media sources, who responded to telephone inquiries so that I could update information from the original chapter by Helen Chapin. Chris Conyebeare of the Media Council Hawai'i and Barry Rivers of the Maui International Film Festival also supplied valuable information.

Rodney Morales consulted several writers on his draft of Chapter 6. He wants to acknowledge assistance in reviewing his manuscript by Eric Chock, Keala Francis, Dennis Kawaharada, Terrilee Keko'olani, John Rosa, and Susan Schultz.

Among those consulted by Anthony Palmer for Chapter 7 are John Starr Alexander ('Iolani School), Mary Jo Freshley (Halla Huhm Studio), Bill Feltz (East-West Center), Aaron Mahi, Lynn J. Martin (State Foundation on Culture and the Arts), Delsa S. Moe (Sterling Scholar Awards), the Office of Hawaiian Affairs, Roy Sakuma Studios, Wendy Schofield-Ching (Native Winds), Tani and others at Punahou School, Cathy Temanaha (professional dancer), and several faculty members from UHM—Peter Coraggio, Jane Freeman Moulin, Sharon Pressburg, Victoria Takamine, Carolyn Leslie Wright, and Noenoelani Zuttermeister.

For Chapter 8, thanks should be extended to Survey Marketing Associates for voting data. Some statistical work was ably performed by Atsuko Sato, another former student of mine. I am grateful for information on the ethnic background of legislators from Abraham Pi'ianai'a, Morris Takushi, and Dwayne Yoshina. Coauthor Dan Boylan has also provided valuable information based on his interviews with journalist Richard Borreca, former governor Ben Cayetano, political strategists Lloyd Nekoba and Andy Winer, and State Representative Roy Takumi.

Special thanks must be extended to Robert Hutchinson, former senior editor at Praeger Publications. His invaluable shepherding from proposal to contract is much appreciated.

I am dedicating the book, written as it is by so many fine scholars of Hawai'i, to those with whom I shared my life as roommates, tenants, or partners during my residence in Honolulu—two Chinese from Hong Kong, a Japanese, a Filipino-Japanese, two mixed Native Hawaiians, a Black Cuban, three Filipino Americans, two Korean Americans, and one Navajo. I remember them fondly as among those who helped to multiculturalize me when I returned home after enjoying days of teaching on the multiethnic campus of the University of Hawai'i, whose students are among the very best and brightest in the world precisely because their sophistication is rooted in the multicultural reality of the Aloha State.

Aloha,
Michael Haas

(*Source*: Factcheck.org [http://www.factcheck.org/UploadedFiles/birth
_certificate_2.jpg])

Chapter 1

Multicultural Barack Obama

Michael Haas

> *I was raised as an Indonesian child and a Hawaiian child and*
> *as a [B]lack child and as a [W]hite child. And so what I ben-*
> *efit from is a multiplicity of cultures that all fed me.*
> (Mendell 2007:32)

What are President Barack Obama's values, his philosophy? What is model of the ideal society? What explains his placid personality?

To understand the revitalization that Obama desires for America and how he attracts such enthusiastic support from millions in the United States and the world, a central fact is that Barack Obama is America's first multicultural president. With relatives on four continents (Africa, Asia, Europe, North America) and the mid-Pacific, he embodies globalization as no president before. Rather than a simple-minded, monocultural outlook, the 6' 2" man from Honolulu brings to the White House a multiplicity of cultural sensitivities and the ability to speak at least four languages (English, Hawai'i Creole, Indonesian, Luo). Indeed, Obama likens his family reunions to a meeting of the United Nations. While journalists trumpet him as "the first African American president," and he has affirmed the same for many years (Fletcher 2009a), he brings to the presidency far more diversity. He is much more than a biracial or even bicultural president (cf. Arcanya 2008). He is the first intellectual, multilingual president who has lived for a time outside the United States since Thomas Jefferson.

Obama's self-described journey has been that of a joyful wanderer. The complexities he experienced during the first 18 years of his life, mostly outside the United States Mainland, were challenges. So were his later years until he settled down, making Chicago his home and Michelle Robinson his wife. It is the task of this chapter to reveal that quest by first presenting facts of his diversity, the meaning of multiculturalism in the land of Aloha, and the enduring values to which he was exposed in the process of self-discovery.

BARACK OBAMA'S MULTICULTURAL BACKGROUND

Similar to more than half the marriages of local residents in contemporary Hawai'i (Table 1.1), Barack Hussein Obama II was the product of mixed-race parents. On August 4, 1961, he was born in Kapi'olani Center for Women and Children, Honolulu. While a boy, his father called him "Barry," his mother sometimes referred to him as "Bar," and

Table 1.1
Interracial Marriages in Hawai'i, 1912–2005 (in percent)

Years	Interracial Marriages
1912–1916	11.5%
1920–1924	18.0
1930–1934	21.6
1940	25.0
1950	29.7
1960	37.3
1970	33.7
1980	37.6
1990	45.2
2000	54.6
2005	53.1
2007	55.0

Note: Figures do not include Filipinos and Mexicans, who are often mixed-race mestizos before arriving in Hawai'i. Including them would increase figures by at least 10 percent in later decades.

Sources: Schmitt (1965); Hawai'i (1970b:Table 5.2; 1980b:Table 5.9; 1990:Table 8.3; 2000:78; 2005:79); *Honolulu Advertiser* (2010).

his grandma used "Bear" (Maraniss 2008; Heilemann and Halperin 2010:425). In Indonesia, he was called "Beri" (Remnick 2010:103).

Obama's parents met while students at the University of Hawai'i during 1960. His father, from Kenya of the Luo ethnic group, enrolled in 1959 as the first African student in Hawai'i.

His mother, Stanley Ann Dunham, was the daughter of two White parents who had married in Kansas during 1941 and later lived in the states of California, Oklahoma, Texas, and Washington before moving to Honolulu. Her parents, Madelyn and Stanley Dunham, passed on their Dutch, English, French, German, Irish, Welsh, and Cherokee ancestries (Caplan and Dell 2008; Hammons 2008). Genealogists believe that Barack has royal blood from William I of Scotland and Henry II of England. His distant cousins include seven American presidents (both George Bushes, Jimmy Carter, Lyndon Johnson, James Madison, Harry Truman, and Woodrow Wilson) and former British Prime Minister Winston Churchill (Morton 2008). One of his mother's forebears was a slaveowner.

Stanley Dunham moved his family to Honolulu in pursuit of economic opportunities in 1960, the year after Hawai'i became the Fiftieth State. Their daughter, previously accepted for admission to the University of Chicago, instead enrolled as a freshman at the main campus of the University of Hawai'i in Mānoa Valley (UHM), where she first decided to call herself Ann.

At the age of 18, Ann met 23-year-old Barack Hussein Obama (Senior) in a Russian class. They courted, he met her parents, she became pregnant, and he proposed marriage. Although her American parents accepted the marriage with quiet misgivings, Obama's father in Kenya did not approve (Obama 1995:125–126). But love prevailed, and they honeymooned on Maui on February 2, 1961. Ann did not know that the Kenyan's first wife had granted him consent to marry again, as Barack told Ann that he was divorced.

The film *Guess Who's Coming to Dinner* (1967) portrays a Black-White couple who meet in Honolulu. The Black man, while attending a medical convention, meets a White tourist. They fall in love and fly to San Francisco, where he meets her parents. The Black man insists they will only marry if her mother and father give approval, which is granted after much discussion. The president's parents met and married under somewhat similar circumstances, though seven years before that classic film premiered. The movie was released during the same year when the U.S. Supreme Court in *Loving v Virginia* (388US1) ruled that marriage is such a fundamental right that no state could prevent two otherwise qualified persons from marrying because of differing racial backgrounds. Of course, no such barrier ever existed in Hawai'i.

Upon graduation in economics in 1962, Barack Senior left Honolulu for graduate studies at Harvard University. Ann and Barry went to Cambridge later in 1962, but Barry's father claimed that his scholarship was insufficient to support them. Ann then took Barry to Seattle, where she enrolled at the University of Washington, but dropped out in 1963 and returned with Barry to be with her parents in Honolulu (Martin 2008). Ann reenrolled at UHM during the summer of 1963 and filed for divorce in January 1964 (Corsi 2009).

Barack Senior, meanwhile, married another Caucasian woman in Massachusetts during 1965, sired two children, but later divorced and married again in Kenya. Since his father had four wives in all, the future president had plenty of relatives to meet some day in Africa.

In 1966, Ann Dunham married another UHM student, Lolo Soetero, who was from Jakarta. In 1967, after a coup, male Indonesian students abroad were ordered home for conscription into the army to fight insurgents, so Soetero went quickly while Ann completed her baccalaureate degree in anthropology at UHM and Barry entered kindergarten at Noelani Elementary in Honolulu. The following year, when Soetero was a civilian again, Ann took Barry to live with her second husband in Jakarta, stopping off in Japan for three days en route. His half-sister Maya, born in Jakarta during 1970, was named after African American poet Maya Angelou.

Barry's experiences in Indonesia included enrollment in the first grade at Besuki Public School and, after the family moved to a better neighborhood, to St. Francis of Assisi School for grades 1–4. At both schools, his nonreligious stepfather listed him as a "Muslim," thereby creating confusion when school records were uncovered by campaign strategists during Barack's presidential campaign. In fact, he took two required hours of instruction in Islam weekly (Davis 2008:24). While learning to speak Indonesian at school and at play, Barry became acculturated. His stepfather told him how Indonesians mistreated other Indonesians, how corruption thwarted opportunity, and at school he even was exposed to political indoctrination classes (Bayuni 2009). Later, he said that his understanding about life was *"permanently altered"* by the experience in Indonesia (Glauberman and Burris 2008:51–55). After being roughed up by Jakarta playmates, his stepfather taught him how to defend himself, from which he developed a certain toughness that would later prove useful in dealing with discrimination as well as in his political career.

Each day, Barry's mother woke him up early in the morning to homeschool him in English and other subjects. Ultimately, she decided that he would be better off advancing his education in Honolulu. Flying with him to Honolulu in 1970, she asked her father if he could secure admission for Barry at Punahou, reputedly the top prep school in the state. Thanks to assistance from Stanley's boss, Barry was accepted into grade 5 for the fall of 1971 and then lived with her parents, nicknamed Gramps and Toot ("tūtū" is short for "grandmother" in Hawaiian). Obama went back to Indonesia at least three times to visit his mom, who in turn flew to be with him in Honolulu whenever she was between jobs in Jakarta or on holidays.

In late 1971, Barry's birthfather suddenly returned to Honolulu to be with him for a few weeks. On one occasion, he insisted that his son should be studying rather than watching television. His mom was already in town for the holidays with Maya, but both went back to Indonesia after the holidays. Barack Senior gave Barry a special present—a basketball. Therein began his fascination with basketball that later involved the dream of becoming a basketball star. Father and son saw never each other again.

After separating from Soetero in 1972, Ann returned to Honolulu with Maya and enrolled as a graduate student in anthropology at UHM. Ann, Barry, and Maya then lived together for the next four years. That summer, Ann took them on a trip to familiarize them with Chicago, Los Angeles, Seattle, and other parts of the Mainland United States.

In 1976, Ann went to Jogjakarta, Indonesia, with Maya in order to complete field work for her master's degree. While there, she was a consultant to the U.S. Agency for International Development, the Ford Foundation, and the Bank of Indonesia. In the latter role, she facilitated microloans for rural women to operate businesses.

Barry stayed on in Honolulu, turning down Ann's invitation to return to live in Indonesia, though Ann visited Barry each year for the holidays until he graduated in 1979 (Scott 2008a). In 1980, she divorced Soetero, who died in 1987.

After graduation, Obama enrolled at Occidental College in Los Angeles. Calling himself Barack for the first time during his sophomore year, he met diverse students and traveled with some of them to México and as far north as Oregon (Wolffe 2009:238). He was challenged in political science courses and crafted an impressive albeit short speech at an anti-apartheid rally.

In those days, Occidental had a program that enabled its students to transfer to Columbia University with relative ease. Obama and a classmate decided to do so in 1981, but beforehand he went to see his mother in Indonesia and Pakistan. While in New York, he buckled down in his studies and graduated in political science in 1983, the same year his mother received an MA in anthropology at UHM.

During 1983–1984, Obama worked for Business International Corporation to provide analyses of investment prospects in Third World countries, a job that he described in a letter to his mother as *"working for the enemy"* (Remnick 2010:119). In 1984, she and his half-sister Maya returned to Honolulu. In 1985, he got a temporary job as a community organizer out of the Harlem Campus of the City University of New York. He so enjoyed his work in Harlem that in 1985 he applied to become a community organizer in Chicago because he *"wanted to make an impact on the world"* (Obama 2010b). He told his future boss that one interest in the position was that he wanted to get material to write a novel, and indeed he later wrote several unpublished short stories based on his experiences.

In Chicago, the son of agnostic parents eventually became a Christian and, for the first time in his peregrinations, felt he had found home, albeit in a Black-and-White environment unlike diverse Honolulu where everyone is *"different looking"* (Draper 2009). His sister visited him in Chicago, where he helped her get her first job, took her to cultural events, and enrolled her in art classes at the Chicago Art Institute (Coleman 2008).

In 1988, he was admitted to Harvard Law School. In the summer before matriculating, Barack went to Europe for three weeks and to Kenya for five weeks, his first trip to his father's homeland. He also visited his mother in Pakistan, and en route toured Bangladesh and India (Wolffe 2009:238). Later that year, his mother and half-sister Maya were in New York (Watanabe 2010), where she had business connected with her work in Asia.

Obama graduated in 1991 as president of the *Harvard Law Review* and took a position in a Chicago law firm. Having met his future wife, Michelle Robinson, during a summer internship in 1989, he dated her and proposed in 1991. After they briefly visited his family in Kenya, they married in 1992. Obama began to teach part-time at the University of Chicago Law School the following year. Their two daughters, Malia Ann and Sasha, were born in 1998 and 2001, respectively. (In Hawaiian, "malia" means "calm" though also a translation of Mary or María, whereas Sasha is a Russian name, short for Alexandra.)

Meanwhile, in 1992, Obama's mother completed her doctorate in anthropology. She worked on a project at Women's World Banking in New York in 1992–1993 and then returned to Indonesia. In 1994, stricken with cancer, she flew to Honolulu. Barack saw her for the last time in a hospital bed but was not present when she died in 1995 (Scott 2008b). Barack's White grandfather had already died in 1992. His White grandmother passed away on the eve of his election to the presidency.

In 1996, Obama's political career began when he was elected to the Illinois State Senate. He served in that capacity until 2004, when he was elected U.S. Senator from Illinois.

In 2003, Barack Obama's half-sister Maya became Maya Soetoro-Ng when she married Konrad Ng, a part-time UHM professor of Chinese ancestry who was born in Canada of parents from Malaysia and later become an American citizen. Their hapa (mixed-race) daughter Suhaila was born in Honolulu during 2005. Maya, a Buddhist, also teaches at UHM.

BARACK OBAMA'S MULTICULTURAL SELF-DISCOVERY

In 1995, Barack Obama published an autobiography, *Dreams from My Father: A Story of Race and Inheritance*, in which he reflects on his early life as a quest for identity. The narrative starts with his life in Honolulu and Jakarta and continues with his experiences in Los Angeles, New York, Chicago, and his sentimental trip to Kenya in 1988.

In Hawai'i, African Americans constitute only 2 percent of the population (Table 1.2), many of whom are stationed on military bases outside town (cf. Jackson 2004). Because Barry's appearance is mulatto and he was often mistaken for Mexican or Puerto Rican, his skin color blended into the mainstream of Honolulu, where those with light skin are easily tanned by the strong rays of the sun and mixtures are the norm.

Barack grew up believing initially that his racial ancestry was unremarkable, later recalling "*That my father looked nothing like the people around me—that he was [B]lack as pitch, my mother [W]hite as milk— barely registered in my mind*" (Obama 1995:9–10). But he saw his father only as an infant and briefly when he was 10. As a child, he lived with a mother who perceived her background as multiracial, evidently because of Native American ancestry from one of her two otherwise Caucasian-appearing grandparents.

While in Indonesia, he encountered both poor and rich Indonesians. Teased by playmates as "Negro," on one occasion he was tied

Table 1.2

Population of Hawai'i by Major Ethnic Group, 1778–2000 (horizontal percentages are in parenthesies)

Year	Total	Hawaiian	White	Chinese	Japanese	Black	Filipino	Mexican	Korean	Puerto Rican	Samoan	Vietnamese	Guamanian
1778	300	**300 (100)**		–			– (–)	– (–)					
1853	73	**71 (97)**	2 (2)	1 (1)			na	na					
1860	70	**67 (96)**	2 (3)	1 (1)			na	na					
1866	63	**59 (93)**	2 (4)	2 (2)			na	na					
1872	57	**52 (91)**	3 (5)	2 (4)			na	na					
1878	58	**48 (82)**	4 (7)	6 (10)			na	na					
1884	81	**44 (55)**	17 (21)	18 (23)	– (–)		na	na					
1890	90	**41 (45)**	19 (21)	17 (19)	13 (14)		na	na					
1896	109	**40 (36)**	22 (21)	22 (20)	24 (22)		na	na					
1900	154	38 (24)	29 (19)	26 (17)	**61 (40)**	– (–)	na	na	– (–)	5 (3)			
1910	192	39 (20)	44 (23)	22 (11)	**80 (42)**	1 (–)	2 (1)	na	5 (2)	6 (2)			
1920	256	42 (16)	55 (21)	24 (9)	**109 (43)**	– (–)	21 (8)	na	5 (2)	7 (2)			
1930	368	51 (14)	80 (22)	27 (7)	**140 (38)**	1 (–)	63 (17)	na	6 (2)	8 (2)			
1940	423	64 (15)	112 (27)	29 (7)	**158 (37)**	– (–)	53 (12)	na	7 (2)	10 (2)			
1950	500	86 (17)	124 (25)	33 (7)	**185 (37)**	3 (1)	61 (12)	na	7 (1)	8 (1)			
1960	633	102 (16)	202 (32)	38 (6)	**203 (32)**	5 (1)	69 (11)	na	na	8 (1)			
1970	774	133 (17)	**255 (33)**	52 (4)	207 (27)	8 (1)	95 (12)	2 (1)	7 (1)	10 (1)			
1980	930	175 (19)	**245 (26)**	56 (5)	218 (24)	17 (1)	134 (14)	9 (1)	11 (2)	20 (2)	11 (1)	3 (–)	2 (–)
1990	1108	205 (19)	**263 (24)**	51 (5)	222 (24)	27 (2)	168 (15)	14 (1)	12 (1)	25 (2)	15 (1)	5 (1)	2 (–)
2000	1212	240 (20)	**294 (24)**	57 (5)	202 (17)	22 (2)	171 (14)	20 (2)	24 (2)	30 (2)	16 (1)	8 (1)	7 (1)

Key: na = Figures not available.

   – = less than 1,000 or less than 1 percent.

   (–) = less than 1 percent.

Notes: Figures are in 000s. Parenthesized figures are percentages of the civilian and military population, and add to 100 horizontally when other ethnic groups are included. For 1778, Stannard (1989) claims 800,000. Figures report U.S. Census data to 1960; because of redefinitions of ethnic categories, the years 1970–1990 are based on the State of Hawai'i Health Surveillance Survey except for blacks, Filipinos (many of whom were improperly classified as "mixed"), and Vietnamese (who were not counted in the Hawai'i survey). "Hawaiian" figures include persons with any Native Hawaiian ancestry, though are undercounted. "White" figures usually include Portuguese and other Caucasians, including Hispanics who self-identify as Caucasian. Figures in boldface identify the highest in each row. Earliest figures for Filipinos and Mexicans are based on historical records. The figure for Mexicans in 1970 is approximated by subtracting Cubans and Puerto Ricans from Spanish speakers.

Sources: Lind (1967:28); Nordyke (1989:178–179,183); Hawai'i (1993–1994:37; 2006:63–67); U.S. Census (1962:17; 1972:199, 205; 1983:16; 1993:6; 2000:DP-1).

up, placed in a stream, and dunked under water (amateur waterboarding). During a visit to a library in Jakarta, he reported once being puzzled upon reading an article in a magazine about Blacks who tried to lighten their skin (Obama 1995:36). But his mom taught him that his African ancestry was special, that Blacks were "superior beings" (Mendell 2007:38) with a "great inheritance" (Glauberman and Burris 2009:69). She evidently inspired his desire to run for the presidency (Plouffe 2009:122).

In Honolulu, due to several awkward incidents, he realized that he was being perceived negatively as a Black person. Two unexpected experiences involved his grandmother and another adult White woman who expressed fear of Black men (Obama 1995:42–45). Others involved students and teachers at Punahou, where Asian and White students were more likely to have pure blood than those in the Honolulu mainstream whom Barry served while working at a nearby Baskin-Robbins. In general, discrimination against African Americans in Hawai'i is sporadic rather than institutional or systematic (Kobayashi 2008), but the incidents gnawed at Barry because he could not get appropriate counseling at home afterward.

Punahou's students, then at least 60 percent White (Glauberman and Burris 2008:86), posed challenges. Barry was more multicultural than most of his fellow students. Indeed, Whites from elite Punahou have not always been respected in the wider community because of their pretensions to superiority (Steinhauer 2007). Those with multiple racial backgrounds in Hawai'i, including Obama's Indonesian half-sister, sometimes have to struggle to find an identity (Petranek 1999), but the only realistic option is to celebrate all cultures that they have in their makeup and thereby to positively value all others (Watanabe 2010).

One time Barry punched a Punahou boy who called him a "coon." He threatened to report the tennis coach, who told him not to touch the match schedule in case his color rubbed off. And he challenged the basketball coach, who once characterized an opposing team with the words, "There are [B]lack people and there are niggers, and those guys were niggers." In return, Obama said, *"There are [W]hite folks and then there are ignorant motherfuckers like you"* (Obama 1995:80–81).

Describing girls who refused to associate with Blacks, a fellow African American student who came from the U.S. Mainland once said, "These girls are A-1, USDA-certified racists. All of 'em. [W]hite girls. Asian girls—shoot, these Asians worse than the [W]hites. Think we got a disease or something" (Obama 1995:73). Yet Barack lived with Whites who were not racists, so he was too sophisticated to subscribe to his friend's characterization and said so quietly in response.

From the age of 13, Barry stopped admitting that his mother was White (Obama 1995:xv). He realized that he was destined to become a Black man in America while living with a family in which nobody had a clue what that meant (Obama 1995:76). Accordingly, he began a quest to find out about African Americans. But he was in Hawai'i, a part of the United States where there is no Black ghetto or residential enclave.

Haunted by the notion, provided by fellow Black students at Puna-hou, that he would be "acting White" if he got good grades, he was a B+ student (Dorning and Parsons 2007:22). Nevertheless, he once surprised his teammates by reading a book when his basketball team flew to Maui for a game (Charlton 2007).

There were few role models for a young Black man in Hawai'i. For-tunately, his grandfather introduced him to African American Frank Marshall Davis, a journalist and poet who retired to Waikīkī from Chi-cago after taking the Fifth Amendment before the House Un-American Activities Committee (Takara 1999). Davis was an intellectual in favor of trade unionism at a time when some labor organizers were under investigation because their rhetoric sounded Marxist. Throughout his teen years, Barry on his own visited Davis, who may have inspired Barry to write a poem, and think big (Glauberman and Burris 2008:110–113). He also sought out gatherings of African Americans on military bases and at the University of Hawai'i, in the latter case to view basketball players recruited from the Mainland. Black military personnel living nearby played basketball, and Barry enjoyed playing with them at public courts in the neighborhood (Purdum 2008).

Television provided role models, such as Bill Cosby on *I Spy*. Mau-reen Dowd (2009) insightfully suggests that Spock (half earthling and half Vulcan) may have been a role model. In fact, Barry was an avid fan of *Star Trek* and, while campaigning for the presidency, gave the Vul-can sign on meeting Leonard Nimoy (Boucher 2009; Meacham 2009b). As for exemplary female African Americans, Uhuru (Nichelle Nichols) caught his interest. Indeed, Chicago-born Nichelle resembles his wife Michelle in many ways.

Fellow students and teachers were unaware that Barry was struggling to find a racial identity (Serrano 2007). He bonded with four Black stu-dents at Punahou, but not enough to form a clique, and he did not fully solve his nagging puzzle about how to conduct himself as a Black man in America (Smith 2008).

As one of the few students at Punahou on scholarship, Barry became aware of different social classes. He socialized off campus with fellow students who came from affluent families. After flirting with fellow student Kelli Furushima, he wrote her a love note upon graduation in 1979, but he never dated her. Nevertheless, she felt that he was "more sensitive than the other guys" (Nichols 2007).

His Black friends had more modest means, as did his grandparents. His grandmother worked her way up from cashier to a position as Vice President of Bank of Hawaii. Gramps managed Pratt Furniture Store when he moved to Honolulu. When that closed down, he tried to sell insurance, but as a relative newcomer to the Islands, he lacked the connections to be successful. Barry apparently realized that Mainland-born Whites experienced some discrimination in Hawai'i (Obama 1995:26).

One summer he met a tourist who impressed him about educational opportunities at Occidental College in Los Angeles, so he applied and was accepted. There, he formed close friendships with other Blacks and realized that his image of being Black was based on false assumptions formed while in Honolulu (Tani 2007). Discovering that fellow Black students had forged their identities in diverse ways, mostly to cope with White discrimination, Barack again found himself trying to establish an identity. One Occidental student called herself "multiracial" because one of her parents was Black and the other was Italian with a smattering of Native American, but she preferred to associate with Whites. Another urged him to just be himself rather than trying to develop his personality on the basis of defense mechanisms (Obama 1995:99–105).

After two years at Occidental, he transferred to Columbia University in New York City, where he first saw Blacks living in abject poverty, both materially and psychologically (Obama 1995:121–122). Accordingly, Obama (1983) felt that his political science courses seemed disembodied from the reality in the streets.

He attempted to date a White woman, the way his father courted his mother. But his monocultural date was baffled by how African Americans perceive that the country has marginalized them, and she did not want to learn more about his perspectives (Obama 1995:211). That ended the relationship.

He concluded that the self-hate among African Americans was rooted in White rejection, thus explaining why Black pride was an obvious antidote (Obama 1995:192–199). Learning about African culture was one way to develop racial pride, he realized in due course (Obama 1995:259).

After graduating from Columbia, he hungered to empower less fortunate Blacks, so he craved for a career as community organizer, a role that his mom played in Indonesia. He was fortunate in landing such a job on Chicago's South Side, an experience that led him to the heart of the African American community, where he at last found a place to feel at home with himself and could firmly claim his African American identity (Watanabe 2010). Two years earlier, Harold Washington had been elected mayor thanks to a multiethnic coalition of voters. Nevertheless, he was frustrated while trying to represent Blacks in City Hall.

Little did he know that as a candidate for president he would later be judged as too Black by some and not Black enough by others (Ifill 2009; Remnick 2010:Ch. 8). After all, he presented himself as a candidate for president rather than as an African American candidate for president. Although the press hammered away at him in the latter role, he avoided calling direct attention to race until the spotlight was directed at his Chicago pastor, Jeremiah Wright. He objected to Wright's remarks as "*divisive at a time when we need unity*" and advocated ending the "*racial stalemate*" that has blocked progress (Heilemann and Halperin 2010:237–238).

According to his sister, he does not think much about his race or "hybridity" and is quite a feminist in light of the two strong women in his upbringing (Coleman 2008). Although he has admitted that many Blacks are biracial (Kaplan 2010), he only checked "Black" in the 2010 census, though he also could have checked "White" (Avila 2010). Ironically, the opportunity to check off multiple races was an innovation in the 2000 census that I originally proposed, based on the longtime practice in racial surveys conducted in Hawai'i (Haas 2010b:Ch. 8).

While living in Illinois, Barack followed the tradition of visiting his relatives in Honolulu for Christmas and New Year's Eve each year. He has drawn continuing sustenance from his Honolulu roots.

Barack Obama's wanderlust journey was not completed until he apparently concluded that Whites of modest means also needed community organizers to uplift them in a country where the middle class was stagnating while the rich had taken control of the levers of government. His candidacy for president capitalized on his experience as a community organizer by appealing to similar needs among White Americans. A primary element in his campaign was grassroots mobilization. And mainstream Americans responded, hungry for someone who said what they felt and promised a dream of something better. Speeches immediately after his nomination and election were new versions of the "I Have a Dream" speech of Martin Luther King, Jr., the oratorical masterpiece of 1963.

WHAT IS "MULTICULTURALISM"?

First-time visitors to Hawai'i on packaged tours often arrive at Honolulu airport, are greeted with leis and music by dark-skinned young people, and are bused to lavish hotels for a week of fun in the sun. They learn about something called the "Aloha Spirit" while on tours and absorb the friendliness of the Islands while observing smiling faces and receiving courteous, seemingly deferential treatment. All too many live in a plastic tourist bubble, unaware that a complex society lies behind what may appear to be a gentle façade.

For broadcaster Cokie Roberts, the Aloha State is a "foreign, exotic place" that was not where a successful presidential candidate should go on vacation (Boehlert and Foser 2008; cf. Alter 2009). Her suggestion that Obama should go to Myrtle Beach instead exhibits a disdain not uncommon on the Mainland, as few commentators have ever wanted to understand the reason why sociologists over the years have marveled at the spirit of Aloha. Indeed, there is not a single entry for "Hawai'i" in the index to the book of a campaign biographer (Wolffe 2009). Two other biographers incredibly emphasize the fact that Obama spent "much of his youth outside the United States" rather than focusing on his life in Hawai'i, the 50th state (Balz and Johnson 2009:381).

In contrast with the touristic image of the Islands, a different Hawai'i is on display a few miles from Honolulu International Airport, where a unique park, known as Hawai'i's Plantation Village, adorns the landscape below an abandoned sugar mill. The park consists of reconstructed plantation houses furnished by eight major ethnic groups of Hawai'i, which, once upon a time, worked side by side in the sugarcane fields. To portray what life was like on the plantations, heritage associations of each group have contributed clothing, cooking implements, photographs, and the like from former plantation workers. Represented are exhibits from Chinese, Filipinos, Japanese, Koreans, Native Hawaiians, Okinawans, Portuguese, and Puerto Ricans. The park does not run organized tours on a regular basis from Waikīkī hotels. Instead, local residents of the Islands, often filled with nostalgia, are the primary visitors. Often, grandparents tell their grandchildren about how for years they suffered in the open sun while saving enough money so that their children could go to college and become, as they have, bankers, corporation executives, physicians, teachers, and members of Congress. The park provides a window into ethnic history that perhaps exists nowhere else in the United States, yet its existence is barely known. As a leaflet provided by the park proclaims, the story behind the village "is the saga of the creation of Hawai'i's unique multicultural society."

Barack Obama has visited Honolulu for every Christmas holiday except 2007, when his campaign for the presidency was underway. According to his spouse Michelle, "You do not understand Barack Obama until you understand Hawaii" (Mendel 2007:20). So what is there about Hawai'i that makes Barack Obama so different from Americans who have lived on the United States Mainland all their lives?

The answer is that Hawai'i's multiethnic society has a distinct culture that differs in fundamental ways from what is encountered within most of the other 49 states. Within the Aloha State, various ethnic groups, many with ancestral enmities, have learned to live together on small islands by developing distinct norms that permit mutual cultural acceptance while not sacrificing cultural identity. As Obama himself said in 1999,

> *Hawaii's spirit of tolerance might not have been perfect or complete. But it was—and is—real. . . . The opportunity that Hawaii offered—to experience a variety of cultures in a climate of mutual respect—became an integral part of my world view, and a basis for the values that I hold most dear.* (Obama 1999; cf. Niesse 2008)

Barack Obama has also referred to the "*legend*" that Hawai'i is "*the one true melting pot, an experiment in racial harmony*" (Obama 1995:24). During the 2008 election, he revised his terminology to say that Hawai'i was neither a melting pot nor a mosaic, but a thick gumbo soup containing large chunks (Wolffe 2009:237).

Conventionally, the term "melting pot" refers to a land where immigrants from different cultures and ethnic backgrounds supposedly created an amalgamated American culture and intermarried. The problem is that the term does not completely describe the American experience, as immigrants during the 19th century were expected to conform to Anglo (English) culture, and only those of European background intermarried. Ethnic identities have not melted, that is, ceased to be remembered, and racial intermarriage is still rare except in Hawai'i. The concept of the "color blind" society is fundamentally antithetical to and disrespectful of distinct cultures.

Hawai'i may appear to represent a true amalgamation, where many races intermarry. Nevertheless, the term "melting pot" is inadequate because what happened in the Islands over the past three centuries was not a "melting" of cultures but a distinct social process that created a new culture without obliterating Native Hawaiian or other cultures. After all, nearly half the marriages in Hawai'i are still monoracial.

Ethnic groups in the Aloha State take pride in their cultural heritage, at least minimally speak the language spoken by their forebears, and have developed a unique "local culture." That the Fiftieth State has serious economic, political, and social problems is undeniable, but the manner in which they are addressed appears exemplary when compared to other parts of the world.

What is problematic is how to characterize the nature of multicultural Hawai'i and how to explain relative success in attaining ethnic harmony. The authors in this volume, who seek to do both, present three approaches. Some sing the praises of the Aloha State with little criticism. Others dwell on serious ethnic problems that fester and await resolution. A middle approach is to note that Hawai'i has had both successes and failures in addressing racial problems.

Still, defining the term "multicultural" is crucial to a better understanding of Hawai'i. The term arose elsewhere in response to a continuing effort to describe (and prescribe) models of ethnic and race relations beyond the doctrine of *assimilationism*, which in the United States demands conformity to cultural traditions brought from England.

The concept of the *melting pot* as a fusion (amalgamation) of separate cultures and nationalities was promoted by French-American farmer Michel Guillaume Jean de Crèvecœur (1782), historian Frederick Jackson Turner (1893), and philosopher Henry James (1907). The term itself was coined by Israel Zangwill in a stage play entitled *The Melting Pot* (1909). The idea was that a new *amalgamated* American culture had developed to replace old ways brought from Europe.

Not all observers, however, were eager to jump into the proverbial melting pot. In a polemic written during the first year of World War I, academic Edward Ross (1914) published a scathing critique of Italians and Slavs as genetically inferior, Jews as greedy, and their presence in the United States as a rootless proletariat threatening skilled native-born workers and relying on political corruption for their advancement. He decried the fact that these groups had not assimilated to American/English culture.

Reviewing Ross's book, philosopher Horace Kallen (1915, 1924) advocated *cultural pluralism*. He believed that an acceptance of diverse cultures coexisting in the United States strengthened rather than jeopardized American solidarity. If one culture insisted on dominating all others, he argued, the result would be continuing disunity and strife. He asserted that assimilationists and amalgamationists not only misrepresented the contributions of immigrant groups but also ignored fundamental American constitutional principles of equality and justice.

Kallen interpreted Ross, the assimilationists, and the amalgamationists as members of an elite Anglo-Saxon class that was losing its dominance and fighting to protect its prerogatives. The uniqueness of America, Kallen felt, was that many streams of immigrants had been enriching the country for more than a century into a mosaic of cultures. Ethnic groups, according to Kallen, have retained what is valuable from their own cultural heritage while accepting a common political culture in the form of democratic principles—representative government under a rule of law that protects individual liberties. ·

Cultural pluralism was later attacked for justifying *cultural separatism*, that is, supporting a transformation to a "nation of nations" similar to Switzerland or a segregated America of ethnically pure residential enclaves. Indeed, perverse cultural separatism is often termed *ultranationalism*.

Accordingly, as World War II was being waged by ultranationalists in Germany and Japan, an obscure book review in the *New York Herald-Tribune* during 1941 advocated *multiculturalism* as an antidote (cf. Safire 1992). The term reappeared during 1965 in the *Report of the Royal Commission on Bilingualism and Biculturalism*, which recommended that "multiculturalism" replace the bicultural policies of Canada that had been granting linguistic equality to English and French (Canada 1965).

Meanwhile, the Civil Rights Act of 1964 outlawed discrimination in employment, government facilities and programs, public accommodations, and voting, thereby serving to end segregation in most areas of public life. By executive order, President Lyndon Johnson in 1965 mandated government contractors to engage in affirmative action, that is, to hire qualified members of minority groups previously excluded. Discrimination was also outlawed in the Immigration and Nationality Act of 1965, which resulted in a considerable increase in non-European immigrants by equalizing country quotas.

The movement that produced civil rights legislation also pressured American universities to establish ethnic studies programs on the premise that the historical status of nonmainstream cultures in the United States had been neglected, so their research agenda was to uncover the contributions of diverse minority groups to the United States, document statistical patterns of discrimination, and otherwise enrich American scholarship by focusing on the diversity of the country. Educational institutions then voluntarily adopted programs of admission by "affirmative action," even though they were not required by law to do so.

Because not all employers voluntarily complied with affirmative action and nondiscrimination requirements, members of minority groups still felt frustrated. So did government officials who monitored lack of progress. Concrete programs were needed to overcome resistance attributable to prejudice, stereotypes, and other factors. Immigrants with behavior patterns that did not conform to the mainstream were particularly disadvantaged.

For example, minority groups traditionally known for menial labor had difficulty being hired for white-collar jobs. In addition, federally funded mental health programs serviced few minorities, in part because the latter arrived from countries where the concept of mental illness was not understood as a treatable medical condition. To overcome favoritism toward the majority group, sometimes called "Anglo Americans", employers and directors of mental health and other government-funded programs were urged to adopt cultural sensitivity training, which relied heavily on scholarship from ethnic studies researchers.

Cultural sensitivity training, however, dealt with adults, and would continue forever as long as children grew up with mistaken and stereotypic ideas about ethnic groups. Accordingly, curriculum reform from kindergarten to college was on the agenda in the 1970s under the banner of "multiculturalism" in order to ensure that young people would have more respect for minority cultures. The ultimate hope was that there would be better utilization of government programs by minorities and less discrimination in employment.

In 1972, the Supreme Court ordered schools in *Lau v Nichols* (414US563) to assist language-minority children, primarily immigrants, through bilingual or English-as-a-second language programs. And the Voting Rights Act of 1975 required ballots printed in the home languages of minorities with substantial numbers in voting districts.

Multiculturalism soon assumed many new forms of government support—approval of radio and television stations in minority languages, funding for minority arts and music, financial aid to minority businesses, scholarships for minority students, and acceptance of holidays for minorities. The establishment of the birthday of Martin Luther King, Jr., as a federal holiday in 1983 is a case in point.

Focus on the special needs of underrepresented groups broadened in scope. Women benefitted, as employment discrimination based on gender was outlawed in the Civil Rights Act of 1964. Other forms of discrimination were banned in subsequent years. The term "multicultural" soon encompassed respect for different ages, physical and mental capabilities, as well as sexual orientations.

Some multicultural innovations were badly designed or implemented, and sudden changes under the name of multiculturalism rankled the mainstream, which resented being labeled as Americentric, Eurocentric, parochial, prejudiced, or otherwise being vilified. The main premise of the counterattack was that the United States was basically a product of Western civilization, so any attempt to divert attention from that foundation imperiled national unity and undermined fundamental values. For the critics, multiculturalism had gone too far (Glazer 1975; Schlesinger 1991).

One value presumably endangered by multiculturalism was said to be respect for competence. Some beneficiaries of affirmative action, notably minority students at leading universities, were teased that they were admitted merely because of their ethnicity, not for their qualifications, as Barack Obama discovered at Harvard (Remnick 2010:187). When private businesses were pressured to fill what they wrongly perceived as ethnic quotas in their workforce, White male job applicants cried out against "reverse discrimination." The same was true of applicants for entry to prestigious universities.

Another criticism of multiculturalism has been that basic knowledge of American history has been eclipsed by too much attention to diverse cultures. Because fundamental principles of American culture and democracy appeared to be treated as an orthodoxy under challenge, critics decried a resulting cacophony and confusion in the minds of students, including members of minority groups themselves.

Multiculturalism was said to unleash identity politics and political correctness. "Identity politics" involved the pursuit of public policies by each ethnic group without cooperating with other ethnic groups, sometimes resulting in advocacy of conflicting solutions and lack of progress for all groups. "Political correctness" meant that one would be accused of being a racist for making factual or scientific statements about group characteristics or merely for posing hypotheses about differences between various ethnic groups.

Philosophically, some multiculturalists were attacked for advocating a relativism in which everything is both true and not true, depending on one's cultural perspective. Social science was questioned as inherently ideological, so college debates between differences of opinion on public policy issues were no longer focused on achieving consensus, but instead on mobilizing support among minorities to prevail over the traditional mainstream view or vice versa, as Obama found among Harvard law students.

In an effort to restore monoculturalism, anti-multiculturalists went too far. In matters of policy, Congress soon became a hyperpartisan arena in which advocates of traditional Biblical and "family values" sought to undermine innovations in order to win a "culture war" against multiculturalists. Passage of legislation no longer sought compromise but instead victory, based on pressures from monocultural interest groups, a tendency that candidate Barack Obama has found deplorable (Obama 2008:12). In response to monocultural extremists, however, former opponents of multiculturalism had epiphanies and joined adherents (cf. Glazer 1997).

Soon, a new concept emerged—*interculturalism*. The view was that members of different cultures should learn from one another rather than having one prevail or allow diverse cultures to become separatist. Interculturalists strive to find commonalities and consider differences as subcultures (Bennett 1998). Interculturalism is particularly meaningful for those who are biracial and multiracial, such as Barack Obama.

Another alternative, *polyculturalism*, insists that the world's cultures have been in flux in part because they have influenced one another for centuries, are interrelated, and therefore possess common values that should be stressed rather than competing for acceptance or dominance (Prashad 2001). Those who have claimed to be world citizens, rather than nationalists, now reside under the banner of polyculturalism. Similarly, Obama's mother saw herself primarily as an internationalist (Wolffe 2009:235). Although Barack Obama stresses his strong roots in America, he declared himself to be a *"citizen of the world"* during his mid-2008 speech in Berlin.

Does Hawai'i illustrate multiculturalism? Yes, insofar as diverse cultures coexist happily and members of ethnic groups intermarry without losing respect for their ancestral cultures. But what is very special is the Aloha State's interculturalism, that is, the openness to learn from other cultures while developing a unique ethos that prescribes norms of behavior.

Relative ethnic harmony appears to exist in Hawai'i as long as principles of a multicultural ethos, to be explicated in the next section of this chapter, are observed. When they are violated, disharmony occurs, whereupon the multicultural ethos is ultimately invoked to bring the discourse back to a more respectful conversation among those of differing perspectives.

White (Haole) dominance of Hawai'i's economy and government before statehood tried to impose American culture onto a non-White population but only succeeded in establishing the legal framework, not a monocultural milieu. After statehood, the first non-White governor, a Japanese American, initially opposed affirmative action as "quotas." But he changed his mind, as Filipinos and other non-Whites demonstrated that the institutional racism established by Whites before statehood still needed to be dismantled.

The election of Barack Hussein Obama in 2008 may have opened a new era of ethnic and race relations in the United States. Some hope that he will adopt "post-racial" public policies that bring Americans together after decades of "culture wars." Having taught American constitutional law with a focus on civil rights, Obama's apparent intercultural message—that diverse Americans should listen to one another in order to achieve pragmatic solutions to festering problems—promised to be translated into action after he became president.

HAWAI'I'S MULTICULTURAL ETHOS

There is a wide consensus that Hawai'i's relatively exemplary race relations can best be explained in terms of shared values (Adams 1926, 1933; Grant and Ogawa 1993; Kirkpatrick 1987; Lind 1969; Park 1938; Wittermans-Pino 1964). Those values may be called its multicultural ethos, though some refer to "local values" (cf. Cayetano 2009:427).

The ethos has developed interculturally by the people (down→up) rather than imposed (top→down) by educators or politicians. Hawai'i's multicultural ethos has evolved from interactions primarily between three strong cultural traditions—American, Native Hawaiian, and Japanese.

Before the arrival of settlers from other lands, Native Hawaiian culture was well established and remains a strong influence for all who live in the Islands. Caucasians (called Haoles) from the United States began arriving in the early 19th century yet had to assimilate to Native

Hawaiian culture in order to fit into the society. At the same time, the indigenous Hawaiians were eager to learn from the Caucasians, who espoused Western values in matters of economics and politics.

From the mid-19th century, several ethnic groups were imported by Caucasian economic interests to work on plantations. The most influential are the Japanese, whose large numbers and political dominance increasingly constituted a major cultural force.

Today, Hawai'i's multicultural ethos is an amalgam of values in the American, Native Hawaiian, and Japanese cultural traditions to which other ethnic groups have had to adjust while retaining their own normative values, such as the veneration of machismo among some of the less dominant groups. Although Filipinos formed a similar amalgamated culture of American, Chinese, Malay, and Spanish influences in the Philippines before they arrived in Hawai'i, they still have had to adjust to Hawai'i's multicultural ethos, while definitely adding to Island joviality.

Barack Obama's family went through an adjustment to Island culture after their arrival in Hawai'i. Barack, however, assimilated to that culture (mixed with an exposure to Indonesian culture) more completely because he did so from a very young age.

Although he matured on the American Mainland, particularly in the rough and tumble of Chicago politics, others on the Mainland clearly perceive in Obama the multicultural values that he learned in Hawai'i, notably Emil Jones, the Illinois State Senate leader who was his political mentor (Burris 2008), University of Chicago Medical Center administrator Eric Whitaker (Alter 2010:144), University of Pennsylvania scholar Kathleen Hall Jamieson (East-West Center 2009), and his biographer Edward McClelland (2010).

Some of the obvious ways in which Obama illustrates the multicultural ethos are noted herein. The most vivid demonstration of how the ethos comes to play in everyday life has been penned by former Governor Benjamin Cayetano in his biography *Ben: A Memoir, from Street Kid to Governor* (2009). A Filipino born in Honolulu, Cayetano demonstrates that culture clash is common in Hawai'i but overcome by finding common values. Cayetano's turbulent early life is in contrast with Barack Obama's more placid youth, but both were influenced by a multicultural ethos that transcended them.

Due to mutual accommodation between disparate cultures, there is a profound homesickness for Hawai'i among its expatriates that is absent among Mainlanders who move comfortably from state to state without any fundamental readjustment problems. Expatriates often realize that they are little ambassadors from Hawai'i, responsible for spreading Aloha to the world. Barack Obama is one of them.

Twelve principles, which capture the essence of what is often called the Aloha Spirit, are identified next, using terms in English, Hawaiian, and Japanese. Nuances of each language may differ somewhat but help to describe the multicultural ethos that pervades Hawai'i:

(1) **Seductive friendliness (akahai) (miryokuteki)**. Giving others a warm welcome is certainly one literal meaning of Aloha, which is often translated as "love" but goes beyond to involve compassion, cordiality, empathy, kindness, and tenderness. An acceptance of what others say and do is one manifestation. Smiling at others and making others feel wanted—and doing so seductively—is in stark contrast with the stand-offishness that people from Hawai'i experience too often when they approach others on the Mainland United States. Failure to smile is interpreted as a sign that something is wrong, so smiling is a way to reassure others. Visitors to Hawai'i are immediately captivated upon observing local persons talking to one another while constantly smiling.

Obama's mannerisms and voice have been described as "loose and inviting" and "mesmerizing" (Abercrombie 2008:vi). In 2004, on a trip to Honolulu, he once said,

No place else . . . could have provided me with the environment, the climate, in which I could not only grow but also get a sense of being loved. There is no doubt that the residue of Hawaii will always stay with me, that it is part of my core, and that what's best in me, and what's best in my message, is consistent with the tradition of Hawaii. (Glauberman and Burris 2008:4)

On his annual return to Honolulu for the holidays, he has not only socialized with family but also with friends in high school with whom he has kept in touch over the decades. During his election campaign, he even flew in longtime friends from Honolulu to join him in basketball (Abercrombie 2008:vii). A consummate networker (Remnick 2010:225, 268), Obama is representative of the typical local guy with a big, friendly smile and lots of boyish charm. He captivated workers on his campaign and voters across the country with his happy-go-lucky demeanor.

(2) **Inclusiveness (ho'opili pū) (hōkatsuteki)**. In Hawai'i everyone is invited and welcome. No group is supposed to be deliberately left out. Although various ethnic groups have their own societies to organize cultural events, they are open to everyone. Those of mixed-race ancestry

go to events of each cultural group as well as those of their mixed-race friends.

Because monoethnic interest groups would raise suspicions, those in charge take extra effort to invite representatives of many ethnic groups into a wider effort. Everyone running for office, for example, proudly advertises a campaign manager or treasurer of a different ethnic background. Yet on the Mainland the overwhelmingly monoethnic composition of various groups, even including Progressive Democrats of Los Angeles, creates no embarrassment or backlash. Such a group would be shunned in Hawai'i for being monoethnic.

Rather than a mere peaceful coexistence or tolerance between the races, intermingling is seen as legitimate, exclusiveness as illegitimate. Indeed, children of interracial marriage often boast lineage from many diverse groups, leaving those who are monoethnic feeling that they should outmarry to overcome their narrower background. Accordingly, teenagers often choose diverse dates in order to sample people of many different cultures.

The reason for the desire to see no barriers between peoples can be explained in different ways. The way in which Native Hawaiians originally welcomed foreigners from Europe and the United States perhaps set the tone, and other groups followed suit.

As Barack Obama once said, *"the multicultural nature of Hawaii helped teach me how to appreciate different cultures and navigate different cultures, out of necessity"* (Walsh 2008). According to his sister Maya, "Hawaii is the place that gave him the ability to . . . understand people from a wide array of backgrounds. . . . People see themselves in him . . . because he himself contains multitudes" (Thanawala 2008). As he once said, *"only in a country in which we can appreciate differences of race and religion and ethnicity while still insisting on our common humanity, will my own soul feel rested"* (Obama 1999). The "culture of inclusiveness attracted [a]cademic Kathleen Hall Jamieson" to buy a second home in Hawai'i (East-West Center 2009).

While in Chicago as a community organizer, Obama wrote to a friend about the Black community: *"I've learned to care for them very much and want to do everything I can for them"* (Remnick 2010:141). He reluctantly objected to the extreme statements of his onetime pastor, Jeremiah Wright during his 2008 campaign.

In Hawai'i, according to Senator Daniel Inouye, "You can't move to the suburbs and live in a mansion. You find it necessary to live with each other" (Glauberman and Burris 2008:109). All the races and members of social classes dine, enjoy entertainment, live, shop, and work in close proximity on small islands. Gossip travels quickly. Reflecting on his diverse experience, Obama says that he is *"constantly looking for links and bridges between cultures and peoples"* (Draper 2009). He admires Abraham Lincoln for not only being self-made but also for *"a deep-rooted honesty and empathy . . . that allowed him to always be able to see the other person's point of view"* (Balz and Johnson 2009:380). He has decried an *"empathy deficit"* in contemporary American politics (Heilemann and Halperin 2010:28).

On November 26, 2008, Obama organized small-group meetings of his supporters across the nation to draw up priorities, saying, *"We want ideas from everybody"* (Carnevale 2008). His management style is summed up with the confession: *"I'm somebody who generally thinks that listening and learning before you start talking is a pretty good strategy"* (Dorning and Parsons 2007).

(3) **Charismatic humility (ha'aha'a) (kenkyo sa).** There is a childlike quality to Hawai'i residents on top of considerable sophistication due to respect for cultural diversity. What makes the humility charismatic is the cheerfulness with which it is displayed. According to his Harvard classmate Chris Lu (Romano 2009), Obama's strong presence was known to all in law school classes. His charisma was already so obvious that he was elected president of the *Harvard Law Review* with strong support from conservative students.

In dealing with others, attitudes of arrogance, pretentiousness, and superiority, which set up hierarchies between people, are disapproved in Hawai'i (Theroux 2009). Commenting on the negative response to arrogance in Hawai'i, Cayetano (2009:159, 204, 254, 286) cites a maxim of court administrator and lobbyist Tom Okuda: "Be patient, be humble and be understanding. And you will be successful in the long run." Humility is perhaps the most difficult trait for Caucasians who move from the Mainland to learn, as they often misinterpret Island diffidence and modesty for inferiority, preferring explicitness over Island implicitness (East-West Center 2009).

The Hawai'i Creole language, often referred to as "Pidgin English," provides a medium of communication for local residents of varying ethnic backgrounds who live in homes where Standard English is not spoken. At school, peer pressure ensures that moderately bright students will not show off good grades, mindful of the common dictum "No make ass" (Pidgin for "Don't make A grades"). Similarly, parents commonly send their children off to college on the Mainland with the injunction, "Be humble!" Those educated on the Mainland have some-times become arrogant and, on returning home to the Islands, fail to demonstrate proper respect for parents and friends. Until his mother insisted that he must go to a good college, Obama thought of himself only as an average student. However, he must have thought that Island culture stressed humility too much, as he encouraged Punahou students in 2004 to entertain *"big dreams"* to realize their full potential. But he felt that those dreams should not be based on materialism or narcissism but instead that *"It is hard to find your individual potential or sense of self-worth unless you are also concerned about the collective potential and self-worth of others"* (Husain and Chang 2005).

At Punahou, he learned that the richest Caucasian students wore T-shirts and faded jeans to show humility, whereas middle-class Asian students dressed up to prove that they were not poor (Glauberman and Burris 2008:11). Narrow apparel standards do not exist in Hawai'i.

During the 2004 Democratic National Convention, Obama referred to himself as an *"unlikely"* person to give the keynote address, a term he used again on election night 2008. While electioneering, he often said, *"This campaign is not about me. It's about you."* His campaign manager, David Plouffe (2009:57) describes his speeches as "quiet[ing] a room, until everyone listen[s] so intently that all else [falls] away." Nevertheless, a presidential aspirant is the antithesis of humble (cf. Goldberg 2010). His candidacy was a bold step that gave him considerable pause before he threw his hat into the ring (Heilemann and Halperin 2010:26, 87, 105).

(4) **Joviality (laupa'apa'ani) (yōki)**. Since all ethnic groups have less desirable attributes, Island humor has developed a fine art of banter in which everyone learns how to tease through ethnic humor. Stereotypes of one's own group are seen as fair game for gentle and harmless ribbing (Serrano 2007). Chinese (known as "pākē") are kidded for being stingy, Caucasians (Haoles) for being pushy, Filipinos for wearing flashy clothes, Koreans for their temper, Portuguese as loudmouths, Native Hawaiians for being lazy, and Japanese for being sneaky. Those of mixed ancestry often characterize themselves as chop-suey, poi-dog, or hapa.

Mainland transplants in Hawai'i are often confused whether being called a Haole is a derogatory term. Yet tone of voice is a clue, with a negative meaning quite obvious from gruff pronunciation. Such charac-terizations might be considered "politically incorrect" on the Mainland, where stereotypic verbalizations are taken seriously rather than inter-preted as amusing reminders of foibles that afflict everyone. Islanders develop thick skins from the gentle ribbing and use of racial terms that would be deeply resented on the Mainland (Davis 2008:50; Associated Press 2010). Although the Hawaiian word "haole" literally means foreigner or without breath, Haoles today are simply understood as non-Hispanic Whites—the equivalent of the nonjudgmental term Anglos in the increasingly Spanish-speaking United States.

Perhaps in this context laughter erupted among classmates when his first Punahou homeroom teacher, on the opening day of class, recited his name, "Barack Obama." During political campaigns he continually referred to his surname Obama as a *"funny name."* When he called himself a *"mutt"* after his election in November, he was probably trying to translate the term used in the local patois of Hawai'i for "mixed race." Not understanding local culture in Hawai'i, at least one person of mixed-race ancestry on the U.S. Mainland (Rhee 2008) took offense from his apparent politically incorrect language, yet he persisted the following year by describing himself as *"mongrel"* (Kaplan 2010). Some misinterpret his genuine sense of humor as unbefitting a president. But perhaps by now they have lightened up, realizing that someone with a good sense of humor has much greater perspective than those easily fazed and too serious.

(5) **Respectfulness ('ihi) (teichō).** Showing admiration for the unique virtues among all ethnic groups is part of the Aloha Spirit. Ethnic back-biting, suspicion, and "talking stink" about others, though sometimes an undercurrent in Hawai'i, are considered improper. "If you no can say nothing good about anyone—no say nothing" is a local maxim, according to former Governor Cayetano (2009:141, 286), whose autobiography is filled with expressions of respect and disappointments over disrespectful actions of others. Honesty and loyalty are highly valued in Hawai'i as a sign of respect for others. But in politics, Cayetano (2009:516) found that they were often lacking or in conflict because of the politics of "going along to get along."

Before entering an abode, residents of the Aloha State take off their shoes, showing respect to the home. And members of one culture tend to defer to the preferences of others rather than considering unfamiliar customs as inferior or odd. Everyone is recognized to have some part of the truth, so views of others are considered important. As his sister Maya observes,

> I think it was Hawaii that made him so broad and spacious and that forced him really to learn how to talk to different kinds of people and to not make assumptions about who they are or what they need. And to also recognize that on a very fundamental level we are

all the same. And I think one of my brother's many strengths is that he is able to help people find common ground. (Chang 2008)

Nobody is supposed to openly contradict anyone else. Relationships with strangers are accommodating, nonjudgmental, and low-keyed, even in the presence of unexpected behavior. Representatives of one culture will seek to avoid offending members of other cultures, something impossible unless all are committed to intercultural learning so that everyone is accustomed to showing mutual respect. Many of those born on the Mainland have difficulty adjusting to the climate of mutual respect, observes Cayetano (2009:530). One of Obama's harshest critics, Bill O'Reilly (2009), admires Obama's repeated stress on showing respect.

Respect for elders is a particularly strong element in Asian and Native Hawaiian families. An older person who has profound wisdom is called "kupuna" in Native Hawaiian culture. In many Asian households, children are not allowed to contradict their elders, who in turn will show respect to their children by sacrificing money and family time together so that the next generation in their family will have more chances for success in life.

Expressing overt anger is discouraged in Hawai'i, particularly by Japanese, who see emotional displays as a sign of immaturity and weakness. Temper tantrums are held back to the extent possible. Many observers of Obama marvel that he can stay cool, relaxed, and unflappable, but that is the way Islanders grow up. He impresses others with his imperviousness in the face of rudeness (Remnick 2010:115, 509).

As Obama says, there is a *"climate of mutual respect"* (Glauberman and Burris 2008:5) in Hawai'i:

> [W]hat people often note as my even temperament I think draws from Hawaii. People in Hawaii generally don't spend a lot of time, you know, yelling and screamin' at each other. I think that there is just a cultural bias toward courtesy and trying to work through problems in a way that makes everybody feel like they're being listened to. And I think that reflects itself in my personality as well as my political style. (Walsh 2008)

While in Chicago, whenever neighborhood residents were angry about their mistreatment by city officials, Obama advised residents to treat those in authority with respect so as to occupy the moral high ground (Wilson 2009b; Remnick 2010:285).

Accordingly, Obama's critique of American politics has focused on the tendency of commentators and politicians to be negative rather than positive. The country, he argued in his campaign for the presidency:

> *can't afford the kind of games we've been playing. . . . It has to do with a politics that is petty, that is small, that is focused on calling folks names and cutting each other up instead of solving the problems of the American people.* (Talley 2007)

His ability to listen approvingly and carefully in order to find common ground is an example of an upbeat approach to others, amazing his interlocutors by demonstrating that he wants to learn from diverse experiences everywhere.

(6) **Nonconfrontational conflict resolution (ho'oponopono) (wakai).** Conflicts are rarely expressed directly. An intermediary is often sought to go between two sides, not only to cool everyone down but also to find a nonadversarial, nonlitigious compromise that will bring parties together again. The mediator will approach the topic gently by encouraging the parties to express opinions before principles in a free-ranging discussion known as "talk story." The ho'oponopono method was indeed used to settle some land claims of Native Hawaiians in the early 1990s (Cayetano 2009:363).

Interpersonal dialog, in short, is seen as storytelling more than struggles to win. Obama avoids confrontation, instead building consensus by listening carefully to both sides of an argument and then extracting points on which they agree (Alter 2010:154–155; Remnick 2010:189–190, 209).

Even when caught in bumper-to-bumper traffic, Honolulu drivers do not honk their horns. Were someone from the Mainland to do so, the local person in front will turn around to see what is the matter and then, realizing that the person is rudely impatient, will give the driver a look of "hush."

Politics, nevertheless, is about the resolution of conflict, which can be very adversarial. Cayetano's analysis of Island politics is particularly acerbic whenever he comments on pigheaded interests that insist on adoption of their proposals without taking the larger context into account. He believes that he persisted in a quest for justice over those who demonstrated unvarnished greed, a conundrum that Obama has encountered as president.

One of Obama's most fascinating autobiographical accounts occurred when his grandfather accompanied him as a young boy to a downtown bar, where a White man complained about having to drink "next to a nigger" (Davis 2008:19). Young Barry then walked over to the man, smiled, and began to talk to him quietly about the foolishness of bigotry and the virtues of equality. In response, the man opened up his pocket and gave him $100!

As a community organizer in Chicago, he impressed others with his desire to be effective without being confrontational (Remnick 2010:164, 179). When Barack Obama became a politician, he observed that most of his colleagues "*have been trained either as lawyers or as political operatives—professions that tend to place a premium on winning arguments rather than solving problems*" (Obama 2008:59). Although he differed sharply from the views of George W. Bush on various matters, candidate Obama stressed that "*we must talk and reach for common understandings precisely because all of us are imperfect and can never act with the certainty that God is on our side*" (MacFarquar 2007).

During 2008 campaign debates, Obama at first seemed ineffectual and passive. He appeared reticent to attack his opponents and considered himself more of a "*storyteller*" than a debater (Balz and Haynes 2009:93). Although apparently grateful when candidate John Edwards attacked Hillary Clinton so that he did not have to do so (ibid., 96–98), he disapproved of negative campaigning and castigated his staff for wanting to run attack ads (Plouffe 2009:44, 73, 323, 357; Remnick 2010:326, 495), preferring a more subtle way to contrast his views with those of his opponents (Heilemann and Halperin 2010:151). Whenever John McCain took the high road, Obama complimented him. A consummate conciliator, he was always the first to congratulate Hillary Clinton on her primary victories, and he made it a point to talk to John McCain soon after his election in November 2008.

(7) **Communitarianism** ('ohana) (kyōdōtaishugi). Caring for others and generosity without expectation of reciprocity are valued interpersonal norms that operate beyond one's family and ethnic group in Hawai'i, where 92 percent of the population continued to contribute to charities even during the Great Recession of 2008/2009 (Vorsino 2009). Ethnic exploitation was experienced on the pineapple and sugarcane plantations in pre-statehood Hawai'i, when non-Whites toiled for Whites in a racist caste system. The Social Darwinist impulse to push one's agenda over others is antithetical to the multicultural ethos, which developed to

end past exploitation and segregation. A sense of commonality pervades today (East-West Center 2009).

Instead of accepting Mainland individualism, the people of Hawai'i are more group oriented, proud of the communities where they live, whether modest or upscale (Theroux 2009). Even though racist comments are made from time to time by employers, politicians, and others, they fail to gain traction and provoke considerable criticism (Kobayashi 2008; Obama 1999).

The Native Hawaiian practice of "hānai" is particularly illustrative. One Native Hawaiian family may allow a son or daughter to be brought up by another family, sometimes because the latter family has no male or female children. Although one result is to complicate genealogies, especially when the adoption is not recorded with the state government, another is to bind Native Hawaiians into a much larger conception of their community, that is, 'ohana.

Reflecting on his first visit to Kenya, where he at first encountered "*the joy of human warmth*," reminiscent of Hawai'i, he later despaired of the "*growing isolation of American life*" (Obama 1995:328–329). He was unhappy when he heard about tribal rivalries in Kenya, scolding his relatives, "*We're all part of one tribe. The [B]lack tribe. The human tribe*" (Obama 1995:348). From his perspective, tribalism has ruined several African countries, whereas the diverse groups in Hawai'i have forged an exemplary sense of commonality. In the Islands, communitarianism cannot be uncoupled from other multicultural values.

Mainland hyperindividualism, as extolled by anti-multiculturalists (Schlesinger 1991:2, 21, 64), finds little place in the Aloha State. Residents of Hawai'i perceive themselves and others as members of groups, not just as individuals, and therefore feel comfortable talking in terms that might be perceived as "politically incorrect" on the Mainland (Okamura 1998:275).

For Obama, "*It is hard to find your individual potential or sense of self-worth unless you are also concerned about the collective potential and self-worth of others*" (Husain and Chang 2005). At a fundraiser, he once said:

> *The essence of Hawaii has always been that we come from far and wide, that we come from different backgrounds and different last names, and yet we come together as a single ohana because we believe in the fundamental commonality of people. . . . We have a sense that beneath the surface of things, all of us share a common*

set of hopes, a common set of dreams and a common set of values.
That's what the Islands have always been about. (Pang 2004)

During his election campaign, when the economy became the number one issue, he talked of *"shared sacrifice and shared prosperity"* to define his economic philosophy (Balz and Haynes 2009:166).

As a candidate, Barack Obama drew fire from Reverend Jesse Jackson for his 2008 Father's Day criticism of African American fathers who abandon their families (MSNBC 2008). Beyond a bit of autobiography in Obama's speech, what Jackson apparently missed was that Obama (2009) considers responsibilities to be just as important as rights.

He endorsed the principle that the world can be perceived as 'ohana when he once said, *"Our diversity defines us rather than divides us"* (Abercrombie 2008). He believes that good parents set an example to their children when they contribute to their communities by coaching Little League events and going to parent–teacher conferences (Obama 2009).

Obama believes that there is a message the world needs to hear from the rainbow people of Hawai'i, namely, that diversity is the hope of the world. His longtime friend Congressman Neil Abercrombie (2008) interprets Obama's keynote address of 2004 as a statement about the American 'ohana. His biographer Richard Wolffe (2009:32) considers that Obama's most important quest was his search for a sense of family, since he grew up with an absent birthfather and a peripatetic birthmother.

When his friendship with Reverend Jeremiah Wright threatened to derail his campaign in 2008, he gave one of the most profound speeches on race relations ever. The following words from that March 18 address sum up his communitarian philosophy:

> *I chose to run for the presidency at this moment in history because I believe deeply that we cannot solve the challenges of our time unless we solve them together—unless we perfect our union by understanding that we may have different stories, but we hold common hopes; that we may not look the same and we may not have come from the same place, but we all want to move in the same direction—towards a better future for our children and our grandchildren.*

Communitarianism, as popularized by sociologist Amitai Etzioni (1993, 2009), is the essence of Barack Obama's political philosophy. In his nomination acceptance speech of 2008, he opposed his predecessor's individualistic "ownership society" as a recipe for *"Pull[ing] yourself up by your own bootstraps even if you don't have boots. You're on your own."* Instead, he identified the *"American promise"* as *"individual responsibility and mutual responsibility."* Columnist David Brooks (2010a, b) also appears to flirt with communitarianism, as he praises British communitarian theorist Phillip Blond (2010).

Communitarians believe that people should join forces together to solve social problems as much as possible outside government. For example, communitarian neighborhood watch groups, numerous in urban and suburban Oʻahu (Vorsino 2010c), can stop and prevent crime with police guidance, whereas conservatives urge individual homeowners to hire private security companies and liberals beef up police forces so that crime fighting is government's sole responsibility. Regarding public defenders' budgets (conservatives wanting less, liberals more), communitarians favor having Bar Associations establish panels of experienced attorneys to serve as pro bono public defenders so that funds can be cut while increasing quality. For Obama, the loss of community in the United States has had tragic consequences.

(8) **Harmony (lōkahi) (wa).** Many ethnic groups came to Hawaiʻi with ancestral histories of antagonism yet now live together peacefully because they value unity over division. Native Hawaiians painfully remember the overthrow of the Hawaiian monarchy in 1893, when Haole business leaders relied on U.S. Marines to arrest the queen and keep her captive until she abdicated. Imperial Japan committed barbarous acts in China, Korea, and the Philippines, and resentments linger among the latters' descendants in Hawaiʻi. Class conflict between rich Whites and poorer non-Whites erupted in labor unrest in the Islands during times past. But that era gave way to a recognition of trade unions and a succession of governors of Caucasian, Japanese, Native Hawaiian, and Filipino ancestry in accordance with the norm that Hawaiʻi must have a peaceful coexistence among the various social classes and ethnic groups.

Barack Obama's change of career from investment consultant in New York to community organizer in Chicago demonstrates his need to bring people together to fight for their rights through normal political channels. He could not abide continued exploitation of the powerless, so he sought to uplift those alienated on Chicago's South Side by bringing them into the mainstream of politics. His vision is that *"people [sh]ould live and work together in harmony."* The *"decision to work in politics, and to pursue such a career in a big Mainland city, in some sense, grows out of my Hawaiian upbringing"* (Glauberman and Burris 2008:5).

According to Obama, *"Hawaii is a fabulous model for the kind of America I hope this campaign will bring about, a place where different cultures can come together in harmony, and a place that rises above the barriers that divide us"* (Glauberman and Burris 2008:4). His belief that Americans should do so is reflected in his most famous quote, presented at the 2004 Democratic National Convention: *"There's not a Black America and White America and Latino America and Asian America. There's the United States of America."*

Nevertheless, there are differences of opinion on many matters throughout the Aloha State. The goal of harmony is not always achieved because of diversity of perspectives. Obama's oft-repeated maxim—that people should *"disagree without being disagreeable"*—is a basic element embodied in Hawai'i's multicultural ethos. Instead of taking sides between those who believe that government is the problem or the solution to the nation's ills, Obama wants government to be effective rather than dysfunctional.

(9) **Serenity (la'i) (hei-on).** For Mainland observers, Obama's most puzzling characteristic is his calm, unflappable demeanor and "unexcitable steadiness" (Zeleny 2008) along with hopefulness and optimism. Local Hawai'i residents have an admirable ability to be patient and understanding, even in adversity, and "wait without impatience and to endure without visible despair" (Broder 2010). When receiving bad news, there is a tendency to say "Minah!" or "Ain't no big ting."

Quick movements in a hot climate result in excessive perspiration, so Islanders are accustomed to move slowly, even gracefully, taking others into consideration along the way. The quiet solitude present in Japanese restaurants carries over to other public places. Signs on public busses warn not to make loud or unnecessary noise. Gym saunas have similar signs so that patrons can use the time contemplatively. Without meditation and *"downtime,"* according to Obama, *"you start making mistakes or you lose the big picture"* (Zeleny 2008).

When George Ariyoshi ran for reelection as governor, his slogan "quiet but effective" summed up the mantra pervading much of Hawai'i. Particularly among Japanese, there is a tendency to eschew negative news, people, and situations, that is, to avoid bad karma. Similarly, the self-described *"serene"* Obama (Heilemann and Halperin 2010:2) insisted that his campaign staff should not dwell on missteps but should instead *"calm down"* (Heilemann and Halperin 2010:375) and keep the focus positive (Plouffe 2009:203).

Governor Cayetano's autobiography reveals much behind-the-scenes wrangling among overheated politicians. Such outlandish behavior is kept out of public view precisely because of the obvious contradiction with prevailing cultural norms.

David Gergen, political adviser to many presidents, referred to incoming President Obama as embodying "Aloha Zen," that is, "a kind of comfortable calm [that] reflects a man who seems easygoing, not so full of himself" (Stolberg 2009). The Zen quality is based on the belief that one must always be positive while persevering in good and bad times. The Aloha quality is that love is anywhere and everywhere. Although journalist Jonathan Alter (2010:Ch. 9) provides extensive commentary on Obama's Zen temperament during his first year in office, that he missed the Aloha element is a sad commentary on how Washington has devoured the young president.

Obama rarely shows emotional passion, but he was visibly choked up about his role as the first African American nominated for the presidency just before delivering his acceptance speech (Balz and Johnson 2009:322). The tears streaming down Barack Obama's face while he gave a final campaign speech after learning of his grandmother's death spoke volumes for how he carried the love of a child into adulthood. His sentimental emotions come to play whenever his family is involved.

(10) **Piety (mana) (ikei)**. Many people in Hawai'i are intensely spiritual without being religious; they live their beliefs without pontification. Native Hawaiians have a spiritual connection with the air, land, ocean, and other people; they believe in a divine power that provides life-sustaining energy (Edwards 2009:63; Zeleny 2008), and provide a special ceremony to bless newly launched undertakings. Although some believe in Pele as the fire god who created the volcanic Islands, most are Christians, and many are Buddhists. Native Hawaiians believe that the land is sacred, and others have joined them in protesting unbridled economic development that turns soil into concrete. As Obama stated at a press conference in May 2010, the indigenous people believe that *"the ocean is sacred."* Native Hawaiians and many Asians also accept the existence of spirits (Grant 2005). Within Hawai'i beliefs coexist in the existence of ghosts, reverence for ancestors, the possibility of reincarnation, and the resurrection of Jesus and other Christian miracles. Human behavior is expected to be based on observing the values of the various religions, such that materialism is secondary to higher values.

In 1997, Hawai'i's spiritual leader, the Reverend Abraham Akaka, died. He was the one who coined the term "the Aloha State." Senator Daniel Akaka, his son, eloquently summed up Native Hawaiian spirituality by quoting his father at the memorial service on September 20:

> Aloha consists of this new attitude of heart, above negativism, above legalism. It is the unconditional desire to promote the true good of other people in a friendly spirit, out of a sense of kinship. Aloha seeks to do good, with no conditions attached. We do not do good only to those who do good to us. One of the sweetest things about the love of God, about Aloha, is that it welcomes the stranger and seeks his good. A person who has the spirit of Aloha loves even when the love is not returned.

Although his mother was a student of comparative religion and read to him passages from many sacred texts (Remnick 2010:174), Barry Obama resisted religious indoctrination at schools in Indonesia. While at Punahou, he attended the campus chapel and took an eighth grade ethics class that required students to think about basic human values. Having converted to Christianity in Chicago, he was exposed to Jeremiah Wright's Black liberation theology. He has frequently lamented the poverty of lives "*geared towards material goods and money*," instead preferring to focus on "*something in the human spirit that can't be conquered*" (Husain and Chang 2005; cf. Parsons and Nicholas 2010).

Obama's vision of the American dream is more than the material aspiration for everyone to live in their own homes. His vision for the United States is of a spiritual transformation, a change in the "*mind-set*" of violence rather than negotiation, greed rather than responsibility (Morris 2010). His strong belief in the basic principles of American government, as embodied in the Declaration of Independence and the Constitution, led him to promise that he would close the Guantánamo prison as contrary to fundamental American principles.

Unlike many in the Democratic Party, Obama is a truly religious president. His religious conversion is genuine. His belief in the need to find common ground amid differences of opinion is rooted in his Christian faith (Remnick 2010:440–442, 458). From the Vermont Avenue Baptist Church in Washington, DC, he confided in January 2010: "*It's faith that keeps me calm. It's faith that gives me peace.*" The same could be said for Native Hawaiians who have persevered in seeking redress since the fall of the Kingdom of Hawai'i in 1893.

(11) **Humanism (lokomaika'i) (jindo-shugi)**. In Hawai'i, people come
before principles. Universalistic approaches that ignore individual cases
enjoy little favor. Dogma is eschewed, according to the multicultural
ethos. Zero-sum decisions are avoided because one size will not fit all in
a diverse society. As a onetime Hawai'i Republican Congressional representative once said, "There is an exception to every rule."

More colloquially, "Don't make waves" is the watchword for caution
in interpersonal relations as well as public policy so that influential people will not harm those who are less powerful and vice versa. Decisions
are ideally made on the basis of a consensus, and building a consensus
requires wide consultation.

Barack Obama has made clear that he is an *"extreme pragmatist"*
(Alter 2010:146) and not ideological. Being result oriented, his test of
success is how a policy benefits people instead of how a policy conforms
to an abstract philosophy. Accordingly, he is unhappy over such dis-
parities as the widening gap of income between owners and employees
(Remnick 2010:285).

Obama's pragmatic approach to the factor of race in politics and society derives in part from the fact that he is of mixed-race ancestry:

> *As the child of a [B]lack man and a [W]hite woman, someone who
> was born in the racial melting pot of Hawaii, with a sister who's
> half Indonesian but who's usually mistaken for Mexican or Puerto
> Rican, and brother-in-law and niece of Chinese descent, with some
> blood relatives who resemble Margaret Thatcher and others who
> could pass for Bernie Mac, so that family get-togethers over Christ-
> mas take on the appearance of a UN General Assembly meeting,
> I've never had the option of restricting my loyalties on the basis
> of race, or measuring my worth on the basis of tribe.* (Obama
> 2008:274)

Native Hawaiians took the lead in marrying outside their race. Filipinos and Mexicans, similarly, have mestizo backgrounds. Interracial
marriage breaks down barriers between races and makes racism seem
irrelevant (cf. Rodriguez 2007).

Obama's experiences outside the United States help him to understand
other cultures. While campaigning in Iowa during 2007, he confessed:

> *If you don't understand these cultures, then it's very hard for you
> to make good foreign-policy decisions . . . . The benefit of my life*

of having both lived overseas and traveled overseas . . . is I have a
better sense of how they're thinking and what their society is really
like. (Agence France Press 2007)

(12) **Boundary maintenance (kapu) (kinshi).** Any culture must establish
ways of preventing the erosion of basic values by enforcing conformity.
Those living in Hawai'i take great pride in the uniqueness of their own
ethnic culture as well as the ethos that binds everyone together. There is
a general recognition that Hawai'i is a "special place" that must be preserved. Island people persist in maintaining their multicultural diversity.

Newcomers (malihini) to Hawai'i, thus, must assimilate to the multicultural ethos in order to become a part of the social mainstream. Mainlanders who try to set up businesses in Hawai'i by cheating customers
will find that word of their improprieties spreads quickly on small islands,
and they will soon end up without customers. Those from the two coasts
tend to have much more difficulty than those from the heartland, where
religious principles are more firmly stressed. The Dunhams, thus, must
have adjusted more smoothly than "Coast Haoles."

Those who play by the rules of Hawai'i's multicultural ethos will be
trusted, but those who refuse to do so are left at the margin, ostracized yet
still given a second chance for inclusion. Those who show contempt for
the rules of the game are likely to suffer discrimination but not disrespect.
The common phrase to describe their misconduct is "How rude!" The
discrimination, thus, is based on cultural grounds, not ethnicity. Many
Caucasians new to Hawai'i are baffled when they are turned down for a
job or quietly hassled at work because their employers and coworkers are
annoyed at an arrogance that they do not perceive in themselves. Often,
they leave the Islands out of puzzled frustration.

Mainland-born Whites sometimes believe that the term "local values"
is racist. Some do not assimilate to the prevailing culture, even after living in Hawai'i for decades.

Clearly, it is an exaggeration to say that the Mainland is the "land of
the free, home of hotheads," as a columnist said after observing town
hall meetings on health care during August 2009 (Rowe 2009a), though
the columnist found support for his view of American culture in the
writings of Alexis de Tocqueville (1835). In Hawai'i, however, hotheads
do not last long.

Obama has frequently referred to his mother's and grandparents'
roots in Kansas. Rather than crediting Hawai'i as the sole wellspring for
his demeanor and values, he often has assigned credit to the heartland of

America. And his supporters from around the country have viewed him as one of them, representing the best of America. Obama has repeatedly complimented the unsung heroes of America, similar to his humble, hardworking, self-sacrificing mother and grandparents. What Mainlanders experience when they move to Hawai'i is that they are rewarded for their positive virtues and gradually weaned away from anything negative, resulting in greater self-fulfillment.

What about the adjustment among Asians from Asia or Asians from the Mainland? Those from Asia join a preexisting ethnic community that can assist in assimilation. Asians from the Mainland, however, have a unique problem because they have already adjusted to Mainland values and may act at first no differently from Mainland Haole transplants. The local term for them is "kotonk"—Asian on the outside but Haole on the inside. However, they find the path to adjustment somewhat easier than Haoles because they still respect ancestral ways that they downplayed in the course of their assimilation on the Mainland.

Ethnic humor serves a useful function as a gentle reminder to avoid culturally annoying behavior (cf. Ariyoshi 2004). Motorists who honk soon learn to be quiet and respectful on the road, yielding to others out of kindness even when they lack the right of way. Although some Mainland transplants in Hawai'i are pleased when politicians are brutally honest, the type of negative campaigning common and effective on the Mainland will boomerang if used openly during election campaigns in Hawai'i (Cayetano 2009:250, 410, 416; cf. Borreca 2010c).

As Obama (1995:270) notes, the culture of Hawai'i is more forgiving of cultural clumsiness. After all, nobody in the Aloha State is truly an expert at intercultural learning. There is always something new to learn and an openness to do so.

Presidents try to be on their best behavior. They are scrutinized as if monarchs setting the tone for the country. Insofar as Barack Obama embraces the 12 principles of Hawai'i's multicultural ethos, he has become a role model for the people of Hawai'i as well as America.

CONCLUSION

One might interpret Hawai'i's 12-fold multicultural ethos as mere personality traits. Nothing could be further from the truth. They represent elements of a distinct philosophy, a mind-set in which interculturalism is the norm, a philosophy known in the Islands as the Aloha Spirit. And they do not represent a rejection of what Will Herberg (1955) calls the

American Way but instead are compatible with respect for life, liberty, and the pursuit of happiness along with generosity, hard work, innovative entrepreneurship, pragmatism, and other quintessential American values. Hawai'i's multicultural ethos is perhaps an improved version of the American Way. Cynics, of course, might dismiss Hawai'i's multicultural ethos, but in doing so they are also rejecting many of the 13 virtues that Benjamin Franklin (1793) espoused—particularly, sincerity, justice, moderation, tranquility, and humility.

Barack Obama grew up in cosmopolitan Hawai'i. Although most residents are classified in the federal census as "Asian and Pacific," those terms are not in currency within the Islands to describe the population (Okamura 1994). Instead, each ethnic group is recognized separately for its own special contributions to the life of the Aloha State.

To enjoy a respite from the stress of electioneering nonstop, Obama returned to Hawai'i in August 2008. During an open-air speech, he told admirers how much he tried to spread Aloha to the rest of the United States during his nomination campaign:

> *I try to explain to them something about the [A]loha [S]pirit. I try to explain to them this basic idea that we all have obligations to each other, that we're not alone, that if we see somebody who's in need, we should help. . . .[M]ost importantly, that when you come from Hawaii, you start understanding that what's on the surface, what people look like, that doesn't determine who they are. And that the power and strength of diversity, the ability of people from everywhere, whether they're [B]lack or [W]hite, whether they're Japanese-American or Korean-American or Filipino-American or whatever they are, they are just Americans, that all of us can work together and all of us can join together to create a better country. It's that spirit, that I'm absolutely convinced, is what America is looking for right now. (Honolulu Star-Bulletin 2008a)*

A consensus exists that there is a unique multicultural ethos in Hawai'i. Lacking a commonly accepted delineation of its content or explanation for its formation beyond the term "Aloha Spirit," this chapter has attempted a comprehensive statement of that ethos. Three cultures (American, Native Hawaiian, and Japanese) have been vying for acceptance of their norms on the basis of their economic and political power in the Islands. Rather than allowing one group to dominate, the multicultural ethos arose. That is, the three main groups decided to adjust to one another without losing their identity, and Caucasians and Japanese have given particularly great deference to the culture of Native Hawaiians.

When Barack Obama arrived in Chicago as a community organizer, he encountered a culture of African Americans who were disempowered and divided. He tried to unite them by *"building a culture"* (Remnick 2010:179). His model was the culture of Hawai'i.

For many observers, Hawai'i is a paragon of ethnic harmony, a thesis on which there is some disagreement inside the Aloha State because of many unresolved political problems. Even the most strident critic of the ethnic harmony thesis admits that relations between the races are better in Hawai'i than on the Mainland (Okamura 1998:274). If so, why? There are several alternative explanations:

Relative ethnic peace is commonly attributed to the fact there is no ethnic majority in Hawai'i. But that explanation is easily contradicted, as the same multiethnic reality exists in California, New Mexico, and Texas without a corresponding cultural transformation.

A persistent explanation is the long acceptance of interracial marriage, as bicultural and multicultural children have blazed a trail of common acceptance (Adams 1926). But Japanese before statehood were treated by the White power elite as out-groups until they achieved political power, and today Blacks, Haoles, members of the military, and even Filipino immigrants are often considered out-groups (Cayetano 2009:252, 531; Okamura 1998:165; Stannard 2005). Sometimes, members of out-groups have been the least likely to be accepted as marriage partners by members of in-groups.

A third view is that the history of the Islands and its political ups and downs has taught everyone not to tread on cultural sensitivities. But an ethnopolitical history arguably shows more problems than solutions (see Chapter 2).

Absorption to a common set of values is perhaps the best way to explain ethnic peace. Public opinion surveys, indeed, prove that opinions held by the people of Hawai'i differ fundamentally from those found on the Mainland (see Chapter 3).

Yet another explanation for relative ethnic harmony is the development of a popular local culture, with acceptance of common customs, folk beliefs, food, jokes, and traditions (Grant and Ogawa 1993:150) as well as heroes (Stannard 2005). One might add the development of a Creole language, the media, local literature, and music (see Chapters 4–7).

A sixth thesis is that less affluent groups have successfully struggled to gain increased status and power. The establishment of labor unions, in turn, led to the election of progressive-minded leaders (see Chapters 8, 9).

Some scholars claim that the rise of Chinese and Japanese from their status as plantation workers to prosperous stalwarts of the Island economy is a valid explanation for the ethnic harmony (Adams 1933:148; Fuchs 1961:449; Lind 1980:901). Statistics can test that explanation (see Chapter 10).

The opportunity for education, which raised the literacy rate of the Kingdom of Hawai'i higher than most countries around the world, provided a path for a better life. Then immigrants from Asia, where education is highly valued as the best hope for social mobility, were recruited to the Islands. The premise that an educated population is likely to behave constructively is nevertheless challenged by the history of public education in Hawai'i (see Chapters 11, 12).

Relatively benign governance is yet another thread that runs through discussions of Hawai'i's ethnic harmony. There appears to be no evidence of discrimination in the way police and courts operate (see Chapter 13).

Accordingly to Jonathan Okamura (1994:165), the power structure has promoted the concept of ethnic harmony to cover up and discourage real grievances and resentments that remain under the surface—in particular, lack of social mobility and justice for certain groups. One reason for failing to meet demands for economic progress can be found in the nature of the world economy, which limits the ability of Islanders to handle their own affairs (see Chapter 14).

Of all the explanations for relative ethnic calm despite ongoing conflicts, adherence to Hawai'i's multicultural ethos is the most fundamental. Indeed, during 1986, state legislators recognized the centrality of the multicultural ethos by adopting what they called the Aloha Spirit Law (see Appendix). The law, which defines some norms of the multicultural ethos, instructs government officials to take the Aloha Spirit into account whenever they make decisions. Presumably, those who fail to carry out the law will be defeated at the polls or be reversed by another branch of government.

Whichever explanation is correct, life in Hawai'i made a profound impact upon Barack Obama. He views Hawai'i as a model for the United States as well as for relations between governments in the international arena. How well has he incorporated his early experience into his administration as America's 44th president? Guided by knowledge of the model that has motivated him all his political life, the reader can make a better judgment in time (see Chapter 15).

Barack Obama is so unlike other political leaders that he appears an enigma. His meteoric rise to prominence has puzzled those who try to understand him, yet fundamentally he is a son of the Fiftieth State and its culture.

But how did that culture emerge? Obama is fortunate to have lived during the transformative 1970s, when multiculturalism blossomed in Hawai'i. To learn how the multicultural ethos arose, one must appreciate the social and political history of Hawai'i. To fully understand Obama, one must trace the pattern of events to which he was exposed while he was growing up. The next 13 chapters indicate what led up to that transformation and what followed, as America may be revitalized when its people learn valuable lessons that President Obama is trying to put into practice.

•

Chapter 2

History of the Struggles
of the Peoples of the Islands

Michael Haas

The ugly conquest of Native Hawaiians through aborted treaties and crippling disease brought by the missionaries, the carving up of rich volcanic soil by American companies for sugarcane and pineapple plantations; the indenturing system that kept Japanese, Chinese and Filipino immigrants stooped sunup to sunset in these same fields . . . all this was recent history. And yet, by the time my family arrived, it had somehow vanished from collective memory.

(Obama 1995:23)

Learning the events of history usually serves to give a sense of identity within the context of one's country. From grades 1–4, Barack Obama's mother homeschooled him in English and the history of the United States, with some emphasis on African Americans, while he was subjected to political indoctrination in Indonesian schools.

After Barry returned to Honolulu to enroll in grade 5 at Punahou, he learned about the history of another country—the Kingdom of Hawai'i. The kingdom, of course, no longer existed. Hawai'i had gone through a transition from Kingdom to Republic to American Territory and finally to statehood in 1959.

The transition of the Islands from an autonomous sovereign country to an American state raises important questions. Why did the indigenous people, the Native Hawaiians, accept the loss of sovereignty without a fight? What issues remain as a result of the fall of the monarchy? Why did the foreign White economic elite, the Haoles, ultimately fail in their efforts to impose institutional racism on imported laborers from Asia and elsewhere? Why, despite unresolved contentious issues, did Hawai'i develop a multicultural ethos that has assured domestic tranquility?

This chapter, accordingly, is a multicultural history of the Islands through its many political reincarnations. The first part deals with pre-statehood Hawai'i. Then the focus shifts to the period of Obama's youth, 1961–1979, perhaps the most fascinating period of transformation, and concludes with what has happened since he left for college, a career, and the presidency.

PRE-STATEHOOD HAWAI'I

More than a thousand years ago, a hardy, seafaring Polynesian people set sail into the South Pacific for an unknown land. After arriving in an isolated archipelago, they developed a unique culture and language. Although accounts of their egalitarian existence evidently inspired Karl Marx and Friedrich Engels (Engels 1884; Harris 1968; Morgan 1870), a class of ali'i (nobility) divided up the land, imposing hierarchical control over maka'āina (commoners), who cultivated food and developed fishing grounds sufficient to feed a population, who increased to at least 300,000 inhabitants and possibly as many as 800,000 by the mid-1700s (Kane 1997:68; Stannard 1989:30).

According to artifacts at the Bishop Museum in Honolulu, the first Westerners to arrive were explorers on Spanish ships (Haas 1991; Knowlton 1991). In 1527, one of three vessels in an expedition led by explorer Álvaro de Saavedra was shipwrecked; two survivors somehow made their way to Hawai'i and intermarried with the local population (Fornander 1880:ii–106). Another Spaniard, Juan Gaetano, landed in the Islands, which in 1555 he named Las Islas de Mesa. In 1567, Álvaro Mendaña de Neira returned to map the islands. Madrid evidently saw no reason to colonize the archipelago, which lay between its larger prizes, México and the Philippines, and kept secret the existence of the Islands, presumably so that no other imperial power would take advantage.

When England's Captain James Cook arrived at Kaua'i in 1778, he named the archipelago the Sandwich Islands after his benefactor, the Earl of Sandwich. In 1779, on a return visit, he landed at the island of Hawai'i, then undergoing civil war. Cook was killed while trying to take a chief hostage in order to retrieve a small ship hijacked by several Native Hawaiian warriors.

The English were eager to expand their commerce, so trading ships soon began to dock in ports for rest and supplies. From 1780 to 1800, Hawai'i was a frequent stopover location in the otter and seal fur trade between North America and China. For the route from Canada to Australia, Hawai'i was in a strategic location. George Vancouver, who sailed to Hawai'i on several occasions in the late 18th century, was astonished when one of the chiefs, named Kamehameha, sought an alliance with Britain so as to prevail in a civil war with rival chiefs on the various islands. Kamehameha even offered to cede the island of Hawai'i to Britain, and although the Union Jack went up in 1794, London was more concerned with European matters, and the flag soon came down (Kuykendall 1938:41).

Meanwhile, two Russian ships visited Kaua'i in 1804, during the reign of Catherine the Great. Small Russia trading posts were established on Kaua'i, but the venture was abandoned by 1817.

Kamehameha I (1795–1819). By 1795, Kamehameha unified most of the Hawaiian Islands under a single political regime. In 1810, when the ruler of Kaua'i agreed to accept Kamehameha's suzerainty, his conquest was complete. He had become ali'i nui (king).

As contact with the artifacts of Western civilization whetted the appetite of Kamehameha to purchase fine clothing and instruments of modern technology, the ali'i followed suit. To obtain Western commodities, including weapons, Kamehameha supplied British merchant ships with sandalwood, in demand within China, and Native Hawaiian maka'āinana (commoners) worked long and hard to provide the treasured resource. Foreign traders offered credit to the monarchy as an advance on the purchase of sandalwood logs.

Kamehameha II (1819–1824). When the sandalwood forest was exhausted, the creditors called in loans of at least $200,000, resulting in onerous taxes on the people (Kuykendall 1938:91–92). The commerce-minded foreigners (Haoles, a term now applied to Caucasians or Whites) lusted to control the economy of the archipelago.

Approximately one hundred missionaries, primarily from New England, began arriving in Hawai'i from the 1820s (U.S. Departments of

Interior and Justice 2000:22). When Kamehameha I died in 1819, his favorite queen, Ka'ahumanu, persuaded the new king to decree an end of the kapu (taboo) system of religious restrictions, which had been violated with impunity by the crews of foreign ships without the dire consequences assumed by the native faith. The people welcomed a new creed when the Christians arrived.

Kamehameha III (1824–1854). After sandalwood, the principal industry was to service whaling ships and their crews, who docked in port from the 1830s. As trade boomed, the Haole population increased (Table 1.2). Western contact meant that new diseases were introduced, but practical measures of public health to cope with various epidemics were insufficient, and the native population fell from 300,000 or more in 1778 to 142,050 by 1823 and 73,000 by 1853 (Nordyke 1989:178).

There were mass baptisms in the 1830s (Meller 1958b:796). The missionaries believed that Christian teaching insisted that good people wear considerable clothing to protect the modesty of their bodies, and they undertook to dismantle the Hawaiian polytheistic religion as idolatrous. Although they introduced public health services, ostensibly to save the indigenous population from extinction, the Native Hawaiian population continued to decline in numbers.

To provide meat for the appetites of the newcomers, cattle were imported. To manage the cattle industry, vaqueros were imported in the 1830s from San Gabriel Mission, California, then under Mexican rule (Table 2.1).

When many missionaries decided to stay in Hawai'i rather than to return to the U.S. Mainland, the American Board of Missions could not support the growing missionary community. By 1837, during a recession in the United States, the Board began to cut financial support, so the missionaries had to become more economically self-supporting. Most embarked on commercial ventures; some became government workers.

British interests were dominant in Hawai'i up to the 1830s. A French ship commander briefly seized the kingdom in 1839, and in February 1843 the commander of a British ship forced the Hawaiian king to grant powers to a British commission. But both Paris and London soon disavowed efforts to claim a colony.

In 1837, Kamehameha III promulgated a declaration of rights. In 1840, he adopted a British-style constitution with an elective seven-member House of Representatives. References to the "Sandwich Islands" ended that year, since the constitution was proclaimed on behalf of the "Hawaiian Islands" (Clement 1980). Concluding that

Table 2.1

Streams of Labor Immigration to Hawai'i by Ethnic Group, 1830–1979

Ethnic Group	Era of Arrival	Number Arriving	Percent Male	Percent Children	Percent of Total
Mexicans	1830s	200	na	na	.1%
Chinese	1852–1885	28,000	89%	5%	7.0
	1886–1899	28,700	na	na	7.2
South Sea Islanders	1859–1884	2,500	87	11	.6
Portuguese	1878–1886	17,500	57	46	4.4
	1906–1913	5,500	60	43	1.4
Norwegians	1881	600	84	20	.2
Germans	1881–1888, 1897	1,300	72	36	.3
Japanese	1868, 1885–1898	45,000	82	1	11.3
	1898–1907	114,000	82	1	28.6
Galicians	1898	370	83	25	.1
Puerto Ricans	1900–1901, 1921	6,000	60	46	1.5
Blacks	1901	200	68	na	.1
Koreans	1903–1905	7,900	90	6	2.0
Russians	1906, 1909–1912	2,400	70	26	.6
Spanish	1907–1913	8,000	56	39	2.0
Filipinos	1907–1932	119,000	92	5	30.0
	1946	7,300	93	12	1.8
Samoans	1919, 1952	na	na	na	na
Vietnamese	1975–1979	3,463	51	48	.9

Key: na = Figures not available.

Notes: "Percent male" is the ratio of male adults to all adults, children excluded. South Sea Islanders came from the countries now known as Fiji, Kiribati, Papua New Guinea, and Vanuatu. Galicia was a part of Poland in 1898.

Sources: Glick (1980:10); Lind (1980:37; 1982:12); Nordyke (1989:91, 253); Schmitt (1977:25); U.S. Census (1902:573; 1922:1180; 1983:13, 66).

they could obtain all they wanted from the Hawaiian Islands without the inconvenience of having to govern the country, Britain and France agreed in November 1843 that Hawai'i should remain independent. Their entente on this matter, formalized by a joint communiqué, was soon accepted by President John Tyler, who extended the Monroe Doctrine to the archipelago (Geschwender 1982:195; Stevens 1945:18–20).

The ruling monarchs, who wanted to avoid being gobbled up by imperial powers, trusted the early missionaries, who did good works but initially took no plunder. Some served as cabinet ministers and in other supporting roles so that the kingdom could more easily govern itself in a manner that foreigners expected. Before taking up official posts, the Americans acquired Hawaiian citizenship. They established a progressive government, becoming the first country in the world to have a ministry of education and a ministry of health. Some intermarried with the native population. At one point, only one-fourth of the king's cabinet officials were Native Hawaiians (Fuchs 1961:14).

Back in 1802, a Chinese merchant decided to mill sugarcane, which had been first planted by a Spanish advisor to King Kamehameha, Don Francisco de Paula y Marín, who later introduced coffee and pineapple to the Islands in 1813. The land proved eminently suitable for large-scale sugarcane cultivation, and by 1835 the first major plantation opened at Kōloa, Kauaʻi. To develop a more extensive sugarcane industry, however, Haole traders could not obtain a sizable foreign bank loan, since they lacked collateral. Land was not for sale in traditional Hawaiʻi but instead was held in common by the monarchs on behalf of the people. An 1841 law allowed aliʻi to lease land to foreigners for up to 55 years, but bankers in the United States were unimpressed. They required transferable assets.

Next, Haole advisers prevailed on the king to introduce a system of private property. Under the terms of the so-called Great Māhele of 1848, the land was divided as follows: 39 percent for the aliʻi, 24 percent for the crown, 36 percent as government land, and 1 percent for the commoners or makaʻāinana (Kent 1983:31), though foreigners still did not own land.

In 1850, when the legislature was increased to 24 members, Haoles held a majority and passed the Kuleana Act, which enabled Native Hawaiians to file a claim for their own kuleana (land where they lived and put to productive use), provided they paid hefty fees to survey the land and register their titles. If they failed to do so, others could file claims of adverse possession. Thus, Native Hawaiians suddenly were allowed their own private property, provided they followed complex legal regulations. Haole entrepreneurs then entreated the Native Hawaiians to sell their ancestral land at profits that seemed staggering. The indigenous population soon became tenants on land owned by foreigners, who controlled two-thirds of the land by 1886 (Morgan 1948:137). Displaced Native Hawaiians then needed to sell their labor in order to feed themselves and pay rent.

For the sugarcane industry, there were not enough Native Hawaiians to work the land, in part because the native population eschewed plantation work. Sugar interests then sought to import workers from China and later from Japan. The king, concerned that the Hawaiian race was dying out, agreed. He evidently thought that the new workers might intermarry with the Native Hawaiians to strengthen the bloodline (Geschwender 1982:208–209). A few Europeans came as contract laborers, too, but the only Caucasian immigrant group of any size was from Portugal, who were not considered Haoles because they worked as plantation workers, albeit as supervisors (Geschwender, Carroll-Seguin, Brill 1988). Thus, Hawai'i developed into a multiethnic society. Most of the population was non-Hawaiian by 1890 (Table 1.2).

In 1850, the Masters and Servants Act legalized a system under which costs of transporting Chinese or other workers to Hawai'i were to be paid by means of lengthy work contracts, which could be broken only under penalty of a jail sentence, thereby creating a condition of legal peonage. The penal code, which established the principle of matching the ethnicity of the defendant with the ethnicity of members of juries (Nelligan and Ball 1992), did not apply to violations of work contracts, however. In 1852, the monarchy and the legislature agreed to election by universal manhood suffrage.

Kamehameha IV (1855–1863). Upon the king's death in 1854, Kamehameha IV (Prince Alexander Liholiho) took over. In 1861, his constitution restricted voting to those who were property owners. He died of chronic asthma.

Kamehameha V (1863–1872). Liloliho's brother, Prince Lot, was his successor. In 1864, he convened a constitutional convention, which was dominated by Haoles. Under the new constitution, voting was restricted by both wealth (income or property ownership) and literacy.

Laborers from China began to leave agricultural jobs to engage in carpentry, cleaning businesses, and rice farming, leaving Japanese and Portuguese on the plantations where wages were based on race: Haoles were paid the most, followed by Portuguese, then Chinese, and finally Japanese (Conan 1946). Hawai'i became a multiethnic caste society in which Haoles and a few upper-status Native Hawaiians lived the good life, Portuguese became plantation supervisors, Asians were plantation laborers, and lower-status Native Hawaiians tried to eke out an existence through traditional subsistence agriculture or as unskilled workers in the towns.

King Lunalilo (1873–1874). Kamehameha V died in 1872 without a successor. The constitution provided that the legislature should name the new king. In an election on January 1, 1873, Prince William Lunalilo and David Kalākaua, who had lesser noble rank, were the candidates.

Suspecting that aliʻi electors had been bribed by Haole commercial leaders to support Kalākaua, Lunalilo's proponents stormed the building where votes were to be announced. The Haole foreign affairs minister then called upon 162 American and British troops from warships in port, and marines occupied the government building. Afterward, the marines withdrew, but gunboats thenceforth were rotated to ensure continuing Haole control.

Lunalilo was proclaimed king but died after a reign of only 13 months. Kalākaua was then elected to succeed him.

King Kalākaua (1874–1891). In 1874, a new constitution abolished property qualifications for voting. Kalākaua traveled to Washington, on behalf of the sugar interests, to secure a common market between Hawaiʻi and the United States. In 1876, Congress ratified the Treaty of Reciprocity, removing trade barriers between the Islands and the United States. In 1885, three of Kalākaua's sons introduced surfing to the United States during a vacation in Santa Cruz (Chawkins 2009).

In 1886, as a condition of renewing the Treaty of Reciprocity, Congress demanded that Hawaiʻi cede to the U.S. Navy exclusive use of the estuary at the Pearl River, now known as Pearl Harbor. That demand led to protests from many quarters, so Kalākaua demurred.

In mid-1887, heads of the largest sugar companies and their Haole allies called upon a group known as the "Hawaiian Rifles" to gain control of strategic locations throughout Honolulu. The king was forced to sign the Reciprocity Treaty and adopt a new constitution. Known as the "Bayonet Constitution," the king remained a constitutional monarch, but qualifications for voting changed: (1) Those born in Hawaiʻi, regardless of ancestry, could vote, even if they were also American or European citizens. (2) Those born in Asia, even if they had Hawaiian citizenship, were disqualified. (3) Voters had to have a yearly income of $600 or own $3,000 in property. Thereby, one-third of Native Hawaiians were disenfranchised.

The Reciprocity Treaty brought so much profit that larger sugar corporations no longer needed foreign bank loans. Haole big businesses then dominated insurance, shipping, and wholesale trade, and by 1904 bought their own sugar refinery (Geschwender 1982:200–201).

In 1889, part-Hawaiian Robert Wilcox sought to put Kalākaua's sister, Lydia Liliʻuokalani, on the throne, as he opposed the way in which

Americans were controlling the destiny of the people. His uprising was crushed by government troops, aided by marines from an American ship.

In 1891, the McKinley Act repealed tariffs on all countries exporting sugar to the United States, while American sugar growers received subsidies. As a result, Hawaiian sugar was too expensive on the Mainland. Through annexation, of course, the trade barrier could be eliminated.

Queen Lili'uokalani (1891–1893). On the death of Kalākaua in 1891, Lydia Kamaka'eha Paki Lili'uokalani ascended to the throne. Lamenting the decline of her people, many of whom were so alienated that they felt driven to despair, drunkenness, and suicide, she contemplated various measures to restore Native Hawaiians to a place of dignity, including abrogation of the Bayonet Constitution.

In early January 1893, in response to a petition signed by two-thirds of the registered voters, Lili'uokalani indicated an interest in changing the constitution to reserve more powers to the crown (McGregor 1991:14). When the Haole cabinet protested, she renounced her intention to redistribute power. However, a secret Committee of Safety formed among 13 persons, including six Haole citizens of Hawai'i, five American citizens, one English citizen, and one German. The U.S. Ambassador to Hawai'i, John Stevens, then assured the conspirators that American troops in port would support a coup.

Coup d'état. On January 16, Stevens ordered 162 troops to disembark from the USS *Boston*, seize the government building, and place the queen under house arrest in the palace, demanding that she abrogate. But Lili'uokalani (1898:Ch. 40–47) relinquished sovereignty to the United States, not to the leaders of the coup, recalling that a British commander who had taken the same action some 50 years earlier was later disavowed by London. After all, the landing of American soldiers was in violation of the Reciprocity Treaty (Dougherty 1992:169). Under arrest, she awaited a similar disavowal from Washington. Her son, Prince Jonah Kūhiō Kalaniana'ole Pi'ikoi, was soon arrested for seeking to restore her to the throne.

Provisional Government. Leaders of the conspiracy, responding to the military action, went to the government building to declare the monarchy dissolved and proclaimed a Provisional Government under martial law, pending annexation by the United States. On February 1, 1893, the American flag went up on the government building, and Republican President Benjamin Harrison submitted a treaty of cession to the Senate.

However, in November 1892, Grover Cleveland, a Democrat, had defeated Harrison's bid for reelection. Five days after taking office in March 1893, Cleveland withdrew the treaty from the Senate and sent to Honolulu an investigator, James Blount, who in turn surveyed the situation, had the American flag lowered, and ordered American troops to return to their ships. The report by Blount (1893) to Cleveland said that most people favored the queen, objected to the coup, and opposed American annexation. Cleveland then characterized annexation as unconstitutional and contrary to international law (Dudley and Agard 1990:25–46).

Republic of Hawai'i. With annexation thwarted, leaders of the coup proclaimed the Republic of Hawai'i on July 4, 1894, while continuing martial law. The Republic then declared crown lands to be government lands, much of which were later sold or leased to plantation owners. Congress, meanwhile, repealed the McKinley tariff in 1894, so the privileged position of Hawaiian sugarcane was restored.

The new constitution establishing the Republic of Hawai'i increased property qualifications for voting, thereby reducing Native Hawaiians to less than 20 percent of the registered voters. Chinese born in Hawai'i were also stripped of voting rights (Glick 1980:224).

Robert Wilcox then mapped a strategy to restore Lili'uokalani through a counterrevolution. When his plot was discovered in 1895, the movement was crushed, and Lili'uokalani was arrested for treason. In 1896, following her abdication, she was released from confinement in the palace and went to Washington to press a claim for Hawaiian independence. But the planters had already been there, lobbying for their interests. Her efforts were in vain.

Annexation. William McKinley was elected president in 1896. After the United States won the Spanish-American War in 1898, Congress voted to annex Guam, Hawai'i, the Philippines, and Puerto Rico. The annexation of Hawai'i occurred without a referendum. Some 38,000 of the 40,000 Native Hawaiians signed a petition opposing annexation (Langer 2008), impressing members of Congress, which had insufficient votes to annex by treaty. Instead, Congress voted to annex by a joint Congressional resolution, a questionable method for transfer of sovereignty under international law.

Territory of Hawai'i. In 1900, Congress passed the Organic Act, establishing Hawai'i as a Territory of the United States. Laws of the previous Republic of Hawai'i were still valid unless they contradicted provisions of the U.S. Constitution. Citizens under the Kingdom were granted American citizenship. Congress declared former crown lands to be government lands, some of which had already been sold or leased to private plantation owners. County governments began in 1903, and the City and County of Honolulu was incorporated in 1907.

Under the terms of the Organic Act, the president appointed Territorial governors, and in 1900 elections were held for local offices and for a nonvoting delegate to the House of Representatives. Knowing that Native Hawaiians accounted for more than two-thirds of the eligible voters, Wilcox now emerged as the standard-bearer of the Home Rule Party on a platform of reestablishing the monarchy. He was elected Congressional delegate, and his party swept elections to the Territorial legislature.

When the legislature convened, Native Hawaiian delegates spoke in their native language. Haole elites then closed ranks in preparation for the 1902 election. The Republicans nominated Prince Kūhiō, erstwhile heir to the throne, as Congressional delegate and thereby attracted Native Hawaiians to vote Republican. Kūhiō defeated Wilcox in 1902 and served until 1921.

From 1902, with Native Hawaiian support, the Republicans thereby attained a firm political hegemony in the Territorial legislature, while electing most Congressional delegates in the next half century. In short, as of 1902, some 29,000 Haoles, of whom fewer than 2,000 were registered to vote, controlled a population of 154,000 (Hawai'i 1902:21). Throughout most of the Territorial era, Native Hawaiians voted Haoles into a dominant position in order to share such rewards of power as contracts and jobs.

Even governors appointed by Democrats Woodrow Wilson and Franklin Roosevelt did not challenge the power of the Haole Republicans, who treated government as an extension of the plantation system of autocratic rule, with elites at the top, virtual serfs at the bottom, and a middle level of professionals and shopkeepers as a buffer between the two layers. Sugar conglomerates and allied Haole corporations assumed oligopolistic control over the Territory's economy (Kent 1983:Ch. 6).

Former crown and government lands from the days of the monarchy and the republic, nearly half the acreage of the Islands, were transferred to the new Territory of Hawai'i. Since most Native Hawaiians were landless and could not live as they had for centuries, Kūhiō felt obligated to do something for his people. In 1919, when nearly all the arable land had been cultivated (Shoemaker 1946:194), the Territorial legislature recommended that some land be set aside for Native Hawaiians. Plantation owners offered to donate their least desirable lands for homesteading by Native Hawaiians (Faludi 1991a).

In 1921, Congress passed the Hawaiian Homes Commission Act, which set aside some 200,000 acres of the nearly 2,000,000 acres of ceded crown lands for 99-year leases by those with at least half-Hawaiian ancestry at an annual rent of $.02 per acre. The rent was to be paid to the Territory's Department of Hawaiian Home Lands (DHHL), which in turn would prepare new land for more occupants with electricity, roads, water, and other infrastructure. In order to raise initial capital to provide infrastructure for homesteaders, DHHL leased more than 60 percent of the land to corporations and wealthy individuals on a long-term basis (Faludi 1991b). The initial rent to corporations was as low as $3.33 per acre, a hefty figure in 1921 but a giveaway by the end of the century, so DHHL increasingly lacked sufficient funds to offer basic services to the homesteaders. Moreover, most homestead land was unsuitable for habitation and was never distributed because no roads, power, or water were available. Only 21 percent of land set aside for homesteading is now being used by homesteaders, and today about 19,000 applicants still await allotments (Hawai'i 1998:172, 199; Pang 2009).

Various developments undermined the ruling coalition before statehood. In 1900, Chinese in large numbers walked off the job on the plantations to join kinfolk who had already started businesses in the cities (Table 2.2). Most Japanese remained on the plantations, but in 1900 they went on strike at almost every plantation for better working conditions. Although they were granted only meager concessions, plantation interests felt that the solution to labor unrest was to bring in more subservient workers, while using police of Native Hawaiian ancestry to break up strikes.

An inflow of workers from Korea, the Philippines, and Puerto Rico soon began (Table 2.3). The plantation owners could deport any alien who refused to accept labor conditions, thereby frustrating trade union organization. As recently as 1969, a report funded by a major plantation corporation characterized a surviving Filipino plantation camp as still remaining in a state of "feudalism" (Moore 1969:34). Strikes occurred throughout the first half of the 20th century, each time eroding the legitimacy of Haole Republican rule when legitimate demands were at issue, such as equal pay for equal work.

Republican leaders were increasingly apprehensive over the future voting strength of Asians. Federal law barred immigrants from citizenship, but their children born in Hawai'i would become immediate American

Table 2.2

Urban Population in Hawai'i by Ethnic Group, 1890–2000 (in percent)

Ethnic Group	1890	1910	1920	1930	1940	1950	1960	1970	1980	1990	2000
Black	na	46.2%	56.9%	57.2%	na	na	26.7%	31.7%	24.2%	19.6%	27.4%
Caucasian	31.9%	39.9	47.4	50.0	49.0%	51.0%	39.7	36.9	42.2	32.1	26.2
Chinese	28.8	44.2	56.9	71.1	78.0	82.5	78.9	68.5	74.0	67.6	70.0
Filipino	na	3.7	.9	7.6	13.1	28.4	32.0	31.4	32.2	27.4	25.3
Guamanian	na	na	na	na	na	na	na	na	40.7	31.1	36.7
Hawaiian	30.6	35.1	42.0	47.0	48.3	48.9	na	na	33.3	24.4	20.6
Japanese	3.1	15.2	22.4	34.0	38.4	50.1	53.5	50.4	52.8	45.6	42.9
Korean	10.1	26.6	40.3	na	na	na	na	na	70.0	63.4	66.2
Mexican	na	na	na	na	na	na	na	na	33.9	24.2	20.5
Puerto Rican	7.9	15.0	33.1	na	na	na	na	na	27.2	19.1	15.4
Samoan	na	na	na	na	na	na	na	na	53.5	41.3	34.5
Vietnamese	na	na	na	na	na	na	na	na	68.0	75.2	76.0
All Groups	25.5	27.2	32.6	37.4	42.4	49.6	46.5	42.3	44.7	36.3	30.7

Key: na = Figures not available.

Notes: Figures report percentages of the Hawai'i civilian and military population living in central Honolulu. The largest groups are in boldface.

Sources: Thrum (1893:12); U.S. Census (1932:48; 1943:5; 1952:35, 37; 1962:17; 1972:28, 47; 1983:11, 13, 16; 1993:5; 2000:Table DP-1).

Table 2.3

Immigrant Population in Hawai'i by Ethnic Group, 1910–2000 (in percent)

Ethnic Group	1910	1920	1930	1940	1950	1960	1970	1980	1990	2000
Black	13.4%	10.6%	6.6%	na	na	na	1.1%	3.6%	3.6%	5.1%
Caucasian	34.3	21.5	11.9	7.7%	5.5%	3.8%	3.3	4.9	4.5	6.2
Chinese	66.8	47.5	27.5	16.8	11.1	9.1	11.1	22.1	28.6	41.5
Filipino	99.8	89.0	83.5	68.1	55.2	41.3	35.3	45.8	44.5	56.3
Guamanian	na	na	na	na	na	na	na	2.8	3.3	3.6
Hawaiian	0.0	0.0	0.0	0.0	.2	.3	.3	.7	.3	.6
Japanese	75.0	55.5	34.7	23.7	16.7	12.1	9.6	9.5	7.7	9.7
Korean	92.0	70.4	46.2	35.8	25.2	27.6	20.6	54.0	54.9	70.8
Mexican	na	na	na	na	na	15.5	12.9	9.2	8.6	14.0
Puerto Rican	na	na	na	na	na	na	na	.8	.6	.7
Samoan	na	na	na	na	na	na	na	28.1	18.2	18.3
Vietnamese	na	na	na	na	na	na	na	86.0	75.3	81.4
All Groups	48.9	34.1	18.6	12.4	15.3	10.9	8.9	14.2	14.7	17.5

Key: na = Figures not available.

Notes: Figures report percentages of the Hawai'i civilian and military population for each ethnic group born abroad. For definitions of ethnic terms, see note to Table 2.1. The largest groups are in boldface.

Sources: Lind (1980:92); U.S. Census (1913:572; 1922:1173; 1932:49; 1943:5, 11; 1952:35; 1962:17, 119; 1972:193, 195–196,201; 1973:178, 180; 1983:38, 65, 71; 1993:58, 124–125, 142; 2000:SF2, SF4).

citizens and would likely vote against the Republicans. An effort to shut down Japanese-language schools in 1925 was reversed by the U.S. Supreme Court two years later in *Farrington v Tokushige* (273US284).

Formal political power resided in the Territorial governor, who by law had to be a Hawai'i resident. The governor could rely on armed forces at the military bases in case of trouble, and Republican business interests could shut down all basic economic services at their whim, thus intimidating members of the Territorial legislature.

A large sector of the Territory consisted of the military population, which was segregated from the mainstream on military bases. One evening in 1931, Thalia Massie, Naval Lieutenant Thomas Massie's spouse, walked home from a nightclub in Waikīkī. Arriving home with her face bruised and her lips swollen, she claimed that she had been raped (Black 2002; Marumoto 1983; Stannard 2005; Wright 1966). At about the same time, police arrested five young local men who were having an altercation with a couple in a car. When police brought them into her hospital room several times, she identified the five as her rapists, but her "eyewitness" evidence was so slim that a jury of local residents refused to bring in a guilty verdict in *Hawai'i v Ahakuelo* (Crim. No. 11782).

Incensed, the Massies sought revenge. With the aid of two subordinate naval officers, the Massies arranged to abduct one defendant, who was tortured and accidentally shot. In *Hawai'i v Massie* (1932), the conspirators were convicted of murder despite an eloquent defense by their attorney, Clarence Darrow. After sentence was passed, Governor Lawrence Judd commuted the sentence to one hour of detention in the office of the State Sheriff. For Asians and Native Hawaiians, this was "Haole justice." The incident raised consciousness among non-Whites that Haoles perceived themselves as above the law.

For many residents, statehood held the best prospect for preventing future Massie cases (Wright 1966), and a poll in 1940 revealed that statehood enjoyed 3:1 support (Schmitt 1977:602). The ruling Haoles, however, were insensitive to such a possible change, continuing to believe that they alone were qualified to hold together what they saw as a fragile multiracial society (cf. du Puy 1932; Tsai 2009).

Anti-Japanese sentiment increased with the bombing of Pearl Harbor on December 7, 1941. When Japanese on the West Coast of the United States were relocated to internment camps in 1942, the head of the Honolulu telephone company and others urged President Franklin Roosevelt to remove all Japanese from the Islands as well (Borreca 1991; Lind 1946:62–63; Matsunaga 1987:A4). Such a remedy was deemed impractical, however, since Japanese comprised about one-third of the Islands' population and operated important businesses vital to the war effort.

Nevertheless, the military were suspicious of the local Japanese. Two hours after the attacks on December 7, some 40 Japanese living near Pearl Harbor were rounded up and driven to the mountains, where they were forced to sleep on the ground for three days under armed guard (Bernardo 2001). Afterward, 320 Japanese were relocated to an internment camp in Honouliuli Forest (Chun 2009). A few were sent to internment camps on the Mainland, about 15 were sent to a facility on Sand Island, and the rest were released. Japanese-language schools were shut down during the war.

Soon, Roosevelt ordered his appointive governor in Hawai'i, Joseph Poindexter, to suspend the writ of habeas corpus and to declare martial law. Lieutenant General Walter Short, the Pacific military commander, then became military governor, but he went beyond martial law to impose military rule—taking control of civilian functions. The military even assumed the power to try civilians in military courts. The press, subject to censure, was prohibited from reporting on court proceedings, in which 99 percent of the defendants were found guilty (Anthony 1955). All residents were fingerprinted. Mail was subject to censure. Sugar workers were forbidden to change jobs. All holidays were suspended. Those out of work were assigned jobs by the U.S. Employment Service. In 1943, when Poindexter demanded the restoration of habeas corpus, he was ignored by the military governor. Thus, the military assumed powers unprecedented in American history, even exceeding those enforced against Southern states immediately after the Civil War.

During the war, the Federal Bureau of Investigation gathered information on individual Japanese who were suspected of conspiring with Tokyo. Although there were no disloyal acts by Japanese in Hawai'i, some 540 were eventually interned in small camps on O'ahu, and 930 were transferred to Mainland camps. Families who lived near military bases continued farming their land, but they were not allowed to live in their homes (Ogawa and Fox 1986). Japanese American members of the Territory's National Guard were dismissed. Many Japanese, living in fear that they would be rounded up, were harassed by persons of other races during the war. In October 1944, when military rule was rescinded by the president, the military returned the situation to martial law. Some 413 internees were allowed to go home, but 50 aliens remained in internment camps, and 67 more Japanese Americans were shipped to the

Mainland. In 1946, wartime military rule in Hawai'i was retroactively ruled unconstitutional in *Duncan v Kahanamoku* (66SpCt606).

There was a bright spot during the war. In February 1942, Japanese American students at the University of Hawai'i formed the Varsity Victory Volunteers (VVV), offering to assist the authorities in strengthening Island defenses. Governor Joseph Poindexter endorsed their proposal, and the military agreed to accept their services. Assistant Secretary of War John J. McCloy, visiting the Islands at the end of the year, was so impressed by the VVV that in January 1943 he gave orders allowing Japanese Americans to enlist in the armed forces to fight in the war. VVVs and members of the 100th Battalion, composed of local Asian residents, were then shipped to the Mainland for basic training, joining volunteers from Japanese internment camps to become the 442nd Regiment of the army, which became the most highly decorated unit of the war.

World War II ushered in other developments. Previously segregated Christian churches, with sermons in English, Filipino, and Japanese languages, offered services in English and became multiethnic (Tangonan 1991). As some Haoles fled to the Mainland during the war, Chinese bought their homes in affluent neighborhoods, thereby effecting housing desegregation.

After World War II, when members of the 442nd Regiment returned to civilian life, they took advantage of the "GI Bill of Rights" and went to college at government expense. The newly college-educated Japanese, however, found that Haole employers in the private sector undervalued their degrees, preferring to hire them at more traditional jobs. Meanwhile, the Ramspeck Act of 1940, which banned racial discrimination in federal government employment, enabled Japanese Americans to get federal civil service jobs and become public schoolteachers in Hawai'i.

During the war, the independent-minded International Longshore and Warehouse Union (ILWU) gained momentum by combining Filipino and Japanese workers into a powerful bloc of workers because the military, not Haole commercial interests, controlled politics. Starting with only 5,000 members in 1943, the ILWU had signed up 33,000 by 1945 (Schmitt 1977:138). Cross-ethnic solidarity was built through such activities as multiethnic baseball and bowling leagues. The ILWU also encouraged Filipino and Japanese members to vote for Democratic Party candidates (Daws 1968:367).

In September 1946, some 28,000 workers went on strike at 33 of the 34 plantations for 79 days. Plantation owners yielded by granting the ILWU the right to represent workers as their exclusive collective bargaining agent. A similar victory was repeated in 1949 after a 178-day strike involving some 2,000 dockworkers (Kent 1983:135).

Solidarity among plantation workers was good news for the Democratic Party. Afraid of losing power, the Haole Republican elites brought the House Un-American Activities Committee to Hawai'i in order to delegitimate the ILWU, whose Haole leaders were vulnerable to charges of sympathy with Marxism. With the pro-union faction of Haole Democrats neutralized thereby, power in the Democratic Party shifted to a cadre of Japanese American war heroes with recent professional degrees, who in turn mapped a strategy for political victory.

In 1952, Congress passed an immigration act that permitted aliens born in Japan to become American citizens. In 1954, after a flood of Japanese in Hawai'i became American citizens (*Honolulu Star-Bulletin* 1954:A3), the Democratic Party achieved a landslide in elections for the Territorial legislature. The 1954 victory, known as the "Democratic Revolution," occurred in part because the Haole oligarchy refused to co-opt Japanese Americans into prominent positions in the Republican Party. As the largest bloc of voters, Japanese cast their ballots largely for the Democratic candidates (Digman and Tuttle 1961). The following year, the legislature adopted a fair employment practice law, banning employment discrimination in the private sector. Nevertheless, the Democrats did not want to antagonize the Big Five (Kent 1983:Ch. 10), who could still pull the plug on the fragile Island economy.

The structure of the economy changed considerably in the 1950s. The Cold War heated up when the Korean War began in mid-1950, resulting in so much military spending in the Islands that the defense sector became the largest source of income (Table 2.4). Meanwhile, as unionization drove up wages on the plantations beyond paychecks of workers in Third World countries, profitability of local agriculture was reduced despite mechanization. The sugar conglomerates soon began to invest in pineapple and sugarcane in Asian countries, diversified their investments, became multinational corporations, and moved many headquarters in due course to the Mainland. Today, only one sugarcane plantation remains.

The campaign for statehood, which began before World War II, accelerated after the war. In 1956, John Burns, a Caucasian Democrat living in a poor section of Honolulu, won election as the Territory's nonvoting delegate to the U.S. House of Representatives, and in 1959 Hawai'i became the Fiftieth State, confirmed by a plebiscite in which support was 16:1 in favor of statehood (Schmitt 1977:602). The United Nations, having monitored the Territory of Hawai'i for some 15 years, then removed Hawai'i from

Table 2.4

Sources of Hawai'i Income by Industry, 1900–2000 (in $000,000s)

Year	Defense	Sugar & Pineapple	Tourism	Total
1900	na	$27 (96)	na	$28
1910	na	43 (93)	na	46
1920	na	98 (93)	na	105
1930	na	94 (93)	na	101
1939	na	89 (76)	$4 (4)	113
1950	$147 (29)	226 (44)	29 (5)	513
1955	273 (37)	261 (35)	55 (7)	747
1960	351 (19)	237 (13)	131 (7)	1,805
1965	430 (17)	293 (12)	225 (9)	2,530
1970	639 (14)	326 (7)	595 (13)	4,427
1975	1,442 (19)	503 (7)	1,360 (18)	7,411
1980	1,865 (15)	821 (7)	2,875 (24)	12,226
1985	2,810 (17)	563 (3)	5,244 (31)	16,875
1990	3,203 (12)	545 (2)	9,739 (36)	26,945
2000	2,878 (7)	176 (1)	10,590 (26)	40,202

Key: na = Figures not available.

Notes: Totals include all industries. Figures in parentheses are percentages of the total and add to 100 percent horizontally when all industries are included. The largest industry is in boldface each year.

Sources: Hawai'i (1901:30; 1910:21; 1920:28; 1931:40; 1940:4; 1970a:65; 1986a:366–367; 1990:344–345; 1993:312–313; 2006:243, 462, 631); U.S. Census (1942:1135; 1943:10).

its list of non-self-governing territories. However, the positive vote came from only 35 percent of all eligible voters, since many Native Hawaiians quietly boycotted because they were not given an opportunity for another choice—a return to the independent Kingdom of Hawai'i that had been annexed by the United States without a plebiscite (Tsai 2009).

STATE OF HAWAI'I

As a state, Islanders could elect their own governor. Federal regulations prevailing within agencies of Territorial government were superseded by laws passed by the new state legislature.

Since most governmental functions before statehood were handled at the Territorial level, Hawai'i's new state government began with more powers than almost any other state. For example, there is a single statewide school district and a centralized public health system. County functions are limited largely to firefighting, police protection, waste disposal, and water distribution. There are no cities independent of counties.

Military bases remained. Since the Defense Department paid no rent to the Department of the Interior, which officially managed the Territory, Hawai'i became the only state that charges no rent for the use of state land for military bases, many of which are on lands set aside exclusively for Native Hawaiians at the time of annexation.

Statehood meant that businesses could relocate from the Mainland to Hawai'i with confidence that they would be subject to the same federal protections and regulations as in any other state. In 1959, Stanley Dunham got word that there was a job managing a Honolulu furniture store. He accepted, and the family packed its bags.

Statehood brought a fundamental demographic change. Whereas Native Hawaiians predominated during the era of the monarchy, and Japanese became the most numerous group in Territorial days, an influx from the Mainland after statehood meant that Caucasians soon became the most numerous ethnic group (Table 1.2), yet without memories of the decline in status of Native Hawaiians or the oppression of Japanese, Filipinos, and others on the plantations.

Governor William Quinn (1959–1962). A Republican, William Francis Quinn was the last appointive governor. When he won the state's first election for governor in 1959, he was committed to what he called a "New Hawaii," promising to change the economic foundation of the Islands, but he was blocked by a Democratic legislature.

The new senators were Democrat Oren Long and Republican Hiram Fong. Although Fong and Quinn urged the Republicans to give prominent roles to non-Haoles, their views did not prevail.

Governor John Burns (1962–1974). In 1962, Democrat John Anthony Burns overwhelmingly defeated Quinn to become Hawai'i's second elected governor. Reelected twice, Burns had strong trade union backing, which brought overwhelming support from Filipino and Japanese voters.

In 1967, the legislature banned housing discrimination on the basis of race, color, religion, or national origin. Over the years, the state employment discrimination law was broadened beyond discrimination based on ethnicity/race and religion to cover age, ancestry, disability status, gender, marital status, sexual orientation, arrest and court records, National Guard participation, and assignment of income for child support obligations. White-only social clubs, such as the Outrigger Canoe Club, where future governor Ben Cayetano's father worked, began admitting non-Whites in the wake of the ongoing civil rights revolution on the Mainland.

Also in 1967, the legislature passed a Land Reform Act to permit leaseholders to buy fee-simple land. Since property taxes in Hawai'i are based on potential use, the taxes on vacant lots and single-family dwellings became so onerous that many owners sold out to commercial investments from the U.S. Mainland as well as foreign countries. Each year from 1971, investors from Japan bought more property for golf courses, while financing hotels and visitor hospitality businesses.

Many Japanese American leaders, with an unparalleled opportunity to influence legislative rezoning to upgrade land use from agriculture to residential, bought wisely and cashed in on a real estate bonanza (Cooper and Daws 1985). Haole Republicans had once showed how to use the political system to enrich themselves, so the new power elites felt no embarrassment in playing by the same rules as they saw them (*Honolulu Star-Bulletin* 1972).

Disenchanted with overcrowded California, stressful cities, or nondescript parts of the Mainland, Caucasians continued to migrate to Hawai'i, filling managerial and professional positions in the expanding statehood economy, thereby producing a boom in luxury housing. Statehood also came as the post-war "baby boom" took off, with an associated need for moderately priced new homes. Because limited land was available to purchase, there was an upward spiral in the price of residences, beyond the reach of most local workers (Kent 1983:167–171). Lacking affordable housing, some poorer neighborhoods deteriorated, in part due to overcrowding.

When Hawai'i became a state, some 1.5 million acres of federal land that had been crown and government land before 1893 were transferred from the Territorial government to the new state government (Table 2.5). The Admission Act of 1959 required that the land be used for various purposes, including the benefit of Native Hawaiians and the general

Table 2.5
Land Ownership in Hawai'i, 1847–1959 (in percent)

Landowner	1847	1848	1898	1959
Crown (royal) lands	100%	24%	0%	0
Island government lands	0	36	0	38.9%[a]
Federal government land	0	0	60	9.8
Large private landowners	0	39	39	46.7
Small private landowners	0	1	1	4.5

[a]Ceded by the federal government to the government of the State of Hawai'i.

Sources: Gomes (2002); Kent (1983:31); Sullam (1976:4).

public. Some Native Hawaiians believed that they had a prior claim to the crown lands, whereas government land was for the general public, but neither Congress nor the new state legislature specified which lands were for which purposes.

When statehood began, some 72 landowners, including the Bishop Estate, controlled 47 percent of the land; on Oʻahu, 22 landowners controlled 72.5 percent (Gordon 2006). The large landowners leased their property for periods of several decades and would not sell. When the long-term leases expired, the land was significantly more valuable than before, so rents for new leases increased astronomically, forcing those living on the land to move.

In 1970, tenant farmers in Kalama Valley on Oʻahu, within the City and County of Honolulu, received eviction notices. The property owner wanted to develop the land for commercial and tourism development and did not care what happened to the Native Hawaiians living there. Soon, an announcement on the radio station of the University of Hawaiʻi at Mānoa invited listeners to meet near campus if they were concerned with "justice for the Hawaiian People" (Akaka 2009). Those who showed up were concerned about the eviction notices. They agreed to picket in Kalama Valley.

In 1971, when bulldozers arrived to remove homes of the predominantly rural Native Hawaiian community, support from many ethnic groups was present, including attempts to sit on top of buildings slated to be demolished. Some protesters were arrested and even received death threats. The bulldozers won, however, and homelessness resulted. The impact on the educational future of children of displaced parents was ignored, as "thousands of children [went] . . . to school from . . . tents, from cars, from caves" (Lilikala Kameʻeleihiwa, quoted in U.S. Commission on Civil Rights 2001:3).

What was particularly offensive about the Kalama Valley eviction was that the landowner was the Bishop Estate, a trust established in 1883 by Charles Reed Bishop on behalf of his wife, the heir to lands controlled by the last king, Kalākaua. The will setting up the trust provided that a school should be established on some of the land to provide education by Protestant teachers; this was the origin of Kamehameha Schools. In 1884, a codicil of the will provided that none of the remaining land could be sold "unless . . . a sale may be necessary for the establishment and maintenance of said schools, or for the best interests of the estate" (Sullam 1976:4–5). In practice, Bishop Estate trustees leased land for a fixed period. Now Native Hawaiians were being evicted from lands that were once the property of the Hawaiian royalty, which had held most of the land in common for the benefit of the people.

Although the Kalama Valley movement failed to preserve ancestral land, new organizations mobilized when similar challenges emerged later in the decade, particularly the successful efforts to block proposed developments that threatened to evict Filipinos at Ota Camp in 1971 and Native Hawaiians at Waiāhole/Waikāne in 1977 (Nakata 1999; Nihau 1999). In 1973, in recognition of strong community spirit, Honolulu's City Council adopted a system of neighborhood boards, which began operation in 1975.

Thus, mass protests occurred while Barack Obama was attending Punahou. That the events made an impact on him is clear from the following statement:

> *Fairly early on, growing up in Hawaii, not only do you appreciate the natural beauty, but there is a real ethic of concern for the land that dates back to the Native Hawaiians. . . . So it was natural for me, I think, growing up, to be concerned about these issues in a way now I think is common across the country but was more deeply embedded in Hawaii at the time* (Glauberman and Burris 2008:80).

Governor George Ariyoshi (1974–1986). During Burns's third election campaign in 1970, he gave the nod to George Ryoichi Ariyoshi as his running mate. The voters concurred.

The year 1974 was a watershed in many ways. Burns's health declined so rapidly that he resigned, making Ariyoshi the nation's first non-White governor. In 1974, the legislature passed the Prepaid Health Care Act, the first state to adopt nearly universal health care. Under the law, all employers were required to provide health insurance options for full-time employees. Later, those less than full-time were allowed to enroll. As an employee of Bank of Hawaii, Obama's grandmother was covered along with her husband.

On Election Day 1974, as investors from Japan were snapping up businesses and major hotels in Waikīkī, voters went to the polls to elect George Ariyoshi for a full four-year term. However, elected along with Ariyoshi was a slate of Japanese Americans, including the lieutenant governor, U.S. Senator, both members of Hawai'i's Congressional delegation, and more than half of both houses of the state's legislature. That one ethnic group was suddenly in charge of the politics of the diverse Aloha State came a shock (Cayetano 2009:265; Kotani 1985; Okamura 1998).

Back in 1965, Congress had passed an immigration act that prioritized family reunions. That is, existing immigrants were able to have members of their immediate personal families join them in Hawai'i as well as on the Mainland. In the Aloha State, Filipinos in particular began to arrive in large numbers (Table 2.3). As immigrants, employers expected them to fill the lowest-paying jobs, and the hotel boom provided plenty of opportunity to make beds, water lawns, and otherwise cater to tourists from around the world. Thus, the ethnic mix after statehood threatened to challenge the power structure of the Democratic Party, based as it was on loyal voting by Japanese Americans, whose relative share of the population was declining (Table 1.2).

While Filipinos and Caucasians increased in population, filling jobs in the private sector at first, many wanted public-sector jobs appropriate to their professional qualifications. Earlier, Haole private-sector employers hired Japanese in subordinate roles, so educated Japanese looked elsewhere and found middle-class government jobs that provided good services for and jobs to local residents. A law passed in 1978 required government jobs to be filled by residents, adversely impacting newcomers. New residents from the Philippines and Caucasians from the Mainland believed that they were treated unfairly when not hired to join the predominantly Japanese American government workforce (Cayetano 2009:249; Haas 1992:Ch. 5–8).

Accordingly, a set of civil rights complaints were filed, charging institutional racism by Hawai'i state government. The institutional practices were mostly established during the period of Haole dominance while Hawai'i was a Territory, but no action had been taken by Japanese American officials to dismantle criteria applied to prospective employees that disproportionately impacted Filipinos, Native Hawaiians, and even Whites.

Many complaints were directed at the state's Department of Education (DOE) for ignoring the needs of Filipinos, especially immigrant Filipino students who lacked programs that might enable them to learn basic English. A different complaint was that the Department of Health (DOH) served a large percentage of Caucasians, who were seeking free mental health services at a level far above their proportionate share of the population, with little outreach to non-Whites. Whereas DOH personnel were primarily Caucasian, the DOE was dominated by Japanese Americans.

Civil rights complaints were vindicated when federal agencies ruled that both DOE and DOH were in noncompliance with civil rights regulations. Millions of dollars in federal funding were also in jeopardy because the state government had refused to adopt an affirmative action plan.

Rather than fighting the rulings, Governor Ariyoshi adopted affirmative action, which he had previously opposed, and the two departments agreed to comply. The new affirmative action plan identified Caucasians, Filipinos, and Native Hawaiians as principal "target groups" (Haas 1992:128).

Many local Japanese took umbrage at the complaints, believing that they were being unfairly accused of being racists. Some developed a counter strategy—to launch a movement touting themselves as "locals," thereby stressing their long struggle in the labor movement and in electoral politics to displace the formerly dominant Haole establishment (Yamamoto 1979). State Representative Roland Kotani, in particular, circulated a pamphlet at the constitutional convention of 1978 entitled *Palaka Power* in the form of a manifesto at a time when Mainland-born Cecil Heftel was a serious candidate to unseat incumbent Governor Ariyoshi.

A subtext of the "local" movement was frustration that Haoles who arrived in Hawai'i after statehood were not assimilating to the multicultural ethos (Manicas 1997). "Locals Only" T-shirts soon appeared, and open discrimination against Haoles increased. After a group of Caucasian dentists, seeking to move their practices to Hawai'i from the Mainland, sued the state for systematic failure to pass licensing examinations conducted by Japanese American examiners in 1973, the issue simmered in the courts until Governor Ariyoshi intervened on behalf of the applicants in 1980. Soon, the "local" movement left the political arena and remained a cultural term used to stress differences between Island and Mainland ways.

The elections of 1976 and 1978 resulted in more diversity in the composition of top officeholders. Tension about what appeared to be a de facto takeover by Japanese Americans subsided.

In 1976, nine young Native Hawaiian community leaders, taking their cue from the occupation of Alcatraz by a Native American group, landed on the uninhabited island of Kaho'olawe, which the U.S. Navy had been using for target practice since December 8, 1941. Although later carried off the island under arrest, they made the point that Native Hawaiian 'aina (land) was being abused. A lawsuit, *Protect Kaho'olawe 'Ohana v U.S. Navy*, charged that the Navy had never prepared an environmental impact statement on the bombing, which was presumably destroying archaeological sites. In 1980, the 'Ohana and the Navy reached a consent decree, placing certain portions of the island under the stewardship of the 'Ohana. President Jimmy Carter then ordered an end to all bombing of the island.

The 1978 constitutional convention was held with a view to revising the basic law adopted before statehood, when Haoles were in control. The *Palaka Power* pamphlet was distributed to members of that body so that the apparent Japanese dominance of state government would be overshadowed by a realization that the constitution had been written to serve Haole interests.

The convention recommended several important changes that were subsequently approved by the state legislature. One change was that English and Hawaiian be the two official languages of the state. Another innovation was a pledge to promote the study of Native Hawaiian culture, including the history and language of the native people. In addition, a special cabinet-level Office of Hawaiian Affairs (OHA) was recommended to look after such matters as income from ceded lands to aid Native Hawaiians (*Star-Bulletin & Advertiser* 1991). But there was ambiguity about how much income OHA could derive and how the funds were to be spent, a question that today remains unanswered.

RECENT HISTORY OF HAWAI'I

When Barack Obama left Honolulu in 1979 for college on the Mainland, Ariyoshi was still governor, but his leadership was under challenge by members of the Democratic Party, Whites and non-Whites alike. The civil rights struggle that occurred while Obama was in the Islands involved Filipinos and Native Hawaiians, not African Americans. Because of annual holiday visits to Honolulu to visit family and friends, he has been able to keep in touch with more recent developments.

Governor John Waihe'e (1986–1994). In 1982, John David Waihe'e III, a Native Hawaiian, was elected lieutenant governor. In 1986, when Governor Ariyoshi was ineligible to run for reelection, having served the maximum number of terms in office, Waihe'e ran for governor and won. Native Hawaiians, heartened that at last one of their own was in charge, had high expectations that he would resolve grievances of Native Hawaiians. In addition, Daniel Akaka elected to the U.S. House of Representatives in 1977, became U.S. Senator in 1990.

On Election Day 1986, voters also selected Ben Cayetano, a second-generation Filipino, as Waihe'e's lieutenant governor. The Waihe'e–Cayetano team was reelected in 1990.

After the first observance of the birthday of Martin Luther King, Jr., as a national holiday in 1986, grassroos pressure insisted that Hawai'i follow suit. Governor Ariyoshi had been opposed, but Governor Waihe'e asked supporters to identify another locally celebrated holiday to drop so that the state would be compensated for the loss of a work day. Native Hawaiians soon had a winning suggestion: Drop Columbus Day, since the discovery of North America had no relation to the Hawaiian Islands. As a result, in 1988 Waihe'e signed the law establishing the King holiday, effective 1989.

Employment discrimination complaints filed with the federal government were a mere trickle until Ariyoshi became governor. By 1988, the backlog of complaints against employers in Hawai'i had become so numerous that an office of the Equal Employment Opportunity Commission was established in Honolulu. Rather than conceding all such cases to the federal office, the legislature set up the Hawai'i Civil Rights Commission, which began work in 1991, the same year when employment discrimination based on sexual orientation was prohibited. Both agencies have received a modest number of complaints each year, with sex discrimination more numerous than race discrimination, though Blacks filed the most cases of race discrimination. White supervisors sent from firms headquartered on the Mainland tend to be charged most often.

In 1987, Dennis "Bumpy" Kanahele, who traces his ancestry to Kamehameha I, led an occupation around Makapu'u Lighthouse by 50 Native Hawaiians. He was arrested and convicted for displaying a shotgun when police approached. Later that year, a constitutional convention for a Native Hawaiian nation met, drafted a constitution, issued a declaration of sovereignty for Ka Lāhui Hawai'i (the Nation of Hawai'i), and elected part-Hawaiian Mililani Trask as kia'āina (governor). She continued to mobilize Native Hawaiians to demand a measure of sovereignty, and in 2001 the Permanent Court of Arbitration at The Hague recognized the existence of the Nation of Hawai'i as a possible international litigant.

In 1988, Congress passed the federal Native Hawaiian Health Care Act. The law authorized funds for nine community-based Native Hawaiian health centers to promote traditional Hawaiian and Western methods of healing.

For many years, observers claimed that the state's Department of Hawaiian Home Lands had breached its fiduciary responsibilities by leasing land for commercial development and neglecting thousands of Native Hawaiian applicants for homesteads, but courts would not allow a class-action lawsuit against the State of Hawai'i. In 1988, Waihe'e waived the state's legal immunity, and the legislature authorized a settlement of individual claims to be settled through mediation (ho'oponopono). As a result, awards were made, totaling nearly $18 million.

In 1990, Congress established the Kaho'olawe Island Conveyance Commission to determine to which agency or organization the island should ultimately have authority. The recommendation of the commission (U.S. Congress 1993), to which President Bill Clinton agreed, was that from 1994 the island would come under the authority of the Kaho'olawe Island Reserve Commission, a State of Hawai'i government entity that would supervise the cleanup of ordinance and the transformation of the island into a Native Hawaiian cultural preserve. The island is to be held in trust until a Native Hawaiian nation entity is established.

Also in 1990, the state legislature clarified that 20 percent of private-sector income from ceded lands should go to the Office of Hawaiian Affairs, and appropriated $7.2 million for the betterment of the conditions of Native Hawaiians. In 1993, the state agreed that OHA would receive back rent of $134 million for the years 1980–1991.

On January 17, 1993, Governor Waihe'e ordered the flag of the Kingdom of Hawai'i raised for five days in order to observe the day when the monarchy was deposed. The events of that day were then reenacted in front of 'Iolani Palace. An international tribunal, with judges from several countries, took testimony that summer throughout the Islands, documenting violations of international law that flowed from the annexation.

In November 1993, Congress officially apologized "that the overthrow of the Kingdom of Hawai'i occurred with the active participation of agents and citizens of the United States and further acknowledged that the Native Hawaiian people never directly relinquished their inherent sovereignty as a people over their national lands." President Clinton then signed what is known as the Apology Resolution.

Later in 1993, "Bumpy" Kanahele organized another occupation at Makapu'u (Tizon 2005), one lasting 15 months, until Governor Waihe'e offered a 45-acre parcel in Pu'uhonua o Waimanalo if the protesters would leave. Kanahele's group agreed and eventually received a renewable 55-year lease at a cost of $3,000 a year (about $60 annually per adult). The state allows the group, which in 1994 proclaimed itself the

Independent Sovereign Nation of Hawai'i, governed by a four-person "council of aunties," to construct structures for its 80 or so residents without enforcing building permits. In 2002, Governor Cayetano (2009:365) pardoned Kanahele for his prior convictions.

In 1994, Waihe'e awarded $600 million to the Department of Hawaiian Home Lands to settle claims of mismanagement and to provide funds for infrastructure necessary for housing (Cayetano 2009:362). He also secured $7.5 million to upgrade the Center for Hawaiian Studies at the University of Hawai'i at Mānoa. Even though Governor Waihe'e pledged to make a final settlement on the ceded lands issue, and offered an additional $66 million in back rent, OHA preferred to settle the issue in court with two lawsuits—one refiled the case demanding 20 percent revenue from ceded lands, and the other asked for injunctive relief in plans to build public housing units on ceded lands located on Maui. Both cases eventually lost.

Governor Ben Cayetano (1994–2002). In 1994, Benjamin Jerome Cayetano was elected governor. With his victory, the mantle has been passed to a Filipino, yet another ethnic group to be so recognized. Also in 1994, "Mufi" Hannemann, became the first part-Samoan (and part-German) to be elected to the Honolulu City Council; he became mayor of Honolulu in 2005.

Cayetano was the first Hawai'i governor to face the full economic impact of the end of the Cold War, when the military began phasing out bases in Hawai'i. Japan's economic troubles during the 1990s meant fewer tourists than before. In a word, he had to cut budgets, a surefire way to make enemies.

Back in 1990, three applications for marriage licenses were denied because the couples were of the same gender, whereupon a lawsuit was filed to insist on the validity of same-sex marriage. One basis for the case was Hawai'i's adoption in 1971 of the Equal Rights Amendment, which amended the state constitution to place gender discrimination on a par with race discrimination. Accordingly, the Hawai'i Supreme Court in 1996 ruled in *Baehr v Miike* that the state could not deny marriage licenses on the basis of gender (74Haw645; 852P2d44) and sent the case back to the lower court for a remedy. However, the ruling sparked considerable controversy.

Trying to forestall the lower court ruling, the legislature adopted the Reciprocal Beneficiaries Act in 1997, establishing a legal basis for unmarried couples somewhat similar to civil unions. The law was trumpeted as an arrangement to cover a single grandparent living with a single grandchild, a situation not uncommon in Asian families, thereby enabling medical, survivorship, and other benefits for both partners. Barack Obama and his grandmother would have qualified except that he was already married and living in Chicago.

The issue of a "gay marriage" law brought much attention to the Aloha State from around the world. In 1998, religious fundamentalists on the Mainland poured money into the state to promote a constitutional amendment to prohibit same-sex marriage. During the same year, Cayetano, whose brother is gay, was up for reelection in a year when Republicans were energized not only to defeat same-gender marriage, but also the Democratic establishment responsible for appointing the judges who made the unprecedented decision. Although Cayetano barely won, the constitutional amendment was also adopted, and many Democrats were defeated in bids for reelection to the state legislature. Same-sex marriage was dead in the Aloha State. In 1999, responding to the apparent will of the voters, the newly elected state legislature failed to reauthorize the medical benefits accruing from reciprocal beneficiaries, though registration continued.

Meanwhile, a backlash toward the sovereignty movement arose (Tizon 2005). In 1996, Harold Rice, a direct descendent of pre-annexation Haoles, sought to register in two elections—to elect OHA trustees and to cast a vote in a plebiscite to determine how Native Hawaiians might form their own semiautonomous entity. When his registration was denied because he was not Native Hawaiian, he sued in federal court. *Rice v Cayetano* ultimately went to the Supreme Court in Washington, DC, which ruled in 2000 that elections could not restrict voters on the basis of race (528US495).

In response, Senator Akaka introduced the Native Hawaiian Government Reorganization Act in 2000. The bill, which passed the House of Representatives but not the Senate in 2010, would authorize the organization of the "Kingdom of Hawai'i" as an entity similar to the various Native American tribal governments, which might then collectively negotiate grievances with the federal government. Obama, once known as the "third Senator from Hawai'i," pledged to sign the bill if approved by Congress (Yaukey 2009).

Cayetano finished his term coping with the economic aftereffects of 9/11, in particular a reduction in tourism and resulting additional cuts to the state budget, which by law must be balanced. Although his lieutenant governor, Mazie Keiko Hirono, ran to succeed him, voters wanted something new.

Governor Linda Lingle (2002–2010). An extraordinary development occurred in 2002, when a Jewish woman, Linda Cutter Lingle, defeated Hirono. A Hawai'i resident for 27 years, and mayor of Maui County from 1990–1998, she had narrowly lost to Cayetano in 1998, but now Lingle became the first Republican governor since Quinn.

When Cayetano (2009:532) once asked Lingle why she was a Republican, given her progressive ideas, her reply was "I didn't feel welcomed by the Democrats." Cayetano acknowledged: "Just as the Republican Party was stereotyped as the party of the Haoles, so too had the Democratic Party become the party of locals and organized labor." Now a new generation of voters, tired of Democratic Party dominance for so long, chose someone who claimed to have brought prosperity to Maui while the rest of the state declined economically.

A legislature dominated by Democrats frustrated many of Lingle's proposals and even overrode her vetoes (Borreca 2005), so she had to work with Democrats. Her careful management of the state's finances in a time of continuing economic downturn was evidently responsible for her reelection as governor in 2006 with the largest margin in state history.

The legislature, meanwhile, revisited discrimination against gays and lesbians. In 2003, benefits accruing from the Reciprocal Beneficiaries Act were renewed. In 2005, Lingle vetoed a bill that would have outlawed discrimination against transgendered persons, but her veto was not overridden, though she signed a law forbidding discrimination based on sexual identity in housing. In 2010, the legislature voted to establish civil unions, but Lingle vetoed the legislation.

The residency qualification for government jobs was finally challenged in 2005. A federal court in 2006 ruled the law unconstitutional. The state's argument, that nonresidents were statistically more likely to quit (cf. Vorsino 2010d), perhaps vindicated the view that recent Mainland Caucasians were hassled on the job (*Honolulu Star-Bulletin* 2010a) but the legislature in 2010 tried to skirt around the decision by requiring 80 percent of all public works employees to be local residents (Honolulu Star-Advertiser 2010c).

During Lingle's administration, issues about Native Hawaiians persisted. In 2002, Kamehameha Schools had admitted a non-Hawaiian student to its Maui campus. His application was accepted because there was still space at the school after all qualified Native Hawaiian applicants had been admitted. But in 2003, two other non-Native Hawaiians applied and were denied, resulting in court cases. The school agreed in out-of-court settlements to allow one student to complete his education up to graduation because he had been approved then denied admission two days before school started, whereas the other received a $7 million settlement.

In 2008, four non-Hawaiian students again challenged the policy of giving preference in admission to Native Hawaiians (*Doe Doe v Kamehameha*). Although the issue currently awaits a final determination in federal courts, another non-Hawaiian was admitted for fall 2010.

The land dispute continued. In 2003, the state legislature authorized back rent payments to OHA for an amount to be determined by a Public Lands Resolution Advisory Task Force, with representation from all stakeholders. Later, the state agreed to pay $200 million to OHA for revenue derived from ceded lands from 1978–2008, but the State House of Representatives and State Senate were deadlocked in 2009 on how much cash and land would be paid (Heen 2009).

Understandable impatience with the failure to provide a definitive redress of issues flowing from the American annexation of Hawai'i was manifest on August 15, 2008, the 49th anniversary of the signing of statehood, when seven Native Hawaiians entered 'Iolani Palace. Led by James Akahi, who claimed to be the heir to the throne of the Kingdom, the group raised the kingdom's flag, chained gates around the palace grounds, and some allegedly roughed up palace employees before being arrested, pending criminal charges (Dooley 2009b).

In 2009, the U.S. Supreme Court dealt another blow to OHA's aspirations to gain ownership of all ceded lands in *OHA v Hawai'i* (07-1372), unanimously ruling that the Apology Resolution did not give OHA the power to stop projects on ceded lands. The case was then sent back to the state Supreme Court. Although one bill in the State Senate in 2009 proposed that any transfer of ceded lands should be first approved by the state legislature, another proposal mandated a moratorium on transfer of all ceded lands until a new Native Hawaiian entity would be established. Should neither bill ever pass, state government would remain in complete control of ceded lands.

Better news came at the end of 2009. Some 2,700 plaintiffs won a class-action lawsuit, *Kalima v Department of Hawaiian Home Lands* (Civil99-04771-12), to settle claims dating back an average of more than two decades on behalf of Native Hawaiian applicants for denial of allotments on Hawaiian Home lands (Pang 2009). Determination of monetary damages is pending.

Governor Lingle ended up in the same situation as Cayetano during her final years in office, confronting a decline in state revenue and a corresponding need to slash expenditures. Her popularity plummeted when cuts were announced in many areas. The loudest complaints were about furloughs for public schoolteachers and pay cuts for University of Hawai'i faculty.

CONCLUSION

As Barack Obama well knows, the history of Hawai'i has many unique elements. An independent kingdom, powerless to defend itself against the United States, was annexed in 1898 without a plebiscite, an action that today would occasion an outcry around the world. Injustices to Native Hawaiians associated with annexation remain largely unaddressed, but rather than mounting a revolution or launching terrorism, they have marshaled support from all other ethnic groups to pressure government to respond to their needs. Most with Native Hawaiian ancestry are racially mixed and have wide social networks.

Obama was present during a fundamental political transformation in which Haoles fell from dominance to a role of accommodation to a multi-ethnic power structure. Some malihini Haoles found the adjustment difficult, but many learned that acculturation to multicultural Hawai'i has brought much happier lives than they would ever have enjoyed on the Mainland.

The history of Hawai'i is perhaps typified by an innovation in 2009, when the state legislature established Islam Day to be on September 24. All groups are welcome.

Whereas Chapter 1 presents a rosy picture of the culture of the Islands, readers of Chapter 2 may be discomforted on learning of injustices meted out to Native Hawaiians over the centuries. When the 50th anniversary of statehood arrived on August 21, 2009, a celebration was not a high priority (Cataluna 2009). A protest of 300 persons organized by several groups who do not recognize the legality of Hawai'i's incorporation into the United States lined the entrance to Waikīkī, conch shells were blown, the hat of an Uncle Sam effigy was knocked off, and the 50th star in the hat was cut off and burned (*Honolulu Advertiser* 2009). The Native Hawaiian people await justice, and two-thirds of the people of the Islands support their recognition for sovereignty similar to Native American peoples (Pang 2010).

Because of the multicultural ethos, the coexistence of Hawai'i's ethnic groups seems to work without embittered rancor despite occasional flare-ups. The prevailing norm is to end racism. The public often seems more adept at achieving multicultural harmony than the leaders, but policy issues, as everywhere, remain (Howes and Osorio 2010). What inspired Barack Obama is that problems are best solved when representatives of various cultures work together.

The history of Hawai'i teaches an even more profound lesson that Obama learned well during Hawai'i's transformative 1970s. Undemocratic societies lack strong intermediate people-power organizations that intervene between the masses and the government. Totalitarian societies survive by banning such organizations, creating what sociologists call a "mass society" (Kornhauser 1959; Mills 1956). The history of Hawai'i demonstrates how strong unions and mass mobilizations have fought for ordinary citizens to make both entrenched economic power and government accountable to the people.

The politics of Mainland America during the same period has been one of a gradual deterioration of trade union influence and inefficacy of mass mobilization efforts in making business and government accountable to the needs of ordinary persons. Barack Obama's journey to the presidency was achieved because of a mass mobilization effort combined with support from citizen interest groups and a widespread yearning on the Mainland for an improved political culture. Today, Obama is in a position to encourage the model of the Aloha State as a way to revitalize American democracy.

Chapter 3

Public Opinion
and Cultural Values

Yasumasa Kuroda

> *Our individualism has always been bound by a set of commu-*
> *nal values.... In every individual, these twin strands ... are in*
> *tension, and it has been one of the blessings of America that*
> *the circumstances of our nation's birth allowed us to negoti-*
> *ate these tensions better than most.*
>
> (Obama 2008:67)

Barack Obama spent nearly the first 18 years of his life outside the
Mainland United States. Fourteen were in Honolulu, and during four
years he lived in Indonesia, which is closer in culture to Hawai'i than to
the United States Mainland. His values were formed as a boy, but he has
adjusted to differences encountered while living in Los Angeles, Cambridge (Massachusetts), New York, Chicago, and now the nation's capital, Washington, D.C. He is the only president who has had to deal with
the tensions between conflicting value systems, all of which he respects.
The following analysis sheds light on Obama's basic values.

Culture offers a way of organizing one's life experience. Key aspects of
culture are the roles that family and self play in experiencing the world.
Barack Obama's Black father and White mother and grandparents provided quite a challenge to him as he shaped his personality in Honolulu
and on the Mainland.

American culture has been known for its emphasis on individualism,
especially from the days of the Western frontier, whereas Asians and Pacific

Table 3.1
Hypothesized Ethnic Culture by Group

Ethnic Group	Priority to Self	Priority to Family
Mainlander	+	−
Local in Hawai'i	−	+

Islanders are believed to stress family or group life more than personal identity (Table 3.1). One hypothesis is that the individualism of Mainlanders is stronger than that of other ethnic groups in the Islands. That is, Mainlanders consider the family or home life to be less important than do locals, who trust family members but not others in general. Mainlanders are often perceived as more secondary-group than primary-group oriented. Previous studies have indeed found that Americans in general are individualistic and optimistic compared with the more anxious and communal-oriented Arabs, Europeans, and Japanese (Kuroda and Hayashi 1995; Kuroda and Suzuki 1991; Yoshino et al. 2002).

Nevertheless, skeptics of sweeping generalizations have a right to demand evidence to support such claims. Statements about attitudes, accordingly, can best be studied through surveys based on random samples. Reported in the following discussion are findings previously reported from surveys of Honolulu voters in 1971, 1978, 1983, and 1988 (Kuroda 1998) plus a study during 2000 in Honolulu and the United States Mainland based on registered voters. The results can serve to test whether a multicultural ethos is truly manifest in Hawai'i.

COMPARISONS BETWEEN HONOLULUANS
AND MAINLANDERS OVER TIME

To compare those living in Honolulu with those on the U.S. Mainland, survey samples are divided as follows: (1) *Honolulu Islanders*, consisting of Hawai'i-reared voters other than Japanese Americans but including other Asians, including local-born Chinese and Filipinos as well as Native Hawaiians; (2) *Honolulu Japanese*, who are almost entirely born in the United States; (3) *Honolulu Mainlanders*, that is, those who hail from the continental United States but live in Honolulu; (4) *All Honoluluans*; and (5) *Mainland Mainlanders*, consisting of those living in the continental United States. Only registered voters are surveyed (Table 3.2), so several groups are left out of the sample—the military, tourists, transients, and noncitizens.

Table 3.2

Psychological Dimensions of Honoluluans and Mainlanders, 1988 and 2000 (in percent)

Survey Question	Honolulu Islanders		Honolulu Japanese		Honolulu Mainlanders		All Honoluluans		Mainland Mainlanders
	1998	2000	1988	2000	1988	2000	1988	2000	1988
If a thing is right, go ahead & ignore custom.	54.7%	53.6%	51.2%	53.0%	72.7%	75.5%	57.1%	58.5%	69.9%
Most people can be trusted.	38.2	56.6	60.5	57.0	62.6	61.8	50.8	57.9	42.4
Most of the time people try to be helpful.	59.6	60.7	58.7	66.9	76.8	73.5	62.7	65.7	53.6
Most like persons who stress interpersonal harmony over rational decisions.	68.4	50.5	71.5	61.6	61.6	44.1	68.1	52.8	47.1
Worry very much about car accident.	40.4	17.3	40.1	21.9	13.1	3.9	34.9	15.8	21.9
Worry very much about war.	30.2	18.4	34.3	21.9	9.1	6.9	27.4	16.9	21.8
To be happy, follow rather than use or conquer nature.	49.8	50.5	50.0	45.7	40.4	55.9	48.0	50.1	25.5
Have religious faith.	80.9	76.7	70.3	69.8	66.7	79.4	74.4	74.9	85.3
Religion is very important to me.	38.7	36.3	24.4	29.8	25.3	21.6	31.0	30.7	47.2
Buddhist	1.8	4.1	29.7	27.8	1.0	2.9	11.3	11.9	0
Catholic	36.4	32.6	7.0	4.0	18.2	22.5	22.6	20.6	24.4
Protestant	27.1	16.1	23.8	19.2	29.3	18.6	26.4	17.7	54.8
No religion	0	7.8	0	13.9	2.0	6.9	.4	9.6	0
Religions teach the same despite many sects.	67.6	58.0	74.4	66.9	59.6	58.8	68.3	61.2	56.5
Desirable to adopt a child to continue family line.	49.3	41.5	32.0	31.8	34.3	37.3	40.3	37.2	52.3
More inclined to honor ancestors.	50.7	52.3	51.7	49.0	35.4	29.4	48.0	46.0	73.1
Choose making more money over more free time.	43.6	52.3	48.8	53.0	45.4	38.2	45.8	49.3	68.3

Note: Figures in boldface are the highest in each row.

Custom. Nearly three-fourths of the Mainlanders, including those now living in Hawai'i, insisted that their opinions are right as opposed to about half of non-White Honoluluans. Those born in Hawai'i often object to Mainlanders for being too pushy with their own ideas. Accustomed as they are to living side by side with people of different races and backgrounds, those who grow up in Hawai'i, are hesitant to speak out. Local-born University of Hawai'i students, for example, rarely raise questions in class, preferring small-group peer interaction. President Obama, who may have surprised Americans of all ages and races with his nonconfrontational approach, provides quite a contrast with Jesse Jackson's combative style of passionate speech.

Trust and helpfulness. Caucasians moving from the Mainland either were attracted to Hawai'i as a place to live because they valued helpful and honest people or they changed their outlooks after settling. Japanese were nearly as trustful and perceived others to be helpful. Non-Japanese Honolulu residents increased from the lowest on trustfulness in 1988 to a middle position in 2000, by which time John Waihe'e and Ben Cayetano had been reelected for governor and lieutenant governor, respectively. Those on the Mainland reported being the least likely to expect trustful and helpful people, a problem that Obama has had to deal with over the years.

Harmony versus logic. Honoluluans, particularly Japanese, chose interpersonal harmony over sticking to principles much more often than those on the Mainland, though there is a decline from 1988 to 2000. Perhaps those in Hawai'i gain an element of wisdom over the years about how to live peacefully with neighbors. A multicultural way of life is needed to live with a minimum of conflict with neighbors on small islands in the Pacific, a quality also needed for a person to be a world leader today. Obama displays the same outlook.

Anxiety. In 1988, Islanders and Japanese had the most worries, but life was viewed as more carefree for all by 2000, when anxieties dropped to Mainland levels. The Cold War apparently was a more important cause of anxiety in Hawai'i than on the Mainland. Nevertheless, those moving from the Mainland to Hawai'i exhibit far fewer worries. Although Obama lived in Hawai'i before 1988, when the Cold War was in full bloom, he appears as free from anxiety as those similar to his mother and grandparents.

Nature. Hawai'i is known for its natural beauty, as portrayed in photographs of Waikīkī Beach with Diamond Head in the background. Perhaps because of the less harsh climate and weather in the land of paradise, twice as many Honoluluans had respect for nature rather than wanting to use or conquer nature, compared with continental Americans. Obama's concern for environmental issues began early in life (Glauberman and Burris 2008:4).

Religion. More than two-thirds of survey respondents declared a religious faith, but more so on the Mainland than in Honolulu. Perhaps because of the multiethnic environment, Honoluluans also placed less importance on religion and its institutions, though few are atheists or agnostics. Somewhat over one-fourth of Japanese professed to be Buddhist, Islanders (mostly Filipinos) leaned toward Catholicism, whereas half of those on the Mainland were Protestant. It is common today to see Japanese Christians go to visit Buddhist temples to pay their respects to ancestors buried there. Honoluluans, particularly Japanese, deemphasized differences and sometime viewed all religions as fundamentally the same.

Family line. Would you adopt a child to continue your family line if you could not have children? More Mainlanders at large would adopt a child than Honoluluans to continue the family line. Over half of the marriages in Hawai'i have partners of different ethnic backgrounds, making the family as an institution quite different from that on the Mainland. To successfully live in a culturally tolerant milieu requires residents to be less arrogant about their ancestry, a trait that goes along with helping and trusting others. Nevertheless, more than one-third of Honoluluans would adopt to ensure that they have children. The most supportive of adoption were Islanders, doubtless Native Hawaiians. One possible reason is the well-known practice called hānai, in which one family shares a child with friends, as when a family with two boys gives a baby boy to a family without a boy. Consistent with a greater concern over thoroughbred pedigrees, Mainlanders had more interest in honoring their genetic forebearers than Honoluluans.

Materialism. Mainlanders more materialistic than Honoluluans, valued the opportunity to enjoy night life, recreation, and other ways to spend their free time. Non-White Honoluluans tended to be less materialistic, in accordance with cultural traditions that emphasize invisible over material things. Native Hawaiians referred to the earliest American and European visitors as "Haoles," meaning "people with lack of breath," that is, those who principally valued things visible and material. Mainland-born residents of Honolulu, however, were the least materialistic. Obama's quest for a career in public service resonates with Island ways of thinking.

In sum, Honoluluans differed from those on the Mainland in significant ways, consistent with Hawai'i's multicultural ethos. Mainlanders moving to Hawai'i apparently assimilate to those values and report living happier lives.

COMPARISONS WITHIN HONOLULU

Insofar as Hawai'i's multicultural ethos pervades the Islands, longtime residents should endorse the 12 principles identified in Chapter 1 more than newcomers from either foreign countries or the Mainland. Surveys available to test that presumption are summarized next.

In addition to the subsamples previously used, the Japanese are divided below into those past or below 50 years of age. The term *Local* is used to refer to Islanders and both older and younger Japanese, that is, everyone but immigrants and transplanted Mainlanders.

Anxiety. Although street crime, particularly muggings, was the number one worry for Honoluluans in 1988, transplanted Mainlanders reported that they were relatively free from daily worries. Locals, particularly older Japanese, were anxious about such matters as auto accidents, nuclear power accidents, unemployment, war, as well as street crime.

In a separate study for 1986, Honolulu residents born on the Mainland reported concern with protecting the environment, having men and women share housework, saving energy, and believing that the arrival of the computer age was desirable and that their health was excellent. Although Locals reported more worries, they tended to believe that the American standard of living has improved and will continue to improve. Mainlanders' values set them clearly apart from Locals, but that was largely a function of higher educational attainments, not ethnicity per se (Research Committee on the Study of Honolulu Residents 1986:106). Barack Obama's carefree demeanor is, not surprisingly, consistent with the thinking of Mainland transplants to Hawai'i.

Employment goals. Mainland transplants looked for "a feeling of accomplishment" in their job, as might be expected of managers and professionals. Locals, particularly older Japanese, were most interested in obtaining safe and secure jobs, whereas Mainlanders were less interested in job security. Even younger Japanese, almost as well educated as Mainlanders, were less inclined to desire a feeling of accomplishment in their jobs. Obama quit a lucrative job in New York for modest employment as a community organizer in Chicago because of a need to achieve something beyond himself, similar to Mainland-born Hawai'i residents.

Lifestyle. Among three lifestyle choices, immigrants were the most interested in working hard to "get rich" and joined older Japanese in being least inclined to endorse the statement "Don't think about money or fame; just live a life that suits your own taste." Older Japanese Americans, who worried more about mundane problems than any other group, most endorsed the statement "Live each day as it comes, cheerfully and without worry"—and by almost two to one over a self-satisfaction lifestyle. Obama has frequently noted that his Mainland-born family worked hard, enjoyed choosing their own paths, and yet did not worry very much.

Social focus. Asking Honoluluans whether they were more focused on their job or their spiritual life, immigrants came out on top in both categories. Religion and church were important to Islanders but less so to former Mainlanders now living in Honolulu and older Japanese Americans. Younger Japanese Americans were the least spiritual. Results were only partly a function of education. Obama was unconcerned with religion as a boy but changed on the Mainland.

Materialism. Should one teach children that money is important? The answer was a resounding "No" for a great majority, especially Mainland transplants, but least so among immigrants. Many immigrants left their homelands to seek a better economic life for their families, indicating that money was important to them, as they remit a large amount to their relatives back home. Older Japanese Americans, many of whom lived through the Great Depression, came closest to the Immigrant group. Barack Obama's American relatives lived modestly, and he could have achieved personal wealth in New York, but he was happier as a community organizer for poor Chicagoans. During his campaign, he stressed the economic perils of the middle class.

Freedom versus responsibility. The American value of individual freedom appears to compete with the Eastern value of responsibility to family. The survey, accordingly, asked about two Eastern and two Western values. The first Eastern value, filial piety, was endorsed by a majority of all respondents but much less by Mainlanders and most by older Japanese. The second Eastern value, social obligation, yielded no group differences.

The first Western value, individual freedom, most attracted former Mainlanders, followed by immigrants, who were doubtless very much aware of limited freedom in their home countries. Locals were least impressed. One possible reason for the difference is that non-Whites were treated unequally for many years before statehood, so reforms by the Democratic Party after overwhelming the Haole Republicans at the polls from 1954 were perceived as attaining their full rights as citizens. There were no group differences displayed in the second Western value, individual rights.

Educational attainments explained the results to a large degree, but not entirely. Obama, the son of an absent Black father, a peripatetic White mother, and down-to-earth White grandparents, has stressed that all four values are important.

Science orientation. Is the advent of the computer age welcomed by everyone or simply accepted as something inevitable by different groups? Most felt computers to be either "desirable" or "inevitable," but immigrants were less welcoming. Nearly two-thirds of Mainland transplants were likely to consider the arrival of the computer age as desirable, compared to only 28 percent of older Japanese, who in turn preferred to say that the advance was inevitable. Barack Obama's love affair with the Blackberry puts him in the Mainland mainstream.

The development of science and technology has made life more convenient, but Japanese Americans most agreed that "a lot of human feeling is lost." Age and education, which are closely correlated, explained preferences to some extent, perhaps because the older a Japanese American respondent, the shorter the length of formal schooling.

Future orientation. Does one have "to live pretty much for today and let tomorrow take care of itself"? Only 6 percent of Mainland-born Honoluluans and 7 percent of younger Japanese agreed strongly, whereas 26 percent of older Japanese Americans did so. Only 12 percent of the Japanese and 30 percent of Mainlanders disagreed strongly.

Will life be happier in the years ahead? Only immigrants thought so. Having hailed from economically stagnant parts of Asia, immigrants hoped for better days in America. Younger Japanese, who have risen in status more than others in Honolulu (see Chapter 10), were slightly more likely than the rest to see better horizons.

Concerning whether "peace of mind" might increase in the future, nearly half of immigrants and older Japanese agreed. Only one-fourth of former Mainlanders said so. The disparity was unrelated to age and educational level. Obama's humble beginnings and extraordinary rise through hard work and careful planning after he left Hawai'i provide one possible explanation for his perennial optimism.

Self versus society orientation. Almost half of older Japanese Americans and immigrants were likely to "follow custom." A large majority of

Mainland transplants would abandon tradition, leaving Islanders and younger Japanese in the middle. Education but not age is a factor in shaping these views to some extent, but so is ethnic culture. Obama's drumbeat about "change" indicates impatience with custom.

To improve life in the United States, some would focus on the individual, others on government. Only 13 percent of Mainlanders believed that the country must improve before individuals could achieve happiness, compared with 42 percent of older Japanese Americans. The other groups fell between. The difference was largely a function of aging and secondarily education among the Japanese Americans. Mainlanders, including Barack Obama, evidently believe that improvements in American life depend on both individual and social or governmental changes, but only about a third of the rest agree. Education appeared to play a minor role in explaining the findings.

Responses by different groups to the survey generally document differences between Mainland versus Local culture. Attitudinally, those coming from the Mainland are more individualistic, whereas others are more tradition bound. Many nuances demonstrate a generation gap within the Japanese American community and hard-working immigrants with idealistic aspirations.

Human relations. Are people helpful or do they just look out for themselves? A majority of Honoluluans viewed one another favorably, particularly immigrants and those coming from the Mainland, who doubtless compared their experience in Hawai'i with what they encountered before. Age more than education was a factor for Japanese Americans, perhaps a reflection of the discrimination that they suffered before statehood, when Whites refused to hire them.

At the same time, Mainland transplants and Japanese Americans believed that most people can be trusted, whereas immigrants and Islanders were more cautious. Responses to this question were highly correlated with education for non-Japanese. Barack Obama's efforts to reach out to Republicans is consistent with the view that people can be trusted to be helpful.

Religion. Honolulu residents overwhelmingly declared themselves to have a religious faith, mainly Christianity. Younger Japanese Americans and those born on the Mainland were least religious. Japanese Americans adopted the host nation's main religion. A generational split was discerned, as nearly half of the older generation of Japanese Americans is Buddhist, and the younger generation Protestant. Some Japanese felt

intimidated during World War II into becoming Christian to avoid perse-
cution. Obama, whose agnostic mother married two nominal Muslims,
adopted the Protestant faith on the Mainland.

Politics. Although only about one-third of the sample professed real
interest in politics; naturalized citizens showed the most, followed closely
by Mainlanders. Locals and Japanese had the least interest, which is surprising in view of their power at the ballot box. There was more interest
in fund-raising events than in politics, suggesting that those attending
enjoyed the entertainment and free food that accompany such occasions
in Hawai'i. Obama has not written that he attended any such events in
Honolulu, but his interest in politics was born in the Islands (Glauberman and Burris 2008:4).

Views of capitalism yield significant differences. Those born on the
Mainland were much more favorable, since many went to Hawai'i to
accept executive or professional positions. The skeptics had personal
knowledge of economic discrimination, whether abroad or on the plantations. Barry Obama, as he was known, was apparently aware of efforts
to protest evictions of Native Hawaiians from their homes by rich landowners and thus of the ravages of selfish capitalists.

Japanese Americans stood out from other groups in choosing the
Democratic Party over the Republican Party. Mainland transplants
occupied the other side of that coin, not far from immigrants. During
the first half of the 20th century, Japanese Americans were maligned by
the Republican Party in Hawai'i, driving them into intense Democratic
Party loyalty, whereas immigrants and Mainlanders are less likely to
know about that history. Those least likely to be Democrats were Chinese and Native Hawaiians. Obama's parents and grandparents came to
Honolulu after the years of bitter racism directed at Japanese and others on the plantations, but he experienced the arrogance and occasional
prejudice of Whites at his mostly Republican prep school, Punahou.

TRENDS

Comparing Honoluluans over time, there were only two significant
changes. That is, responses rarely differed 20 percent or more from the
years 1983 to 1988 to 2000 (Table 3.3).

First of all, feelings of anxiety declined sharply from 1988 to 2000.
Between those two years, the Soviet Union collapsed, and the Cold
War ended. Honolulu is a dangerous place in time of war because of its
strategic position. Military bases have numerous nuclear devices, and

Table 3.3

Psychological Dimensions of Honoluluans, 1983–2000 (in percent)

Survey Question	1983 Survey	1988 Survey	2000 Survey	Difference From 1983 to 2000
Anxiety: Worry much about				
1. Car accident	**35.0%**	**35.0%**	15.8%	−19.2%
2. Nuclear power	**41.0**	34.0	17.8	−23.2
3. Serious illness	**36.0**	31.0	31.2	−4.8
4. Street crime	**43.0**	41.0	22.3	−20.7
5. Unemployment	**28.0**	15.0	16.5	−3.5
6. War	**44.0**	27.0	16.9	−27.1
Most important two values:				
1. Filial piety	54.0	**77.7**	69.4	+15.4
2. Repaying obligation	19.0	**56.8**	33.1	+13.1
3. Individual rights	**79.0**	25.2	27.6	−51.4
4. Individual freedom	45.0	32.8	**62.3**	+17.3

Note: Figures in boldface are the highest in each row.

military-related activities make up a major part of Hawai'i's economy. Honoluluans not only felt more at ease about war and peace issues in 2000, but also about such mundane problems as street crimes and car accidents.

Obama, having spent much of his childhood in Honolulu, may have acquired values that have led him to use diplomacy as a favored tool of American foreign policy, whereas his predecessor administration launched unilateral wars. Indeed, Islanders are less confrontational in dealing with others when compared with Mainlanders in that they tend to trust others, and are more flexible and less rigid in dealing with others or insisting on one's own values. Accordingly, Obama's olive branch diplomacy contrasts with his predecessor's declaration that "you are either with us or with the terrorists."

The second difference was a dramatic drop in concern for individual rights. Previous findings reported that Islanders held civil liberties in much greater esteem than Mainlanders. What happened after 1983 and occurred before 1988 is an ethnic political succession of governors.

Although Japanese American George Ariyoshi was governor in 1983, in 1986 and 1990 his successor was John Waiheʻe, the first Native Hawaiian head of government since the days of the monarchy. His running mate both years, Filipino American Ben Cayetano, was elected governor in 1994 and reelected in 1998. Waiheʻe and Cayetano represented two among the least economically affluent ethnic groups, most of whose members live outside Honolulu (Table 2.3). Just as Obama's election excited Whites to imagine that the United States lives in a "post-racial" world, so White and non-White Honolulu residents may have thought that the elections of Waiheʻe and Cayetano were significant victories in the attainment of equal rights.

CONCLUSION

Mainlanders tend to possess a clear, distinct, positive, and powerful concept of self, whereas Islanders' self is more diffuse and extensive and less salient. Major sources of the local concept of self are likely to be rooted in the cultures of the Native Hawaiians and Asians. Such concepts as Aloha and ʻohana (family) also resemble key elements of Japanese culture, which emphasizes the importance of family and group memberships over the individual. Chinese often speak of keeping dirty linen within the family and prefer the middle way, avoiding extremes. Japanese place a premium on harmony, the most cherished value that Prince Regent Shôtoku enunciated in 704, when he promulgated a 17-article constitution that provided a basis for governance. Japanese today avoid open conflict and confrontation and prefer to work out solutions through consultation and mediation.

Thus, Hawaiʻi has developed a variant of communitarianism (cf. Etzioni 1993, 2009). Compared with interviewees in France, Germany, Japan, the United Kingdom, and the U.S. Mainland, Honolulu residents are happier, healthier, and more optimistic and relaxed (Kuroda 1993:17–19). In Hawaiʻi, personal happiness is shared, and sadness is easier to bear when there are sympathetic ears. Honoluluans have a generally positive orientation toward other people.

A separate poll, conducted in 1997, revealed that more than 80 percent of Hawaiʻi residents believe that the "Spirit of Aloha" is an important part of their lives and that people get along regardless of race and ethnicity, both on the job and in the neighborhoods where they live (Dingeman 1997). They want the Islands to remain a special place, that is, a refuge from the conflict-oriented Mainland.

Although no ethnic group is free from discrimination in Hawai'i, the extent of relentless racism is less than on the Mainland. Islanders pay more attention to the feelings of other ethnic groups. For example, an African American on the Mainland may openly and proudly vote for a fellow African American candidate. In Hawai'i, no one will openly declare political support on the basis of race or ethnic origin. Because of historical reasons, Hawai'i has several chambers of commerce based along ethnic lines. However, such groups as the Chinese Chamber of Commerce admit non-Chinese. The Japanese Chamber of Commerce has even elected a Caucasian as its president.

There is a heightened sense of alienation in modern America, as manifested in the rise of divorce and family violence. In Hawai'i, human bonding remains stronger than on the U.S. Mainland.

The data presented in this chapter prove that there is a deeply rooted Aloha Spirit in Hawai'i. The people of Hawai'i are more likely to express their trust in other people, show respect for others, are flexible and less definitive in expressing themselves, and value free time over money, being less materialistic. They are optimistic and less confrontational. Such values are consistent with the multicultural ethos described in Chapter 1 and the state law that mandates Aloha as a norm (see Appendix). No other state codifies kindness and nonconfrontational conflict resolution into law.

Anyone moving from the Mainland to Hawai'i or vice versa is likely to run into a certain amount of "culture shock." Mainlanders who relocate in Hawai'i are to a certain extent already attuned to the multicultural ethos or adjust admirably. Those moving from gentle Hawai'i to the harsh Mainland have a more difficult time. Barack Obama made that trek at age 18, but his Aloha Zen values were already a mixture between Hawai'i- and Mainland oriented because of those with whom he lived and where. He remains a multicultural icon for the country and the world today.

Chapter 4

The Multilingual State

Lāpaki

> While campaigning in Virginia during 2008, the greeting of
> Aloha Kakou! [Aloha to everyone!] brought an immediate
> smile to Obama's face. He responded with a popular greet-
> ing of his own that is unique to Hawaii: "Howzit!" (How is
> it going?), together with a friendly Hawaii-style thumb and
> pinky greeting gesture known as the "shaka."
>
> (Finin 2008)

Visitors to Hawai'i will immediately hear an English that is at once
exciting and friendly. The musical sounding of "eeeeee" instead of the
Mainland "ee" in such words as "believe" provides a sweetness to conversation that can only be articulated with a broad smile. The legato way
in which words are articulated by hotel employees and television newscasters provides a relaxing contrast with the staccato manner in which
Mainlanders often string words together as if firing pistol shots at interlocutors. In addition, frequent nonverbal gestures have the appearance
of hugging everyone in a conversation of joy known as "talk story."

   From birth, Barack Obama was accustomed to a standard form of
English from his parents and grandparents, but some acquaintances
and playmates in Honolulu spoke a Creole language unique to Hawai'i
with varying degrees of fluency. Then for four years from the age of 6,

he learned Indonesian at school and with playmates in Jakarta, while his mom awakened him at 5 A.M. to teach him English. Somewhere on the Mainland, he picked up the African American patois (Barabak and Fausset 2009; Remnick 2010:361, 500), often dropping the "g" at the end of an "ing" word or using the expression "y'all." Later, on the campaign trail, he would often say that his accent was from Kansas. As president he has addressed foreign leaders by saying "hello" and other key phrases in more than a dozen languages (Alter 2010:238). Obama's multilingualism typifies the mélange of languages spoken in Hawai'i.

The Hawaiian language prevailed long before Captain James Cook dropped anchor in 1778. English was introduced by a small minority as a new tongue. Chinese, Japanese, and other plantation workers, who entered later, were mostly denied the opportunity to learn English, Hawaiian, or languages other than their own in a divide-and-conquer strategy by their employers.

Yet the various non-White groups could communicate so well with one another that they were able to join together culturally, politically, and socially. Why? The answer is that they developed a new language indigenous to the Islands—a fascinating Creole language now spoken by an estimated 600,000 (Sakoda and Siegel 2003:1) of the 1.1 million Island residents as their first or second language. "Howzit" or "hauzit" (meaning "How are you?") is only one of thousands of words in that language, now known as Hawai'i Creole English (HCE) or, more colloquially, Pidgin. The federal government does not recognize HCE, so census statistics (Table 4.1) are incomplete. Throughout the Islands, immigrant groups eventually learned exemplary English, have had their languages accepted, and have made English and Hawaiian official languages of the Fiftieth State.

Longtime residents of Hawai'i are proud of their multilingualism, and their English tends to be mostly free from foreign-sounding accents. They refer to one another in slang words derived from Hawaiian or Pidgin—as Haole (White), Japanee, Kānaka (Native Hawaiian), Pākē (Chinese), hapa (mixed race), Pōpolo (Black), Yobo (Korean), Bukbuk (Filipino), Portagee (Portuguese), and Borinque (Puerto Rican). References to ethnicity are usually spoken with a smile. Hawai'i is not a color-blind society because members of each group respect other groups, an inevitability given a mixed-race population living in close proximity.

Language is an integral part of the observance of Aloha. Obama's engaging demeanor at the podium demonstrates how well he has incorporated communication skills acquired while a boy in Honolulu and

Table 4.1

Linguistic Abilities in Hawai'i Households, 2000 (in percent)

Ethnic Group	Monolingual English	Monolingual Non-English	Bilingual or Multilingual
Black	90.3%	4.1%	15.6%
Caucasian	81.9	4.0	14.1
Chinese	37.8	42.2	20.0
Filipino	17.1	28.6	54.3
Guamanian	32.7	21.4	45.8
Hawaiian	69.5	6.1	24.4
Japanese	65.0	15.1	19.9
Korean	20.6	55.5	23.8
Mexican	48.8	19.3	31.9
Puerto Rican	71.8	6.8	21.4
Samoan	11.8	34.6	53.6
Vietnamese	4.6	78.7	16.7
All Groups	59.7	14.7	25.5

Notes: Except for rounding errors, figures sum to 100 percent in each column.

Figures in boldface identify the highest in each column.

Source: U.S. Census (2000:PCT41).

rooted in a culture that developed after the English language was introduced on the island where he was born.

The language situation in Hawai'i argues strongly against the validity of the "English-only" position, which holds that social and cultural integration cannot proceed unless all languages but the dominant one are ruthlessly suppressed. Indeed, efforts to impose monolingualism in Hawai'i have failed completely.

HISTORY OF LANGUAGE CONTACT

For almost a century after the arrival of Captain James Cook in 1778, the predominant means of contact, first between Native Hawaiians and Euro-Americans, was a pidginized variety of the Hawaiian language (Roberts 1995a, b;1998). Robert Jarman (1838:124), a whaler who visited Hawai'i in the 1830s, reported: "Their [Hawaiian] language is particularly easy to learn. During the short time we lay here, almost all acquired a smattering of it, enough to get ourselves into trouble, or conciliate, as we chose best."

Richard Henry Dana gave further evidence in his novel *Two Years before the Mast* (1840), in which he puts the following words into the mouth of a Native Hawaiian sailor:

> Now got plenty money; no good, work. *Mamule* ["Later"] money *pau* ["finished"]—all gone. Ah! very good: work!—*makai hana hana nui*! ["good work a lot"] . . . Aye! me now that. By –'em-by money *pau*—all gone; then Kanaka ["Native Hawaiian"] work plenty . . . Aole! Me no eat Captain Cook! (Roberts 1998:14)

Today, most of the italicized words are still in common use, including the ubiquitous "em," (as in "book-em Dano" from the original *Hawaii Five-O*), sprinkled with English.

New England missionaries who came to Hawai'i in the 1820s also began by picking up Pidgin Hawaiian. Soon, some graduated to fluency in vernacular Hawaiian.

Originally, the missionaries tried to promote education and literacy in the Hawaiian language. They were the first to produce written versions of Hawaiian, to translate the Bible into Hawaiian, and to preach in Hawaiian. Their children, who included the founders of many of Hawai'i's larger businesses, were another matter. Already by the mid-19th century there was emerging among them, and among others who sought their fortunes in the Islands, a vision of Hawai'i's future that did not include the Hawaiian language—a vision of a docile, well-educated population that could compete commercially in international trade.

But the majority of early non-English-speaking newcomers never progressed past a pidginized version of Hawaiian. Pidgin Hawaiian stabilized toward the middle of the 19th century.

The first sugar plantation opened in 1835, employing Native Hawaiian laborers. Chinese immigrant laborers arriving in the 1850s soon picked up a Pidgin Hawaiian to communicate with both Haole bosses and Native Hawaiian coworkers—and even with speakers of mutually incomprehensible Chinese dialects (Spear 1856:58). The Hawaiian Sugar Planters' Association, from its establishment in the 1830s onwards, drew the technical language of the sugar industry almost exclusively from Hawaiian, that is, from a pidginized rather than a vernacular version of that language. Nevertheless, Pidgin Hawaiian was the second but not the first language of anyone throughout most of the 19th century.

Most Native Hawaiians were not upset about the development of a pidginized Hawaiian. If there is a continuum of attitudes from those least tolerant of grammatical error (such as the French) to those most tolerant, Native Hawaiians are on the latter end. Their tolerance, which allowed newcomers to enter (or to feel they had entered) Native Hawaiian society, however, was a two-edged sword, bringing about a superficially harmonious society but at the cost of diluting Hawaiian language and culture, and allowing alien values and attitudes to infiltrate the community.

English replaced Hawaiian in 1854 as the language of instruction in many public schools for the upper strata of Native Hawaiians (Day 1985; Kimura 1985). In the 1860s, the Kingdom of Hawai'i's Ministry of Education made determined efforts to reverse the trend, but the effort was short-lived.

During the last quarter of the 19th century, more immigrant laborers were recruited by plantation owners to the Islands, with far-reaching linguistic consequences. Pidgin Hawaiian continued to supply one mode of interethnic communication, especially on the plantations. However, the torrent of newcomers was obliged to communicate with one another (and with residents and previous immigrants) before they had had either time or opportunity to acquire even a pidginized version of Hawaiian let alone English.

Portuguese parents on the plantations petitioned the government to enable their children to learn English (Sakoda and Siegel 2003:14). From 1878–1888, children in schools where English was allegedly the language of instruction outnumbered those where the language of instruction was Hawaiian.

But many English teachers knew little more of the language than their students. In 1888, a writer in the daily *Pacific Commercial Advertiser* noted that "English was stopped like the study of Greek when the lessons were over," and that all the children played either in their own languages or in Hawaiian (Nemo 1888). Children may not have taken seriously their studies in Chinese- and Japanese-language schools, as their playmates were using Pidgin.

By the mid-1880s, a "macaronic Pidgin" developed, that is, a structureless jumble of words drawn from several languages. The Hawaiian language still predominated, but English played a gradually increasing role as more English-speaking supervisory staff entered the plantation system. However, many utterances contained ingredients drawn from three or four languages, such as "You nani hana hanahana?" ("What work do you do?"), which was composed of the following:

you [from English]
nani ["what" in Japanese]

hana ["work" in Hawaiian]
hanahana ["work" in Pidgin].

Immigrant laborers, of course, used their own languages wherever they could. Older residents, particularly Native Hawaiians, picked up small numbers of useful words from each of the major immigrant languages.

When one's own language failed, the prevailing strategy was to try to speak the other person's language. If that failed, words from other languages were spoken until understanding was achieved.

Although English ingredients of the macaronic Pidgin gradually increased, the Hawaiian component still outweighed all others. In verbatim quotes from defendants and witnesses within criminal trials, Hawaiian words outnumbered English until the early 1890s by at least a 4:1 ratio, though Pidgin was also used. Haoles were still obliged to communicate through some form of Hawaiian. Nevertheless, English-language schools increased from 1878 while Hawaiian-language schools decreased (Sakoda and Siegel 2003:6).

THE ROLE OF CHILDREN

In the 1880s, the principal linguistic medium regularly available on the plantations was the unstructured, highly variable macaronic Pidgin. But that Pidgin lacked most resources available to all natural languages, having a very limited vocabulary and a virtual absence of syntactic structure. The latter limitation made utterances more than four or five words long almost impossible to express or interpret.

During most of the day, when their parents were at work, immigrant children were in public schools run by English-speaking authorities. After school, according to the dictates of their parents, they might attend private schools to learn their native languages. One parent could have spoken English or Chinese, another Hawaiian. At play, children facilitated linguistic unity by speaking a Pidgin that incorporated both languages as well as some Portuguese. Then they played with one another, speaking a pidginized English, until their parents returned home, when the children communicated—and taught—Pidgin to their parents. Japanese, however, had much less influence on the development of Pidgin as a separate language.

While learning the structure of English, children transformed the macaronic Pidgin into a full-fledged Creole language. Exposed to English words and grammar at school, they developed a Pidgin that used English

words, but often with very different meanings, along with words from
Chinese, Hawaiian, Japanese, Portuguese, and other languages. The new
language, today known as Hawai'i Creole English (HCE) or Hawai'i
Creole or just Pidgin, gradually acquired its own grammar, sound system, structure, syntax, and word meanings—the ingredients of a separate language. From 1905–1920, HCE became the first language of
immigrant children and their parents (Sakoda and Siegel 2003:10), even
off the plantations as many workers left for the cities after their work
contracts expired.

Linguists define a Creole language as a Pidgin with substantial monolingual speakers. Hawai'i Creole English shares many features with Louisiana Creole French and the Gullah of the South Carolina Sea Islands,
the other two indigenous American Creoles, as well as with Papiamentu
in the Dutch West Indies, Jamaican Creole, Haitian, and many similar
languages worldwide. Indeed, what happened was a repeat of events
in dozens of similar colonial plantation cultures worldwide (Bickerton
1983). HCE's rapid delivery and complex sentences contrast strongly
with the slow, hesitant delivery and short, simple utterances of old, true
Pidgin-speaking immigrants, very few of whom survive today.

HCE's uniformity meant that in the early 1900s, for the first time,
a bond of unity existed between almost everyone who could call the
Islands home, regardless of skin color, cultural heritage, or any other
determinant. Those moving to Hawai'i later in life, however, were left
outside the Pidgin linguistic community, for no schools have ever existed
to learn Hawai'i Creole. Newcomers have only been able to pick up
words and phrases—more if their children were born in the Islands and
have attended public schools. Little Barry Obama, thus, would have
been able to teach HCE to his mother and grandparents.

LANGUAGE AND OFFICIALDOM

In the golden age of imperialism, Hawai'i appeared an anomaly—an
independent, indigenously governed state that was separated from the
rest of the world only by water. No matter that Honolulu residents
had electricity, streetlights, and telephones before most in the United
States. No matter that Hawai'i's literacy rate was the highest in the
world. Such advances, prominent Haoles argued, could owe nothing to
the qualities of the Hawaiian nation, but must have come about solely
through the actions of Haole advisers and experts who had managed
to insinuate themselves into the self-destructively tolerant Kingdom

of Hawai'i government. Therefore, the Haole elite strongly urged that the Islands be Americanized—which meant, of course, linguistically Anglicized—as rapidly as possible. From 1870, English was the original language on many government documents (Day 1985; Kimura 1985).

A writer in *The Friend* (1887:63) claimed, "English is already settled in its place as the controlling language of the country. It is the governing language of the laws and of the courts. It is supreme in business and in journalizing." Such statements were propaganda, designed to encourage active American support for the military coup that Haole business leaders were contemplating.

After the overthrow of the monarchy in 1893, the pace of Anglicization stepped up. In 1896, the Hawaiian language was all but made illegal in schools and was discouraged elsewhere. Native Hawaiians increasingly abandoned or concealed the use of their language. English was enshrined in 1898, when Congress annexed Hawai'i by joint resolution. By 1900, there were fewer pure Native Hawaiians than those with mixed Hawaiian ancestry, such as Caucasian Hawaiians and Chinese Hawaiians (U.S. Census 1902). Within a few decades, the number of Hawaiian speakers had shrunk to a few thousand in isolated areas.

From 1900, when the Territory of Hawai'i was officially established, English was the medium of instruction in government-run schools. The Haole establishment hoped that English would fill the vacuum resulting from the decline of Hawaiian, but such a view was unrealistic, since native English speakers made up only 5 to 6 percent of the population. Instead, that vacuum was quickly filled by the new language that spread quickly among locally born speakers of all ethnic groups—HCE. As new immigrants from Korea, the Philippines, Puerto Rico, and elsewhere arrived in the Islands, they learned the Creole language that was common everywhere.

Chinese and Japanese continued to maintain their languages by sponsoring private schools taught exclusively in their own languages after normal school hours. Some Japanese even sent their children back to Japan to receive secondary or even primary education. But local language schools had only limited effectiveness, due to antiquated teaching methods and the desire of students to get ahead in English.

In 1921, Congress passed the Hawaiian Homes Commission Act to enable those with at least half-Hawaiian ancestry, many destitute or homeless, to live in homes on ceded crown lands for an annual rent of $.02 per acre. Those who took advantage were thereby isolated from the rest of the population, further decreasing the likelihood that the Hawaiian language would play an important role in the continuing development of HCE.

After annexation, and particularly from the 1920s, new employees were recruited from the Mainland to run the Territorial government at all levels. Those at the top could send their children to Punahou. Children of middle-class parents who could not afford Punahou's tuition went to public schools and brought home what the Haole establishment decried as "Pidgin English." Accordingly, a decision was made in 1924 to establish "English Standard Schools" (ESSs) within the public school system so that Caucasians of more modest means could learn proper English. "Nonstandard" schools, where local students were denied an opportunity to perfect their English skills, thus became incubators of the further spread and development of HCE.

The separation gradually eroded as non-Whites passed qualifying exams to attend ESSs. Some non-ESSs even established ESS tracks, to keep the races apart within the same schools. From 1920–1930, nevertheless, HCE was the language spoken by most Island residents (Roberts 2000). Hawaiian homesteading and ESSs cemented the dominance of HCE.

In 1925, the Territorial government restricted Japanese-language schools by various regulations, suspicious that they were instilling patriotic attitudes toward Japan. But in 1927, the U.S. Supreme Court overruled the action in *Farrington v Tokushige* (273US284), asserting that there was a fundamental right to language and language instruction. Nevertheless, attendance at language schools declined between the two world wars. In the tide of xenophobia that accompanied World War II, all were closed by the government. From 1943, students below the fifth grade were statutorily prohibited from studying a foreign language, so a Chinese-language school took the Territorial government to court, which overturned the ban in 1947 in *Stainback v Mo Hock Ke Lok Po* (74FSupp852). Although the Territorial legislature later amended some of the more objectionable provisions of the 1943 law, which was finally repealed in 1959, foreign language schools never regained their earlier rates of attendance.

During World War II, many Haole families returned to the Mainland, whereupon enrollment in ESSs declined so precipitously that non-Whites were admitted in larger numbers. Then in 1947, a decision was made to abolish ESSs on a grade-by-grade basis each year until the last ESS classes received their diplomas in 1960.

As with all attempts to extirpate languages and dialects, the campaign to stamp out HCE failed completely. As a result, code-switching (changing one's variety of speech according to social context) became a sine qua non. The same children who were berated by teachers as substandard language speakers were in fact prodigies of linguistic virtuosity—re-pidginizing their Creole for the benefit of immigrant grandparents, switching into standard English (or something close to it) at their white-collar jobs or in court, and then returning with visible relief to their natural HCE speech with friends and younger relatives.

Similar to many stigmatized languages and dialects, HCE is at one and the same time (and often by the same people!) despised as some kind of uneducated "broken talk" and admired as a bonding mechanism among the locally born as well as a mark of working-class toughness and anti-Haole solidarity. The main social role of HCE has been as a badge of community identity—"local" (that is, raised in Hawai'i, even if one happens to be that apparent oxymoron, a "local Haole") as against the rest of the world. It is almost impossible to pronounce Pidgin words without smiling, knowing that in so doing the speaker is self-identifying as a local person. Although HCE in its original form is spoken only in predominantly agricultural areas by working-class people in their sixties or older, some younger working-class locals have attempted to halt HCE's decline by accentuating whatever is left of the Creole features in their speech as a boundary marker against younger Mainland-born Whites, who increasingly compete with them for less-skilled jobs.

Local people traveling on the Mainland United States while operating in standard English mode will immediately switch into HCE if, while in transit at some airport, they happen to bump into the merest acquaintance from the Islands. Even expatriates who move to the Mainland find much difficulty in dropping words and phrases from HCE, thereby bemusing both English-speaking interlocutors and friends who have recently arrived from Asian countries and are trying to learn the difficult English language.

With some 25.5 percent of the population bilinguals and multilinguals, Hawai'i is one of the most linguistically diverse states in the Union, even if one does not count HCE as a separate language. Only five other states have higher percentages of persons who exclusively speak a language other than English at home, but Hawai'i has the most bilinguals and multilinguals (Table 4.2).

Within the major ethnic groups, Blacks and Whites live in the highest percentage of monolingual English households (Table 4.1). More than three-fourths of Vietnamese and half of Koreans exclusively speak their

Table 4.2

Linguistic Abilities in Households within Selected States, 2000 (in percent)

State	Monolingual English	Monolingual Non-English	Bilingual or Multilingual
Arizona	66.2%	18.7%	15.1%
California	52.0	**31.3**	16.7
Hawai'i	59.7	14.7	**25.5**
New Mexico	51.4	25.5	23.1
New York	65.0	22.3	12.7
Texas	61.3	24.4	14.3

Notes: Except for rounding errors, figures sum to 100 percent in each row.

Figures in boldface identify the highest in the two relevant columns.

Many other states have higher percentages of monolingual English.

Source: U.S. Census (2000:PCT41).

own language at home. More than half of Filipinos live in bilingual and multilingual households, followed closely by Samoans.

LANGUAGE IN HAWAI'I TODAY

Linguistically, the years when Obama was at Punahou—the 1970s—were transformative. In 1978, the constitution of Hawai'i was amended to make English and Hawaiian as official languages of the Fiftieth State (even though HCE is perhaps spoken by more than either). The Hawaiian language has been revitalized over the last decades, particularly since publication of the *English-Hawaiian Dictionary* (1964) and the *Hawaiian-English Dictionary* (1965) by Mary Kawena Pukui and Samuel H. Elbert.

After leaving Honolulu for college, Barack Obama would have noticed superficial signs during holiday visits that Hawaiian is an official state language. The spelling "Hawai'i" emerged in the late 1970s, using the 'okina (' mark) indicating a glottal stop to be observed when pronouncing separate syllables of a word or between words. The same gradually applied to other place and proper names, such as "Wai'alae Avenue" and "Governor Waihe'e." From about the year 2000, the macron (ˉ) began to appear on such street signs as "Kalākaua Avenue" to indicate pronunciation of a vowel longer than normal.

Congressional statutes from the 1970s have been interpreted to mean that any program financed by federal funds must provide language assistance to groups that make up 5 percent of the potential population to be serviced or (where the population is more than 20,000) at least 1,000 persons. By that standard, language assistance to at least seven ethnic groups qualifies (Table 4.1).

A significant influx of Japanese tourists occurred in the 1970s. Signs in Japanese emerged ubiquitously throughout Waikīkī. Third-generation Japanese Americans found themselves learning a language better than their parents to cash in on new jobs in the tourist industry.

In 1980, the Hawai'i Department of Education acknowledged that HCE "is the first language of many children" (Hawai'i 1980a:4). In 1987, more than half the students in certain rural parts of the Islands were considered monolingual in HCE (Reyes 1987). Yet even by 2010, census enumerators were not asked to identify speakers of HCE—or even for the Hawaiian language.

Meanwhile, the Hawaiian language is destined to strengthen its position. One reason is the revival of public school teaching in the Hawaiian language since 1987. Students can now opt to enroll in a school where Hawaiian alone is spoken until grade 5, when English is introduced for the first time.

An endorsement of HCE appears in a popular work, *Pidgin to Da Max* (1981). Written by artist Douglas Simonson with assistance from Ken Sakata and Pat Sasaki, the illustrated book was revised in a second edition in 1992 (*Pidgin to Da Max: Hana Hou*) and a third edition in 2005, with over 200,000 copies sold. The cover conveys much humor and irony, featuring a local mother, who says to her children in HCE, "How many times I tol' you .... No talk li' dat!"

The most accessible way for Mainlanders to hear a bit of Pidgin today is to attend a performance of Frank De Lima. Of Portuguese, Hawaiian, Irish, Chinese, English, Spanish, and Scottish heritage, Frank Wilcox Napuakekaulike De Lima presents himself self-deprecatingly as a "Portagee." His stand-up comedy shows bring down the house in Hawai'i as well as on the Mainland, liberally using Pidgin and utilizing Island humor that pokes fun at ethnic stereotypes while also celebrating them. De Lima has spawned a new generation of stand-up comedians, including Filipino Andy Bumatai, one of whose routines is to make fun of ethnic accents, referring to those who speak the language spoken by his parents as sounding like "boiling water."

However, there are signs that "progress" is achieving what several generations of prescriptivist teachers failed to achieve. Every year, one hears less HCE spoken in public places. The increased population from the

Mainland United States since statehood has given speakers of American English an increasing plurality, if not yet a majority of the population.

Continued pressure comes from corporations and government agencies that are unwilling to take on employees who deal directly with the public if they have even a distinguishable local accent. Some unfortunate legal decisions have upheld the prerogative of employers to refuse to hire speakers with non-Mainland accents. In *Kahakua et al. v. Friday* (876F2d698), two Hawai'i-born weather forecasters brought suit against their employers, the National Weather Bureau, for failure to promote them to the position of recorded forecasters. The Bureau claimed that their accents would be unintelligible to nonlocals in vessels at sea. The forecasters lost their case in 1989, the same year when the City and County of Honolulu won a court case, *Fragante v Honolulu*, filed by a job applicant who was turned down for a position because of his "heavy Filipino accent" (699FSupp1429; 888F2d591).

To demonstrate continuing use of HCE lingo, on July 29, 2009, there was a Craigslist ad from a 26-year-old male at Kahalui, Maui: "loko braddah hea lookn fo same . . . if datz u den hit me up." (Local brother here looking for same . . . if that's you, then send me e-mail.)

A perceptive reader (and listener) will notice the New England accent, with the broad "r," originally brought by missionaries in the 1820s that prevails mostly among those who have attended Kamehameha Schools, whereas more recent migrants keep accents from either the Western United States or their home countries. In addition, a sing-song accent has continued through generations of Japanese American females. Old-country accents from other languages are also heard.

From 1998, Professor Kent Sakoda has convened a weekly meeting, known as Da Pidgin Coup, on the Mānoa campus of the University of Hawai'i with the aim of discussing educational, linguistic, and social issues concerning Pidgin on a professional level. *Pidgin Grammar: An Introduction to the Creole Language of Hawai'i* (2003) is written by two linguistics professors, Sakoda and Jeff Siegel.

Today, despite the growing percentage of Mainland Whites among Hawai'i's people, HCE will persist, albeit in a somewhat diluted form, for as long as those born and raised in Hawai'i identify with the local culture and feel the need to distinguish themselves from the rest of the population. "Pidgin light," interspersed with a clear pronunciation of English, and vice versa, is commonly spoken by members of all ethnic groups, binding everyone together as special people in a special part of the world.

Could the fact that Hawai'i is also the most linguistically diverse and racially harmonious of the 50 states be nothing more than mere coincidence? Hawai'i's experience suggests that proponents of "English-only" policies need to do some serious thinking about the effect that such policies have on racial tensions in Mainland America.

Chapter 5

The Media: A Mixed Plate

Helen Geracimos Chapin

*[T]he media [are] splintered into a thousand fragments, each
with its own version of reality, each claiming the loyalty of a
splintered nation. . . . For the broad public at least, I am who
the media says I am.*

(Obama 2008:151, 121)

When Barack Obama was growing up in Honolulu, his parents and
grandparents listened to the radio, watched television, and subscribed
to one or both of the two daily newspapers. Barry found out about the
world from the usual news sources in Honolulu, even if just to find out
when the next basketball game might be held on the Mānoa campus of
the University of Hawai'i, where his mom had enrolled.

Because of his conversations with his mom and counterculture labor
journalist/poet Frank Marshall Davis, he must have developed a healthy
skepticism about mainstream news. Nevertheless, in his pursuit of identity, he felt that *"TV, movies, the radio . . . were the places to start"*
(Obama 1995:78). Whether he was aware of media written for various
ethnic groups is unknown, but many Island residents relish the variety
because they want to learn from what interests others so that they can
show more understanding.

Hawai'i, an isolated, preliterate society—oral, memory based, communal, with a nature-based religion and a barter economy dependent upon
food yields from the ocean and land—was washed over after contact by

Christianity, money, a market economy, private property, printing, and literacy. Newspapers entered the Hawaiian Kingdom in 1834, radio in 1922, television in 1952, and the Internet by 1988. Although different technologies, they share in common that they are imported, intrusive forces that impact even as they record history. Their separate and joint histories carry many paradoxes.

Perhaps the most important aspect of the media in Hawai'i is that the tone is cheerful and positive. On radio and television there is a friendliness and sense of joy from local broadcasters. Those who move from Hawai'i to troubled parts of the Mainland are shocked by so much negative news. The metaphor most applicable to media in Hawai'i today is the ever-popular "mixed plate," that is, a meal with a variety of foods, such as Japanese rice, Chinese noodles, Hawaiian-Japanese teriyaki steak or chicken, Korean kim chee, and Euro-American salad and bread.

In contrast, the original printed media were divisive. Those in power who could not read Chinese or Japanese media would have been fearful of what was being said. How the Islands developed multilingual media is the story of this chapter.

NEWSPAPERS

The printing press entered the Islands in 1820 with American Protestant missionaries from New England (Chapin 1996). Appearing first in Hawaiian, then in English, an astonishing 1,000 separate newspaper titles have appeared during two centuries in Hawai'i. More than 100 titles have been produced in Hawaiian, plus some in 11 other languages or in English for various ethnic groups.

Missionary printers, from 1834, taught young Native Hawaiian males at Lahainaluna School on Maui to write, set type, and produce the four-page *Ka Lama Hawai'i* (The Hawaiian Luminary), written in Hawaiian. Later that year appeared the first regularly published newspaper, *Ke Kumu Hawai'i* (The Hawaiian Source). One aim was to spread Christianity by stimulating a desire for literacy. As of 1887, there were more newspapers in Hawaiian than in English (Bickerton 1998:61).

More than one-third of all the newspapers over the years have represented ancestral tongues other than English—Chinese, Ilocano, Hawaiian, Japanese, Jewish, Korean, Portuguese, Samoan, Spanish, and Vietnamese. Fully one-third of Hawai'i's publications have been bilingual and even trilingual, that is, printed in two or three different languages or dialects—Japanese and English, for example. Thus, while newspapers were imported from the United States into what was first thought to be an outpost, later an integral part of America, they have encompassed diversity and multiculturalism from their earliest days.

Four categories may be used to classify newspapers—establishment, opposition (or alternative), official, and independent. Newspapers may shift and overlap across the four types as they change within the context of their times, contributing further to diversity.

Establishment press. Also called the "commercial" or "mainstream press", establishment periodicals were instituted in the Hawaiian language by the missionaries soon after their arrival. By 1836, the first foreign-language paper appeared—an English language periodical backed by American business interests, who were gaining influence in the growing port town of Honolulu. Called the *Sandwich Island Gazette and Journal of Commerce*, the publication lasted only three years.

The weekly English language *Pacific Commercial Advertiser* began in 1856 as a bilingual newspaper. Five years later, the Hawaiian portion of the *Advertiser* was spun off into the independent Hawaiian language *Nūpepa Kūʻokʻa* (The Independent Press) (1861–1927). Both were edited by missionary descendants fluent in Hawaiian and by ardent Native Hawaiian Christian news reporters fluent in English.

Future King David Kalākaua was one of the editors on *Nūpepa Kūʻokʻa*. In 1870, he became the sole editor of *Ka Manawa* (Time), the first daily newspaper run by Native Hawaiians.

Plantation periodicals produced by sugar and pineapple management, with columns in Ilocano (the language of the northern Philippines) and Japanese, were aimed at ethnic groups entering Hawaiʻi as plantation labor to propagandize them of the superiority of American values. Inadvertently, while wielding economic, political, and social power, the establishment thereby added to multiculturalism.

Responding to economic realities, the metropolitan dailies and weeklies, although predominantly in English, have come to include over the decades multicultural editorial and advertising content. To identify just a few, supermarkets and restaurants advertise specific ethnic foods, and Saturday church columns promote services from Korean Christian to Samoan Mormon and Greek Orthodox. Features appear on Black History Month, St. Patrick's Day, and other ethnic holidays. Discussions often cover Native Hawaiian sovereignty issues.

In 1921, the morning daily changed its name from *Pacific Commercial Advertiser* to *Honolulu Advertiser*. In the afternoon, what began in 1882 as the *Evening Bulletin* competed with the *Hawaiian Star*, which started in 1883 (*Honolulu Star-Advertiser* 2010a). The two merged in 1912 to become the *Honolulu Star-Bulletin*. During the period of Haole dominance in the first half of the 20th century, both newspapers were frankly racist, but that changed after World War II. Editors with new outlooks were hired—George Chaplin at the *Advertiser* and Bud Smyser at the *Star-Bulletin*—and both newspapers became much friendlier to the local population.

Honolulu managed to maintain two newspapers through creative managerial decisions until mid-2010, when the owner of both merged them into the *Honolulu Star-Advertiser*, which also publishes *MidWeek* (1984–), a weekly with ads and features mailed to 270,000 Honolulu residents (Boylan 2009). Although the major newspapers are published on Oʻahu, they cover some news from Neighbor Islands but inevitably miss matters of local importance, leaving room for other island newspapers (Table 5.1). All newspapers cover ethnic events as well as "mainstream" news. Letters to the editor in the remaining daily occupy more space than in the *Los Angeles Times*, but, in accordance with the multicultural ethos, "personal attacks will not be published."

Alternative newspapers. Non-Whites have had newspapers of their own. Some were opposition newspapers that did verbal battle with and resisted the Haole establishment. Over two centuries, indigenous and ethnic language opposition papers have contributed to the Islands' racial amalgam.

A 19th-century example set the model for racial blending, when two Haole journalists, the Swedish Abraham Fornander and the American Henry Sheldon, published *Honolulu Times* (1849–1851). Both married

Table 5.1
Mainstream Newspapers in Hawaiʻi Today

Periodical Title	Principal Market	Year Launched
Cop-Out	Lānaʻi	1970
Garden Island	Kauaʻi	1902
Hawaiʻi Tribune-Herald	Hilo	1923
Honolulu Star-Advertiser	Oʻahu	1856[a]
Maui News	Maui	1900
Molokai Advertiser-News	Molokaʻi	1985
West Hawaiʻi Today	Kona	1997

[a]Originally *Pacific Commercial Advertiser*, but merged with another newspaper in 2010.

Native Hawaiian women and challenged rising American dominance. Acceptance of English enabled English-language newspapers to flourish.

Initially, the *Pacific Commercial Advertiser* railed against the sugar barons, opposed importing laborers from Asia to work on the sugarcane fields, and also attacked the hula as a pagan ritual. Sugar giant Claus Spreckels, with the aid of Kalākaua, bought out the newspaper to still the protests of its editor, Henry Whitney, and adopted a pro-royalist editorial policy from 1880. In 1888, when Spreckles sold the paper to Lorrin Thurston, he invited Whitney back, and he served as editor for another five years.

Native Hawaiians, who avidly adopted literacy, produced from 1861 a nationalist press of some 20 newspapers that challenged the promotion of imperialist American interests. In Hawaiian and English, this press articulated arguments for keeping Hawai'i an independent country. In the 1890s, Hawaiian nationalist papers reached their height of influence. Such journalists and political activists as Robert and Theresa Wilcox, who co-published several papers, and John Bush, editor of *Ka Leo o ka Lāhui* (Voice of the Nation) from 1889 to 1896, were expertly bilingual. The influence of both papers decreased rapidly after annexation, when English was no longer regarded as a foreign language—a process identified as "linguistic genocide" (Day 1985).

Print fosters independent thinking, but it also enables government to centralize and oppress. The most blatant examples occurred after the overthrow of the monarchy, when the oligarchy eliminated guarantees of free speech, and arrested, fined, and jailed a dozen Native Hawaiian and allied Caucasian oppositionists for "seditious libel" and "conspiracy"—that is, for pro-Hawaiian sentiments.

In defiance of the Haole takeover, Joseph and Emma Nawai, brought out *Ke Aloha 'Āina* (Love of the Land), during 1895. They sought a return to the monarchy, but their last issue was published in 1920.

Other alternative newspapers arose in ethnic languages. Produced by educated cadres, they have played a dual, paradoxical role—to foster pride in the home country by keeping readers in touch with their roots, and to inform readers of the new land's customs and practices, thereby helping to acculturate or assimilate. Ethnic periodicals were an outgrowth of the recruitment for plantation labor. Hawai'i may claim to have one of the most numerous ethnic language presses in the world (Beechert 1985).

The first Chinese newspapers were issued in 1881. To date, there have been at least 26 Chinese or Chinese-English papers.

The first Portuguese newspaper was printed in 1885. *O Luso Hawaii-ana* (1895–1924) was the longest lived of some 13 different titles. No Portuguese papers are in print today.

More than 120 papers have appeared in Japanese or Japanese and English since 1892. In their heyday, the 1920s to the 1940s, the papers reached one-third of the population, reflecting the Territory's demographics.

Japanese newspapers illustrate another dynamic. Ethnic or indigenous language papers usually do not speak in a single voice, for there are differences of opinion within almost any cultural group. The establishment, by contrast, is often unified in its determination to retain power. Accordingly, the oligarchy applied a divide-and-conquer strategy by fomenting dissension among the Japanese-language newspapers, accusing the "rabid Japanese press" of "trying to stir up agitation" (*Pacific Commercial Advertiser* 1919).

In 1912, Frederick Shinzaburo Makino, the offspring of a Japanese mother and an English father, began publication of *Hawaii Hochi* (Hawaii News Record). After World War I, he agitated in the newspaper to gain citizenship for Japanese who fought in the American army. In 1924, he backed strikes for better pay and working conditions, while *Nippu Jiji* (Japan-Hawaii Times) (1906–1985) editorially counseled moderation. When the Territorial legislature banned Japanese-language schools, Makino led the fight to save them all the way to the U.S. Supreme Court, which, in 1927, declared the law unconstitutional. Still published today, articles are in English and Japanese.

After the December 7, 1941, attack on Pearl Harbor, the military government shut down all ethnic-language papers. When the military government realized there was no other way to inform immigrants, four were allowed to reopen (two in Japanese and one each in Chinese and Ilocano) under strict censorship.

After the war, Japanese-language papers receded in influence. The principal one, the semimonthly *Hawaii Herald* (1980–), in English and occasional Japanese, reaches younger generations of Japanese Americans, and remains an important voice for ethnic pride, the transmission of cultural values, and intergenerational dialogue.

Korean newspapers have numbered about 30. They have been chiefly interested in politics in Korea.

Newspapers for the Filipino community have had a historic role since Pablo Manlapit brought out *Ang Sadata* (The Sword) in 1913 to protest unfair conditions of Filipinos on the plantations. A lawyer, he was disbarred, arrested for subornation of perjury, and released to take a one-way ticket to the Mainland. At present, such periodicals as the *Fil-Am Courier* (1986–) and the more popular *Hawaii Filipino Chronicle* (1993–) reach new immigrants from the Philippines as well as the Filipino community in general.

Other periodicals include *Hawaii Jewish News* (1977–), with content on Hawai'i and Israel. *Mahogany* (1988–) features primarily Latinos, but also other people of color—African Americans, Filipinos, Native Hawaiians, and Samoans. Still another ethnic paper is aimed at the visitor or tourist market—*Waikiki Bīchi Purisu* (1971–), the Japanese-language counterpart of the English biweekly *Waikiki Beach Press* (1960–).

In the last third of the 20th century, such ethnic papers as the *Hawaii Herald* have become part of the establishment because of political ascendancy by non-Caucasians. There is a paradox here, too. The ethnic press reflects the continuation of immigration into the Islands. But Hawai'i also has the highest ratio in the nation of mixed marriages—about 50 percent. Thus, the papers are simultaneously ethnic enclaves with multicultural outreach. They are concerned with the histories of their own groups locally but report outside events.

Organized labor, too, has shifted roles from opposition to establishment. From the 1930s to 1950s, union newspapers served as organizing tools across racial lines struggling against an exploitative management. The *Honolulu Record* (1948–1958), sponsored by the International Longshore and Warehouse Union, was especially effective. As editor of the *Record*, Nisei (second generation) Koji Ariyoshi, advocated racial equality and a free press. One columnist on the newspaper, Frank Marshall Davis, was mentor to Barry Obama.

Official newspapers. The Kingdom of Hawai'i had its own newspaper, the *Polynesian* (1841–1864), founded by Henry Whitney. One reporter, Elizabeth Swain Jarves, was Hawai'i's first female journalist. When her husband left the Islands to seek medical care, she ran the paper. Whitney's spouse issued a feminist newspaper, the single issue *Folio*, in 1855.

Hawai'i is arguably the most militarized of the 50 states, so military newspapers are an active presence. They represent an equal-opportunity service whose enlisted personnel are more than one-third non-Caucasian. Accordingly, *Stars and Stripes* promotes a combination of ethnic pride and patriotism, and claims to be free from censorship, though published by the Department of Defense. First issued in 1942 for soldiers in Europe, the Hawai'i version, which focuses on Asia and the Pacific, has been published since 1945, superseding the wartime *Midipacifica*.

From 1980, *Ka Wai Ola* (The Living Waters) has been produced by the Office of Hawaiian Affairs and printed in English but with columns in Hawaiian. A tabloid distributed free around the Islands, the publication prides itself on "featuring Native Hawaiian news, features, and events," thus aiding the sovereignty movement and providing news of general interest. In addition, several small anti-establishment newspapers are printed by Native Hawaiians.

Independent newspapers. Some publications are not beholden to any special interest. The best contemporary representative is *Ka Leo o Hawai'i* (Voice of Hawai'i), the student-run newspaper at the University of Hawai'i at Mānoa. Published since 1922, the periodical is overseen by a publications board but left alone editorially. Over the years, *Ka Leo* has been a model of multiculturalism in content and multiethnic staffing. Residents and tourists alike rely on *Honolulu Weekly* (1991–), which lists events in great detail and also has serious articles on various subjects and allows letters to the editor.

Internet publishing. From the 1990s, many periodicals described herein have posted Internet editions. Today, everyone can be a journalist by establishing a weblog, that is, a website to which news and opinion can be posted as often as the owner or manager of the website desires. Today, there are more than 100 million blogs around the world. Hawai'i has hundreds. *Hawaiinews.com* boasts that it was the first Island blog, having begun in 1994. On *hawaiiweblog.com*, Ryan Kawailani Ozawa lists the "Top 10" among a long list of Island blogs. Hawai'i news can be obtained on the national news weblog *examiner.com* by a simple mouse click, as is true of *craigslist.com*, where free advertisements have cut into the profits of newspaper classified ads. Those who subscribe to a blog can sometimes receive regular e-mail postings. Much of the mobilization of support for Barack Obama in Hawai'i and elsewhere occurred through such e-mail mailings.

RADIO

Although printed media survive, only perhaps 20 percent of those in Hawai'i read newspapers (Hawai'i 1992:382–406). Radio and television have more listeners.

In 1898, news of the American annexation of Hawai'i took seven days to arrive in the Islands by steamship from California. On New Year's Day 1903, the Pacific Cable, containing electronic circuitry, was installed—a technologically significant act that connected the Islands in seconds to the Mainland United States, Europe, and other countries and continents. That cable, which was superseded in 1951 by other communication methods, now lies unused at the bottom of the ocean.

The first known commercial radio program in the United States was a Christmas Eve broadcast in 1906 from Brant Rock, Massachusetts. On May 11, 1922, the Islands' first commercial stations, KGU and KDYX (from 1930, KGMB), blurted out "Hello, hello," and "Aloha" (Schmitt 1978:107). Originally owned by newspapers, KGU affiliated with the National Broadcasting Company (NBC) in 1931, followed by other affiliations interconnecting radio stations with the Mainland.

After World War II, radio stations burgeoned. Honolulu, with a population of 905,037 in 2008, has 56 stations. In addition to commercial stations, in 1996 two noncommercial stations began—Hawai'i Public Radio and the radio station of the University of Hawai'i at Mānoa (KTUH). Both now have four channels. On the Neighbor Islands, there are 28 radio stations on the island of Hawai'i, 14 on Kaua'i, and 21 in Maui County (including the islands of Lāna'i, Maui, and Moloka'i).

Radio fits into four broadcast categories—commercial, noncommercial and public, professional, and amateur (ham radio). Similar to newspapers, the Islands contain a surprisingly large number of radio stations that have been multicultural from their first days.

From the beginning, radio owners perceived that, to attract advertising revenue, the appeal should be to all listeners. White-owned, pro-establishment English-language stations have aired Hawaiian music, Sunday sermons in Japanese, and Filipino cultural programs. The nationally popular *Hawaii Calls*, featuring Hawaiian music, beamed to Mainland and worldwide audiences from 1935 to 1975.

The 1960s, when Barack Obama's parents and grandparents first arrived in Hawai'i, were a turning point because ethnic and indigenous stations first came on the air. The rise in consciousness of "roots," the resurgence of Native Hawaiian identity in the 1970s, and continued migration into the Fiftieth State have contributed to an increasing number of language and cultural programs on the English-language stations and to other stations dedicated exclusively to individual ethnic groups, principally Filipinos and Japanese.

One especially interesting type of multicultural outreach is "local programming" focused on non-Haoles who have forebears connected to the plantation experience. The Creole tongue pervades most radio stations in the Islands.

Local radio has attached itself to the automobile in Hawai'i. Due to heavy Honolulu traffic, motorists getting up early or being caught in bottlenecks relished the opportunity listen to Brooklyn-born Hal J. "Aku-head Pupule" Lewis on KGMB-AM after World War II. In 1983, after Lewis died, he was replaced by a duo—Mainland-born Michael W. Perry and Hawai'i-born Pidgin-speaking Larry Price. From 1991, KSSK-AM has been the top station during peak hours from 6 A.M. to 10 A.M. and overall in the Honolulu market (Engle 2009). Perry & Price, as they are known, introduced the "phone posse," an informal but potent volunteer community assemblage of 60,000 listeners, who use cellphones to report speeding vehicles, accidents, and car thefts, which they then relay to the police. Other drive-time stations have followed suit.

Attesting to the immediacy of radio and multiculturalism, KIKI found itself in a major flap in 1993, when what appeared to be anti-Hawaiian remarks were broadcast. What happened was that KIKI's general man-ager, Lee Coleman, advised a Mainland advertising agency to aim its Acura ad campaign at professional, high-income, white-collar Cauca-sian and Japanese, and not at the Native Hawaiian population. In a singular exaggeration and simplification of sovereignty goals, Coleman described the movement as one "where Hawaiians want to retake the Islands and remove all foreigners and foreign business." Protests poured in from the general public (Fernandez 1993; Tanahara 1993). KIKI pub-licly apologized and agreed to help the public have a greater understand-ing of issues relating to sovereignty. For a year, the station aired "Historic Notes," prepared by the Hawaiian Historical Society, on a wide range of cultural and historical subjects.

An important outreach audience consists of Native Hawaiians. From 1990, KCCN-FM has played Hawaiian music, conducted interviews, aired education and informational programs, and broadcast from out-side the studios on special occasions. Two other Hawaiian music stations are KINE-FM and KKNE-FM.

The first Filipino-owned station was KISA, which began in 1950, but changed to Korean-language programs in 1982, when some of its celebri-ties and staff moved to KNDI. Since 1960, KNDI has provided program-ming for Filipinos, who are primarily from the Ilocos Province of the Philippines and speak Ilocano, though programs also have been available in two other Philippine languages: Tagalog and Visayan. Today, KNDI is broadcast in eight languages with a religious format. In 2008, KPHI began as a Filipino station, broadcast in Tagalog for recent immigrants.

Two AM stations broadcast in Korean. KHRA began in 2008 as an affiliate of KMPC-AM in Los Angeles, which relays programs produced in California. KISA changed its call letters in 2000 to become KREA.

Radio also targets Japanese and the visitor market from Japan. KOHO-AM, which later became KORL-AM, began in 1959, appealing to Japanese visitors in the 12- to 44-year-old bracket with programs featuring music, sports, entertainment tips, and lessons in Hawaiian. After expanding to a 24-hour four-language format that reached three islands, and advertising itself as a "talk and multicultural" station, KORL-AM shut down in 2002. From 1963, KZOO-AM has continued to broadcast in Japanese, with Japanese pop and variety music today. Non-Japanese Island residents have tuned in both stations to enjoy Japanese music.

New populations bring new markets. One long-underserved market consisted of Southern military personnel stationed in the Islands. In 2005, KHCM began broadcasting country music. In 2010, KORL-AM was back on the air as a Spanish-language religious station.

On the Neighbor Islands, several stations call themselves "Hawaiian," air Hawaiian music, and highlight news and features of interest to Native Hawaiians. In fact, most "mainstream" stations on the major islands include substantial Hawaiian, "local," and ethnic language and cultural broadcasting.

KLHI-FM began in Honolulu during 1989, featuring contemporary rock, but the owners moved to Maui in 1996 as KORL-FM. The format changed to daytime multicultural programming with nighttime and weekend smooth jazz. In 2008, multicultural programming ended.

In 1991, KONI-FM on Lāna'i signed on, featuring oldies. In 1997, KAYI (now KTOH) began operating on Kaua'i with country music programming. Two more stations began in 1997—KAWT (now KITH-FM) with "world ethnic" programming and KAWV (now KJMQ) with adult contemporary music.

Consolidations in radio ownership have occurred in Hawai'i as elsewhere, but diversity in programming remains. As of the mid-1990s, radio listening of the average person was 22 hours per week (Harada 1996).

Oceanic Cable Televisions, a subsidiary of Time Warner, provides several channels for radio programs. There are no Hawai'i satellite radio stations, but residents can receive Sirius.

In addition to Internet broadcasting provided by existing AM and FM stations, there are some exclusive Internet radio stations. From O'ahu, *NorthShoreRadioHawai'i.com* features Asian, Hawaiian/Pacific, and contemporary reggae music, while *HawaiianRainbow.com* originates on Maui with Hawaiian music. *Pipeline2paradise.com* also features Hawaiian music.

Finally, ham radio is also popular in Hawai'i. Ten clubs exist on various islands. KWHR broadcasts religious programs on six shortwave bands from Southpoint on the island of Hawai'i.

TELEVISION

Television was technically feasible by 1931, but did not broadcast until April 30, 1939, at the opening of the New York World's Fair. By mid-1940, there were 23 television stations in the United States. World War II brought all activity to a halt, but from 1946 there has been phenomenal growth of television. Television broadcasting began in Hawai'i during 1952, immediately initiating ethnic programming.

On O'ahu, there are 17 broadcast stations, including one public or noncommercial. Of the 35 stations on the Neighbor Islands, all but two (a jewelry channel and a religious station) relay programs, including public television, from the major network stations from O'ahu. An estimated 97 percent of Island households receive television (Hawai'i 1992:382–406).

While the Mainland enjoyed the television series *Hawaiian Eye* (1959–1963), most locals resented the subordinate role played by non-Whites. The same phony racial stereotyping occurred in *Hawaii Five-O* (1968–1980), a series coinciding with most of Barry Obama's years in Honolulu that was relaunched with a new cast—but not yet with a meaningful representation Island people—in fall 2010. Although *Magnum PI* (1980–1988) tried to regain the audiences of *Hawaii Five-O*, and the local characters were somewhat less stereotypic, they still did not project a multicultural message. In 1994, a family-oriented *Byrds of Paradise* sought to do so by depicting a family moving from the Mainland to Kaua'i that had to learn how to adjust to life in the multicultural Aloha State. Although reminiscent of the famous *Ozzie & Harriet* show, the *Byrds of Paradise* folded after a seven-week run. Then two crime dramas tried to exploit the scenery—*One West Waikiki* (1994–1996) and *Hawaii* (2004)—but again Mainland writers did not know how to portray Island culture.

In 1976, KITV fired an all-White news team and opened its evening news with four non-White newscasters (Chinese, Filipino, Native Hawaiian, and Japanese). Along with the rest of Hawai'i, Barry Obama must have been dazzled by their presence. Subsequently, announcers from several ethnic communities appeared on all the local network news shows.

Once described as "the most cabled state in the world" (McLaughlin 1989), there are 41 commercial cable stations. Some stations receive transmissions directly from Japan, Korea, the Philippines, and Taiwan by satellite.

The public access channel 'Olelo, financed jointly by private and public funds and incorporating "narrow casting" (meeting the needs of audiences who otherwise would not have voices on television), currently has six channels. The four main county governments also have their own cable channels. In addition, Cinemax, HBO, and Showtime provide "Pay TV."

Although noncommercial television stations are the most multicultural, KIKU offers Japanese programming, KBFD provides Korean programs, KHLU services the growing Spanish-speaking community, and NATV focuses on the Native Hawaiian Community. Cable Channel 16 on Oceanic Time Warner has programs for several ethnic groups. Of course, with the purchase of a of satellite dish, all languages are now available.

An overview of a typical week's programming illustrates that commercial television is also multicultural. Food and cooking shows are enormously popular. Programs offer movies in Cantonese, Japanese, Korean, Mandarin, and Tagalog, as well as Chinese opera, Philippine soap opera, *Samoan Highlights*, karate, and sumo. *Soul Train*, which Barry Obama evidently watched from its beginning in 1971, was carried on Hawai'i television during its record 35-year run. One disappointment came at Christmastime 1971, when his father, who unexpectedly popped into town, ordered him to study in his room instead of watching *How the Grinch Stole Christmas*. Now compared to First Officer Spock, Obama was an avid fan of the television series *Star Trek*.

From 1982–1999, after Obama was already on the Mainland, Hawai'i Public Television launched *Spectrum*, an award-winning program on a full range of cultural subjects that appealed to audiences of Island groups. Appearing on commercial and noncommercial stations are such local comedians as Frank DeLima, who lightheartedly spoofs himself and all racial groups.

Today, Internet television programming and podcasting provides many new outlets, whether on Twitter, YouTube, or other video websites. The cooking show *BenWongTV.com*, for example, offers viewers an alternative way to view his program. Among the new video websites, *HawaiiTVNetwork.com* broadcasts Maui TV news programs and stockpiles other video shows for viewers to watch whenever they wish.

Some programs on the newer media are television reruns or consist of longer presentations that were cut to fit limited time on network or cable television programs. The democracy of the newer media is that almost anyone can become a broadcaster.

FILM

Hawai'i has occasionally been portrayed in film. According to the International Movie Data Base (*www.imdb.com*), some 332 movies have featured Hawai'i. The first was *The Beachcomber* (1915). A series of 36 murder mysteries from 1931 to 1949 featured Charlie Chan, a brilliant Chinese detective from Honolulu who spoke in broken English. Yet both actors who played Chan were Caucasian, and film viewers learned little about Hawai'i, since Chan often went to various foreign locations, such as Berlin, to solve murders (Huang 2010).

Hawai'i was the venue for some World War II films. One of the most memorable during the war is Howard Hawks's *Air Force* (1943). After the war, the most notable is perhaps *From Here to Eternity* (1953), but the focus in James Jones's tale, as brought to the screen by Fred Zinnemann, was mostly on military personnel who lived on a military base. The same can be said of *Tora! Tora! Tora!* (1970), a coproduction directed by Richard Fleischer, Kinji Fukasaku, and Toshio Masuda.

Elvis Presley was so entranced by Hawai'i that he produced *Blue Hawaii* (1961), capturing the imagination of many around the world, and he returned for two more films. James Michener's famous novel *Hawaii* (1959) inspired two films focusing on the interplay between ethnic groups in the Islands—*Hawaii* (1966) and *The Hawaiians* (1970). The complexities of multicultural Hawai'i are perhaps best portrayed in Alan Parker's *Picture Bride* (1994), in which a Japanese woman is imported to Hawai'i in 1918 to marry a Japanese plantation worker.

In 1981, the East-West Center launched an annual international film festival, attracting a wide variety of documentaries and feature films, many from Asia. Both the festival, now known as the Hawai'i International Film Festival (HIFF), and a later annual Maui International Film Festival (from 1999), also offer local film makers an opportunity to present their productions to a wider audience. Two smaller film festivals are The Rainbow Film Festival (from 1989) for gay and lesbian films and the 'Ōiwi Film Festival (from 2010) for Native Hawaiian filmmakers. Many documentaries have focused on the Islands over the years (cf. Weber 2004).

The latest film of relevance to Hawai'i, which appeared commercially in 2010 after a première at HIFF, is Marc Forby's *Princess Ka'iulani*. The film depicts the princess's education in England and her efforts to save the Kingdom of Hawai'i from annexation by the United States.

As a student, Obama played a small role in *Narc Squad*, an independent film made at Punahou. Among his favorite films are *The Godfather*, *Casablanca*, *One Flew Over the Cuckoo's Nest*, and *Lawrence of Arabia* (Alter 2010:303). He has been featured in several documentaries about his presidential campaign and inspired the character of Matt Santos in *The West Wing* (Remnick 2010:422–423). In 2010, Indonesian film director Damien Dematra began shooting *Obama, The Menteng Kid*, a movie based on Obama's four years in Indonesia.

MEDIA COUNCIL HAWAI'I (MCH)

In 1970, when Honolulu Mayor Frank Fasi decided to ban individual reporters from his press conferences, the Honolulu Community-Media Council was formed, and a court case forced Fasi to rescind the ban. The oldest of the five volunteer media councils in the United States, members include individuals from the community and the media industry.

In 1999, renamed Media Council Hawai'i, the organization formed Save Our Star-Bulletin to block Gannett Corporation from acquiring the *Honolulu Star-Bulletin* with the intention of shutting the newspaper down. As a result, Honolulu remained a two-newspaper town for another decade.

In 2007, Micronesians United complained about a *Honolulu Advertiser* reporter who wrote what they considered a derogatory news article about the use of homeless shelters by Micronesians. With MCH's assistance, an apology was issued.

MCH successfully lobbied the state legislature to pass a Shield Law in 2008 that protects journalists from being forced to reveal their sources in state courts. As a result, journalist Keoni Kealoha Álvarez was exempted from answering subpoenas in a 2009 civil suit.

MCH demonstrates how multiethnic citizen action protects the media in Hawai'i. MCH aims at broadening public understanding of the role of the media, improving public access to information, promoting accurate and fair journalism, and strengthening public support for First Amendment rights and freedoms through public forums and sponsorship of a hotline.

Today, all Hawai'i's commercial broadcast stations are owned by Mainland or international conglomerates. In 2009, perhaps reflecting competition with the new media, a merger of the newsrooms of three separate television stations to cut costs was proposed, whereupon MCH filed a complaint with the Federal Communications Commission that resulted in disclosure of several documents, but the merger went ahead.

CONCLUSION

Greater diversity was accelerated by statehood. Various ethnic groups have felt free to start newspapers and publishing businesses. Radio stations and television programming became more diverse. With the advent of Internet blogging and programming, there is no limit to opportunities for a rainbow of media producers. Media pluralism, a vital force that can unite scattered communities, has long done so in Hawai'i.

The media in the Islands are proud of their multiculturalism. Prejudices are occasionally articulated, but are very unpopular, and dissenting voices are given media time. During Obama's childhood, newspapers ran stories about the transformative politics of the 1970s, radio programming became increasingly multilingual, television newscasts featured multiethnic reporters for the first time, and MCH began.

What is the future? Worldwide, the infinite reach of media may ultimately lessen ethnic conflicts and hostility. While a candidate and later as president, Barack Obama has accepted the diversity of media as a strength of America. Hawai'i's media, in which all groups have access both as producers and consumers, offers a viable intercultural model wherein everyone can learn and respect the cultures of everyone else.

Chapter 6

The Emergence
of Local Literature

Rodney Morales

*I gathered up books from the library—Baldwin, Ellison,
Hughes, Wright, DuBois. At night I would close the door to
my room, telling my grandparents I had homework to do, and
there I would sit and wrestle with the words, locked in suddenly desperate argument, trying to reconcile the world as I'd
found it with the terms of my birth. But there was no escape
to be had. In every page of every book . . . I kept finding
the same anguish, the same doubt; a self-contempt that neither irony nor intellect seemed able to deflect. Even DuBois's
learning and Baldwin's love and Langston's humor eventually
succumbed to its corrosive force, each man finally forced to
doubt art's redemptive power . . .*

(Obama 1995:85–86)

WHO GETS TO TELL THE STORY?

Hawai'i is a place claimed as home by many people, both native and
nonnative, local and nonlocal. The largest group consists of descendants
of immigrants—Chinese, Filipinos, Japanese, Portuguese, Puerto Ricans,
and others—who came to Hawai'i to make money by laboring on the

sugarcane and pineapple plantations over a century ago. To tourists and newcomers, if not themselves, the descendents of plantation workers form a "local community," a group with a common language (Hawai'i Creole English, or Pidgin), a lifestyle often termed as "laid-back" (lots of sun and surf), and a common diet (most often the plate lunch, a combination of rice, salad and meat, or the ubiquitous Spam).

Both the mainstream media and the Hawai'i Visitors and Convention Bureau promote the image of the Hawaiian Islands as a multiethnic, multicultural paradise. Tourists from all parts of the world are enticed, invited to come and, upon arrival, are entertained within the framework of such portrayals. For the visitor who can get past the unexpected charges on the hotel tab, and hasn't been unduly shaken by encounters with the homeless while cruising the wrong beach on the wrong island, or inundated by people selling everything from T-shirts to timeshares on the sidewalks of Waikīkī, or turned off by the concrete and the traffic and other evidence of development gone awry in Honolulu, Hawai'i is just that—a paradise. Weather and lush greenery aside, Hawai'i is touted as a model for diversity, a place that has transcended the usual race/class markers. The Islands form the Aloha State, and its Aloha-Spirit-driven, multicultural lifestyle seems clearly evident in the workplace; at shopping malls; at sports and cultural events in parks, stadiums, and arenas; at restaurants and movie theaters; and at beaches.

Those with a more intimate understanding of Hawai'i's sociopolitical culture, at least those who have been able to experience the Islands absent any filters, especially those delivered by the mass media and corporations bent on profit making, are keenly aware of the rips and snarls in the seemingly seamless social fabric of the multicultural state called Hawai'i.

Hawai'i is the birthplace of the 44th president of the United States, a man who happens to be of mixed race—fitting in a state where one-half of the population is born multiethnic. No other state even comes close. Hawai'i has given the United States not only its first Black or mulatto president, but also its first multiethnic and multicultural president. His small role in an unprecedented historical occurrence has put Hawai'i in the national and global spotlight.

Here's an example of the kind of coverage given to President-Elect Barack Obama by a Mainland journalist when he vacationed in Hawai'i during December 2008:

> In his two weeks in Hawaii, Barack Obama has oozed island cool:
> the black shades and khaki shorts, the breezy sandaled saunter that

suggested he had not a care in the world. Who said anything about the presidency? He strolled shirtless near the beach, enjoyed a shave ice and a local seaweed-wrapped delicacy called Spam musubi. One day, the president-elect flashed the friendly "shaka" sign, shaking his pinky and thumb in a local surfing gesture. (Rucker 2009a)

No doubt many readers were taken by how the journalist captured and distilled Obama's temperament and daily routines while vacationing on the Windward side of O'ahu, the island where Obama spent most of his childhood. The soon-to-be president was exotic in so many ways.

Readers in Hawai'i probably thought the same, except for a detail or two. That very specific and delicate paper-thin slice of dried seaweed is called nori (don't forget to roll that "r"). And the ubiquitous "shaka" sign is not a local surfing gesture. What's the source of that bit of (mis)information? At the tail end of an inoffensive and sometimes laudatory description there is something that seems, well, made-up. A small thing. A very small thing. No harm intended. No intentional misreading. (Unlike that comment by FOX News' E. D. Hill about Michelle and Barack Obama's fist bump, where the alleged journalist termed an innocent, somewhat hip gesture, a "terrorist fist jab." And although Hill apologized, the damage had been done (Sweney 2008). *They're not like us,* was her implicit comment. *We can't trust these people.*)

Small things, but part of an ongoing pattern, a pattern established well over a century ago. Whether the person writing or saying such things is a journalist or novelist passing through, whether a Mark Twain or a Jack London, both of whom visited Hawai'i eons ago, one before achieving fame (Twain) and one at the apex of such (London), and, while falling way short of their usual abilities in their articulations and analyses of what they saw, each was read widely. Or a Paul Theroux, a contemporary part-time resident whose fame preceded his stay in Hawai'i, which may partly explain the condescending way he has written about Hawai'i's local community. Or someone *born* but not raised in Hawai'i, such as poet Garrett Hongo (e.g., 1995). Or *born and raised* in Hawai'i but long gone from its shores, for example, novelist Kiana Davenport (e.g, 1994). These two, along with other opportunistic writers, have spun tales set in the Hawaiian Islands, not only with not-so-surprising inaccuracy, but also with a proprietary sense of place.

And then there's someone who has spent her formative years on some other island than the one she is writing about, namely, Lois-Ann Yamanaka (2009) and her expounding in the *New York Times* on whether Barack Obama is a "local" or not. The fact that she's the go-to person for the mainstream media says a lot about how, to use a phrase Obama seems particularly fond of, they don't "get it." In all the aforementioned cases, there is an annoying pattern of *someone not exactly qualified being authorized to comment.*

So Islanders overreact, it appears. Everyone is claiming authenticity, and it does seem to matter. The central subject is usually the failure to give voice to those born in the Islands with long local roots. And although just about everyone gets something wrong at some point or other, the grasp for authenticity, for legitimacy, is the common thread in ongoing discussions of literature in Hawai'i.

The feeling among longtime Hawai'i residents, especially those who make up its literary community, can be summed up thusly: *People have gotten us wrong since time began. We haven't had the chance to tell our own story. And when we tell it . . .* (Well, let's save this part for later.).

Who gets to tell the story? Winston Churchill (and countless echoing voices since) reportedly said, "History is written by the victors." With literature, the story has been no different. The story of the first 200 years, bookended by the arrival of Captain James Cook and his crew and the Talk Story conference two hundred years later, is just that, a tale told by colonizers—and their representatives—frankly, mostly Haole male authors. It's not that non-White people in Hawai'i did not write. Whether Native Hawaiian or immigrant, they have literary histories going back hundreds, if not thousand of years. They simply haven't had, for social, political, and economic reasons, a voice in the marketplace about Hawai'i.

It is no wonder, then, that the contemporary Local Literary movement, to be described in this chapter, is a by-product of the Black studies, ethnic studies, and feminist movements that coalesced in the 1970s. At the University of Hawai'i, the newly formed Ethnic Studies Program's rallying cry "Our History, Our Way" was in reaction to history being told by the so-called victors. Whether Hawaiian history, or plantation history, the perspective hadn't been that of the victims, but that of the perpetrators of the alleged crimes.

The political, cultural, and intellectual climate in Hawai'i in the 1970s, which included the *Palaka Power* tract by Roland Kotani (1978) and a cultural awakening that came to be known as the Hawaiian Renaissance, inspired the formation of Local Literature, a literary movement that in name clearly identified the community from which it was generated.

THE "TALK STORY" CONFLUENCE

> For entertainment there were Hawaiian songs and a ceremonial hula. When later, the Mainlanders began to stroll through the gardens, they found mangoes, ripe and gorgeously multicolored, lying on the ground, theirs for the taking. It was the quintessential Hawaiian Dream! (Newman 1979:47–48)

It's often been declared that "Local Literature" emerged as a recognizable and viable entity as a result of the Talk Story Conference of June 1978 held at Mid-Pacific Institute in Mānoa Valley, not far from the main University of Hawaiʻi campus. Known more formally as "Talk Story, Our Voices in Literature and Song: Hawaiʻi's Ethnic American Writers' Conference," the groundbreaking conference brought together many writers of local heritage, who for the first time had an opportunity to network, find some common ground, organize, and become agents of their own agendas. Following the emergence of Black studies and ethnic studies programs across the continental United States, the local community had begun to assert itself culturally. Local writers now wanted to play their role, according to the Talk Story media guide, in "confront[ing] the plantation owner aesthetic of Haole arbiters in the University of Hawaiʻi's Department of English."

Two of these "Haole arbiters" were A. Grove Day and Carl Stroven, longtime members of the Department of English at the University of Hawaiʻi at Mānoa (UHM), who edited *A Hawaiian Reader* (1959). The anthology presented an exotic collection of ship's logs, diaries, poems, short stories, folktales, and essays, written mostly by "histouricists," a term coined by Pacific scholar Paul Lyons (2006:21) and derived from the notion that "most of the canonical U.S. writers about Oceania were literally tourist boosters . . . native informants to metropolitan areas" and they were invested in a "national narrative" that espoused a "model of triumphalist 'history'," in which, as Hawaiian activist-scholar-poet Haunani-Kay Trask notes, "a rich historical past became small and ignorant . . . a few authors—the most sympathetic, have recorded with deep-felt sorrow the passing of our people. But in the end, we are repeatedly told, such an eclipse was for the best" (Trask 1993:149). Histouricists have included Jack London, W. Somerset Maugham, Robert Louis Stevenson, and Mark Twain, all highly recognizable names on literary maps of the Western world. Collectively, their works painted a misleading, racist, and often lurid portrait of Hawai'i and its unique multicultural mix.

Jack London's *Koolau the Leper* (1909) is a superficial depiction of Hawai'i's notable flora and its locales, an exaggerated portrayal of those afflicted with leprosy—all Native Hawaiian—as well as a superimposition of an individualistic, gunslinging Western hero (also Native Hawaiian) into a communal setting. What is worse, according to Lyons, is that "London projects into the mind of Ko'olau, so that it seems the reader overhears the representative Hawaiian freedom-fighter speaking the doom of his own race." Ko'olau marvels at the tenacity of the [H]aole, and finds it to be a fault and a virtue that "his own kind lacked."

W. Somerset Maugham, in his story *Honolulu* (1921), depicts the town as a creepy place populated by hare-lipped "Chinks," "cross-eyed niggers," and a native doctor a "with the face of a monkey" who looked "hardly human." The very word *Honolulu* seems to be uttered with a shudder by the protagonist as he recalls his experience with "primitive superstition."

One would think that by 1959, when Hawai'i became the Fiftieth State, the blatant racism of early-20th-century writers would have been called out, to say the least. For Day and Stroven to give life to 50- to 100-year-old stories ensured that the triumphalist message would continue to be the dominant narrative through the first decades of statehood. And to call the text *A Hawaiian Reader* [emphasis added] was even more audacious. The foreword was written by award-winning novelist James Michener, author of *Hawaii*, a thousand-page opus also published in 1959.

In recent years, another histouricist, Paul Theroux, has been staking ground in such works as *Happy Isles of Oceania* (1992), in which Pacific Islanders are portrayed as unintelligent Spam-eaters, with Spam being a link to their alleged cannibal past (Spam, of course, was meat that could be stored in plantation houses, which lacked refrigeration), and *Hotel Honolulu* (2001), wherein the poor writer from the continent has to endure the inanities of the ignorant natives. Even *Publisher's Weekly*, which presumably has no axe to grind regarding Hawaiian issues, states in May 2001, "Theroux, never one to tread lightly, often portrays native Hawaiians, including the writer's wife, as simpleminded, craven souls." Such recent instances of travel channel journalism and less than equally opportunistic social satire reveal that, in some far-reaching circles, the national triumphalist narrative continues unabated.

Another obstacle to breaking free from triumphalism was the Hawai'i Literary Arts Council (HLAC). Founded in 1974, HLAC was created to support the literary arts in the Islands. It is a volunteer, nonprofit organization supposedly made up primarily of teachers and writers from "the community," though until 1980 non-White writers were shut out of "the community." HLAC was using grant monies from state and federal agencies to bring acclaimed national and international writers to Hawai'i for readings and publicized other literary happenings. HLAC board members selected the winners of the one major literary award, the Hawai'i Award for Literature.

A counter narrative was needed. And by the late 1970s, emerging local writers, disenchanted with the cultural imperialism that came with statehood, set about to create one.

The prime movers of the Talk Story conference were the cofounders of Talk Story, Inc.—writer-scholar Marie Hara, writer-storyteller-curator Arnold Hiura, and writer-scholar Stephen Sumida, the latter the first credentialed commentator on Hawai'i's literary scene, most notably with his later collection of essays on the literature of Hawai'i, *And the View From the Shore: Literary Traditions of Hawai'i* (1991). The three brought in writers who had some link to Hawai'i or the Asian literary community of the West Coast. Among those included were Asian American author and then-Hawai'i resident Maxine Hong Kingston, who, while she had dubious *local* credentials, having grown up in Stockton, California, was already a literary star, thanks to her award-winning novel-passed-off-for-marketing-purposes-as-memoir *The Woman Warrior* (1976); retired University of Hawai'i novelist-microbiologist O. A. "Ozzie" Bushnell, author of five historical novels centering on Hawai'i (e.g., 1971, 1972); playwright Aldyth Morris, author of *Captain James Cook* (1955) and *Damien* (1980); and novelist Milton Murayama, whose self-published *All I Asking For Is My Body* (1975) was becoming an Island classic, and, validated by sales volume and critical attention, would later be published and distributed by University of Hawai'i Press. Also attending the conference were many aspiring young writers, including several who have come to be associated with Bamboo Ridge Press.[1]

Katherine Newman, editor of a couple of anthologies on American ethnic literature and creator of the Society for the Study of the Multi-Ethnic Literature of the United States rightly observes that Michener's *Hawaii* "was very conspicuous during Talk Story—by never being mentioned at all" (quoted in Sumida 1991:68).

Agency was the operative word that emerged from the conference. Local writers learned that they had to take matters into their own hands. One obvious way to do just that, when the outside world is ignoring you and your kind, is to start your own press and publish your own work and that of artists whom you respect and wish to support. The founders of Talk Story, Inc., began doing just that while the conference was still in the planning stages. Thus, not long after the conference, they published *Talk Story: Big Island Anthology* (Hiura, Sumida, and Web 1979), a collection of drama, fiction, and poetry by writers who had been involved with the conference, as well as by other locals deemed worthy of attention.

Soon afterward, several small, independent journals emerged, publishing some form of local literature. The most notable among these are *Bamboo Ridge: The Hawai'i Writers' Quarterly*, edited by poet Eric Chock, and playwright-fiction writer Darrell Lum; *Seaweeds & Constructions*, edited by poets Richard Hamasaki and Wayne Kaumuali'i Westlake; *Ramrod*, edited by poet Joseph P. Balaz; and *Hapa*, the brainchild of poet-novelist-lawyer Michael McPherson. All four journals complemented the already established *Hawai'i Review*, student edited and funded by the University of Hawai'i's Board of Publications (cf. Hamasaki 1993).

The first four journals were later supplemented or supplanted by others. *Tinfish*, a series of chapbooks and journals, is published by University of Hawai'i poet/professor Susan Schultz. *'Ōiwi* features Hawaiian authors exclusively, its primary architect being poet and essay writer Mahealani Dudoit. Kalamakū Press and its imprint *Noio* are funded and published by writer-scholar Dennis Kawaharada. And *Hybolics* is funded and published by self-described "pidgin guerrilla" poet-fiction writer-essayist Lee Tonouchi (2005). In addition, several community college-based literary journals reach small, yet no less significant, audiences.

Undoubtedly the most successful press to come out of the tangible assertion of local literature was Bamboo Ridge. Today, editors Chock and Lum, along with guest editors, have produced more than 90 volumes of fiction, poetry, single-writer collections, and special-themed issues that allow for a wider range of groupings and genres, including screenplays, works by children, compilations of speeches, photographs, and drawings. Many local writers have found their first pieces of poetry, drama, and fiction in their pages. One of their more recent books is a collection of stories, entitled *Islands Linked by Ocean* (2009), by Hawaiian-Chinese-Japanese-Filipino Lisa Linn Kanae.

The rise of local literature hasn't been easy, not just a matter of printing some books but a matter of altering consciousnesses. The UHM English Department, which originally supported the histouricist enterprise, refused for far too many years to let local literature be taught in the English Department, ignoring the growing presence of local writers, many as credentialed as any on their creative writing staff, and, perhaps most egregious, not allowing even one local writer to teach among them until the mid-1990s, when the English Department morphed into a strong supporter of local writers, making a concerted effort to remedy the slight imposed upon the very community that it purported to teach, and began to hire not only Hawai'i-born scholars and creative writers, but also those from as far-off places as New Zealand and Pakistan. The department also created the annual (now semiannual) Fall Celebration of Writers, and has successfully recruited writers from all over the globe.

According to Stephen Sumida, who was a UHM lecturer before going on to get his PhD at the University of Washington in Seattle, the brush-off of local writers affected their self-esteem:

> Told all my life that Hawaii's Asian Americans did not write—and were not verbally skillful enough even to understand—imaginative literature, I frankly was astounded by what we found. I realized how deeply I too had taken the claim for granted, or, worse, had always been afraid that it was true: that locals could never hope to write decent literature. (Sumida 1986:317)

Except for the disturbing conflation of the terms "Asian American" and "local," Sumida speaks for writers who grew up in Hawai'i during the pre-"Talk Story" era, when a deep-seated feeling was that maybe local writers weren't up to speed. Inundated as Hawai'i's local people were with American pop culture, its images filling television screens, movie screens, and the radio waves, local writers seemed to know more about mainstream America than themselves. A lack of self-assurance, a relinquishment of authority, was commonplace. Promotion of local literature and culture was seen as essential to reclaiming collective identity.

In 1980, writers associated with the fledgling Bamboo Ridge Press staged a "revolution" at the polls. Frustrated by what they perceived as Haole dominance of the local literary scene, they went after the Honolulu Literary Arts Council. Those connected to Bamboo Ridge Press organized their own HLAC membership drive, signing up friends and relatives, got them to vote in the annual board election, and succeeded in voting in a slate of writers and scholars. Bamboo Ridge editor Eric Chock became HLAC president.

Today, HLAC is much more supportive of locals. Having added the Elliot Cades Award for Literature as a way of giving recognition and support to Hawai'i-based writers, HLAC can now boast of wider community representation, a more inclusive spirit. HLAC's website states, "Most important, HLAC is open and fair."

One area touched upon by newly installed president Eric Chock in his acceptance speech was the lack of support in Hawai'i for the arts. In those days, Bamboo Ridge Press could barely pay its bills. As the years went by, Bamboo Ridge Press was able to leverage some steady funding and did fairly well with book sales. In recent times, funding has been scarce, so Bamboo Ridge, always enterprising, has relied more on fundraising activities. How the press has endured for so long, in a world where such community-driven presses are short-lived, is nothing short of remarkable.

OBAMA'S QUIET LITERARY QUEST

In 1974, when HLAC was founded, Barack Obama, then known as Barry, was in 7th grade, well beyond the age where his favorite childhood story, *Where the Wild Things Are* (Sendak 1963), would provide any lasting comfort. Four years later, when writers in Hawai'i began to be vocal about asserting their local identity, and had found in Talk Story a venue, Barry was moving in a different direction.

Although he had grown up in the multicultural environment of Honolulu, he apparently was oblivious of the local literature literary movement. Attending Punahou, an elitist, Haole-dominated private school, Barry was hard-pressed to find any role models. He found one outside of school, Frank Marshall Davis, a poet who helped the young Obama with his poetry, including "*dirty limericks*" (Obama 1995:77).

Obama was also evidently unaware of Kathryn Takara, a UHM ethnic studies instructor of African American descent who had interviewed Davis a number of times between 1972 and 1987 and was a poet herself. Sometimes before an interview at Davis's pad in Waikīkī, she would run into Obama's grandfather Stanley, but never Barry.

Honolulu lacked a substantial community of African Americans, and in 1979 Obama looked elsewhere for college. As he later reflected:

Hawaii lay behind me like a childhood dream; I could no longer imagine settling there. . . . [I]t was too late to ever truly claim Africa as my home. And if I had come to understand myself as a

[B]lack American, and was understood as such, that understanding remained unanchored to place. What I needed was a community. . . . A place where I could put down stakes and test my commitments. (Obama 1995:115)

At Occidental College, he took a course in creative writing and wrote a few poems. At Columbia University, he took a course in modern literature. When he applied for a job as a community organizer in Chicago, he said that he wanted to gather material for some short stories, and he penned a few before going off to Harvard. Then Barack (no longer Barry) put down stakes in Chicago, which Frank Marshall Davis once called home.

So exit Obama, and enter Bamboo Ridge Press. The historical impact of the "passing in the night" in 1979 may perhaps be integrated into future discussions of the literature in Hawai'i. Honolulu did give the future president a "culture" to participate in, but what kind of culture? If reduced to shaka signs, such foods as shave ice and Zip Min, beach attire, and Pidgin phrases that fit tidily on souvenir cups ("Ass Why Hard" and "Badda You," for example), there seems to be little of substance. Add a bit of Hawaiian music and a touch of the hula, and you have a bit more.

But unless you add a literature to the mix, and allow it to entertain, engage, challenge, disturb, and teach—it's only then you're talking about something of substance that a culture can be built upon. And culture is fundamental to survival. Without self-expression, as Islanders learned in difficult ways, there really is no identity.

Such a truism was not lost on our current president, for he noted thoughts on identity in his memoir: "*Only [W]hite culture could be neutral and objective. Only [W]hite culture could be nonracial, willing to adopt the occasional exotic into their ranks. Only [W]hite culture had individuals*" (Obama 1995:100). But his *Dreams from My Father*, published in 1995, proved otherwise.

THE FLOWERING OF LOCAL LITERATURE

Around the time Obama left Hawai'i, leaving his place of birth behind "*like a childhood dream*," writers began not only to tell their own stories and were encouraged by institutions to do so, even if some of the writing called for the dismissal of the very same institutions. And, as writers and their small press publishers began to understand better how to distribute their stories, a culture began to assert itself.

In the 1980s, there seemed to be a flowering of literature in Hawai'i. Elder statespersons Ozzie Bushnell, John Dominis Holt, and Milton Murayama were still producing texts that served to inform and instruct, and they were assisted by a growing number of young poets, fiction writers, playwrights, critics, and scholars.

Writers dealt with universal themes as well as issues that were decidedly place specific. Collectively, they brought a level of verisimilitude not seen in the works of histouricist writers—and a level of self-awareness.

Many stories and poems published by Bamboo Ridge Press focused on "small kid time," a somewhat idyllic, somewhat shared past. The past (the pre-Talk Story era) was a time when there were few avenues for self-expression, and no such a creature as local literature. Writers looked back to their formative years, often writing through the lens of a child, recalling a less hostile, a more innocent world. Times were better, writers kept insisting, because although threatening forces were out there, in the small worlds of friends and families people treated one another with more Aloha, with more of a kindness of spirit. In Darrell Lum's "Beer Can Hat" (1986), a local favorite delivered entirely in Pidgin, we're left wondering what will happen to Bobo, an abused special-needs kid. In "Primo Doesn't Take Back Bottles Any More" (1986), protagonist Rosa Kamahele learns, when his world is going to hell, that the one place he thought he had left, the one place he thought he could turn to, is under new management. Anyone paying attention to the demise of Aloha Airlines due to the predatory practices of Mesa Air Group and its subsidiary airline, Go!, or the corporate takeover of family-owned supermarket chains, or the ever-growing presence of big-box stores, knows exactly what he meant.

In Eric Chock's "Tūtū on the Curb" (1986b), a smartly dressed elderly Native Hawaiian woman is caught in the stinky exhaust fumes of a passing bus. A troubling moment points to how the most cherished aspects of the past are being recklessly overrun. And in a similarly themed work, Chock's "Poem for George Helm—Aloha Week 1980" (1986a), the beautiful concept of Aloha has been commodified. Chock conjures up revered Native Hawaiian activist George Helm, who disappeared in March 1977 off the island of Kaho'olawe, an island that was being used for target practice by the U.S. Navy, and asks whether, should he return, would he like what he would see?

By the 1990s, such fiction writers as Gary Pak (e.g., 1992) focus on development gone awry, destruction of the environment, and homophobia—and sometimes in a magical realist style. Poet and fiction writer R. Zamora Linmark dared to disturb with his downright funny and provocative look at growing up gay and Filipino in Kalihi Valley, a working-class enclave in Honolulu, in his *Rolling the Rs* (1995).

And along came Lois-Ann Yamanaka (1993, 1996) with an energetic style of poetry, and then fiction, which seemed to pull out all the stops. Her work shouted in a big, sometimes disturbing way. A talented writer, she sometimes hit her target and sometimes missed, to the point that one had to wonder where she was aiming. Although she showed at times a tendency to succumb to stereotypes, Yamanaka had few equals in displaying defense mechanisms that locals developed in youth to mask problems with self-image.

Countless local residents in Hawai'i can attest to being inundated and immersed in American pop culture, both with joy and peril. Having been written about and portrayed in negative terms for generations, then having been exposed through film, radio, and television to lifestyles and mores that were not their own, local citizens felt that they could not live up to the standards being presented in various media. Having been told the Hawai'i was always a few years behind the Mainland, the term used for the U.S. continent (because wasn't it the *main* land?), and believing Hawai'i was behind, local people said so out loud, to one another, accepting that the Islands were some backwater doomed to playing catch-up. In Hawai'i, father didn't know best, and he often came home in a puka (tattered) shirt all drunk. The multiethnic local majority was *working class*. Young girls didn't look or act like Gidget. In the few instances when locals were the focus of attention, when Hawai'i got to be the star of the film or TV show (notably the original *Hawaii Five-O*), the depiction was so distorted, so laughably out of focus, that locals knew *intuitively*, even before they knew *consciously*, thanks to the literature they now had to help make sense of things, that outsiders didn't get it, that they did not understand, or did not have an investment in understanding Hawai'i's local community. Indeed, the success of the early *Hawaii Five-O* was precisely based on its depiction of non-Whites as having difficulty with English and accepting a subordinate status, thereby offering a nostalgic look backward for those seeking relief from the tensions of the Mainland civil rights struggle.

One sees an impressive body of work produced by Bamboo Ridge Press during the 1980s and 1990s. As with any good literature, the themes were timeless and universal, the content quite place specific. Hawai'i's location in the middle of the Pacific, a confluence of East and

West, allowed for a wide range of influences in the riveting poems and stories that shed light into every aspect of how locals lived and who locals were—just about everything under the Hawaiian sun.

So at the end of the day, all was copacetic.

Or was it?

CONSCIOUSNESS AND CONFLICT

As local literature was making headway into the consciousness of Hawai'i's citizens, many in the indigenous community felt they were being left out of the discussion. Bamboo Ridge Press was primarily publishing local Asians (though not exclusively), and some thought that the press's claim to represent all locals, as formulated in its mission statement, simply wasn't true. To add fuel to the sparks, some Kānaka Maoli (the preferred term of many Native Hawaiians; maoli, meaning "the real" or "genuine," and kānaka, "people") or Kānaka 'ōiwi ('ōiwi being a shortcut for the indigenous population of the Hawaiian Islands) writers claimed they were unfairly treated by the likes of Bamboo Ridge Press, which they felt had become a vehicle more for Asian Americans than the wider community of locals that included indigenous Hawaiians (cf. Young 2004:31).

While writers associated with Bamboo Ridge often dealt with Native Hawaiian culture sympathetically, the occasional stereotypical treatment of Native Hawaiians and Hawaiian culture by a non-Hawaiian writer made some Kānaka Maoli feel like they had a new oppressor. And while many Native Hawaiians were writing creatively, they somehow, with a few exceptions, weren't making it in the pages of the journal that was widely seen as the most successful representative of local literature. Nevertheless, Eric Chock later reflected, Bamboo Ridge had indeed published Native Hawaiians in several of its journal issues, and that the Bamboo Ridge publication *Mālama: Hawaiian Land and Water* (1985) featured a Native Hawaiian editor, Dana Naone Hall. But this did not satisfy some Native Hawaiians authors. They clearly wanted a say, on their own terms.

In 1994, Dennis Kawaharada, onetime managing editor for Bamboo Ridge Press, went on to form his own press, Kalamakū. He criticized writers associated with Bamboo Ridge Press for having abandoned the working-class solidarity with Native Hawaiians and for succumbing to American notions of individualism and middle- and upper middle-class success. In "Towards an Authentic Local Literature of Hawai'i" (1994), published by HLAC, Kawaharada talked about how the local literature that had been developed by the "grandchildren of Asian immigrants" was constructed upon a "nostalgia for family and homeland," and then stated, "and if you write it in [P]idgin English and refer to local landmarks like King Street and Diamond Head or Tantalus, you've got a regional flavor that has some appeal for a local, if not a national, audience. . . . But this literature is not local in the same sense that Hawaiian stories are local" (Kawaharada 1994:58). Kawaharada went on to claim that Bamboo Ridge Press literature was "neo-colonial" partly for "embod[ying] values of the American way of life." He suggested that local Asians could learn a lot by studying Hawaiian language, Hawaiian folktales (mo'olelo), and other aspects of Hawaiian culture. After all, they did live in Hawai'i.

Kawaharada, following his own advice, and with assistance from Hawaiian language instructor Esther Mo'okini, edited and published ancient Hawaiian tales that he thought should see the light of day (Kawaharada 1999).

Darrell Lum (1998:11), in the anthology *Growing Up Local* (Chock, Harstad, Lum, and Teter 1998), offered a kind of response. He begins his introductory essay "Local Geneaology: What School You Went?" by citing Stephen Sumida (1991:xvii):

> [I]n the native-Hawaiian way, personal introductions include these questions: What are you called (i.e., your given name)? Who is your family (i.e., your surname and genealogy)? Where are you from (i.e., your neighborhood or district)? And who is your teacher (i.e., your school or the way of thought to which you are loyal)? . . . without their knowing its Hawaiian origins, locals expect this genealogical exchange. . . . It is a way to begin weaving their histories together—and this defines friendship, or an aspect of it, local style.

In other words, nonindigenous locals had unconsciously adopted Native Hawaiian ways through some curious form of osmosis. Lum goes on to explain (pp. 12–13) that the "What school you went?" question has its roots in the Native Hawaiian way of identifying oneself by geography and genealogy. Lum goes on to talk about how "local culture's resistance to the dominant Western society" is tied together by the bond of "common values, common history, and common language (Pidgin or, more correctly, Hawai'i Creole English)."

Native Hawaiian scholar Kuʻualoha Hoʻomanawanui (2008:126–127) replied,

> Lum tries to tap into the Kānaka Maoli worldview linking Kānaka to ʻāina through genealogy when he describes settler writers as having a "distinct sensitivity to ethnicity, the environment (in particular that valuable commodity, the land), a sense of personal lineage and family history." But the problem with Lum's attempt at expressing aloha ʻāina and equating settler sentiment for ʻāina with that of Kānaka Maoli is that he describes the "beloved" land we share in colonial sentiments: it is a "commodity," not an ancestor; it is an environment, a settling, a landscape, not a family. And its value is not in its ability to provide food, or to nurture life, but in its monetary worth.

Hoʻomanawanui considered Lum presumptuous for equating the theft of Kānaka Maoli political power through the overthrow of the monarchy to the immigrants' struggles and hardships. She accused Lum and others of "[pretending] to side with Kānaka Maoli against the alleged 'common enemy'—[H]aole," while in actuality they are linked to the Haole because of their shared American values. Hoʻomanawanui didn't stop there. Further along, she accused Bamboo Ridge critic Dennis Kawaharada of usurping the native voice:

> Kawaharada's *Storied Landscapes* is disturbing because it perpetuates settlers' practice of claiming Hawaii for their own. By asserting himself as the narrator throughout the essays, Kawaharada reframes the view of the ʻāina for the reader through a non-Native lens; while Kānaka Maoli are present (such as Nainoa Thompson, the master navigator of the voyaging canoe "Hōkūleʻa"), they are not permitted to speak or share their manaʻo (thought, idea, belief) of the ʻāina to which they are genealogically connected." (p. 142)

Kawaharada, in response, indicated that he just wanted "to narrate how someone whose grandparents arrived in the Islands in the early 20th century came to learn about and love the Islands, while paying homage to the much longer presence of Hawaiian families and their traditional knowledge, language and beliefs."[2]

Somewhere, somehow, a separation began to occur, a split in the local writing community. Was the split always there?

Sociologist Andrew Lind (1938) and historians David Stannard (2005) and John Rosa (2000) have all explored the genesis of local identity, which they date back to the 1930s, a time when this new self-identifier, "local," began to upstage ethnic/race signifiers as the way many who grew up in the Islands wished to be perceived. This was a pan-ethnic, essentially non-White coalition, brought about by mutual circumstances and one that in many ways still resonates to this day, in terms of language(s) spoken, foods eaten, daily activities, and marriages consummated irrespective of racial differences. But the threads of disenchantment also go back at least to the 1950s, when the descendants of immigrant plantation workers, the majority of whom were Asians, seemed to be more engaged in bettering their lives economically and hoping to prosper from statehood than in asserting native rights. Native Hawaiians, on the other hand, were fighting for cultural and land rights, which included the perpetuation of Hawaiian language, the assertion of hula and Hawaiian music, and rights of access to the mountains and the beaches. Local literature found itself caught between two contending narratives—one that still celebrated local culture and put on the face of Aloha, claiming to embody its spirit as it promoted the *Hawai'i as multicultural paradise* framework, and the other, which recast the non-Hawaiian "local" community as "settlers," a strategy to pull the land from under these usurpers, and re-label the notion of a local culture as illusory and/or short-lived.

In recent years, the term "settler," especially as attributed to the local Asian community, has gained traction as an often-articulated, seemingly *more correct* phrase, in terms of defining those who aren't indigenous, no matter how long or short their residency in the islands. In a *Honolulu Weekly* interview, cultural studies scholar Candace Fujikane, was quoted as saying:

> The UH ethnic studies fight in the 1970s had a slogan: "Our history, our way," and "We built Hawaii" [sic]. But what these local Asians were saying was colonial, implying that there was nothing before. There was no perception that Hawaiians have their own struggle." (Seeto 2009)

Davianna McGregor, UH professor in the Ethnic Studies Department and a Native Hawaiian, responded:

> Dr. Fujikane mistakenly attributed our department's slogan, "Our History, Our Way" to local Asians who[m] she called colonial with

"no perception that Hawaiians have their own struggle." First of all, myself and other Kānaka 'ōiwi (Pete Thompson, Kehau Lee, Terrilee Kekoolani, Soli Niheu) were at the forefront of the struggle and the formulation of our slogan. Second, the slogan is inclusive of Kānaka 'ōiwi history. Our ethnic studies courses on Hawaiians and land tenure were the first to challenge the dominant historical narrative, which characterized Native Hawaiians as compliant, childlike natives who embraced Christianity and American settler civilization. (McGregor 2009)

"Sadly," McGregor went on to say, "Fujikane's statement is yet another example of how labeling Asian immigrant workers and their descendants as colonial 'settlers' is ahistorical, narrow-minded, lacking in class analysis, and too simplistic to explain our complicated islands' society."

For some, the "settler" thesis was a discussion among scholars, mostly (relish the irony) Asian and Native Hawaiian scholars. The idea was getting no traction in working-class communities, or communities where Native Hawaiians were the majority population, where Pidgin is the primary language.

Supporters of the "settler" idea would say otherwise, of course, and would continue to push the idea that the concept of "local" is a deliberate strategy linked to political control, a way to continue oppressing Native Hawaiians. But everyone agreed that the "settler" term is divisive.

But why? Why now?

The "settler" concept is merited in that it *reminds* people that an indigenous culture that has been ravaged by outside intrusion is still suffering, as statistics citing high incarceration, poor health, and lower educational attainments make quite clear. So even if locals intermarry, dine on each other's native foods, dress alike, talk alike, engage in activities raging from surfing to soccer and other sports, attend or participate in 'ukulele and hula festivals and so on, there *is* something separating the people of Hawai'i. For political purposes—issues related to ceded lands, assertion of culture, and the like—a distinction between settlers and natives can be useful indeed.

On the other hand, any rich literary tradition relishes irony and nuance. Binary thinking (good/evil, Black/White, rich/poor, native/settler), generalizations about places and people, and rigid ideas that lead to self-censorship and/or the muting of voices have little place in literary art. Art and literature do not go for easy answers. According to cultural studies theorist Stuart Hall, whom John Rosa (2000) cites in his "Local Story" essay, cultural identity should be viewed in more complex ways, not simply *us* versus *them*.

Bamboo Ridge Press, which in the 1990s took hits from some in the local literature community for allegedly appropriating the term "local" under an Asian rubric, while ignoring other non-White authors, has made a point in the first decade of the 21st century to showcase Native Hawaiian authors in quite prominent fashion, with single-author texts such as Lisa Linn Kanae's *Islands Linked by Ocean* (2009) and Lee Cataluna's *Folks You Meet in Longs* (2005), as well as a landmark text, *He Leo Hou: A New Voice—Hawaiian Playwrights* (Apio 2003). With the Kānaka Maoli literary journal '*Ōiwi*, and the presence of Native Hawaiian authors in just about every other Hawai'i-based press, literature in Hawai'i has taken on the curious look of inclusivity. One could add the seismic shift sparked by the Hawaiian Renaissance— the surging numbers of Hawaiian-language students, the revival of the hula, the popularity of authentic Hawaiian music, with such players as Israel Kamakawiwo'ole, John Cruz, Willie K., and Raiatea Helm getting national and international attention. Add the support that many non-Hawaiians bring to the fight for indigenous rights, whether it be nationhood, or the Kānaka Maoli claim to the Hawaiian Kingdom's crown and government lands (ceded lands), or cultural primacy. Enough? Probably not. But no doubt gigantic steps have been taken in the right direction. Many in the wider Hawai'i community would not like to undo the cross-ethnic alliances, the coalitions that were formed, and still choose to believe in what they see before their eyes—a multicultural and multiethnic community.

In "Kamau," playwright Alani Apio (2003) depicts a young Native Hawaiian man, Alika, who works as a tour guide to support his family, including the child he adopts after her father, his cousin, commits suicide. He would like to quit his job, but can't afford to. Then he learns that the tour company has bought his family's land. In trying to placate the young man, he offers his cousin Michael a job. Michael goes ballistic, accuses Alika of selling him out, and later attacks the security guards watching what used to be family property. Michael ends up in prison, a familiar place for so many Native Hawaiians. Alika is distraught and quits his job, but as reality kicks in and he has to choose between the immediate needs of his family and the compelling need to practice his Hawaiian culture, he chooses family. And that's just Part One.

Similar nuanced storytelling has appeared in the writings of Lee Cataluna (2003, 2005), Lisa Linn Kanae (2009), and the late Wayne Kaumuali'i Westlake (Hamasaki and Siy 2009). And historian/biographer Gavan Daws and publisher Bennett Hymer have put together *Honolulu Stories* (2008), a book so large (1,120 pages) it seems to include every writer who has ever set foot in the Islands.

And there's so much more.

Haole authors who have been longtime residents, as well as Haole writers born and raised in the Hawaiian Islands also have made making substantial contributions to local literature. Longtime Hawai'i resident and creative writing professor Ian MacMillan (e.g., 2009) has contributed several book-length texts that help dispel the notion that Haoles only fit some histouricist model. Sensitive to the languages spoken in these Islands, and wary of the issues involving indigenous culture, MacMillan's short stories and novels, particularly those situated in the Hawaiian Islands, show that while he came here to teach, he also came here to learn. Also worth noting is MacMillan's role in mentoring so many local students who have become leading writers in this community. Poet and teacher Susan Schultz has a similar track record, and while her creative work rarely features Hawai'i, she has also created the previously mentioned *Tinfish*, a marvelous venue for up-and-coming local writers, including the aforementioned Lisa Linn Kanae, and self-described Pidgin-guerrilla Lee Tonouchi (2005).

Alexei Melnick, J. Freen (a pen name), and Chris Kelsey are among the most notable among the growing list of Haole authors who could quite easily fit the seemingly oxymoronic term "Local Haole." Each writer grew up in the Hawaiian Islands, and each has shown significant talent. Melnick has already displayed such an impressive range of voices in his short stories and in his first novel, a work that takes readers into the hell that is crystal meth addiction, that he may be the most promising writer of his generation.

To scan the "Hawaiiana" section of any bookstore in Hawai'i is to be intimidated by the sheer quantity of texts, a lot of them commercial and trashy. While it's good to have abundance, the danger is getting lost in the mix. Local literature, despite its vast productivity, is still relegated to the margins, so local writers can't be complacent. Despite the battles won, many are still to be fought.

OBAMALAND (OR SHOULD WE CALL IT BARRYTOWN?)

> In the beginning we recall that the word was hurled
> Barrytown people got to be from another world.
> (Steely Dan 1974)
> If "news is the first draft of history," you hold in your hands a hard
> copy of material assembled when Barack Obama was on the cusp
> of becoming the most heralded person in world history. (Jacobs
> 2009:15)

No doubt, Hawai'i's been overwhelmed by the success of one of its own, reconstructing narratives in a new light. But *Obamaland? Most heralded person in world history?*—the things people say to sell a book (Jacobs 2009)!

Dreams from My Father is selling amazingly well, thanks in part to the newfound fame of its author, and deservedly so. It is a stirring and compelling memoir, one that conjures up the likes of James Baldwin. He continues his literary output with *Of Thee I Sing: A Letter to My Daughters* (2010a), a book of children's stories that he promised his publisher in 2004, and a nonfiction work that he has pledged to write after he leaves office (Associated Press 2010a).

But is *Dreams* an example of local literature? Contrary to what some may think, Obama was born and raised in Hawai'i. In his memoir, however, he scarcely deals with the place in which he spent most of his childhood, except as a dream left behind. He may one day put Hawai'i in the center of a narrative. He's talented enough of a writer to do a great job of relating a fuller story of what it was like to grow up on O'ahu, critically examining the good parts as well as the bad. In the meantime, he's busy running a country.

And as far as Obama's "local identity" goes, Susan Schultz in a recent interview says:

> I do think Obama deals pretty well with being a non-local, non-
> [Native] Hawaiian resident of Hawaii. If there's any sense of post-
> racial to come with Obama, we might also look to a post-local, if
> not as fact, then as an idea worth considering. That's where I'd like
> to go with this, in *Tinfish* and in my teaching. Because I no longer

think that splitting people into groups like "local" or "Hawaiian" or "Haole" work. . . . I would suggest we need to break these categories up, again, and reconceptualize our alliances so that groups of us, regardless of ethnicity, etc., can face up together against militarization, Republicanism, boring literature, and so on!

CONCLUSION

So what's so special about local identity and local literature? Who or what is represented? Histouricist authors will doubtless continue to hold up clumsy mirrors to the local community and its artists. There's nothing in place to stop them, and why should there be? They can be ignored. And no doubt some scholars and political activists will invent newer ways to divide and incite local writers. Some will play well and some won't.

All in all, it seems that the intensity of Hawai'i's literature and its literary currents has a lot to do with knowing a place, respecting and caring for a place, and having Aloha for that place. Just listen to the deep and poignant voice of Iz (Israel Kamakawiwo'ole), a haunting voice that goes so deep it gives you "chicken skin."[3] You hear it in the chants of Charles Ka'upu. You see it in the stories told by the hands of authentic hula dancers. You see it in the faces of the homeless who walk our city streets. And, to quote Michael McPherson (n.d.), "It helps to know of what and whom you speak."

In the end, is Hawai'i a place where, everywhere you look, if you lift up the rocks and the sheets or drive over to the less beaten tracks, you find contentiousness and cynicism gone rampant? Is that why Barack left? Or is it an idyllic paradisiacal place where tolerance overrides the problems and multiculturalism happens? Beyond visiting family and friends, is that why Barack has kept returning?

So we end where we began. Who gets to tell the story?

Who indeed.

NOTES

1. Much of the write-up on the conference has focused on the influence of Asian Americans from the Mainland on the budding local literary movement. Such writers as Jeffrey Paul Chan, Lawson Fusao Inada, and Shawn Wong seemed to function as mentors to the young local writers, many of them Asian.

Also intriguing is the attention given to non-attendee Frank Chin for his long-distance (and long-running) attack on Maxine Hong Kingston (for what Chin claimed were inauthentic portrayals of Chinese culture). A related and much-covered "event" is Chin's stint as a visiting writer the following year, when he took a number of local writers under his wing. Chin, who constantly emphasized to local writers the need to cast minority characters in heroic light, chastised Darrell Lum for writing stories that put Hawai Creole English into the mouths of losers (Fujikane 1994:64).

2. When asked why he chose to call his book *Storied Landscapes* and not, say, *Wahi Pana*, Kawaharada said that he chose an English title because the book was written from a nonnative point of view, in the colonial language of English. He noted that Kānaka Maoli photographer Kapulani Landgraf, whose photo appears with her permission on the cover of Kawaharada's book, used "Wahi Pana" in the title of her own book, *Nā Wahi Pana: ʻO Koʻolau Poko: Legendary Places of Koʻolau Poko* (1994), in which she included Hawaiian language text. He added that his use of "landscapes" (as opposed to ʻaina or land) indicates that he is not of the land, but views it from the outside, and that "storied" suggests that the writer is learning to read the landscape by reading native stories (primarily in translation by colonial settles), rather than by learning about the land directly from his parents or ancestors, who are not native and did not know much about Hawaiʻi or Native Hawaiian traditions. Thus, had Kawaharada used the "proper" term, he would have been accused of appropriating a Hawaiian phrase—a case of damned if you do, equally damned if you don't. One step further, taking into account Kawaharada's criticisms of the local Asian community (which Hoʻomanawanui curiously echoes) is a slippery slope where the inevitable result is the Japanese American editors of *Asian Settler Colonialism* (Fujikane and Okamura 2008), the book in which Hoʻomanawanui's essay is featured, being criticized for speaking on behalf of Native Hawaiians.

3. "Goosebumps" is the Mainland equivalent of the local term "chicken skin."

Chapter 7

Hawai'i Calls:
Musics of the Islands

Anthony J. Palmer

> *When I was a kid . . . you always had an art teacher and a*
> *music teacher. Even in the poorest school districts, everyone*
> *had access to music and other arts. . . . People understood that*
> *even though they hadn't done all the scientific research . . .*
> *children who learn music actually do better in math and kids*
> *whose imaginations are sparked by the arts are more engaged*
> *in school. . . . Our art, our culture . . . that's the essence of*
> *what makes America special, and we want to make as much*
> *of that as possible in the White House.*
>
> (Goodale 2009)

Music is a window into the hearts of cultures and people, especially
in Hawai'i. An important way to understand the personality of Barack
Obama is to examine his musical choices and early experiences. From
media reports, Obama listens to music regularly. His adult tastes in
music were formed from his early days in Hawai'i. The way in which
various cultures have impacted Island music, bringing a sense of calm
friendliness, has shaped not only Barack Obama's demeanor but has
provided the United States a multicultural genre that is enjoyed around
the world.

What effect on musical preferences did many years spent in the Fiftieth State have on Obama's charismatic and historic path to the presidency? How did Hawai'i's musical environment influence Obama? Some questions can be answered by assumptions, others in part by information from the media or from his autobiography, *Dreams from My Father*, but there are prior questions: How did the Hawai'i in which he lived develop so much musical diversity? And why was that diversity so accessible to Obama? And why did he have so much affinity to jazz?

During his first 18 years, Obama lived beyond the mainstream continental culture of Mainland America except for the usual interaction with movies, music broadcasts, television programs, recordings, visiting artists, and tourists who visited the Islands. After his first 6 years in Honolulu, Obama accompanied his mother, Ann Dunham, to join her second husband in Jakarta, where music is an integral part of the culture, and he heard a different kind of music from what is normally heard in the West. Most certainly, he would have heard the gamelan performances, ubiquitous in those islands, possibly predisposing him to a broader palette of music than continental American youngsters. Then in the 1970s, he was back in Honolulu.

Had he been born on the Mainland, he would have grown up with appreciation for African American and mainstream pop music. Instead, he was exposed to a multitude of musics not normally encountered on the Mainland. A review of the musics of Hawai'i is therefore imperative to gain some insight to the president's predilections for musical variety and the excitement that music holds in the lives of residents of multicultural Hawai'i. The musical history of Hawai'i can shed light, especially the contributions of particular ethnic groups and institutional supporters of music. But what is most fascinating is how musical traditions interpenetrate the lives and souls of a people who love the opportunity to choose and mix their music without prejudice or restraint.

THE IMPORTANCE OF MUSIC IN HAWAI'I

Musical expression is as natural to Island residents as politics is to Washington, D.C. Hawai'i is a musical state with more performers (dancers and musicians) per capita than any of the 50 states (National Endowment for the Arts 2008:10) or almost any place in the world.

Hawai'i's Aloha Spirit is complete only with the inclusion of music and dance as preeminent means of expression. Island residents' diversity in ethnic and nationality backgrounds has fostered an enjoyment of differences and a willingness to be open and explorative in the arts, particularly music and dance. The general positive regard for artistic expression is manifest in several ways:

1. Native Hawaiian culture held music and dance in high esteem. Consequently, the revival of that tradition from the 1970s has blossomed into the wide acceptance of music generally and Hawaiian music specifically in everyday life in private and public venues, notably at the state legislature, symphony concerts, church services, and schools.
2. A vast array of musical multiculturalisms exist side by side, occasionally interacting, yet retaining their uniqueness and individuality.
3. Music is taught and carried on by a wide array of people who are not necessarily ethnically identical to the music they represent.
4. Students range across Hawai'i's spectrum of ethnicities. Japanese, for example, study hula. Native Hawaiians and Asians study Western music. Westerners study any number of Asian and Pacific musics. Accordingly, the term "Hawaiian music" refers to the full array of musics found in the Islands and is broader than "Native Hawaiian music."
5. Musical hybrids have arisen, such as hapa Haole (English-language songs about Hawai'i, such as *Pearly Shells*) and Jawaiian (Hawaiian reggae), as a consequence of the crossroads nature of the Islands.
6. The people of Hawai'i resist being categorized and separated by ethnicity. There are simply too many mixtures and intermarriages of nationality and language, culture, and identity to challenge any ideas of purity. Although recent arrivals in Hawai'i maintain purity of culture for a short time, within a generation or two the bonds begin to loosen and ethnic purity, especially for the children, becomes difficult.
7. Nevertheless, cultural identities coincide with musical traditions for a number of reasons, not the least of which is language and knowledge of tradition. Western classical and popular music, Hawaiian and Pacific regions, and Asian and other world traditions are among the contributions.
8. Institutions unique to the Islands have invited nonresident groups to further enhance the musical palette. The University of Hawai'i, for example, has hosted an annual series of concerts of chamber music groups from the Mainland.

9. Tourism, a high economic priority, has broadened the entertainment venues for a variety of musics, principally Hawaiian.

Then as now, the center of musical activity is Honolulu, whether talking about music or government. Honolulu contains the primary concert house, Blaisdell Auditorium. West of Honolulu, the auditorium at Leeward Community College plays host to a wide variety of music and dance performances. Also, recently built is the Pearl City Community Cultural Center, albeit with a fine auditorium that is too small to accommodate the larger audiences necessary to sustain a professional company. A decade ago, the old Hawai'i Theater—a 1,400 seat house in the downtown area—was renovated and plays host to a variety of musical events.

The Neighbor Islands are not devoid of artistic activity, but the numbers of audience and appropriate venues are insufficient to compare. A fine arts center on Maui, opened during the mid-1990s, plays home to the Maui Symphony Orchestra, a community orchestra, and other performance groups.

Any of the Hawaiian styles of music can be found at various hotel and lounge venues in Waikīkī and on the other islands as well. Throughout the Islands, the small lounge group has been an important aspect of Hawaiian music. Such groups have been requirements at lū'au dinners and ship tours of the harbor at night. Aaron Mahi, former director of the Royal Hawaiian Band, joined George Kuo to perform regularly at the Marriott Waikiki Beach Hotel. Hotel lounges regularly feature outstanding performers, who display the more popular vocal and instrumental music for listening and dancing, covering most styles of top 40, jazz fusions and other cross-over types, ballad, and salsa and other Latino musics. Although all the music played, sung, and danced in hotels is considered to be more for tourists than for local aficionados, their roots and spirit are distinctly Hawaiian.

June 11 is a state holiday known as Kamehameha Day, which celebrates King Kamehameha's birthday. In 2009, Maui held a colorful parade through Lahaina featuring Pa'u riders on horses decorated with exotic flowers representing each major island. The parade included marching bands, and floats honoring King Kamehameha's families.

Contemporary Hawaiian music draws on numerous influences just as it has since Western contact. The conditions remain dynamic, and the Hawaiian spirit prevails through the many different styles adapted for various uses. That spirit is exemplified by Aloha, variously defined as affection, generosity, love, and openness (Kanehele 1979:10), which will

continue as the force that drives Hawaiian music. Bishop Museum eth-
nomusicologist Elizabeth Tatar sums up the essence of Hawaiian music
as follows:

> Hawaiian music is not a simple tune sung to the strum of an
> 'ukulele. A typical melody, harmony, or text is not going to define
> Hawaiian music. Nor is a Hawaiian voice quality without the typi-
> cal musical trappings to accommodate it going to define the music.
> It is the right combination of typical musical features, representa-
> tive instruments, and unique Hawaiian voice qualities sparked by
> the creative individual genius of the Hawaiian artist that makes the
> music unquestionably Hawaiian. (Kanehele 1979:xxx)

Institutional support for music over the years has been provided by
Kamehameha Schools, public schools, the University of Hawai'i, the
East-West Center, and many private music schools. The state legislature
has also provided subsidies.

EARLY PERIODS OF MUSIC IN HAWAI'I

The foundation upon which the present state of music rests is the music
of Native Hawaiians, who arrived as early as 300 CE (Kirch 1985:285,
298). Native Hawaiians developed a unique culture long before 1778,
when the expedition of Captain James Cook arrived. While significant
differences presently exist between Hawaiian music and other Polynesian music, evidence from Captain Cook and the subsequent missionary
arrivals in the early 19th century shows that their roots are recognizably
East Polynesian (Tatar 1993:307–309).

Hawaiian musical culture in 1778 consisted of various drums, non-
pitched idiophones, a small number of aerophones, a few chordophones,
and most prominent of all, the voice (Roberts 1926). The origin of the
hula, the all-encompassing music and dance tradition of Native Hawaiians, is steeped in various legends describing a divine source through Pele,
Goddess of Fire, Creator and Destroyer (Hopkins 1982:20–23). From
the origins of the hula, which became the complete expression of Native
Hawaiian spirituality, only chants are preserved in oral tradition, but that
body of chant is the basis for a modern reconstruction that is vital today.
Male hula developed from ancient Native Hawaiian martial arts.

Native Hawaiians placed such a high value on music and dance that
they were receptive to a variety of musical influences. The post-contact

period of Hawai'i's musical history is characterized by several distinct periods with approximate dates listed as follows:

1820–1872. Although sailors from Captain Cook's ships in the 1770s and their brethren over the next few decades brought a modicum of Western music to Hawai'i, March 30, 1820, marks a significant date when the music from the West began to influence the Islands. On that day, a large party of New England Congregationalists landed on the Island of Hawai'i.

Kamehameha the Great had died the previous year. Liholiho reigned as Kamehameha II. Within a year's time, the missionaries gained a permanent status in the Islands. Eventually, the missionaries saw that the only way to convert the large masses of people was to convert their leaders, but Liholiho was not a willing student. His death in 1824 cleared the way for the mission to succeed under Kamehameha III. In a short time, schools and churches were built. Imperatives to obey the Sabbath, attend school and church, and to become Christian were then established (Daws 1968:61–74, 85).

The solemn and straight-metered hymns were principal staples of conversion material. Native Hawaiians, already musically advanced, learned quickly, and the hīmenī (hymn) became the fundamental musical style of the new converts. Other Christian groups followed within a couple of decades, with music an indispensable part of worship. Churches today remain centers of musical activity.

New musical instruments came by sea traffic (bass viol, violin, guitar, piano, accordion, and flute). Church music was of American origin—unadorned, soulful, sober New England harmony. Secular music soon came from Europe and Asia, including German, Italian, and Mexican instrumental and vocal ensembles to Burmese singers. Except for a short revival of chant under Kamehameha III in the 1830s and 1840s, Native Hawaiian traditions were discouraged.

1872–1895. Composers known as Na Lani 'Ehā (the Royal Four) are credited with creating the climate for a rich musical tradition through personal musical contributions and by providing support to chanters, composers, dancers, instrumentalists, poets, and singers. They consisted of David Kalākaua, his sisters Lydia Kamaka'eha Paki (Lili'uokalani) and Miriam Likelike, and his brother William Pitt Leleiohoku, the youngest.

Although the Royal Hawaiian Band traces its roots to 1836, the band took shape in 1872, when Henry Berger was appointed conductor. King Kamehameha V had asked the Prussian Ministry of War to send a band leader, and Berger was ordered to perform a concert soon after his arrival with just five days of rehearsal (Kanehele 1979:336). From the meager beginning of just 10 young men assigned to Berger on his first day, the band grew into a fully professional group that today numbers 40 regular members with others added for special events.

Although many pieces written during the days of Berger and his successor, Charles King, were with Western instrumentation, the compositions were influenced significantly by traditional Native Hawaiian stories, texts, and subject matter. Subsequently, the band moved to more regular Western fare but still keeps within its repertoire the standard pieces from a century ago. Every concert closes with *Aloha 'Oe*, the famous farewell song that was composed by Queen Lili'uokalani. Band members today include members of many ethnic groups.

During these years waltz music was in fashion. Pianos and zithers accompanied prolific compositions of royalty. Beyond hymn harmony, wider possibilities were achieved in melody. Hula ku'i (falsetto style of singing) also appeared.

Common folk embraced the guitar during these years. Most probably, the guitar made its way to Hawai'i through the influx of Mexicans to Hawai'i from California in the early 1830s. The term "paniolo" (Hawaiianized term for español) is now applied to their songs, which are chronicled in the booklet *Nā Mele Paniolo* (Trimillos 1987).

The guitar was gradually adapted into Hawaiian music through the slack key guitar and steel guitar. The slack key guitar tradition emanates from the retuning of the regular Spanish guitar by slackening the strings to sound a major chord, enabling a player to use the lower strings open while stopping the upper strings in various chord and melodic formations. Many tunings exist to adapt various songs. The most famous of the slack key guitar masters are Fred Punahoa, Leonard Kwan, Peter Moon, Raymond Kāne, Sonny Chillingsworth, and the latter's student, Matthew Swalinkovich, whose Hawaiian name is Makana.

As for the steel guitar, Joseph Kekuku claimed to invent the technique in 1885 at age 11 and then developed the technique over the next seven years (Kanehele 1979:367–368). With the electrification of the steel guitar in Texas around 1935, the sound became instantly recognizably Hawaiian, while also becoming established in Mainland country music to great effect, especially during its heyday (1900–1930). The Hawai'i Steel Guitar Association was established in the mid-1980s and has more than 600 members throughout the world. The Steel Guitar Hall of Fame is in St. Louis, Missouri.

1895–1915. American urban music, ragtime, and Hawaiian quintets (typically an ensemble of strings) were in great demand as dance bands. Although of Portuguese origin, the 'ukulele was developed in the Islands. The Roy Sakuma 'Ukulele Studio, established in Honolulu in the early 1970s, now has a faculty of approximately 20 instructors in several locations and annually teaches thousands of students. The Hawaiian-made Kamaka factory has been turning out 'ukulele since 1916 and sells a few thousand per year, mostly in the Islands.

In 1900, the Honolulu Symphony Orchestra began a history of music making in Hawai'i. The oldest symphony west of the Rockies, the symphony was originally an amateur group, with concerts on an irregular basis. One difficulty was in finding wind players. The symphony's extensive education programs are fundamental to their mission, and programs for children began in 1906. The orchestra underwent a hiatus in 1914, when World War I began.

Previously, most songs of Native Hawaiians were in the Hawaiian language. In 1912, a Broadway stage play, Bird of Paradise, featured musicians from Hawai'i playing such hapa Haole music (half Hawaiian and half English) as Mauna Kea, Old Plantation (Ku'u Home), and Wai'alae. The performance was so successful that the play toured around the Mainland. Jazzed-up Tin Pan Alley versions of hapa Haole music spread to Mainland America, particularly after the 1915 Panama-Pacific International Exposition in San Francisco, where George E. K. Awai led the Royal Hawaiian Quartette in a show of hula and music from Hawai'i.

1915–1930. In 1915, Diamond Head Theatre brought musical theater to the Islands. Known as the Broadway of the Pacific, the theater produces musical productions each year. Although productions on the Mainland would cast Caucasians to play appropriate roles, there is a shortage of qualified Whites in Hawai'i, so non-Whites often end up in the title role of Phantom of the Opera and similar productions. Talent trumps ethnicity in dramatic as well as musical performance in the Islands. Diamond Head Theatre is one of several dozen companies and venues in the Islands for musicals and plays.

In 1924, the Honolulu Symphony was reinstituted on a more solid financial foundation and presaged the future multiethnic makeup by having a Japanese-American violinist. The wind player problem was solved by borrowing from military groups, always a large presence in Hawai'i.

1930–1960. The golden age of Hawaiian music, according to some observers, occurred during the three decades before statehood. Full orchestras added slick Hollywood sounds to Hawaiian songs. Radio, movies, and television coverage peaked. Revues with apparent Hawaiian musicians were featured performers at hotel venues across the Mainland and the world. Mainland musicians adapted Hawaiian songs to Big Band music.

Hapa haole music became big business, particularly after Nebraska-born Harry Owens arrived in Honolulu in 1934 and hired schoolteacher Hilo Hattie to sing and dance in performances at the Royal Hawaiian Hotel. The genre was first developed by Sonny Cunha in 1903 and became popular after 1935, when the radio program *Hawaii Calls* was beamed to the Mainland and later to the world from the Moana Hotel. Owens and Hattie performed on the program from time to time. Also a comedian, her trademark song was *When Hilo Hattie Does the Hilo Hop*. In 1937, Owens won an Academy Award for the song *Sweet Leilani*, which Bing Crosby sang in *Waikiki Wedding*. Owens also appeared in the film *Cocoanut Grove* (1938). Owens took his song repertoire of some 300 hapa Haole original songs on tour around the world with Hilo Hattie, popularizing Hawaiian music and dance. A decade after statehood, both retired. *Hawaii Calls*'s final radio show was in 1975, when the state government subsidy lapsed.

The symphony shut down during World War II but began again in the 1950s. Functioning at first with a large number of amateurs, the orchestra became a union closed shop in the 1960s. New conductors began to recruit professional musicians, and the quality improved markedly.

The Honolulu Chamber Music Series, which began during 1955 in a private home, was soon hosted at the Mānoa campus of the University of Hawai'i. About six top international chamber music groups, from the Beaux Arts Trio to the Tokyo String Quartet, perform in the fall and winter months. Now a separate self-functioning organization, known as the Hawai'i Chamber Music Society, performances are held at the Honolulu Academy of Arts, which also carries a high-level concert series of various constituencies, from solo performers through small ensembles.

In 1955, the Islands' only nonprofit professional source of dramatic productions was formed. Known as Hawai'i Theatre for Youth, the organization not only has productions for the public, but also offers professional training in drama for children in private and public schools. Budding playwrights also have opportunities to develop and premier their creative talents.

In 1957, Hilo-born Filipino American jazz musician Gabe Baltazar left for the Mainland and performed in the Stan Kenton Orchestra from

1960 to 1965. He came back in 1969 after recording many records, and in 2007 he received the Hawai'i Academy of Recording Arts' Hanohano Lifetime Achievement Award in 2007. He continues to be a mainstay at many commercial jazz ventures and also contributes annually to jazz festivals held at various places in the Islands. Barack Obama's interest in jazz music developed two years after Baltazar returned to the Islands, when his father took him to his first jazz concert (Remnick 2010:74).

MUSIC SINCE STATEHOOD

When the Dunham family arrived in Honolulu during 1960, one year after statehood, they were present at the beginning of perhaps the most significant transformation of music in Hawai'i.

1960–1969. When statehood was granted in 1959, there was a surprising lack of interest in Hawaiian music. Hawaiian radio featured only about 5 percent Hawaiian music. Rock and roll dominated, possibly because Hawai'i caught the attention of Elvis Presley, who fell in love with the Islands during his first visit in 1957, returned several times over a 20-year period, and made three films in Hawai'i, the first of which was *Blue Hawaii* (1961). His most famous live concert, held on January 14, 1973, was broadcast worldwide as "Elvis, Aloha from Hawaii." Elvis captured the attention of the people of Hawai'i, who particularly mourned his death on August 16, 1977.

Statehood attracted an influx of tourists, eager to enjoy sun, surf, and musical entertainment. One of the first shows, which continued for decades, was that of Don Ho in Waikīkī's International Marketplace. Others included Danny Kaleikini at the Kahala Hilton, and the Cazimero brothers performed at the Royal Hawaiian Hotel. The big shows today are Jimmy Buffet's at the Beachcomber, the Society of Seven at the Outrigger Main Showroom, and Magic of Polynesia starring John Hirokawa at the O'ahu Waikiki Beachcomber.

Don Ho, Hawai'i's longtime "Ambassador of Aloha," often performed on the Mainland. His 1966 debut at Hollywood's Cocoanut Grove broke records. He performed regularly at the Sands in Las Vegas, but also at Harrah's at Lake Tahoe, the Palmer House in Chicago, and the Americana Hotel's Royal Box in New York, popularizing his song *Tiny Bubbles*. His television appearances (including his own show on ABC-TV for the 1966/1967 season) and 15 records further made Hawaiian music a major genre in the country. His mellifluous voice captivated audiences and introduced Mainlanders, whether in Waikīkī or elsewhere, to many aspects of Hawai'i's multiculturalism. Of Hawaiian, Chinese, Portuguese, German-Dutch ancestry, Donald Tai Loy Ho's performances for locals first became popular at his parents' nightclub in Windward O'ahu when he started to sing quietly and sensually. Soon he began to perform hapa Haole music in Waikīkī for tourists (though locals came), introducing them to the "shaka" sign, providing tidbits about local culture, and amusing his audiences with local humor. He sang, playing an organ keyboard, at first alongside his mother and father and later with his 10 children in various roles. He was accompanied by the multiethnic Fabulous Ali'is (Joe Mundo playing piano, Al Akana on drums, Benny Chong on guitar, Manny Lagodlagod on bass, and Rudy Aquino on xylophone, percussion, and half-a-dozen other instruments). Audiences were packed three shows a night, seven days a week, and he always made the management happy selling drinks by singing *Suck 'Em Up!*. He was greatly mourned on his death in 2007.

In 1961, the Hawai'i Opera Theatre began, at first allied with the Honolulu Symphony. The premier production was of *Madame Butterfly*, appealing to Japanese Americans. Also in 1961, the opera announced auditions for children to sing in *La Bohème*. So many children showed up that the Hawai'i Youth Opera Chorus was founded to serve the need for a regular supply of children for the chorus. Nola Nahulu now leads the chorus.

In 1964, the Honolulu Symphony moved into its own home, the new Blaisdell Concert Hall. Also that year, the Hawai'i Youth Symphony, a statewide organization recently under the wing of Henry Miyamura, was another addition to the concert fare. Both the Youth Symphony and the Hawai'i Youth Opera Chorus offer frequent public concerts, have large followings, concentrate on Western and Island repertoire, and develop young musicians, many of whom succeed to professional careers as music teachers and performers. Students represent the full ethnic spectrum in the state.

In 1964, the Merrie Monarch Festival began as a tourist attraction for visitors to the Island of Hawai'i. Now an annual three-day event, the festival honors King David Kalākaua, who was given the name "Merrie Monarch" for his lavish parties and celebrations in which he brought back the hula. He was an accomplished musician and composed both chants in Hawaiian and songs in the Western mold with Hawaiian text. The festival's website contains a telling motto: "Hula is the language of the heart, therefore the heartbeat of the Hawaiian people."

In 1969, a group of graduate students at the University of Hawai'i founded the Hawai'i Performing Arts Company. After meeting at various venues around Honolulu, funds were raised by 1983 to build Mānoa Valley Theater to continue offering traditional drama and musicals.

The 1970s. When Barry Obama returned to Honolulu in order to enroll at Punahou, he gravitated toward music:

> *Pop culture was color-coded, after all, an arcade of images from which you could cop a walk, a talk, a step, a style. I couldn't croon like Marvin Gaye, but I could learn to dance all the* Soul Train *steps.* (Obama 1995:78)

Whatever Barry thought of Hawai'i when he left at the age of 6, he returned with a broader view stemming from his Indonesian experience. He was only one of four African Americans at the Punahou prep school in 1971, and he suffered somewhat of a crisis of identity throughout those years because of his very different experiences.

Included in Obama's Punahou experience was a year spent in Boys Chorus, followed by a year in Concert Choir. He apparently turned to sports in his 11th and 12th grades, but sometimes fired up his team-mates with the music of Earth, Wind & Fire (Serrano 2007). At home, he watched nightly television programs, including *Soul Train*, and often fell asleep in his room to the Top 40 tunes that were popular during the 1970s. His tastes were certainly varied, presently reflected in his listening patterns, which include jazz and country western. He can still sing such songs as *Hawai'i Aloha*, a kind of national anthem in the Islands.

One picture unearthed by Punahou School shows Obama apparently addressing some large group unseen in the photo. He is draped with a traditional flower lei but also a lei made of leaves from the maile vine, a rare rainforest plant. Both are honorific and contain great cultural significance. Receiving a flower or maile lei can make one feel very honored. Wearing the natural beauty and fragrances will change one's vision and relationships to others and to the Islands.

Obama was not alone in his search for ethnic identity and pride. Parallel to the development of Black Pride and similar movements on the Mainland, there was an energetic revival of early indigenous music (Kanahele 1979:xxv–xxvi) due to a groundswell of support in the community for Native Hawaiian music, hula, and the Hawaiian language. The fear was that native speakers of Hawaiian would be lost before they had an opportunity to pass on their legacy (Hawai'i 1986b:I–1). The state legislature provided critical aid at a most opportune time, and activity to recover lost repertoire—dances, chants, music, and related expressions—was launched. The era is remembered as the beginning of the Hawaiian Renaissance.

In 1971, a hula contest was introduced at the Merrie Monarch Festival. Only nine dancers performed, but the response was so considerable that the contest soon became the main event, with increasing numbers of performers (Hopkins 1982:125) featuring numerous performances equally divided between ancient and modern, solo and group. Different dance groups are represented, male and female. All age groups perform, including keiki (children) through professional-level adults. The festival is sold out long in advance.

Today, hula is respected throughout the state as a true Island treasure, involving dances, chants, instrumental accompaniment, costumes, and decorations. There are hundreds of hālau, the name for schools where hula is taught. The Office of Hawaiian Affairs has compiled a directory in the hope that more will be known about teaching aspects of hula. Hula is of great value to other nations, as hundreds of schools in Japan and México teach hula to millions.

In 1978, Krash Ke'aloha established the Na Hoku Hanohano Awards, Hawai'i's version of the Grammy Music Awards. The public elects the favorite entertainer of the year by voting on ballots that are distributed through record stores and radio stations in Hawai'i one week prior to the awards. Local residents also vote for the best recording artists, engineers, graphic artists, line note annotators, producers, studio technicians, writers, and others with local recording credit. Members of the Hawaiian Music industry vote on the remaining 21 categories, which include best albums for Hawaiian, jazz, reggae, religious music, and rock music.

In due course, the group Big Island Conspiracy was formed, a musical group seeking to mobilize Native Hawaiian resistance to the colonization of the Islands. One famous line, "We are the evidence, not the crime," was composed by Keli'i "Skippy" Ioane. In due course, rap music developed, and protest music was established as an integral part of the music of Hawai'i.

In 1978, the O'ahu Choral Society began as the choral partner of the Honolulu Symphony. Recently conducted by Rachel Samet of the University of Hawai'i Music Department, the chorus has had a varied history and was reorganized under Timothy Carney in 1995 as a nonprofit organization. In addition to providing choral accompaniment to the Honolulu Symphony, various concerts have been given to an array of community functions, from funerals for notable Island personalities to visits of President Bill Clinton and His Holiness the Dalai Lama. The chorus is highly representative of the Island ethnicities and races.

In 1979, Barry Obama left Honolulu for college in California. While waiting for his flight, others from the Islands were doubtless also bound for the Mainland. He may have witnessed a repeated story that unfolds at Honolulu airport each year. A group will gather at one of the airport gates to say farewell to a young man or woman departing for the Mainland for college. The young person will be loaded with leis riding high from shoulders up to his or her face. The group will be quite diverse, representing a wide variety of ethnicities and races. In addition, there will be a small instrumental group, perhaps composed of four 'ukulele. The group will sing *Aloha 'Oe*, the Hawaiian farewell song. Obama may have been so honored when he left, but years after he boarded the plane he must have realized that, in many hours spent in airports across the country, he would never witness a musical offering of that sort until he returned to the Islands. Ever since, he has made an annual pilgrimage to refresh his soul in the place that shaped his dreams and values.

1980 to the present. Musical activity after Obama left Hawai'i continued to develop along the lines set down in earlier years. Among the new developments was the decision of the Hawai'i Opera Theatre in 1980 to become independent of the Honolulu Symphony as a nonprofit organization. In 1982, Chamber Music Hawai'i was founded from a consortium that soon included four groups of musicians—Galliard String Quartet, Honolulu Brass Quintet, Spring Wind Quintet, and Tresemble (a mixture from the three preceding groups). The groups, composed of members of the Honolulu Symphony, decided to pool their advertising and perform on alternate weekday evenings.

Composer Dan Welcher debuted his work at the Honolulu Symphony on the legend of Maui and the sun, part of the Hawaiian cosmogony. In 1991, he received an award for adventuresome programming of contemporary music, particularly American works.

In 1994, the Hawaiian Music Hall of Fame was established to confer awards to outstanding past and present musicians of Hawai'i. Four years later, the Hall opened an exhibit at Palikū Theater in Kāne'ohe.

The economic downturn of 2008 adversely affected music. In 2009, Honolulu Symphony filed for bankruptcy with plans to downsize the number of performances each year. Ballet Hawai'i, which for 15 years performed *The Nutcracker* with the symphony, was also affected. Similar reductions in performances have affected Hawai'i Opera Theatre and Mānoa Valley Theatre (Tsai 2010).

CONTRIBUTIONS FROM BEYOND THE ISLANDS

The chronological history of music in Hawai'i has focused primarily on Native Hawaiian and Western music. When various groups migrated to the Islands as agricultural laborers, immigrants, or as students, they brought musical traditions that sometimes predated Native Hawaiian and Western cultures. Many of their contributions have blossomed from the 1980s (Palmer 1998). From the Pacific Islands, solid contributions have been made by Tongan multipart polyphonic singing that existed prior to European contact. Samoan music is strongly choral singing, and is frequently accompanied with dance.

East Asian contributions include music from Japan, notably summer-time O-bon festivals, Okinawan cultural organization festivals, music at many temples associated with Japanese Buddhism and Shinto sects, and taiko (Japanese drum) groups. Perhaps the most outstanding example of an ethnic crossover is the Korean Dance Studio of Halla Huhm, which was run by Mary Jo Freshley when Huhm died in 1994, and was honored with a "Save America's Treasures" grant in 2000 to work on the Halla Huhm Dance Collection. Barack Obama's mother met both women at the East-West Center. Three other Korean contributions are the traditional musical forms of P'ansori (stylized speech, gesture, and song by a soloist accompanied by a drum), Sanjo (solo instrumental playing on the plucked zither called "kayagûm"), and church music.

Chinese have also perpetuated the original culture:

> They formed fraternal societies, established Chinese language schools, supported Chinese opera, and perpetuated special cultural celebrations. In addition, Chinese families maintained some of their ancestral traditions, such as customs surrounding childbirth, birthdays, marriages, and funerals. (Martin 1994:59)

In 1970, Hardja Susilo brought Indonesian gamelan music, which Barry Obama doubtless encountered while a boy in Jakarta. Music from Indochina (Laos, Thailand, and Vietnam) can be found among the music and dance offerings. Due to their smaller numbers, their performances are usually for members of their own groups.

Filipino culture, although Southeast Asian, is permeated by Spanish music and traditions. The major musical tradition, rondalla, is largely accompanied by plucked stringed instruments, with an occasional accordion. In recent years, other instruments have been added, such as banjo, flute, mandolin, saxophone, 'ukulele, and violin. The long-standing Pearl of the Orient Dance Company was led for many years by now-deceased Orlando Valentin and his spouse Pat.

Filipino American Joel Jacinto has a most fascinating story. Born in San Francisco, he learned the hula at a hālau organized in California by a woman from Kaua'i. In 1981, while attending UCLA, he attended a Filipino student organization and realized the special value of learning Filipino dance and music. After graduation, members of the hālau, mostly of Filipino ancestry, entertained on tourist cruise ships off Honolulu and Kona. On shore, Jacinto performed at the Royal Hawaiian Hotel and joined the Pearl of the Orient. In 1988, he even performed at the Merrie Monarch Festival. In 1990, he formed Kayamanan Ng Lahi, a Philippine dance group in Hawai'i that regularly performs at Filipino fiestas and other events (Arcayna 2002).

Puerto Rican music in the Islands is more related to the Spanish heritage than the subsequent African influence in Puerto Rico, and consequently owes its allegiance to the plucked string variety of instruments. Mexicans have recently formed Los Amigos Ballet Folklórico Dance Team of Hawai'i, which parallels the famous group based in México City. At the suggestion of a Mexican American priest, the familiar Las Posadas celebration (the journey by Mary and Joseph looking for shelter in Bethlehem) has been performed by St. Anthony's Church in Kailua. In 2004, the Mexican vocal group Internacionales Pasteles won a Hawai'i Music Award for the best Latin album, *Umores de Hawaii*. Salsa music is also found at hotels. Otherwise, at least one Mexican restaurant features live Mexican music, and mariachi bands have performed at various locations.

Native Americans have been supported by the now-defunct Intertribal Council of Hawai'i, which was active when Native Americans were more numerous in the armed forces stationed in the Islands. Even so, 808NDND, a drum group on O'ahu, keeps the pow-wow alive. The American Indian Pow-Wow Association has held an October gathering on O'ahu for more than 30 consecutive years.

The International Folk Dancers sponsor Eastern European music and dance events. Celtic culture is supported by the Caledonian Society, which sponsors the Highland Games annually. A Swedish dance group performs regularly. A Greek festival is held each year.

Middle Eastern music is found in various avenues, frequently religious, such as the half dozen Jewish temples and synagogues. On the secular side, belly dancing has been found at Middle Eastern restaurants.

The African American community, although small in number, makes its presence felt through church congregations that serve permanent residents and those on military duty. Trinity Missionary Baptist Church of Honolulu, founded some 40 years ago, is well known for its Trinity Choir. Young Barry Obama apparently attended events where African American music from the Mainland was featured.

Perhaps the most important developments in contemporary music throughout Hawai'i are more subtle because they are transcultural. Consider the case of Cathy Temanaha. Of Chinese and Native Hawaiian descent, she began studying hula at five years of age, and at 17 joined a troupe going to Japan to present Polynesian music and dance. Additionally, she had to learn Samoan, Maori, and Tahitian dance. While she continued all her dance interests—joining a troupe back in the Islands that performs regularly—, she especially developed Tahitian dance, married a Tahitian living in Hawai'i, and with husband Charles developed a Tahitian show in 1987, which for a time played regularly in Waikīkī. Their show was composed solely of Tahitian musicians, experts in the various instruments used in the music and dance, and the group was representative of the Islands, with its range of ages from 9 to mature adults, with various ethnic backgrounds. Her frequent trips to Tahiti keep her current on Tahitian dance, and she regularly travels to México and Japan to lead workshops in Tahitian dance. A highlight of her activities was a recent three-month USO tour of Europe, visiting troops in nine countries, adding Egypt to the tour to cap off a successful venture. Her activities in the Islands focus on teaching and special events.

Jane Freeman Moulin, of English American background, approached Polynesian studies from a different contact point. Now a professor in ethnomusicology as a specialist in French Polynesian music, she gained expertise by spending four years in Tahiti with Te Maeva and Tahiti Hui dance troupes. She was also part of the Pape'ete-centered Royal Tahitian Dancers' tour to South America. Finding her niche in the Islands, Moulin writes and lectures extensively on Tahitian music and dance, and teaches Tahitian dance among her many ethnomusicology courses at the University of Hawai'i.

THE LONGER VIEW

This chapter demonstrates that Hawai'i is indeed multicultural to a major and important degree, not because distinct cultures are present, but due to the crossovers that enable residents to sample from a vast variety. Music, in the end, is a reflection of deeper psychic processes than the mere sounds that one hears. Each tone is selected in combination with others, held in specific durations that make up the rhythms of a people in their interpretation of natural and social phenomena that they experience daily, expressed through timbres to which a group claims ownership, adding precise inflections in phrasing that are recognizably theirs, and formed to mirror their innermost psychic needs as a people. While the musics present in Hawai'i are now easily recognized for their ethnic origins, the future belongs to the intercultural cross-fertilizations of the people and their newly developing collective psychic makeup.

The future is impossible to predict, for the millions of variables that enter into the continuing fructifying of Hawai'i's multicultural society are vibrant, allowing the voice of the people to speak loudly through chosen pathways that feed the individual and collective soul. That soul, because of the unique experiences of the individual parts put into collective ensemble, will always be Hawaiian, typified perhaps by the heavenly sound of the voice of the late Israel Kamakawiwo'ole and the multiple musical styles of Scott Katsura.

Likewise, Barack Obama's psyche consists of 50 years developed over a broad range of foreign and national experiences, starting with his youth in which he spent four years in a foreign nation and 14 years in a non-continental state of the United States. He is a product of those years. As has been reported many times by cable news commentators, Obama manifests Aloha in his public appearances, although described in different terms—cool and in control, yes, but most importantly, friendly, outgoing, and inclusive.

Although open to all kinds of experiences in the arts, Obama sought out African American music in his youth. He has continued his musical eclecticism throughout his life. While campaigning, National Public Radio's *All Things Considered* reported the music preferences of the presidential candidates. On August 1, 2008, the program listed Obama's Top 10, which included everything from Frank Sinatra, through the Rolling Stones, the hip-hop group Fugees, doo-wop singer Marvin Gaye, and Bruce Springsteen. His iPod has songs by Sheryl Crow, Bob Dylan, Springsteen, Stevie Wonder, and Jay-Z (Alter 2010:303).

His campaign song *We Are the Ones We Are Waiting For* (1980) is from the female group Sweet Honey in the Rock. Another song, *Yes We Can*, inspired by a talk that he delivered just before the New Hampshire primary, was written by Will.i.am (2008). During his campaign,

Hawai'i-born singer Scott Katsura and David Velarde rewrote the "rap without gripes," *Mahalo America*, to promote his candidacy, giving a new title as the *Barack Obama Song*. During a fund-raiser in Honolulu, Barack sang *Hawai'i Aloha* with Raiatea Helm (2008).

Although he once scolded a fellow Punahou student that his musical tastes went beyond Stevie Wonder, when he accepted the Democratic Party nomination for president at Invesco Stadium in Denver, Stevie Wonder performed, as he did at his inauguration. Although Obama did not indulge in Bach or Beethoven or Brahms or Bartók in his youth, he recognized the value of classical music at his inauguration, including the piano chamber group of Gabriela Montero, violinist Itzhak Perlman, clarinetist Anthony McGill, and cellist Yo-Yo Ma. John Williams offered a new composition at the inauguration ceremony. Another highlight was Aretha Franklin's rendition of *My Country 'Tis of Thee*. Several others performed, including Pete Seeger and Bruce Springsteen. Ten official inaugural balls hosted a variety of popular American musicians and singers from earlier to recent fame. Subsequently, concerts scheduled at the White House have included all the forms easily found on radio, television, and other media. He has also commented on rappers Jay-Z and—notoriously—Kanye West. In 2009, the White House sponsored a master music class for 120 students, featuring violinist Joshua Bell and others. He danced at a Latino event and entertained the national conference of governors by organizing a bipartisan conga line.

David Plouffe (2009:76) describes Obama's campaign style as follows: "Barack was a jazz musician, riffing, improvisational and playing by ear." David Remnick (2010:537) regards his oratory before a teleprompter as similar to "a well-rehearsed musician glancing at the score." Indeed, those who listen to cool jazz often hear a musician trying to find sonority from disparate themes, just as Obama sought an identity while growing up with the ambiguity of someone perceived as Black while living with Whites in a multiethnic society where everyone can easily access musics of other cultures. The cerebral quality of the jazz that fascinated Obama appears to mirror his intellectual approach to problem solving.

Chapter 8

Electoral Politics: Post-Racial?

Dan Boylan and Michael Haas

*[P]olitics has become [a dead zone] ... in which narrow inter-
ests vie for advantage and ideological minorities seek to impose
their own versions of absolute truth. Whether we're from red
states or blue states, we feel in our gut the lack of honesty,
rigor, and common sense in our policy debates, and dislike
what appears to be a continuous menu of false or cramped
choices ... I reject a politics that is based solely on racial
identity, gender identity, sexual orientation, or victimhood
generally.*

(Obama 2008:12, 16)

When Barack Obama came of age politically in Hawai'i's transformative 1970s, he read in the newspaper and saw on television a Japanese American governor, George Ariyoshi, whose quiet political style
embodied the principles of Hawai'i's multicultural ethos. In Hawai'i,
lieutenant governors are selected independently in party primaries, and
Ariyoshi was elected with Japanese American Nelson Doi as his running
mate in 1974.

In 1978, the year before Obama left the Islands for college, voters
picked mixed-race Jean Sadako King (Japanese-White) as Ariyoshi's
running mate. If non-White and mixed-race candidates could be elected
to high offices in Hawai'i, why not an African American president?
Obama, we now know, thought about becoming president at an early

age (Coleman 2008). To entertain such an ambition, he must have conceived the possibility of a "post-racial" politics. Indeed, the polls showed that Ariyoshi enjoyed support from all ethnic groups. Obama grew up in an environment of political inclusiveness, not division (East-West Center 2009).

But politics was the principal means by which a system of ethnic dominance and subordination was enforced in Hawai'i not long after the arrival of Haole settlers in the Hawaiian Islands during the 1820s. Although Native Hawaiian monarchs were officially in control, they listened to and acted on advice from the Haoles without prejudice, including the law in 1848 that enabled land held in common by the monarch to become private property, a decision that soon made Haoles economically dominant.

Mutual trust between the ethnic groups was jeopardized in 1887, when the king signed the "Bayonet Constitution," which established property qualifications for voting, thereby disenfranchising many Native Hawaiian voters for the benefit of a small Haole commercial elite seeking to maximize profits by exploiting Chinese, Japanese, Native Hawaiian, and Portuguese plantation workers. And the coup of armed Haoles who overthrew Queen Lili'uokalani in 1893 is clearly an example of racism.

What happened between the imposition of monocultural White rule over a multiethnic population in 1893 and the 1970s? To answer that question requires an understanding of political party loyalty, ticket balancing, ethnic bloc voting, and candidate characteristics in Hawai'i elections, factors well understood by Barack Obama in his election to office in Illinois and later in his quest to become president.

ETHNIC SUCCESSION

Within national politics, most presidential candidates have been Anglo-Saxon Caucasian Protestants. The first German descendant, Dwight Eisenhower, was elected in 1952. The first Catholic, John Kennedy, won in 1960. The first mixed-race president was Barack Obama. Ethnic succession has been slow, but as the non-White and Hispanic populations inexorably increase, the long dominance of White presidents is fading.

In Hawai'i, the succession has been more dramatic. After the coup by Haole settlers in 1893, a Haole-dominated Republic of Hawai'i ruled until 1900, when free elections were held in the newly constituted Territory of Hawai'i. The Native Hawaiian-backed Home Rule Party then swept Territorial elections, calling for a return of the monarchy. In 1902, Haole Republicans captured control with Prince Kūhiō Kalaniana'ole as delegate to Congress at the head of the ticket by beguiling Native Hawaiians into believing that their best interests were served by Haole Republican rule.

Native Hawaiians continued to be the largest voting bloc until the 1930s (Table 8.1). Then in 1954, Japanese Democrats were voted into power in the Territorial legislature and have maintained a plurality ever since (Table 8.2).

Another peculiarity of the political history of Hawai'i is that before 1964, the most populous island (O'ahu) was underrepresented in the state legislature. Neighbor Islands, predominantly Democratic and non-White, had more power than their relative share of the population. The U.S. Supreme Court's one-person-one-vote ruling in 1962, *Baker v Carr* (369US386), required voting districts to have roughly the same population. The percentage of Japanese legislators declined, as the Caucasian population was increasing (Table 1.2). The result of legal and demographic trends has been more ethnic diversity in office holding, though ethnic succession still has not passed from the hands of Japanese in the legislature.

Since statehood, Hawai'i has produced many firsts. A colorful variety of office seekers has emerged from primaries to run in the general elections. Beyond Caucasians in public office, Hawai'i can boast the first Chinese American U.S. Senator (Hiram Fong); the first Japanese American member of the United States House of Representatives and Senate (Daniel Inouye); the first Native Hawaiian member of the House and Senate (Daniel Akaka); the first Japanese American female member of the House of Representatives (Patsy Takemoto Mink); the first Filipino (Ben Cayetano), Native Hawaiian (John Waihe'e), and Japanese (George Ariyoshi) governors; and the first part-Samoan mayor (Muliufi Francis "Mufi" Hannemann) of a big (12th largest) city. Voters in the Aloha State today accept diversity as a fact of life in culture, politics, and society.

Comparing legislators with registered voters (Tables 8.1 and 8.2), the overall match appears reasonably close, though Caucasians and Filipinos are underrepresented, and Japanese and Native Hawaiians are over-represented. Meanwhile, the gubernatorial torch passed from a White Republican to a White Democrat in 1962, then to a Japanese in 1974, a Native Hawaiian in 1986, a Filipino in 1994, a female White Republican in 2002 and a White male Democrat in 2010.

Table 8.1

Registered Voters in Hawai'i by Ethnic Group, 1887–2008 (in percent)

Year	Caucasian		Chinese		Filipino		Hawaiian		Japanese	
1887	31.4%	(48)					65.3%	(100)		
1890	27.4	(36)					75.4	(100)		
1892	28.0	(40)					69.9	(100)		
1894	77.1	(100)					18.0	(23)		
1897	55.1	(100)					41.8	(76)		
1902	30.0	(44)	1.1%	(2)			68.8	(100)		
1904	28.2	(40)	1.3	(2)			69.8	(100)		
1906	22.4	(32)	1.6	(2)			71.0	(100)		
1908	30.4	(45)	2.0	(3)			67.6	(100)		
1910	30.6	(46)	2.7	(4)			66.6	(100)	.1%	(–)
1912	34.3	(55)	3.2	(5)			62.1	(100)	.3	(–)
1914	37.4	(64)	3.7	(6)			58.2	(100)	.6	(1)
1916	34.5	(61)	4.1	(7)			56.7	(100)	.9	(2)
1918	39.7	(73)	4.7	(9)			54.2	(100)	1.4	(3)
1920	37.5	(67)	4.3	(8)			55.6	(100)	2.5	(4)
1922	40.1	(77)	4.6	(9)			51.8	(100)	3.5	(7)
1924	41.2	(86)	5.8	(12)			48.0	(100)	4.9	(10)
1926	38.0	(87)	7.2	(17)			43.8	(100)	7.6	(17)
1928	39.8	(97)	8.6	(21)			41.1	(100)	11.7	(28)
1930	**39.1**	(100)	8.4	(21)			38.1	(97)	13.5	(34)
1932	**39.8**	(100)	8.4	(21)			33.8	(85)	17.7	(44)
1936	**34.6**	(100)	8.6	(25)	–	(–)	28.9	(84)	24.9	(72)
1938	**32.3**	(100)	8.6	(27)	.6%	(2)	26.7	(83)	28.5	(88)
1940	30.2	(97)	8.5	(27)	–	(–)	24.7	(80)	**31.0**	(100)
1961	28.9	(73)	13.3	(34)	6.2	(16)	7.5	(19)	**39.5**	(100)
1970	20.0	(44)	5.3	(12)	9.7	(21)	16.9	(37)	**45.8**	(100)
1974	32.5	(89)	7.4	(20)	7.9	(22)	9.9	(27)	**36.7**	(100)
1976	29.0	(75)	7.2	(19)	9.7	(25)	12.2	(32)	**38.6**	(100)
1990	28.0	(80)	8.0	(21)	10.0	(29)	10.0	(29)	**35.0**	(100)
2008	29.1	(na)		na		na	5.0	(na)		na

Key: na = Figures not available.
    – = less than 1% but more than 0.
    (–) = less than 1% of top group.

Notes: Except for 2008, figures report percentages of voting-age persons within each ethnic group who registered to vote, and add to 100 percent horizontally when other groups are included. For 1961, figures exclude Kaua'i, Lāna'i, and Moloka'i. For 1974, figures exclude Lāna'i and Moloka'i. For 1990, the combined count of Chinese and Koreans was 10 percent, so Koreans were allocated 2 percent of voters. Figures in parentheses are normed, with 100 assigned to the group with the highest percentage of registered voters; other groups are expressed as a percentage of the top figure. For 2008, the figures are for eligible voters who may not be registered. "Hawaiian" figures include persons with any Native Hawaiian ancestry. "Caucasian" figures include Portuguese, Puerto Ricans, Spanish, and other Caucasians. Figures in boldface are the highest in each row.

Sources: Coffman (1973:11); Hawai'i (1932:21; 1934:10; 1940:15; 1977:87); Kuroda (1998:145); Lind (1967:98); Meller (1955:265); Oshiro (1976:A3,10); Schmitt (1961:5–6; 1977:55–56); Pew (2008).

168

Table 8.2

Legislators in Hawai'i by Ethnic Group, 1901–2009 (in percent)

Year	Caucasian		Chinese		Filipino		Hawaiian		Japanese	
1901	16.7%	(0)					73.3%	(100)		
1905	37.8						62.2			
1909	37.8						62.2			
1913	42.2						57.8			
1917	37.8						62.2			
1921	37.8						62.2			
1925	42.2						57.8			
1929	46.7		4.4%				46.7			
1933	33.3		4.4				51.1		8.9%	
1937	48.9		6.7				35.6		6.7	
1941	42.2		8.9				33.3		15.6	
1945	46.7	(63)	6.7	(7)			46.7	(26)	.0	(0)
1949	46.7	(48)	6.7	(3)			20.0	(17)	26.7	(28)
1953	37.8	(56)	6.7	(4)			13.3	(11)	37.8	(30)
1955	33.3	(30)	2.2	(7)	2.2%	(0)	13.3	(10)	46.7	(53)
1959	31.0	(25)	7.9	(6)	2.6	(4)	14.5	(6)	46.1	(58)
1963	28.9	(21)	7.9	(10)	2.6	(4)	6.6	(4)	50.0	(62)
1967	26.3	(15)	11.8	(13)	5.3	(6)	5.3	(4)	50.0	(62)
1971	21.3	(14)	10.7	(10)	2.7	(8)	12.0	(4)	50.7	(65)
1975	23.7	(15)	10.5	(11)	1.3	(2)	13.2	(11)	46.0	(57)
1979	15.8	(12)	6.6	(7)	2.6	(3)	14.5	(13)	47.4	(55)
1983	17.1	(14)	7.9	(8)	7.9	(10)	19.7	(22)	38.2	(41)
1987	23.7	(18)	7.9	(10)	6.6	(8)	18.4	(18)	36.8	(45)
1991	21.3	(14)	9.3	(11)	8.0	(9)	17.3	(20)	42.7	(45)
1995	25.3	(20)	9.3	(9)	9.3	(11)	12.0	(12)	44.0	(48)
1997	21.3	(11)	6.7	(8)	8.0	(10)	16.0	(15)	46.7	(55)
1999	26.7	(14)	8.0	(10)	5.3	(6)	6.7	(6)	53.3	(62)
2001	29.3	(19)	9.3	(11)	8.0	(11)	6.7	(17)	44.0	(58)
2003	32.0	(16)	6.7	(7)	9.3	(13)	8.0	(7)	41.3	(54)
2005	28.0	(17)	8.0	(8)	8.0	(10)	9.3	(10)	46.7	(53)
2007	28.0	(22)	6.7	(6)	5.3	(11)	5.3	(8)	42.7	(49)
2009	25.3	(20)	6.7	(6)	10.7	(12)	10.7	(9)	41.3	(46)

Notes: Figures not in parentheses report percentages of legislators within each ethnic group and add to 100 percent horizontally when other groups are included. Figures in parentheses are percentages of legislators for each ethnic group in the majority party and add to 100 percent horizontally when other ethnic groups are included (but are unavailable from 1905 to 1941). Figures in boldface are the highest in each row. Hawaiian" figures include persons with any Native Hawaiian ancestry, and "Caucasian" figures include Portuguese, Spanish, and other Caucasians.

Sources: Fujiyama (1967:111, 123, 135, 147, 159, 171, 183, 195, 207, 219, 231, 243); Hawai'i (1932a:21; 1934:10; 1976:181; 1977:189; 1979:246; 1981:336; 1983:396–397; 1985:255; 1987:280; 1990:253); Meller (1955:267; 1958a:104; 1961/62:47); personal communications from various sources.

Table 8.3
Ethnicity and Party Preference in Hawai'i, 1976 and 1986 (in percent)

Ethnic Group	Party Preference	1976	1986
Caucasian	Democratic	49%	33%
	Republican	30	43
	Independent	26	24
Chinese	Democratic	40	37
	Republican	29	20
	Independent	31	43
Filipino	Democratic	77	41
	Republican	9	24
	Independent	14	35
Hawaiian	Democratic	49	46
	Republican	17	21
	Independent	34	33
Japanese	Democratic	58	68
	Republican	11	9
	Independent	31	23
Total	Democratic	52	45
	Republican	18	27
	Independent	30	28

Note: Figures in boldface identify the top preference for each ethnic group for each year.
Source: Boylan (1992:71).

Japanese are still the largest ethnic group in the electorate (Table 8.1) and in the majority Democratic Party (Table 8.3). Since statehood, while about two-thirds of the Democratic candidates have been Japanese, nearly half of the Democrats winning major primary elections have been Japanese (Table 8.4). Polling by Representative Roy Takumi reports that Japanese vote at higher percentages than all other ethnic groups. Even so, their percentage in the electorate has slipped as more Caucasians have moved to the Islands after statehood. Unfortunately, more recent figures are unavailable, but the victories of a White Republican governor in 2002 and 2006 indicate that new factors are at play.

Beyond ethnic diversity in officeholding, is Hawai'i truly an example of "post-racial politics," that is, a politics in which citizens no longer vote on the basis of race? Why do voters appear to vote so many members of different ethnic groups into office? What motivates voters? What are the decisive factors for victory at the polls?

Table 8.4

Ethnic Representation of Major General Election Candidates within Hawai'i, 1959–2008 (in percent)

Ethnic Group	Democrats	Republicans
Caucasian	30.5%	**64.8%**
Chinese	.0	4.4
Filipino	4.2	.0
Hawaiian	15.8	16.5
Japanese	**48.4**	13.2
Samoan	.0	1.1
Mixed	1.0	.0
Total	99.9	100.0

Notes: Except for rounding errors, figures sum to 100 percent in each column. Figures in boldface identity the largest ethnic group in each column.

   Most knowledgeable observers today believe that ethnicity is not the most important factor for Hawai'i voters. According to successful campaign strategist Lloyd Nekoba, other factors are experience, local identity, political party, and reputation. "Local identity" refers to the way in which the hapa (mixed-race) population sees itself today. That is, someone with a White father and Japanese mother, or vice versa, may prefer to identify as "local" rather than as Japanese-Caucasian, mixed, or even hapa. But of course, to be "local" also means speaking Hawai'i Creole English, eating mixed-plate meals (with food from several cultures on the same plate), going to a high school in Hawai'i, and giving the "shaka" sign with a big smile. Being local is also subscribing to Hawai'i's multicultural ethos. Indeed, Obama is still a local at heart, displaying as he does the "shaka" sign (Finin 2008).

POLITICAL PARTY PREFERENCE

Most observers believe that political party preference is the most important factor in voting within Hawai'i. Before statehood, Caucasians and Chinese leaned toward Republicans, Filipinos and Japanese preferred Democrats, while Native Hawaiians split between the two political parties. However, voters on the plantations were carefully monitored. Pencils tied with string onto an overhead cable were positioned so that the Republican side of the ballot could be marked with ease. Any movement of the pencil meant a vote for the Democratic Party and possible disciplinary action, such as being fired from work and blackballed from future employment in the Islands (Fuchs 1961:179).

Clearly, the most dramatic succession in political power was from Republicans to Democrats in 1954. By 1976, Democrats were the first choice of all ethnic groups. In 1986, some Caucasians defected to the Republicans, and more Chinese considered themselves independents. Figures for 1996 and 2006 are unfortunately unavailable to determine whether the trends continue, but successful Japanese Republicans and White Democrats in primary elections are still numerous enough to suggest that party preference continues to override ethnic loyalty (cf. Haas 2010b:Ch. 2).

The most successful Democratic candidates in general elections are Japanese (Table 8.5). Although Republicans elected to office are equally represented by Caucasians, Chinese, and Native Hawaiians, they need more support from non-Whites to win. Whites, meanwhile, do equally well in both political parties. Japanese Democrats are almost three times more likely to win than Japanese Republicans.

Although a Republican governor was elected in 2002 and 2006, Democrats continue to outnumber Republicans in the state legislature, so the Democratic Party remains dominant. During 2008, when Barack Obama was elected president, his coattails in Hawai'i resulted in a decline from 12 to 10 Republicans and an increase from 63 to 65 Democrats among the 75 members of the State Senate and House of Representatives.

Overall, the odds favor the Democratic Party, backed by a highly unionized workforce and a "political machine" to get out the vote.

Table 8.5

Ethnic Representation of Winners of Major General Elections in Hawai'i, 1959–2008 (in percent)

Ethnic Group	Democrats	Republicans	Total
Caucasian	27.4%	27.3%	27.4%
Chinese	.0	27.3	3.2
Filipino	4.8	.0	4.2
Hawaiian	17.9	27.3	18.9
Japanese	48.8	18.2	45.3
Samoan	.0	.0	.0
Mixed	1.2	.0	1.1
Total	100.1	100.1	100.1

Notes: Except for rounding errors, figures sum to 100 percent in each column. Figures in boldface identity the largest ethnic group in each column.

According to former Governor Ben Cayetano (2009:81), the Democrats in Hawai'i have formed the longest lasting political machine still operating in the United States. He should know, as he was twice elected governor with the support of the machine.

BALANCED VOTING SLATES

What is perhaps most fascinating, therefore, is to trace whether voters prefer balanced (multiethnic) or unbalanced (monoethnic) slates, as ticket balancing connotes inclusiveness. Few candidates for governor have endorsed lieutenant governors, so voters nominate candidates for both positions independently. Although candidates may independently decide to run for office, what often emerges from primary elections is a balanced slate of officeseekers. The result is not entirely accidental, as candidates seeking individual offices in Hawai'i often advertise backers of various ethnic backgrounds to signal a multiethnic base of support.

Prior to the 1980s, many legislators ran in multimember districts, electing two members to the State House of Representatives. Ticket balancing was therefore possible, as one political party could officially back two candidates of different ethnic backgrounds in the same district. But in 1982, a federal judge in Honolulu ruled that multimember districts were unconstitutional, based on *Mobile v Bolden* (446US55), a decision by the Supreme Court of the United States two years earlier.

Accordingly, there were fears that minorities would suffer from single-member districts in which the ethnic group with a plurality of votes could outpoll smaller ethnic groups (Cayetano 2009:216). Nevertheless, the fears were unfounded. Chinese, Filipinos, and Native Hawaiians have fared slightly better in legislative representation than before 1982 (Table 8.2).

In 1959, Hawai'i's first election as a state, Democratic statewide candidates consisted of three Whites and two Japanese, while Republicans balanced the ticket with a Chinese, a Japanese, a Native Hawaiian, and two Whites. The Republicans won the positions of governor, lieutenant governor, and senator, while the Democrats won one seat each in the House of Representatives and the U.S. Senate.

Learning their lesson (Boylan 1992:76), the Democrats fielded a more balanced gubernatorial ticket in 1962—Caucasian John Burns and Native Hawaiian William Richardson—and defeated Republicans, who fielded all White candidates except for one Native Hawaiian (for lieutenant governor). In 1966, Burns's lieutenant governor was Tom Gill, a fellow Caucasian, but they defeated a Republican White-Native Hawaiian team. In 1970, Governor John Burns was eager to have a Japanese lieutenant governor, so he endorsed George Ariyoshi, while the White Republican also ran a Japanese lieutenant governor candidate but lost.

In 1974, Burns resigned because of poor health, whereupon Lieutenant Governor George Ariyoshi became governor. Later that year, Ariyoshi ran for a full term as governor but refused to endorse lieutenant governor candidates. On primary election night, he discovered that voters had nominated Japanese Americans for governor, lieutenant governor, senator, and two members of the House of Representatives, while Republicans selected only Whites for the same races. Of the two unbalanced slates, the Democrats won in the general election.

In 1978, the Democrats' balanced ticket (Ariyoshi and mixed-race Jean Sadako King for lieutenant governor) defeated two White Republican candidates for governor and lieutenant governor. In 1982, Native Hawaiian John Waihe'e joined the Democratic ticket as Ariyoshi's running mate and defeated a White-Japanese Republican combination.

In 1986, Republicans nominated two candidates of Portuguese ancestry for governor and lieutenant governor—Andy Anderson and John Henry Felix. They were opposed by an ultimately victorious Democratic team of Native Hawaiian John Waihe'e and Filipino Ben Cayetano. The "Ariyoshi/Burns machine" had become a multiethnic "Democratic machine."

In 1990, Republican gubernatorial Caucasian candidate Fred Hemmings, Jr., urged primary voters to choose Billie Beamer, a Native Hawaiian, as lieutenant governor. Leonard Mednick, who was also a candidate for lieutenant governor, then charged Hemmings with discrimination for failing to endorse him as a running mate because he was Caucasian (Borreca 1990). The Republicans were later defeated by incumbents Waihe'e and Cayetano.

In 1994, Pat Saiki was the Republican choice for governor and stalwart Hemmings was her lieutenant governor running mate. In another balanced ticket, Cayetano ran for governor, and Democratic primary voters selected Mazie Hirono as his running mate. To pull the rug from underneath both parties, which failed to have Native Hawaiians on either ticket, longtime Honolulu Mayor Frank Fasi chose Native Hawaiian entertainer Danny Kaleikini as his running mate on the short-lived and unsuccessful Best Party. Cayetano and Hirono won.

In the 1998 election, the team of Cayetano and Hirono brought together the principal ethnic groups that worked on the plantations. The

Republicans ran Jewish candidate Linda Lingle for governor with Japanese Stan Koki for lieutenant governor. Lingle had strong ties with a prominent local business, had married and divorced a Native Hawaiian, and was a popular mayor of Maui. The margin of Cayetano's victory was 5,254 votes (1.2 percent), which was a wake-up call for Democrats that moderate voters were defecting from the Democratic Party.

Although Cayetano was elected governor by the Democratic machine in 1994 and 1998, the margins of victory were so thin that the machine was on life support and finally died when Republican Governor Linda Lingle was elected in 2002 and reelected in 2006, both times with Native Hawaiian James "Duke" Aiona, Jr., as her running mate. The Democrats in 2002 nominated Mazie Hirono for governor, but her running mate was another Japanese, Matt Matsunaga. The balanced Republican ticket then defeated the unbalanced Democratic slate.

In 2006, Democrats nominated another Japanese, Randy Iwase, for governor and Native Hawaiian Malama Solomon for lieutenant governor. Despite two balanced tickets, the Democrats lost again, raising the question whether the political machine that elected Democrats for so long could ever be reincarnated. But in 2010 two White Democrats (Neil Abercrombie and Bryan Schatz) defeated a balanced Republican ticket (Aiona and Filipina Lynn Finnegan). Voters usually prefer inclusive politics (Table 8.6).

The 2008 election demonstrated the success of ticket balancing at the national level. Whereas 90 percent of John McCain's supporters were White, Obama's voters were 61 percent White, 23 percent African American, and 11 percent Hispanic (Todd and Gawiser 2009:29). McCain captured 55 percent of all White voters, but that was not enough. The demographics of America are changing, so the McCain-Palin ticket painted itself into a White ethnic enclave while the mixed-race Obama-Biden team had wider appeal. In 2008, some 26 percent of the voters were non-White, whereas in 1976 the corresponding percentage was 10 percent. Black voter turnout in 2008 exceeded all previous elections. The Republican choice of a White woman for vice president may have

Table 8.6
Ticket Balancing for Governor and Lieutenant Governor in Hawai'i, 1959–2010

Electoral Result	Balanced Tickets	Unbalanced Tickets
Success	11	3
Failure	9	5

sought to tap into disappointment that Hillary Clinton was not on the Democratic ticket, but voters were insufficiently impressed.

Obama, of course, grew up in a state when Japanese American voters had the reputation of being quietly decisive in electing statewide and national candidates. That is, their votes were crucial but they refused to make ethnicity central. In Hawai'i, successful politicians must think of a politics of 'ohana, not a politics of division. Obama had established an ability to appeal to Black voters in Chicago and White voters in down-state Illinois as *"the son of a Black man from Kenya and a White woman from Kansas."* He did so again in 2008, and the voters responded with landslide support.

As an astute biographer has observed:

Obama wouldn't have developed his ability to bridge racial divides if he had been a [W]hite politician who could take [B]lack Demo-cratic votes for granted rather than a [B]lack politician who had to work hard in order to overcome the suspicions of [W]hite voters and media toward [B]lack politicians. It is not Obama's race that matters, but how Obama's race taught him so much about Ameri-can values. (Wilson 2008:80)

ETHNIC BLOC VOTING

Whereas some White opponents of statehood feared that non-White ethnic bloc voting existed in Hawai'i, those supporting statehood denied that there was ethnic bloc voting in Hawai'i. The latter view still persists to bolster Hawai'i's image of a land without discrimina-tion (Boylan 1992:73–77), but the evidence suggests that both views are incorrect.

Many politicians admit that subtle ethnic appeals are central to their campaigns (Boylan 1992:73; Cayetano 2009:328–329). But an open ethnic appeal by one candidate risks political suicide by alienating vot-ers of other ethnicities.

To measure bloc voting, there are two scientific methods. The aggre-gate method is to correlate percentages of an ethnic group across pre-cincts with percentages of votes by candidates of the same group. A second method is to examine opinion surveys. Corroborating informa-tion comes from campaign managers and politicians whose observations are based on private polls.

In what became a Democratic state after statehood, the most important contests are the primary elections. If ethnic bloc voting exists, primaries are where ethnicity is likely to play a crucial role. When there were multimember districts, voters were suspected of "plunking," that is, voting for candidates of their own ethnicity and not casting a second vote for candidates of other backgrounds who were running in the same district. Now that single-member districts exist, many observers believe that there is a clear correspondence between the ethnicity of victorious candidates and the largest ethnic group in corresponding districts.

Correlating ethnic composition of precincts with successful candidates by ethnicity, sociologist Andrew Lind (1957) found considerable bloc voting in Hawai'i from 1928 to 1938. But his analysis of voting in 1947 came to an opposite conclusion.

Three later multivariate statistical studies found much ethnic voting. In 1954, when the Democratic Party displaced the Republican Party to become the dominant party in the legislature, there was a clear polarization between pro- and anti-Japanese precincts, though party preference was a better predictor of voting than ethnicity (Digman and Tuttle 1961). In one precinct that year, where voting officials identified each voter's ethnicity, the ethnicity of voters correlated directly with the ethnicity of candidates supported. In 1956, they found a similar pattern (Digman and Tuttle 1959).

The election of 1970 was a watershed in many ways. Two White Democrats vied for the governorship. Incumbent John Burns courted Japanese and other non-White voters, implying that his Hawai'i-born opponent, Lieutenant Governor Thomas Gill, was the darling of upper-status Haoles and recent arrivals unassimilated to the local culture of the Islands (Coffman 1973:Ch. 17). The victory of working-class Burns, who lived in Hawai'i from the age of 4, signaled that Filipino and Japanese support for Democrats remained solid.

On closer examination, a multivariate analysis of aggregate precinct voting in 1970 demonstrated a polarization between Caucasian-dominated precincts supporting Caucasian Republican candidates and Japanese-dominated precincts favoring Japanese Democrats, while several other factors linked ethnicity of candidates with the ethnic composition of precincts (Haas 2010b:Ch. 2).

Statistical correlations of precinct characteristics, however, may be challenged because they lack the sensitivity of polls, which directly measure public opinion. There is a peculiarity about surveys in Hawai'i, however. When polls are taken early in the year of an election, a sizeable percentage do not choose a candidate. Many non-White voters, busy with family and work, are unable to prioritize their time to decide on political choices until an election draws near. Politicians, therefore, must shift into high gear late in the election campaign to reach voters and must participate in many tiring after-dinner "coffee hours" throughout the Islands in the hope of making the sale. Because Caucasians generally decide early, White candidates appear to take the lead for major political offices but often lose when late deciders go to the polls.

Public opinion surveys, nevertheless, largely agree with the multivariate statistical studies. In 1950, four years before the first Democratic landslide, a survey found that Japanese preferred the Democratic Party, and Caucasians showed even more preference for the Republican Party (Territorial Surveys 1950), a finding that has been repeated in many subsequent studies.

The next major sample survey of voters in Hawai'i occurred in 1970, when Caucasians preferred Gill to Burns in the primary. Native Hawaiian Republican gubernatorial hopeful Samuel King lost to Burns in the general election that year. Non-Whites, especially Filipinos and Japanese, supported Burns in both the primary and the general elections (Table 8.7).

In the 1974 Democratic primary, Ariyoshi was opposed by Gill, but Honolulu Mayor Frank Fasi, a Sicilian American from Hartford, Connecticut, who came to Hawai'i as a marine in World War II, threw his hat into the ring as well. Whereas Ariyoshi sought to attract the Democratic non-White voting bloc that had brought victory in every gubernatorial election from 1962, middle-class voters showed a preference for Gill, and Fasi made a populist appeal targeted at non-Caucasian working-class voters as well as to alienated Mainland-born Whites.

Ariyoshi's campaign manager then urged State Senator David McClung, a Caucasian from Michigan, to enter the race in order to split the Caucasian vote even more. Revealing the offer on television, McClung threw his support to Gill (Burris 1974). At one point in the campaign, Gill evidently came close to comparing Fasi with Benito Mussolini, the former fascist leader of Italy, whereupon the mayor bristled that a "slur on one minority is a slur on every minority" (Kakesako 1974:A1). When Ariyoshi supporters spread the word that the meaning of the election was to determine whether Japanese were good enough to be elected governor (*Honolulu Advertiser* 1974b), Fasi retorted that "nobody should get elected to any office in Hawaii because of his racial or ethnic or national origin" (Kakesako 1974:A1).

Table 8.7

Gubernatorial Support from Voters in Hawai'i by Ethnic Group, 1970–1978 (in percent)

Election	Candidate	Party	Race	Caucasian	Chinese	Filipino	Hawaiian	Japanese	Other	Total
1970 primary	Burns	D	W	19%	na	na	na	**33%**	na	25%
	Gill	D	W	29	na	na	na	**36**	na	33
	Burns	D	W	35	na	55%	50%	**58**	na	na
	Gill	D	W	**59**	na	40	41	35	na	na
1970 general	Burns-Ariyoshi	D	W-J	45	48%	**61**	48	59	55	58
	King-Kiyosaki	R	H-J	50	42	33	47	35	39	42
1974 primary	Ariyoshi	D	J	14	na	21	na	**36**	na	26
	Fasi	D	W	**33**	na	31	na	26	na	29
	Gill	D	W	**35**	na	23	na	22	na	26
	Ariyoshi	D	J	13	*	23	*	**41**	23	35
	Fasi	D	W	**35**	*	32	*	25	30	31
	Gill	D	W	**36**	*	25	*	23	27	30
1974 general	Ariyoshi-Doi	D	J-J	25	*	*	*	**72**	47	49
	Crossley-Dillingham	R	W-W	**57**	*	*	*	14	31	33
1978 primary	Ariyoshi	D	J	17	*	*	*	**59**	32	29
	Fasi	D	W	**65**	*	*	*	17	44	39
	Ariyoshi	D	J	14	*	*	*	**55**	23	34
	Fasi	D	W	**74**	*	*	*	19	54	44

Key: See Table 8.3.

    * = included in "Other" column.

    na = Figures not available.

Notes: Figures report percentages of each ethnic group preferring one of the candidates or candidate slates and add to 100 percent vertically when other candidates and nonascertained preferences are included. When two or more sets of figures are reported for the same primary, the topmost is from the earliest sample. Figures in boldface identify the highest in each row.

Sources: Coffman (1970; 1973:181, 203); Keir (1974a:A4; 1974b:A4; 1974c:A1,3; 1978a:A17; 1978b:A4).

Then, in a close vote, Ariyoshi squeaked to victory over his two White opponents. According to a public opinion poll, Japanese supported the two White gubernatorial candidates by a 48-41 percent margin over Ariyoshi, Filipinos went 57-23 percent for the White candidates over Ariyoshi, and Caucasians voted 68-14 percent against Ariyoshi (Table 8.8). In the general election, Japanese overwhelmingly supported Ariyoshi over his Republican opponent, Randolph Crossley, a White business executive who attracted a larger share of Caucasian voters than had King in 1970.

Had there been one White candidate instead of two in the 1974 primary, armchair observers speculated, Ariyoshi might have lost. In 1978, there was an opportunity to test that hypothesis, since Fasi was Ariyoshi's major opponent. Opinion polls released before the election even predicted Fasi's victory (Keir 1978a, b). But there were two problems with the polling that year (*Honolulu Star-Bulletin* 1978). First, 26 percent of the Japanese voters refused to state a preference. Second, the sample was drawn from all potential voters, even from those not registered to vote in Hawai'i, so the influence of respondents in the military, who generally vote by absentee ballots in other states, distorted the sample. Fasi won on O'ahu by a few votes but lost decisively on the primarily non-White Neighbor Islands, so Ariyoshi was renominated in the primary. In the general election, Ariyoshi defeated State Senator John Leopold, a Republican born in Pennsylvania.

In 1982, Ariyoshi faced opposition from his lieutenant governor, Jean King. No relation to Republican Samuel King, she became Ariyoshi's lieutenant governor in a close election in 1978 as "Jean Sadako King," so voters correctly suspected that she was of mixed White-Japanese ancestry. In 1982, however, she inexplicably dropped "Sadako," her pale face looked more White than Eurasian, and solid backing from Japanese voters carried Ariyoshi to victory. Fasi, tired of losing in Democratic primaries against Ariyoshi, formed the Independent Democratic Party. In the general election, the Republican gubernatorial challenger, State Senator Andy Anderson, a Caucasian with Portuguese ancestry, picked a Japanese running mate, Pat Saiki, another state senator. Together, the Independent Democrat and Republican tickets won majority support from all groups but Japanese (Table 8.8), who had sufficient voting strength to reelect Ariyoshi for a third term.

According to the newly revised Hawai'i constitution, Ariyoshi was ineligible for reelection to a fourth term. In 1986, John Waihe'e, Ariyoshi's lieutenant governor from 1982, then sought to run as the heir to the Burns-Ariyoshi tradition. One of Waihe'e's primary election opponents was Chicago-born Cecil Heftel, a White business executive who operated a network television station, often editorializing on political issues during prime time. Heftel won election to the first Congressional district (urban Honolulu) in 1976, and was reelected to Congress four times. A third gubernatorial candidate in 1986 was Japanese—Patsy Takemoto Mink, formerly elected to the second Congressional

Table 8.8

Gubernatorial Support from Voters in Hawai'i by Ethnic Group, 1982–1990 (in percent)

Election	Candidate	Party	Race	Caucasian	Chinese	Filipino	Hawaiian	Japanese	Other	Total
1982 primary	Ariyoshi	D	J	30%	*	*	45%	**84%**	48%	**52%**
	King	D	WJ	**54**	*	*	40	11	37	35
1982 general	Anderson-Saiki	R	W-J	**44**	*	*	25	17	27	28
	Ariyoshi-Waihe'e	D	J-H	19	*	*	31	**65**	31	38
	Fasi-Piltz	I	W-H	**34**	*	*	**37**	10	33	27
1986 primary	Heftel	D	W	**60**	*	*	**59**	44	**57**	**54**
	Mink	D	J	13	*	*	3	**13**	8	10
	Waihe'e	D	H	11	*	*	**29**	21	15	18
1986 general	Anderson-Felix	R	W-W	**59**	*	21%	49	21	*	39
	Waihe'e-Cayetano	D	H-F	23	*	**35**	32	**60**	*	**41**
1990 general	Waihe'e-Cayetano	D	H-F	46	na	63	66	**78**	na	na
	Hemmings-Beamer	R	W-H	**46**	*	*	*	20	29	30
	Waihe'e-Cayetano	D	H-F	42	*	*	*	**71**	66	**60**

Key: See Tables 8.3 and 8.8
  I   = Independent Democrat.
  na = Figures not available.
  x-x = ethnicities of gubernatorial and lieutenant gubernatorial candidates.
Notes: Figures report percentages of each ethnic group preferring one of the candidates or candidate slates and add to 100 percent vertically when other candidates and nonascertained preferences are included. When two or more sets of figures are reported for the same primary, the topmost is from the earliest sample. Figures in boldface identify the highest in each row.
Sources: Keir (1978b:A4; 1982a:A4; 1982b:A4; 1986a:A1,A3; 1986b:A4); Kresnak (1990:A3); Burris (1990:A4).

district (rural Hawai'i), who had lost a bid for a U.S. Senate seat in 1976 and now wanted to make a political comeback. Despite an early poll showing that Heftel would be the clear winner among all ethnic groups (Table 8.8), Waihe'e mobilized a majority in a primary in which charges of racial prejudice leveled at Heftel played a role, albeit mostly in private conversations (Hartwell 1987). On the Republican side, Andy Anderson ran again—and lost—for governor in 1986.

A more interesting race developed for lieutenant governor that year. Mayor Fasi encouraged Maria Victoria ("Vicky") Bunye, the Filipina head of his Office of Human Resources, to run for lieutenant governor (Borreca 1985), saying that he did not want an "all-Caucasian" Republican ticket (*Honolulu Advertiser* 1986), as Republican gubernatorial candidate Andy Anderson endorsed John Felix for lieutenant governor. During the campaign, Bunye cited statistics on Filipino underrepresentation in jobs with Hawai'i state government and urged Filipinos to switch to the Republican Party (Takeuchi 1986a). Ben Cayetano, a Filipino candidate for lieutenant governor in the Democratic primary, then attacked Bunye for injecting the issue of race into the campaign and for dishonoring Japanese Americans, who applied for government work because of discrimination in the private sector and had become a "great American success story" (Takeuchi 1986b). As a result, support for Cayetano shot up in the polls (Cayetano 2009:248–249). (In his autobiography, nevertheless, Cayetano [2009:328–329] admitted that only in Hawai'i, where he knows that race is a factor in elections, did he experience racial discrimination.)

Cayetano became Waihe'e's Democratic running mate, but Bunye lost in the Republican primary. The Waihe'e-Cayetano ticket then defeated Anderson and Felix in an election in which Japanese votes were again decisive (Table 8.8). Republicans remained political dinosaurs at the statewide level despite electing mayors on Maui and O'ahu.

In 1990, the Waihe'e-Cayetano team faced token opposition in the Democratic primary. In the general election, they attracted about as many Caucasian votes as their Republican opponents, Caucasian State Senator Fred Hemmings, Jr., and Native Hawaiian Billie Beamer, to win the first overwhelming landslide election since statehood (Table 8.8).

Following the tradition established by Ariyoshi, Gill, King, and Waihe'e of having lieutenant governors run for governor, Ben Cayetano was the Democratic choice in 1994. For Cayetano to win, however, he would have to defeat not only Republican Pat Saiki, but also an independent challenge by Frank Fasi's newly formed Best Party.

The first survey to appear, in November 1993, showed that Saiki was popular within all ethnic groups but Filipinos, who preferred Cayetano (Table 8.9). Saiki's overall lead was 2:1 over both Cayetano and Fasi (cf. Yuen 1993). One year later, however, Cayetano emerged on top. Although many Caucasian Republicans defected from Saiki to Fasi, the biggest switch was Japanese from Saiki to Cayetano: Japanese were evenly split between Cayetano and Saiki in early September, but they were almost 2:1 for Cayetano-Hirono over Saiki-Hemmings two months later. Were Japanese returning to traditional Democratic Party loyalties or instead attracted by the addition of Mazie Hirono as Cayetano's running mate in

Table 8.9
Gubernatorial Support from Voters in Hawai'i by Ethnic Group, 1994 (in percent)

Election	Candidate	Party	Race	Caucasian	Chinese	Filipino	Hawaiian	Japanese	Other	Total
1994 primary	Cayetano	D	F	21%	*	**39**	31%	23%	21%	24%
	Fasi	B	W	20	*	6	**32**	8	25	20
	Saiki	R	J	46	*	22	31	**48**	29	**40**
	Cayetano	D	F	17	*	**51**	19	21	20	22
	Fasi	B	W	23	*	14	**27**	6	16	19
	Saiki	R	J	**52**	*	31	40	**64**	56	51
	Cayetano	D	F	13	*	*	**17**	16	16	18
	Fasi	B	W	24	*	*	**26**	13	26	22
	Saiki	R	J	39	*	*	30	**43**	36	36
	Cayetano	D	F	20	16%	**57**	33	29	na	28
	Fasi	B	W	22	**24**	8	16	17	na	20
	Saiki	R	J	**38**	**38**	14	25	28	na	31
1994 general	Cayetano-Hirono	D	F-J	19	na	**42**	25	32	na	30
	Fasi-Kaleikini	B	W-H	25	na	19	**27**	16	na	23
	Saiki-Hemmings	R	J-W	33	na	11	18	25	na	**34**
	Cayetano-Hirono	D	F-J	19	na	**61**	45	45	na	35
	Fasi-Kaleikini	B	W-H	**27**	na	na	21	na	na	20
	Saiki-Hemmings	R	J-W	**40**	na	na	21	32	na	31
	Cayetano-Hirono	D	F-J	16	25	**47**	33	**46**	na	31
	Fasi-Kaleikini	B	W-H	**36**	24	21	22	10	na	24
	Saiki-Hemmings	R	J-W	31	28	3	18	26	na	24
	Cayetano-Hirono	D	F-J	17	16	**48**	17	41	na	27
	Fasi-Kaleikini	B	W-H	33	32	17	**38**	10	na	26
	Saiki-Hemmings	R	J-W	35	31	6	22	27	na	26

Key: See Tables 8.3 and 8.8   na = Figures not available.
B = Best Party D = Democratic Party R = Republican Party
Notes: Figures report percentages of each ethnic group preferring one of the candidates or candidate slates and add to 100 percent vertically when other candidates and nonascertained preferences are included. When two or more sets of figures are reported for the same primary, the topmost is from the earliest sample. Figures in boldface identify the highest in each row.
Sources: Yuen (1993; 1994a, b); Burris (1994a, b); Kresnak (1994); *Honolulu Advertiser* (1994a, b).

Table 8.10
Gubernatorial Support from Voters in Hawai'i by Ethnic Group, 1998
(in percent)

Candidate	Party	Race	Caucasian	Filipino	Hawaiian	Japanese
Cayetano	D	F	20.6%	**44.3%**	32.8%	**41.1%**
Lingle	R	W	**68.2**	26.2	**52.3**	33.1

Key: See Table 8.3.
Note: Figures in boldface identify the highest in each column.
Source: *Honolulu Advertiser* (1998:A18)

the primary election? Survey data strongly suggest that Cayetano needed Hirono to divert Japanese voters from Saiki.

For many years, the *Honolulu Advertiser* contracted with a polling company to survey likely voters, and results by ethnicity were published in the morning newspaper. From the mid-1990s, however, the survey contract went to another firm, and results by ethnicity have been published only for one gubernatorial and two mayoralty elections. Instead, vague descriptions of ethnic leanings in other races have been reported in the text of the articles rather than presented in tabular form. As a result, there is no precise way to track later shifts in ethnic voting patterns.

In 1996, incumbents for Congress were reelected, so voting patterns were unlikely to have changed very much. A July 1998 poll indicated that Democratic incumbent Ben Cayetano mobilized the Filipino-Japanese coalition, while his Republican opponent Linda Lingle got primary support from Caucasians and Native Hawaiians (Table 8.10), but the race was close. Particularly notable in the poll was that one-third of the Japanese supported Lingle and about one-sixth would not declare a preference. In late September, six weeks before the 1998 general election, after voters selected lieutenant governor running mates, the ticket of Cayetano and Mazie Hirono trailed the Republican opponents, Lingle and Stan Koki, by 7 percentage points.

Cayetano's campaign staff in 1998 included the famed international political consultant Joe Napolitan, who said:

Lingle's got a big lead over you with the [W]hite voter. . . . Right now you're getting about 22 percent of [W]hite vote, and I doubt that you'll get any more than that . . . so we got to get Democrats—especially the Japanese voters—to come back in greater numbers than they are now. We need 65 percent of them. (Cayetano 2009:414)

They indeed came back, and Cayetano eked out a 5,000-vote victory over Lingle.

Also in 1998, Congressional incumbent Democrat Neil Abercrombie defeated Republican Gene Ward for the First Congressional District. Abercrombie attracted all non-White ethnic groups, Ward the Caucasian vote (Dayton 1998). Both Caucasians, incumbency must have carried the day.

In 2000, Congressional incumbents were reelected. In 2002, Japanese American Patsy Mink, longtime member of Congress died a few days before the general election. In a special election during late November, voters preferred well-financed Caucasian Ed Case from a field of 27 candidates of various ethnicities and political parties, including her Caucasian husband, John Mink.

The big news in 2002 was that Linda Lingle won the governor's race with James R. "Duke" Aiona, Jr., as her lieutenant government. Lingle, now the successful "Great White Hope," mobilized both Caucasian and Native Hawaiian voters, with some White Democrats crossing over to support the Republican candidates (Cayetano 2009:527). Adding disaffected Caucasians to disgruntled Native Hawaiians, in other words, yielded enough votes to win. Lingle claimed that her policies accounted for much prosperity on Maui, where she had been reelected mayor, and the economic situation was in some decline as the military was closing down bases in the post–Cold War era.

In 2004, Ed Case was reelected to Congress. His Republican opponent, of mixed Samoan-Caucasian ancestry, Mike Gabbard, stressed anti-gay themes in his campaign, and voters preferred the candidate who did not run a negative campaign. According to Cayetano (2009:413), the Republican Party had lately become dominated by religious conservatives. Gabbard typified that ideology.

In 2006, Lingle and Aiona were reelected in a landslide. Once again, she had a winning coalition, even a majority of the various Asian groups, according to a cable news network that used Mainland-style ethnic categories (Table 8.11).

Meanwhile, in the Second Congressional District (rural Hawai'i), voters replaced Case, who ran for Senator, with the unsuccessful gubernatorial candidate of 2002, Mazie Hirono. Senator Dan Akaka defeated the Republican candidate, Cynthia Thielen, with traditional strength from

Table 8.11

Support from Voters in Hawai'i by Ethnic Group, 2006 (in percent)

Election	Candidate	Party	Race	Caucasian	Asian	Latino	Other	Total
Governor	Iwase	D	J	30%	40%	37%	31%	35%
	Lingle	R	W	65	60	59	69	62
	Total			32	32	9	25	
Senator	Akaka	D	H	44	67	68	69	61
	Thielen	R	W	55	31	27	28	37
	Total			31	33	9	24	

Key: See Table 8.3.

Notes: Figures add up to 100 percent in each column when votes of other political parties are included. Figures in boldface identify the highest in each row.

Source: Cable News Network (2006)

Asian ethnic groups and more Caucasians than the former Democratic candidate for governor, Randall Iwase (Table 8.11).

In 2008, Congressional incumbents were reelected, and ethnicity appeared again to have been a strong predictor of electoral success for the State House of Representatives. The elected representatives came from the largest ethnic population in 27 of the 51 districts. On the Island of Hawai'i, four of the seven came from the largest ethnic group in their respective districts. For example, Japanese American Clifton Tsuji held the seat in Hilo, which has a population of 6,800 Japanese-Americans, 2,600 Caucasians, 2,000 Filipinos, and 1,900 Native Hawaiians. The sustained support for Japanese American candidates from the district has garnered the title of "Shoyu Alley." (*Shoyu* is the Japanese word for soy sauce.) In Hawai'i Island's tourist-oriented West Hawai'i, the Caucasian population equals or exceeds that of Japanese, Filipino, and Native Hawaiian populations combined, and the representatives are Caucasians Bob Herkes, Denny Coffman, and Cindy Evans.

The pattern holds throughout the state, not restricted to Japanese and Caucasians. Thus, Filipinos are predominant residents where Filipinos hold the seats. When incumbent attorney Alex Sonson gave up his seat in District 35 to run for the State Senate, six Filipino candidates sought the office— five Democrats and one Republican. No other ethnicities decided to apply. O'ahu has a "Shoyu Alley" of its own, running from Ai'ea to Waipahu, where Japanese Americans are the largest ethnic group by a significant margin, and each district elects a representative of Japanese heritage.

Table 8.12

Support for Mayoralty Candidates from Voters in Honolulu by Ethnic Group, 2004 and 2008 (in percent)

Year	Candidate	Race	Caucasian	Chinese	Filipino	Hawaiian	Japanese	Other	Total
2004	Bainum	W	28%	8%	17%	12%	27%	5%	na
	Hannemann	SW	20	7	14	25	16	7	na
2008	Hannemann	SW	52	na	64	63	60	na	58%
	Kobayashi	J	41	na	24	30	27	na	33

Key: See Tables 7.3, 7.8.
        na = Figures not available.
        SW = part-Samoan and part-White.
Note: Figures in boldface identify the highest in each column.
Sources: Brannon (2004); Boylan (2008a)

A more subtle examination of ethnic voting can be discerned in non-partisan elections for Honolulu mayor in polls conducted during 2004 and 2008 (Table 8.12). In 2004, Caucasian Duke Bainum initially led in all ethnic groups but Native Hawaiians, but part-Samoan "Mufi" Hannemann won by stressing his roots as a local-born Polynesian. When he ran for reelection, Hannemann gained support from all groups. The underfinanced Japanese candidate, Ann Kobayashi, failed to attract a majority in 2008 from her own ethnic group to defeat him.

In sum, ethnic bloc voting in Hawai'i is best explained as a situation in which the two largest groups, Caucasians and Japanese, have respectively sewed up control of the Democratic and Republican parties. The presumption that some ethnic groups vote together has long enabled campaign strategists to perceive each group as a building block from which they add other ethnic groups to form a coalition of at least 50.1 percent of the voters (Haas 1992:Ch. 4). But that pattern is changing.

In a recent interview, Representative Roy Takumi agreed that ethnicity "is a huge factor in campaigning. It's never blatant. When you're running, you try to appeal to everybody. But your ethnicity is your base." Once in office, pressures come from all groups. Once a politician is elected, according to Takumi, "there's none of this talk about ethnicity. There's a lot of talk about local identity." Now in his eighth term in the legislature, Takumi distinguishes between ethnicity's role in campaigning and in policy making:

When you're running, ethnic voting is alive and well. For example, in elections for the Board of Education, where you don't know anything about the candidates, you often make your choices on the basis of ethnicity.

Once in office, policy making is done on the basis of class, not ethnicity, according to former governor Ben Cayetano (2009).

CANDIDATE CHARACTERISTICS AND OTHER POST-ETHNIC INFLUENCES

Cultural and ethnic interpretations of Hawai'i elections may square with the popular understanding in the Islands, but other factors loom much larger than before, in part because approximately half the population born over the past decades is of mixed ethnic ancestry. When Waihe'e and Cayetano were in office, politics appeared to have become post-ethnic, as the two major ethnic groups (Caucasian and Japanese) no longer visibly held onto power. The earlier judgment that "blood runs thick" in Hawai'i elections (Boylan 1992) was no longer true, at least in the major political contests.

Answers to questions in sample surveys that correlate ethnic background of voters with ethnicity of candidates may be misleading. Party orientation in Hawai'i has been predominant in presidential elections. In local elections, however, personal attributes perceived by voters about candidates, such as whether those running for office observe the principles of the multicultural ethos of the Islands, may have been more important influences on voting than either ethnicity or party preferences.

On the Mainland, the focus on divisive ethnic politics has long been a major reason why politicians have been able to steer clear of class politics in local and national elections (Key 1949). Meanwhile, Japanese in Hawai'i benefited economically after the 1954 Democratic landslide, advancing into middle-class status (see Chapter 10). Rather than moving into the Republican Party, as might be expected of successful ethnic groups on the Mainland, Japanese remained loyal to the Democrats and gracefully passed the mantle in the 1980s to a Native Hawaiian and a Filipino rather than infiltrating a Haole-dominated Republican Party that showed little sign of becoming truly multiethnic until the close election of 1998. Meanwhile, Democratic Party leaders became more conservative, that is, so entrenched that their policies supported the status quo.

Few understand the dynamics of Hawai'i's ethnic politics better than attorney Andy Winer, who has served as campaign manager in three recent elections. According to Winer,

[A] political consultant has to have the right ear for the cultural filters.
Those are more important than individual ethnic group voting. Ethnic voting still plays an important role in Hawaii politics, but there's
not the ethnic crusade you saw in the 1960s or 1970s. There are ves-
tiges of it, but it's more bloc voting by up-bringing and culture.

Winer goes on to report, "AJAs [Americans of Japanese ancestry] are no
longer monolithic. . . . You can tease out the threads that tie together the
65-plus and 45–65 year-olds. But the younger ones are more difficult."
    Honolulu Star-Advertiser political writer Richard Borreca, who was
also interviewed for this chapter, concurs with Winer:

The AJA vote isn't as strong as it used to be. . . . Japanese-American
enclaves like Mānoa Valley have become leisure worlds of older
Japanese. And their vote isn't always about ethnicity; it's about
culture. If a candidate is not a Japanese American, they have to
demonstrate Japanese cultural values or achieve them. Japanese
value loyalty, education, responsibility to the group. If a candidate's
qualities resonate with the values of the group, Japanese will tend
to vote for him. That works for other groups as well. If a candidate
is forthright, speaks his mind, and not afraid of a fight, he's likely to
appeal to Caucasians. And today, Caucasians make up the biggest
ethnic voting bloc in the state.

    Back in 1980, in an effort to cultivate a successor, Ariyoshi supported
the candidacy of his Director of Finance, Eileen Anderson (no relation
to Andy), for mayor of Honolulu over Fasi. After winning, rather than
returning the favor by working closely with the Ariyoshi administration, she operated independently. In 1982, Ariyoshi's running mate
was instead Native Hawaiian John Waiheʻe. In 1984, when she sought
reelection, Ariyoshi's support was absent, and Fasi returned to City Hall.
Anderson's future was doomed by a failure to show loyalty.
    Loyalty and respect for elders was a factor, according to Winer, in
a campaign during 2006, when two-term Congressman Ed Case challenged incumbent Dan Akaka's bid for a third term in the U.S. Senate.
Case, a bright, articulate attorney, is some 30 years Akaka's junior. On
the heels of a *Time* magazine article that named Akaka one of the five
worst members of the United States Senate, a poll showed Case beating
Akaka and a weakness among Japanese American voters. According to
Winer in the same interview,

Case started advertising a quotation from Governor Ariyoshi's memoir about its being time for the next generation to take over. . . . Ariyoshi became really angry that Case didn't ask him for his permission to use the quote. He called a press conference and laid into Ed for being disrespectful and dishonorable. Here was an older Japanese man calling out a Caucasian candidate for being disrespectful. Akaka's numbers among AJAs shot up during the next two weeks.

Case was born in Hawai'i, but voters believed that he failed to show proper respect for his elders (kūpuna, in the Hawaiian language). Case's challenge constituted, according to Winer, "an affront to local rules."

At the same time, in order to win the tight Democratic primary for Akaka in 2006, Native Hawaiians had to come out to vote for their native son. Winer admits:

We targeted ethnically. . . . We identified 55,000 Hawaiians. Over the previous two election cycles, they had four opportunities to vote. We isolated the names of 26,000 who had voted only one or two times. Each of those Hawaiian voters received seven pieces of mail before primary election day, six or seven telephone calls, and two or three offers of a ride to the polls on Election Day. Akaka won by 17,000 votes. You could argue that they were all to be found in our targeting of Hawaiians.

There is a tendency for Hawai'i voters to support candidates who show humility by working their way up the ladder rather than those who appear as upstarts (White 2009). Cayetano, for example, began in the State House, then ran for the State Senate, next for Lieutenant Governor, and finally for Governor. Case lost against Akaka because voters, unable to find a reason to vote against Akaka, remained loyal supporters of the incumbent.

Running an overtly negative campaign to tarnish a candidate's reputation can backfire, as challengers to Senator Inouye found out in 1992, when allegations about an extramarital affair were touted by an unsuccessful Republican opponent. Nevertheless, covert smears are more likely to pick on Caucasians as not "locals," that is, not born in the Islands.

A test of loyalty occurred in the caucuses to choose delegates to the Democratic National Convention in 2008, when Winer managed the campaign for Obama. According to Winer,

We went on-line with the Obama campaign in December 2007. . . . The Mainland people asked us what issues were important for Hawaiʻi. We told them to forget it. That's too complicated. The only thing that was important in a Barack Obama–Hillary Clinton contest for Hawaiʻi's delegates to the Democratic National Convention is that he's from here, and she isn't. Although Clinton enjoyed the endorsement of Hawaiʻi's most respected Democratic politician, Senator Daniel K. Inouye, the Hawaiʻi-born Obama swamped her at the Party's February precinct caucuses. Voters of every ethnic, racial, and cultural background lined up in school cafeterias around the state to vote, and they voted overwhelmingly for the keiki o ka ʻāina (child of the land) in the race. Obama received 75 percent of the caucus votes to Clinton's 25 percent. In the general election we didn't have to do anything. . . . After winning the nomination, Obama came out to Hawaiʻi for a vacation. He went body-surfing at Sandy Beach, said he was going to buy a plate lunch at Rainbow Drive-in. That's all it took. The national campaign offered to send some celebrities to speak on his behalf, but we had his sister Maya (a local private school teacher) and raised money to send to the national campaign.

"Local counts in Hawaiʻi politics as well as ethnicity," says Winer. In the current state legislature, only 17 of the 76 members of the House and Senate are not locally born, though more than half of the state's population was born elsewhere.

Those of mixed-race ancestry often prefer to identify themselves as "local," a cultural concept. Ben Cayetano, similar to all other politicians in Hawaiʻi, never had a "Filipinos for Ben" organization. As he described his life growing up:

Asato, Ching, Hayashida, Koda, Mau, Okuda. Pratt, Tavata and Steinhoff—those were the last names of my close childhood pals. . . . [I]f asked about our ethnicity, we would answer: "Chinese, Filipino, Japanese, Hawaiian-Chinese," whichever the case may have been, but we were different from our Mainland counterparts. Indeed, it would have been more accurate to describe us all as "local," rather than by our ethnicity, for we were born and raised in Hawaiʻi, spoke Pidgin, loved local food, and had a greater affinity for the Hawaiian culture . . . than for the ethnic culture of our grandparents' homelands, about which most of us knew little or nothing. (Cayetano 2009:9)

Cayetano's 28-year political career is a refutation of ethnicity as political destiny. Filipinos are notorious for forgetting to vote on either primary or general Election Day. Yet he won every election in which he ever ran. In his first campaign for public office, Cayetano ignored the wisest political counsel, when political veterans told him he should run in a working-class and heavily Filipino district of Honolulu (Kalihi). Cayetano chose instead to stand for election in a multimember Pearl City district for the State House in which Japanese Americans names dominated the voter rolls. With law degree in hand and an attractive young family campaigning beside him, he won one of the two seats available, placing second behind an equally attractive young Japanese American candidate.

Two years later, in his reelection bid, Cayetano got the most votes. In 1978, Cayetano sought a seat in the State Senate. Again, he led the Democratic ticket, finishing ahead of two Japanese Americans and two Chinese Americans. In his campaign for lieutenant governor in 1986, he stressed his local roots by calling out an immigrant Filipina for questioning the competence of Japanese American school personnel, became the lieutenant governor candidate, and won as the running mate of John Waihe'e.

In 1994, on the advice of storied Hawai'i political consultant Jack Seigle, Cayetano ran for governor. Again, the analysis was ethnic. "I think the time is right," Cayetano (2009:326) quotes Seigle as saying:

> You've won every one of your past elections because you've been able to get good support from the different ethnic groups. In fact, you're one of the few [Filipino-American politicians] who've been able to get strong AJA [Americans of Japanese ancestry] support. That vote along with the Filipino vote will give you a good shot at winning the Democratic primary. Frankly, I think you should go for it. I don't think things will get any better for you.

And he easily won the Democratic primary. In the general election, he defeated Honolulu Mayor Frank Fasi (running as an independent) and former Congresswoman Pat Saiki (running as a Republican). But he won the three-way race with only 35.8 percent of the vote.

"Local" identity attracts longtime residents of Hawai'i to vote against more recent arrivals and vice versa (Oi 2010). In 1986, for example, Waihe'e bested Cec Heftel in a classic kama'āina (local) versus malihini (newcomer) contest.

Similarly, in the race for Mayor of Honolulu in 2004, "Mufi" Hannemann was opposed by Duke Bainum, both members of the City Council. A native of Arkansas, Bainum brought his education as a physician and great family wealth to Hawai'i. He started as a legislative intern, was elected to the State House and the Honolulu City Council, and then announced for mayor. As a Caucasian, Bainum came from the largest ethnic group in the state. On the other hand, Harvard-educated Hannemann's father is German and his mother is Samoan, the latter group numbering about 20,000 (Table 1.2), of whom two-thirds are from American Samoa, and the rest work in Hawai'i on green cards because they are from the independent nation often known as Western Samoa. American Samoans are American nationals, but few have become American citizens and thus cannot vote. So, in essence, Hannemann had no ethnic base, but he advertised himself as a "proud Polynesian." By 2004, Hannemann had been running for office since the mid-1980s—twice without success for Congress, successfully for the city council, and unsuccessfully for mayor. He also held a cabinet-level state job in two Democratic administrations. Bainum had money and ethnicity on his side in 2004—conceivably enough to win the election. But he was not local, and the electorate was reminded of that every time he opened his mouth, as he talked with a pronounced Southern twang. Hannemann beat him by 1,000 votes. Local identity trumped both money and ethnicity.

In 2010, Neil Abercrombie ran for governor against Mufi Hannemann in the Democratic primary. Abercrombie, who served in Hawai'i's Congressional delegation from 1991, was born outside the Islands. Hannemann, however, appeared to be supported by Senator Dan Inouye. Those born in Hawai'i want to keep the Islands multicultural, and a Samoan governor would carry on the tradition of rewarding all ethnic groups with high political office. Although early polls showed that Abercrombie's solid support was with Caucasians, whereas Hannemann got the non-White "local" vote (Borreca 2010a), Abercrombie won by a nearly 2:1 landslide after Inouye criticized Hannemann for playing the race card in his campaign (Sonmez 2010) and was elected governor.

Ed Case, meanwhile, ran for the Congressional seat vacated by Abercrombie in a special nonpartisan election during May 2010 against Senate President Colleen Hanabusa. Case was supported by Cayetano, who was annoyed by Hanabusa's support for special interests while governor (Cayetano 2009:517). But Akaka and Inouye endorsed Hanabusa, as Case had run against incumbent Akaka for Senator in 2006. Although

Hanabusa got more votes than Case, they split the vote and trailed Republican Charles Djou, who won with less than half of the vote. Born in Hawai'i, Djou's father is Chinese, his mother is Thai, and his wife is Japanese. Case then withdrew from the Democratic primary for the November 2010 election, when Hanabusa defeated Djou.

Aside from loyalty and local roots, campaign financing also plays an important role. In 1988, for example, when 39 percent of the incumbents in the state legislature ran unopposed, most had formidable campaign war chests to deter challengers (Boylan 1992:78).

ISSUE ORIENTATION

Are Hawai'i voters issue-oriented? Definitely. Voters in the election of 1900 wanted to reverse the declining role of Native Hawaiians. From 1902 to 1950, the Haole-Native Hawaiian coalition was forged by per-suading Native Hawaiians that their best interest to land government contracts and jobs was to go along with Republican Party leaders, and that the national Democratic Party supported racial segregation and was openly racist.

After the victory of the Democratic Party in 1954, some Democratic Party leaders used their position to create wealth for their friends or themselves—for example, by buying agricultural property, having the government rezone the land for housing, and then selling the property to real estate developers at extraordinary profits (Cooper and Daws 1985). Many Democratic Party candidates made sure that government contrac-tors contributed to the party coffers in order to finance election cam-paigns and otherwise cozied up to local business interests.

Filipinos, Native Hawaiians, and smaller ethnic groups once thought that the Democratic Party was their best hope for social advancement. The elections of Waihe'e and Cayetano kept those groups inside the Dem-ocratic coalition, but their socioeconomic status has barely improved since statehood (see Chapter 10).

In 1998, Democratic voters began to switch to the Republican Party candidate for governor, Linda Lingle, in the hope that she could revive the health of the economy. But she could not. Nevertheless, with the com-position of the winning ethnic coalition in Hawai'i reshuffled because Republicans have gained ground, the future is more unpredictable than ever before. In 2010, the Democratic Party's biggest split on issues was on civil unions for gays and lesbians (Borreca 2010b).

CONCLUSION

Here is how Barack Obama announced his candidacy for president at Springfield, Illinois, on February 10, 2007:

In the face of a politics that's shut you out, that's told you to settle, that's divided us for too long, you believe that we can be one people, reaching for what's possible, building that more perfect union.

Obama was commenting on the Republican strategy of appealing to less-affluent Whites who prioritize social issues over economic issues and then blame "tax-and-spend" Democrats for their economic woes. His candidacy attracted the less affluent. His description fit the coalition building in which candidates of every major ethnic group in Hawai'i have been elected on the basis of multiethnic support.

There has never been a backlash to the construction of winning ethnic coalitions in Hawai'i. Politicians have learned not to tread on the toes of any ethnic group too openly. Through electoral politics, the politicians and voters have interculturally learned from one another. In fact, one faction of the Democrats once achieved a majority to organize one house of the legislature by offering some Republicans to head committees, and they accepted. Because one political party overwhelmed the other from the 1950s to the 1990s, there was little cause to engage in partisan bickering until 1998, when some Republicans decided to latch onto divisive religious fundamentalist sentiments during the second gubernatorial election campaign of Ben Cayetano (2009:143). That nasty current, however, has not become a torrent in Hawai'i.

Barack Obama should be understood as a politician who would easily fit into Hawai'i politics as a leader with special sensitivity to Native Hawaiian, Japanese, and other local cultures. But what would have made him ordinary in Island politics made him special in national politics.

Chapter 9

The Strength of Organized Labor

Edward D. Beechert

> *[M]embers of every minority group continue to be mea-
> sured largely by the degree of our assimilation—how closely
> speech patterns, dress, or demeanor conform to the dominant
> [W]hite culture—and . . . impact on the often snap decisions
> of who's hired and who's promoted.*
>
> (Obama 2008:279)

One of the best ways to trace the progress of race relations in Hawai'i
over the years is to focus on how laborers have been treated and how
they have reacted. The story begins with exploitation on the sugarcane
plantations and ends democratically with laborers controlling political
power and setting terms for management. Through the window of organized labor can be seen the rise of the multicultural ethos that binds the
people of Hawai'i together today and the way in which young Barack
Obama has viewed labor-management relations.

When Obama was growing up in the transformative 1970s, he was
affected by the most important legacy of that struggle—the importance
of the working class and its union organizers in shaping the political
agenda of the Islands. To appreciate the inclusiveness of class-based politics in Hawai'i, one must reflect on the history of the Islands. An understanding of President Obama requires an appreciation of that struggle.

THE PLANTATION SYSTEM

Sugar plantations have traditionally used coercive labor systems, ranging from the mildest form of indentured labor in Hawai'i to slavery in the United States and Latin America. The range of repression has varied according to location and historical circumstance (Lal, Munro, and Beechert 1993; Tinker 1974). The gap between Cuba's extreme chattel slavery and the Solomon Islands' savage indentured labor and Hawai'i's indentured labor system was very wide.

Native Hawaiian people were caught up in a violent political and dynastic struggle when Captain James Cook arrived in 1778. Western military tactics and weapons were injected into what had been a traditional conflict. The new weapons were purchased with drafts of labor and goods produced by the commoners. Under normal conditions, the people could have produced easily for their own subsistence (Beechert 1985:10–11; Kamakau 1976:34), but now they began to sell their labor.

Cook's arrival also brought about an increasing number of ships calling at Hawai'i ports. The new demand for supplies for foreign visitors further converted the commoner into a laborer status rather than sticking to traditional agriculture. Production was no longer for the mutual support of the community and ruling class, but was now for the power and prestige of the chieftain (ali'i) class (Sahlins 1958:1,412).

The ali'i sought symbols of prestige and power—weapons, Western clothing, furniture, and jewelry. As the Islands became a winter rendezvous for ships trading and fishing the Pacific, the Native Hawaiian population was decimated by famines induced by the diversion of commoner labor from agriculture and the arrival of European diseases.

Two further steps were needed to convert Native Hawaiian commoners to the status of wage laborers. First, taxes payable in cash were levied. Then, in 1848, some land held in common by the king was converted to fee-simple holding. But privatization of land resources did not consider water and access rights and thus left the commoner with small plots of useless land in most cases (Kelly 1956:131). As a result, Native Hawaiians had to resort to wage labor to meet the head taxes imposed.

The reluctance of Native Hawaiians to work for low wages or under intolerable conditions soon made clear the necessity of imported labor to put vast tracts of unoccupied land to profitable use. Importation of Chinese, which began in 1852, trailed off as the sugar boom of the 1850s faded (Table 2.1). When the American Civil War closed off sugar production in the South, prospects for sugar from Hawai'i to penetrate

Mainland markets in the North loomed. The reciprocity Treaty between Hawai'i and the United States allowed Hawaiian sugar into the American market duty-free. Given the protective tariff on imported sugar from other parts of the world, the treaty provided a bonus profit of two cents per pound to Hawaiian growers (19 U.S. Statutes at Large:200; Kuykendall 1967:III Ch. 2).

Plantation acreage then increased rapidly, as did the numbers of imported Chinese workers. Anti-Chinese sentiments in Hawai'i prompted the search for other labor sources. Portuguese from the Azores and Madeira, and small numbers of other European workers were recruited, and in 1885 plantation workers began to come from Japan (Table 2.1). In part because Native Hawaiian authorities tried to limit the power of the planters to recruit more Chinese, the planters used the threat of armed insurrection to force a new constitution in 1887 on the king and the legislature. The new "Bayonet Constitution" greatly limited the power of the king.

When Congress passed the McKinley Tariff of 1891, the subsidy of the Reciprocity Treaty ended. Hawai'i suffered a severe depression, and the importance of becoming a part of the United States was abundantly clear. The uncertainty of labor supplies meant the threat of higher wages and some restriction of production. The loss of the subsidy was unacceptable to the growers, as were plans of Queen Lili'uokalai to draw up a new constitution more favorable to her people (Taylor 1935:68).

In 1893, the monarchy was overthrown by what amounted to a joint conspiracy between the sugar planters and members of the U.S. military. Ruling by executive committee decree, the new Republic of Hawai'i quickly reduced labor indenture to a condition of servitude, restricting imported workers to plantation work on threat of deportation. The importation of Chinese workers was accelerated. Given the high rate at which imported indentured workers left the plantations for the cities, sugar planters faced a continual shortage of labor, resulting in a competition for labor and higher wages than they wanted to pay. Despite draconian efforts of the Republic of Hawai'i to impose strict controls on labor, however, slightly more than half the plantation workforce consisted of free day workers.

ANNEXATION

In 1898, Congress declared that Hawai'i was annexed by the United States. Under the Organic Act of 1900, establishing the Territory of

Hawai'i, the American Constitution and Congressional law opened the possibility of labor organization with some protection of civil rights. The careful control that the planters managed to exert was severely challenged by more permissive federal law. Accordingly, the struggle to control the job site was fought vigorously from 1900, when Japanese went on strike on almost every plantation, albeit without much immediate success.

The O'ahu strike of Japanese workers in 1909 was also nominally unsuccessful, when measured in the traditional way, because their union was not recognized, no bargaining took place, and demands were not met. The leaders were prosecuted under a variety of charges and jailed. However, the strike for the first time inflicted considerable damage on sugar production. In response to the strike, planters changed the discriminatory wage structure and improved social and living conditions. Japanese strikers won the sympathetic support of the fledgling Honolulu Central Labor Council, which was an important step toward cross-ethnic unity (Beechert 1985:174–176). The social demands of the workers outnumbered the economic demands, since the growing number of married Japanese workers created a pressing need for better housing, roads, and schools. Above all, the workers proved that they could organize, formulate demands, and take action, demonstrating skills and power that surprised plantation owners.

One outcome of the 1909 strike was a renewed search for new labor supplies to marginalize Japanese. Recruitment from Puerto Rico, the scene of the first effort, was grossly mismanaged. The pacification of the Philippines opened the door to a new possibility.

Spurred by the strike of 1909, planters began to import Filipino workers. By 1920, Filipinos formed a significant portion of the workforce. When the Federation of Japanese Labor presented demands for higher wages and improved living conditions, the Filipinos joined, forming a somewhat impromptu Filipino Labor Union, and they were supported by housing and rations from the Federation of Japanese Labor (Beechert 1985:196–215).

Unified multiethnic labor cooperation confirmed the worst fears of the planters. The strike of 1920 created a wave of hysteria in the Honolulu press and the Hawaiian Sugar Planters' Association (HSPA), which portrayed the Japanese as conspiratorial, degraded, evil, and stupid, and denounced their leaders as gangsters preying on otherwise docile workers. The Filipinos were largely portrayed as primitives with little understanding. The thoroughly frightened establishment resorted to repressive labor legislation, including a criminal syndicalism statute modeled on Mainland laws, but otherwise improved social conditions (Beechert 1985:206; 1988).

The Filipino sugar strike of 1924, the most massive and lengthy strike in Hawai'i up to that point, put an end to such ideas. Over a period of eight months, though ill planned and conducted, Filipino workers struck 23 of the 45. Particularly disturbing to the plantation owners in the 1924 strike was evidence of considerable economic support from the non-striking Japanese community in the form of money and food supplies. Industry efforts to step up labor scabs from the Philippines and vigorously prosecute strikers and strike leaders did nothing but prolong the strike. Non-struck plantations were discovered to have greater losses in production due to the steady diversion over nine months of new labor supplies and the steady out-migration of Filipinos from the sugar industry.

Native Hawaiian plantation workers, from 1853 forward, suffered no restrictions on their movements in and out of plantation work. Such agricultural areas as cattle raising, coffee farming, dairying, independent cane planting, and pineapple cultivation offered an alternative to sugar plantation work. Accordingly, some Filipinos took advantage.

Because many Filipino workers left for the Mainland, the planters tried to restrict their out-migration. Although noncitizens, Filipinos were American subjects, needing no visa to leave Hawai'i for the Mainland. Rising opposition to this immigration resulted in Congressional efforts to keep out Filipinos, a goal that was reached by the Philippine Independence Act of 1934, which cut off Filipino emigration to the United States while promising the Philippines independence by 1944. As a result, the plantations could only import citizen labor—a condition impossible for any plantation economy (Benn 1974; Thompson 1975:115).

In 1926, the HSPA contracted a massive study of the sugar industry. The resulting report cited serious inefficiencies in both mill and field operations and noted the contradiction between the welfare-community programs and day-to-day operation of the plantations. The recommendation for improvement in managerial personnel was particularly strong, as field foremen were held to be responsible for many of the difficulties in production efficiency (HSPA 1926:I iv–v). The basic recommendations, too radical for the industry, were rejected. Improvements in medical care and housing were instituted, however, and efforts to mechanize the more difficult tasks increased. Then came the Great Depression.

THE BEGINNING OF TRADE UNION ORGANIZING

From 1911, craft unions were established at Pearl Harbor, where construction began at the naval base. Traditionally, the American Federation of Labor (AFL) excluded Asians from membership and, due to federal requirements, also barred noncitizens. Shortly after annexation, Honolulu had a Central Labor Council, made up entirely of AFL craft unions. Although the national construction unions barred Asians from membership, Carpenters Local 745 began admitting Chinese as early as 1906. Such names as "Young" appeared to the parent organization as Caucasian, but they were likely to have been Chinese, Chinese-Hawaiians, or Korean. The first explicitly Chinese name appears on the membership roles in 1919, followed by a Japanese name in 1920, along with eight Native Hawaiians, six Portuguese, and one Chinese (Beechert 1993:16–17). These admissions defied an order from the International Brotherhood of Carpenters and Joiners and AFL President Samuel Gompers to exclude such members.

The dockworkers of Hilo and Honolulu joined the International Longshoremen's Union (ILU) as early as 1911. Despite ILU anti-Asian resolutions of 1912, they asked for permission to admit Japanese workers in order to prevent the plantations from using them as strikebreakers. ILU delegate Moses Keohokalole succeeded in gaining permission to admit Japanese members, with the proviso that they would be denied transfer-membership into Mainland locals (ILA 1912:73). Following a strike by dockworkers in Honolulu during 1916, the ILU local demanded the rehiring of several Japanese dock foremen who had earlier been fired for sympathy toward the strikers.

A significant if temporary step toward racial unity occurred when George Wright, who chaired the Central Labor Council, worked actively to support the Filipino and Japanese sugar strikers in 1920. Following that strike, he formed the Hawai'i Workers Union in 1921, dedicated to the inclusion of all workers, in a "rank and file" union (Beechert 1985:212–214; cf. Reinecke 1979:318–319).

During the rest of the 1920s, Hawai'i experienced savage anti-labor legislation. What remained of the early organizing efforts was a spirit of racial unity. What was lacking was any formal organization to implement that unity. In 1929, according to the U.S. Commissioner of Labor, there were no union contracts in force within Hawai'i.

During the 1930s, the administration of President Franklin Delano Roosevelt brought a new power to Hawai'i—federal regulation of local economic affairs. The subsidy arrangements for sugar, the Agricultural

Adjustment Act, the National Labor Relations Act, and the Social Security Act, all of which came in 1935, transformed the economy of Hawai'i along with industrial relations. Although the conventional wisdom of sugar industry lawyers was that the laws would be declared unconstitutional, the sugar industry had to comply in order to receive a subsidy. The Fair Labor Standards Act of 1938 also imposed minimum wage standards. Hearings to enforce compliance soon brought about major changes.

Dockworkers in Hilo and Honolulu were again in the vanguard of organizing. Harry Kamoku went to Hilo, determined to organize his fellow workers along the lines of the San Francisco dockworkers, but Hawai'i locals were only recognized after formation of the International Longshoremen's and Warehousemen's Union (ILWU) in 1936. ILWU leader Jack Hall (1968) describes the racial situation in Hawai'i during the 1930s in the following terms:

> In the past, Hawaii's power structure has dealt as badly with minorities as the [W]hite power structure in Alabama, Mississippi or Chicago. It was not until the minorities themselves did something about their situation that this was changed and we have finally ended up today where there is no serious discrimination based on race per se either economically, politically or socially—where Hawaii's minorities are now hailed as the "golden people." . . . It was not always so.

Plantation organizing began in 1937, when the United Cannery, Agricultural, Processing, and Allied Workers of America issued a charter for organizing on Kaua'i. At the first National Labor Relations Board hearing in Hawai'i during 1937, the ILWU local in Honolulu successfully proved unfair labor practice charges against a subsidiary of one of the sugar conglomerates (NLRB 1937, Region 12, Case XX-C-55:3). ILWU's Jack Hall made sophisticated use of the new federal legislation by adding a new element to Island politics when he successfully organized political action and ousted two leading planter-politicians from the Territorial Senate in 1938 and 1940. In 1940, a contract was successfully negotiated with Kaua'i Pineapple Company.

In 1938, the Roosevelt administration undertook a major expansion of Pearl Harbor. As a result, the Pacific Contractors' Consortium brought Mainland construction workers with their union contracts and wages to Hawai'i.

During World War II, when Hawai'i was under military rule, chainstore and other commercial interests brought Mainland construction practices and wage scales to the Islands, effectively breaking the long-standing monopoly on the retail sector of the economy by the main Haole-dominated companies. The military had no interest in maintaining the local commercial power structure.

Most important of all was the arrival of effective organizing of the agricultural economy under the leadership of the ILWU, which recognized the importance of bringing all ethnic groups into the union. After the lifting of military rule over Hawai'i in 1944, the ILWU International Executive Board, pushed by insistent demands of Hawai'i dockworkers, set up a Hawai'i division under the leadership of Jack Hall as division director and Frank Thompson as field organizer. The ILWU achieved overwhelming victories during 1945 and 1946, winning union recognition elections at all plantations but one small company on Kaua'i (Beechert 1985:289–310).

In September 1946, some 28,000 workers went on strike at 33 of the 34 plantations and held out for 79 days. After the planters hastily imported 6,000 Filipino workers as potential scabs to counter the impending strike (U.S. Department of Labor 1948:51–55), they all joined the union as willing strikers (Beechert 1985:299). The 1946 strike resulted in a uniform contract for the sugar industry and uniform job classifications. More importantly, the union was recognized as the bargaining agent for all workers in the sugar industry. The unity of the workforce was an impressive demonstration of the union's effort to eliminate ethnic rivalries that had plagued some earlier strikes.

The urban unions, primarily in construction and the tourist industries, also made progress toward ethnic unity. In 1944, Art Rutledge of the Hotel Employees and Restaurant Employees union (HERE) defied the president of the Hotel Workers' International, who objected to his placing Japanese Americans in culinary jobs (Stern 1986:15).

Spurred by activities after World War II on the plantations, road workers in Hilo wanted to organize, so the AFL in Honolulu sent Don Owens. The road workers were tired of the old system of being at the disposal of county politicians, that is, hired before elections and laid off after the election. They refused the AFL, wanting to join their plantation friends. The ILWU turned down their request, pointing out that there was a Congress of Industrial Organizations (CIO) government employees union, which they promptly contacted. Henry Epstein of the CIO's State, County, and Municipal Workers of America then arrived in Hawai'i on May 2, 1947, with a charter for Local 646, which later became the United Public Workers of Hawai'i (UPW). From that beginning, Epstein (1975) went on to organize hospital workers, refuse collectors, custodial people, prison guards, and private hospital workers, becoming basically a blue-collar union with a good mixture of the Hawai'i population.

The climax of labor organizing came in 1958 in the so-called "Aloha Strike," for which the ILWU won improvements to the pension plan and generous severance pay for workers displaced by advancing mechanization. The union's presence was never again seriously contested by management. The strike was in many ways the culmination of union strength and maturity. The ILWU doctrine of racial equality then quickly spread to other sectors of the community.

END OF THE AGRICULTURE-BASED ECONOMY

In the 1960s, sugar and pineapple employment declined due to mechanization of the work processes. Thousands of workers were pushed into urban and public-sector employment. In addition, Hawai'i agriculture lost comparative economic advantage to tropical countries, and there was pressure on land for development and tourism. Barry Obama was present during the most sweeping economic transformation of the Islands since the arrival of Captain Cook.

The ILWU began a serious effort to organize the service sector, primarily the tourist industry. Rutledge's HERE continued to organize workers. But, citing preferences of Mainland visitors, hotels had long confined Filipino and Japanese workers to "back-of-the-house" positions. Both HERE and the ILWU emphasized the importance of ending the crude, racist practices of the tourist industry, but by 1970 HERE and the ILWU were able to organize only the larger hotels (Reinecke 1970:25–26; Stern 1988).

If the tourism-service sector economy was the "new plantation" for workers, public employment became a second major source of employment in Hawai'i. Following the lead of Epstein's UPW, a state law in 1970 permitted the organization of public employees, creating overnight a major labor union sector. Two unions now dominate this field—the Hawai'i Government Employees Association (HGEA) and UPW. Both are affiliated with the American Federation of State, County, and Municipal Employees (AFSCME). In addition, public schoolteachers were organized into the Hawai'i State Teachers Association (HSTA), and University of Hawai'i faculty members formed the University of Hawai'i

Professional Assembly (UHPA). Both HSTA and UHPA have organized strikes over the years but are not linked to national labor organizations, as members have voted down AFL affiliation.

HGEA was originally a traditional government employees association, specializing in insurance, political lobbying, and travel. As reorganized in 1970, HGEA now dominates the clerical sector of public employment.

Important changes also came in the construction unions. Under the leadership of Walter Kupau, the Carpenters Union Local 745 initiated far-reaching programs of change, including a community service program to bring families closer to the union. An effective apprenticeship program took advantage of the construction boom of the 1970s. The labor-management Joint Training Program enrolled more than 1,000 students through the University of Hawai'i community colleges. In 1987, a special effort in the program was made to reach out to women and minorities (Beechert 1993:74–75).

Both the HGEA and UPW engage heavily in political lobbying, since bargaining is largely a matter of convincing legislators and the governor to make desired concessions. For two decades, bargaining seemed always to result in higher wages, improved benefits, and liberalized work rules. The union's insistence on including a statement of nondiscrimination in all contracts, though fiercely resisted by employers, was generally accepted by the public.

Unions further cemented their public approval in 1974, when they secured passage of the Prepaid Health Care Act, which required all employers to provide health insurance for their full-time employees, the only state ever to do so. When Obama was barely 13 years old, the unions brought about a universal health care insurance plan in the Islands that served as a model for the rest of the country after he was elected president.

THE FUTURE OF THE LABOR MOVEMENT

From the 1990s, the pattern has been sharply reversed. The end of the Vietnam War in 1975 and the end of the Cold War in 1989 had their toll, reducing the role of military spending in the Islands. A massive state budget deficit and falling tax revenues of local governments resulted in major layoffs in 1995 (*Honolulu Advertiser* 1996). The worldwide recession of 2009 has also put Hawai'i's economic plans in a shambles. The decline in tourism and the corresponding decline in employment resulted in a sharp decline in state tax revenue and talk of furloughs, layoffs, and salary reductions.

One is tempted to use the popular phrase "back to the future" in describing the present. The tourist industry, particularly large hotels, has come to rely heavily on part-time labor, frequently made up of Mainland Caucasians who finance short-term vacation visits with work in hotels and restaurants, and thus tend to regard the unions as unimportant. Local residents regard the transients' attitudes as hindering their achievement of reasonable working conditions.

Resentment among some ethnic groups threatens the outwardly calm labor and social situation. Filipinos resent the domination in the unionized state civil service by Japanese Americans. Other minorities, such as Samoans, lack opportunities for advancement. In recent years, the Native Hawaiian nationalist movement has gained impressive strength. Underlying demands for sovereignty is the fact that many have been systematically shut out of adequate housing, denied access to land, and shunted into low-paying occupations. Although Native Hawaiians have raised public consciousness about their plight, resolution of their demands has been frustrated by fiscal crises.

Construction, public and private, and the continuous expansion of the tourist trade are no longer viable means for sustaining employment. Faced with economic and political obstacles to organizing, labor now confronts the rising demands of ethnic groups left behind. The observations of Jack Hall of the ILWU in 1968 remain a valid observation of the situation today:

> It is important to realize that the Aloha Spirit grew out of struggles to eliminate injustice. New forms of injustice, which are present in Hawaii today, can destroy it if they are not remedied. Even today certain deprived groups among us tend to fall into racial categories. . . . The Aloha Spirit will flourish to the extent that all elements of our community are able to participate in the good things of life. (Hall 1968:5–6)

Clearly, political tensions in Hawai'i are growing as the global economy worsens. The tourist industry is particularly vulnerable to economic downturns. A mistaken belief is that tourists will flock to Hawai'i if only there were more advertising, a "solution" that implies that "those who lack the means for an Hawaiian vacation might be persuaded to come to Hawai'i to spend money they don't have for a vacation they can't afford" (Stern 1988:124).

A wide-ranging survey of the challenges facing Hawai'i today presents a very mixed bag of conclusions. One of the more perceptive analyses concludes:

> The crucial point is to recognize the existence of some positive ethnic and racial patterns; the persistence of some long-standing negative ones; the threats imposed by new developments; and, most important, the need for policy considerations to protect and enhance our ability to tolerate and respect different heritages and aspirations. (Odo and Yim 1993:229)

OBAMA AND THE LABOR MOVEMENT

Hawai'i residents were understandably elated by the election of the first hapa to the presidency of the United States. Barack Obama's election in November 2008 raised the hopes of many in the labor movement, both in Hawai'i and on the Mainland, for a better tomorrow.

When the Prepaid Health Care Act passed in 1974, employees of Bank of Hawaii and other businesses were covered by state-mandated health insurance, which was designed not just for union members but also for the middle class into which he was born. Since his grandmother worked for the bank, she was covered. Later, when his half-sister and brother-in-law were employed at the University of Hawai'i, they could become members of a public employee union, UHPA, and were covered by the same health insurance plan.

In Barry's youth, his grandfather introduced him to African American poet Frank Marshall Davis, a columnist on the radical newspaper the *Honolulu Record.* Davis took an interest in the young Black man, telling him something about being Black in America and life in multiracial Hawai'i. The formative teen years saw Barack experiencing firsthand the subtle discrimination against Blacks in Hawai'i.

Barack Obama lived in Hawai'i during a time of strong union organization and the political influence of the ILWU. He could hardly fail to note the union attitude toward the dignity of the multiracial workforce, as he was employed part-time at Baskin-Robbins in Honolulu. The union's views on race, social class, and discrimination were widely known and must surely have influenced the young Obama's views on politics and society. His grandfather's friendship with and frequent visits to Davis would have exposed Obama to the dominant ILWU views on race and society.

Hawai'i, similar to the rest of the United States, is moving toward a structure of employment ever more dominated by poorly paid jobs with little or no future. Workers are not generally happy with the rapid development of the service sector's low-wage, low-security employment. Although labor organizing and collective bargaining face massive hostility from corporations busily "downsizing," one cannot assume that history has stopped or that the basic struggle of class interests has ceased. Organized labor, for all its faults and weaknesses, is a key point around which ethnic minorities in Hawai'i can continue their struggle so long in the making. And without organized labor solidarity, rooted in intercultural cooperation and learning, the Aloha Spirit might have no steady mass-based institutional support.

To understand Hawai'i politics, one must appreciate the role of the trade unions and the way in which the White power structure was humbled by non-White plantation laborers. Barack Obama was never a member of a union, but he benefited from the inclusive way in which organized labor brought the working and middle classes together by identifying common ground and forging mutually beneficial solutions. Obama has never forgotten that lesson, one that much of the rest of the United States needs to learn.

Chapter 10

Social Structure
and Social Mobility

Michael Haas

> [T]he ambitions they [my grandparents] had carried with
> them to Hawaii had slowly drained away . . . . They would
> occasionally grumble about how the Japanese had taken over
> the islands, how the Chinese controlled island finance.
>
> (Obama 1995:57)

During his youth, Barack Obama's principal understanding of the social
structure in Hawai'i, based on what his grandparents said, was that there
was a caste system of sorts. In their view, Japanese controlled politics
and Chinese dominated economics. Although he has not commented in
depth on the role of other ethnic groups, in *Dreams from My Father* he
contrasts the status of his middle-class White family with his ultra rich
(mostly White) classmates at Punahou and the humble status of African
Americans in Hawai'i.

Accordingly, Obama's remarks raise several questions about the social
structure of the Islands. Did Chinese and Japanese, who were imported
as unskilled manual laborers in the late 19th century, rise quickly in
social standing during the 20th century—and how? Why have other
groups apparently failed to do so? Why have differences between ethnic groups and social classes failed to undermine the social fabric that
appears to support Hawai'i's multicultural ethos?

SOURCES OF SOCIAL MOBILITY

Six explanations or theories have been advanced to account for the apparent success of Chinese and Japanese, while other groups have lagged behind: (1) One possibility, according to Obama's grandparents, is that Japanese utilized *political power* to enhance social mobility for their members. (2) A second explanation, *capital accumulation*, is that over time entrepreneurial Chinese accumulated sufficient capital to set up businesses in the cities, and then Japanese did the same. (3) *Institutional racism* is a third explanation, as advantaged groups did whatever they could to perpetuate their status (Akaka 2009). Just as Whites discriminated against non-Whites before statehood, Japanese resisted affirmative action programs after statehood that would have dismantled institutional biases in governmental procedures (Haas 1992). (4) *Economic transformation* may be responsible, disfavoring social mobility. As the main sector of the economy has changed from agriculture to military spending to tourism, the newer occupational opportunities in hotels and restaurants have offered even lower pay than on the plantations. (5) *Migration longevity* may be an explanation, as an influx of less skilled and less well-educated members of certain races might dilute any incipient progress of certain ethnic groups. (6) Finally, there is a *cultural* explanation. Native Hawaiians, it is claimed, have been left behind because other groups have been more aggressive, arriving with the explicit goal of making money and then doing so.

Which explanation is correct? Can the social structure today be attributed to politics, capital accumulation, institutional racism, economic transformation, migration, or culture? The first task is to identify whether ethnic social differentiation has existed, using income and occupational data. The second task is to analyze educational opportunities, the principal route to advancement for most persons.

Inevitably, census statistics can be misleading. Different definitions are used from census to census. Census statistics have historically counted Hispanics as Caucasians, and part-Hawaiians have often been apportioned to the non-Hawaiian race of a parent, thereby arbitrarily miscategorizing offspring of interracial marriages. A further problem is that substantial members of the lower-paid military, primarily Blacks and Whites, are isolated from the local mainstream but are included in the data for Hawai'i (Table 10.1). Unfortunately, ethnic data were not a priority for the 1960 and 1970 censuses, during the years when Barry Obama was going to school in Honolulu, and therefore the press did not

Table 10.1

Persons Housed in Military Barracks in Hawai'i by Ethnic Group, 1950–2000 (in percent)

Year	Black	Caucasian	All Groups
1950	na	na	3.0%
1960	na	na	4.2
1970	27.1%	7.3%	3.2
1980	25.1	5.1	2.4
1990	15.0	3.7	1.7
2000	11.6	3.2	1.2

Key: na = Figures not available.

Note: Figures represent percentages in military barracks for each group.

Sources: Schmitt (1977:8,660); U.S. Census (1973:247; 1983:36; 1993:50; 2000:PCT17A, B, PCT1).

report or otherwise deal with the subject. His impressions about social mobility were derived from anecdotes and personal experiences.

INCOME ATTAINMENTS

Hawai'i has the highest percentage of millionaire households of the 50 states (Phoenix Marketing International 2009), but in comparing family and household income statistics by ethnicity and race, the principal pitfall is that some families are larger than others, and women have more incentive to work in support of families when their husbands have lower-paid jobs. To minimize noncomparabilities, male income is examined (Table 10.2).

Tracing median income levels over time, Chinese males were substantially above other groups before statehood and continued for a decade afterward, when they were succeeded by Japanese at the high point of their political dominance. The relative decline of Chinese is associated in part with the arrival of immigrants after passage of the Immigration Act of 1965 (Table 2.3).

Caucasian male median incomes evidently rise and fall with the size of the military population, which tends to be underpaid, as they peaked before the Korean War and after the Vietnam War, and between those years they fell below Chinese and Japanese. Koreans did slightly better than Whites in 1979 and 1999. Native Hawaiian males were nearly equal

Table 10.2

Median Income of Males in Hawai'i by Ethnic Group, 1949–1999

Ethnic Group	1949		1959		1969		1979		1989		1999	
Black	na		$1,982	(39)	$3,227	(40)	$6,879	(47)	$15,554	(61)	$29,017	(62)
Caucasian	$2,856	(98)	3,649	(73)	6,173	(77)	11,444	(78)	22,322	(87)	38,431	(82)
Chinese	2,964	(100)	5,096	(100)	8,000	(100)	13,915	(95)	22,570	(88)	43,777	(94)
Filipino	1,995	(67)	3,071	(60)	5,252	(66)	9,511	(65)	16,640	(65)	29,061	(62)
Guamanian	na		na		na		9,887	(68)	18,728	(73)	40,682	(87)
Hawaiian	2,369	(80)	na		6,835	(85)	11,054	(76)	19,030	(74)	34,801	(75)
Japanese	2,427	(82)	4,302	(84)	7,839	(98)	14,597	(100)	25,587	(100)	46,653	(100)
Korean	na		na		na		11,535	(79)	20,592	(80)	40,563	(87)
Mexican	na		na		na		7,430	(51)	17,246	(67)	26,135	(56)
Puerto Rican	na		na		na		9,038	(62)	16,728	(65)	29,806	(64)
Samoan	na		na		na		7,577	(52)	13,393	(52)	26,984	(58)
Vietnamese	na		na		na		4,798	(33)	10,265	(40)	24,969	(54)
All Groups	2,340	(79)	3,717	(73)	6,528	(82)	11,505	(79)	21,095	(82)	36,808	(79)

Key: na = Figures not available.

Notes: From 1949 to 1959, figures report median incomes of full-time male workers aged 14 and over. In 1969, figures are for males aged 16 and over except for Blacks and Caucasians, which are for males aged 14 and over. From 1979, figures are for males 15 and over. Figures in parentheses are normed, with 100 assigned to the top group and other groups expressed as a percentage of the top group. For 1969, data for Koreans ($8,510) apply only to Honolulu. Figures in boldface identify the highest in each column.

Sources: U.S. Census (1952:150; 1962:72, 248; 1972:423; 1973:15, 74, 133, 179, 181; 1983:50, 68, 74; 1993:63, 132–133, 150; 2000:PCT133).

to Japanese in 1949 but declined in the 1970s and have not improved since.

Black males, with the highest density in the military population, have incomes substantially below the average, though they have experienced relative improvement over the years. They remain below Filipinos, who have continued to derive less than two-thirds of the median income of the top groups and have not advanced. The arrival of a large number of unskilled immigrants from the Philippines after 1965 may be one explanation (Table 2.3). Puerto Rican males are about at the same place as Filipinos in the pecking order, and they have been swamped by the arrival of newcomers.

Mexican and Samoan males rank below the groups thus far mentioned. Except for a high point for Mexicans in 1989, they have not advanced relative to the top group, though Samoans increased somewhat in 1999.

Two groups have achieved remarkable improvement—Guamanian and Vietnamese males. Blacks and Koreans, as already noted, have also consistently improved relative to the top group. Guamanians now are comparable to Koreans, whereas Vietnamese still remain the least affluent of the 12 major ethnic groups in Hawai'i.

The other side of the income coin is poverty (Table 10.3). Patterns in poverty statistics appear similar to those from median incomes. Families least likely to have extremely low incomes are Caucasians, Blacks, Chinese, Filipinos, and Japanese. Filipino families avoid poverty despite substantially lower median incomes for males because many Filipinas are gainfully employed.

Thus, income data show considerable social mobility for Japanese, other groups to a much lesser extent, but a relative decline and stagnation in the income levels for Native Hawaiians. Poverty data show improvements for groups with lower income levels. Samoan family decreases in poverty level are not reflected in better income for Samoan males, however.

Improved income rankings for some groups suggest the possibility that they are moving into the middle class. Accordingly, occupational data are examined next.

OCCUPATIONAL STATUS

The highest status jobs are administrative, executive, and managerial positions. Barack Obama's father arrived in Honolulu as the manager

Table 10.3

Families Below Poverty Level in Hawai'i by Ethnic Group, 1969–1999
(in percent)

Ethnic Group	1969	1979		1989		1999	
Black	15.6%	11.5%	(4.4)	5.6%	(3.3)	5.6%	(2.4)
Caucasian	9.1	7.4	(2.8)	5.0	(2.9)	5.5	(2.4)
Chinese	na	5.1	(2.0)	5.0	(2.9)	6.1	(2.7)
Filipino	na	8.5	(3.3)	6.4	(3.8)	5.7	(2.5)
Guamanian	na	8.9	(3.4)		*	21.4	(9.3)
Hawaiian	na	15.1	(5.8)	14.1	(8.3)	14.1	(6.1)
Japanese	na	2.6	(100)	1.7	(100)	2.3	(100)
Korean	na	10.6	(4.1)	9.1	(5.4)	12.3	(5.3)
Mexican	na	18.3	(7.0)	7.7	(4.5)	13.3	(5.8)
Puerto Rican	na	19.3	(7.4)	17.3	(10.2)	20.2	(8.8)
Samoan	na	37.5	(17.4)	30.4	(17.9)	27.8	(12.1)
Vietnamese	na	**40.6**	(15.6)	**36.0**	(21.2)	25.8	(11.2)
All Groups	7.4	7.8	(3.0)	6.0	(3.5)	7.6	(3.3)

Key: na = Figures not available.

   * = Figures for Guamanians in 1989 are left blank because too few families were sampled.

Notes: Figures in boldface identify the highest in each column. Figures in parentheses are derived by dividing each group by the figure for the top group (with the fewest families below poverty).

Source: U.S. Census (1973:466–468; 1983:33, 52, 69, 75; 1993:39, 108–109, 134–135, 152; 2000:PCT157).

of a furniture store, but when that business closed, he tried to sell insurance, a job with lower status, and had much difficulty. While his status and income declined, Obama's grandmother's status increased. She rose from bank teller to vice president of a bank, though she was passed over many times because of her gender (Heilemann and Halperin 2010:350). To raise extra money for the family, Barry sold ice cream in a nearby store, and he later experienced upward mobility after becoming a lawyer in Chicago.

Among the executive positions, the most desirable is to head a business. Historically, Caucasians from Europe and the United States set up shop in Hawai'i first. Chinese left the plantations to open food stores, restaurants, and other businesses, and then Japanese followed.

According to census data (Table 10.4), however, Chinese are not the most entrepreneurial, and Japanese in the 1970s evidently did not use

Table 10.4

Self-Employed Workers in Hawai'i by Ethnic Group, 1980–2000 (in percent)

Ethnic Group	1980	1990	2000
Black	3.3%	4.1%	5.2%
Caucasian	8.0	10.0	5.6
Chinese	5.9	6.9	13.0
Filipino	2.3	2.6	4.0
Guamanian	2.4	1.6	3.0
Hawaiian	3.1	3.6	5.9
Japanese	5.4	5.4	9.2
Korean	7.6	11.9	20.4
Mexican	6.5	5.8	8.8
Puerto Rican	3.2	3.2	6.7
Samoan	1.6	2.3	2.5
Vietnamese	1.6	**16.0**	22.0
All Groups	5.5	6.5	10.0

Notes: Figures in each column represent percentages of workers of ethnic groups who are self-employed. Figures in boldface identify the highest in each column.

Sources: U.S. Census (1983:42, 66, 72; 1993:62, 128, 146; 2000:PCT87).

politics to open a raft of new businesses. In 1980, Caucasians were more likely to own their own businesses than members of other ethnic groups, but by 1990 they were out percentaged by Koreans and Vietnamese. Most groups have improved over time. Although groups with higher percentages of business ownership tend to have higher median incomes, that generalization obviously does not apply to those in very smallest businesses, notably Vietnamese.

Regarding occupational social status, data are available from 1896 to 2000 (Tables 10.5a, b). In 1896 (during the Republic of Hawai'i), Chinese males were the principal professionals, and Japanese males were the main agricultural workers. After annexation to the United States, an influx of White male professionals displaced the ranking for Chinese.

As plantation laborers were recruited from the Philippines during the first half of the 20th century, they displaced Japanese. After Japanese left plantations in large numbers, they gradually increased their share of professionals. Native Hawaiian professional males, meanwhile, consistently declined percentagewise up to statehood, while their share of laborers was relatively steady, even increasing somewhat after statehood.

Table 10.5a

Male Occupational Distributions in Hawai'i Across Ethnic Groups, 1896-1960
(in percent for each column)

Ethnic Group	Professionals					Laborers				
	1896	1910	1930	1950	1960	1896	1910	1930	1950	1960
Caucasian	24.8	**46.7**	**42.3**	**47.9**	**40.0**	10.5	12.0	3.8	8.2	12.3
Chinese	**38.4**	6.8	6.3	9.9	11.6	34.1	11.6	3.2	1.6	2.0
Filipino	na	na	6.5	3.4	3.0	na	na	**63.8**	**49.1**	**44.8**
Hawaiian	22.5	20.7	13.0	8.4	na	9.7	8.0	5.1	10.8	na
Japanese	11.3	23.3	29.2	28.4	37.7	**44.9**	**59.0**	19.8	27.4	24.3
Korean	na	na	.5	.2	na	na	na	1.8	.6	na
Puerto Rican	na	na	.5	.2	na	na	na	2.3	3.1	na
All Groups	100	100	100	100	100	100	100	100	100	100

Key: na = Figures not available.

Notes: Figures in each column add up to 100 percent when other groups are included.

Definitions of each occupation vary over the years.

Figures in boldface identify the highest in each column.

Source: Lind (1967:77, 82).

Distributions *within each occupation* only hint at social mobility. What is more revealing is to see percentages *within each ethnic group* over time in order to determine trends. Fortunately, statistics on occupations of males date from 1896, so generational trends can be discerned (Table 10.6a, b). In the following analysis, an ethnic group that is most prevalent in a particular occupation is said to be "concentrated."

The data reveal that *Caucasians* (including Portuguese) have dominated the two upper-status collar occupations, with a surge in professionals, subordinate white-collar jobs, and service personnel after statehood. They remain concentrated in top-level positions.

Although *Chinese* have been most concentrated in clerical/sales jobs, they have ranked just below Whites in executive jobs over most years. Their numbers on the plantations dwindled markedly, first after World War I and then more so after World War II. After statehood, their numbers increased considerably in the professions. Chinese moved up the ranks quite rapidly.

Japanese mirrored Chinese in exiting from manual labor jobs after the two world wars, and then were concentrated in skilled labor jobs before statehood. They have almost doubled in clerical/sales positions since statehood and have steadily gained in executive and professional

Table 10.5b

Male Occupational Distributions in Hawai'i Across Ethnic Groups, 1980–2000 (in percent for each row)

Ethnic Group	Executive, Administrative, Managerial			Professionals			Sales, Technical, Administrative support, Clerical			Craft, Precision production, Repair			Operators			Service			Laborers		
	1980	1990	2000	1980	1990	2000	1980	1990	2000	1980	1990	2000	1980	1990	2000	1980	1990	2000	1980	1990	2000
Black	12.4	10.9	14.1	9.9	9.5	20.8	21.3	**31.2**	18.6	14.8	13.8	10.8	11.2	8.8	10.0	20.6	19.0	19.3	9.8	6.8	6.4
Caucasian	**18.6**	17.4	17.7	15.3	**16.8**	24.0	20.1	21.1	16.3	17.2	18.0	14.9	7.7	6.9	8.7	12.5	12.8	15.6	8.6	6.3	2.8
Chinese	18.0	16.1	17.2	14.5	14.6	23.1	**24.9**	25.3	20.6	13.3	13.1	9.7	6.1	6.8	8.5	16.8	19.6	19.0	6.2	4.3	2.0
Filipino	5.2	6.7	6.6	2.6	3.3	7.9	12.3	15.4	14.5	19.1	18.4	16.6	16.8	14.8	12.5	22.0	25.3	**34.1**	**21.9**	**16.7**	7.8
Guamanian	10.1	4.9	7.5	1.4	3.3	**32.2**	19.4	22.8	14.6	21.7	**36.3**	17.3	14.3	8.1	9.2	16.6	13.7	15.6	16.6	10.9	3.7
Hawaiian	9.3	8.9	9.6	5.7	6.3	9.5	12.7	15.1	14.0	19.8	21.4	18.6	19.3	15.4	15.7	17.7	19.3	25.6	15.1	13.2	7.0
Japanese	16.9	**17.9**	**19.2**	10.3	12.8	30.2	23.6	26.7	21.4	23.9	19.6	15.5	7.7	6.6	7.6	9.9	10.5	13.1	7.3	5.6	3.1
Korean	16.2	13.7	16.4	11.2	10.4	14.4	22.1	26.3	**25.5**	19.8	15.1	13.3	9.2	11.9	9.9	14.8	17.2	18.9	7.8	4.9	1.7
Mexican	10.6	10.4	10.3	11.8	9.9	9.7	9.2	16.4	19.9	**26.2**	24.4	**18.7**	9.0	8.6	8.1	22.4	20.1	28.1	10.8	10.6	5.2
Puerto Rican	5.7	5.5	6.7	3.1	3.9	9.6	8.9	14.4	15.9	25.1	22.9	17.4	21.4	18.0	14.1	15.5	20.0	26.9	19.9	15.0	**9.4**
Samoan	4.3	5.3	6.6	4.7	7.4	6.0	10.8	12.1	14.2	16.1	15.8	15.2	**23.3**	16.0	18.5	24.7	**28.1**	32.1	14.8	15.5	7.4
Vietnamese	10.1	5.5	6.7	8.4	4.5	6.1	13.4	28.3	15.6	13.8	5.8	5.4	17.2	**29.1**	**28.1**	**29.3**	22.3	30.9	7.8	3.2	7.3
All Males	15.0	14.2	13.8	10.5	11.8	16.6	19.3	21.4	17.5	19.6	18.5	16.1	10.5	9.4	10.4	14.4	15.9	20.9	10.4	8.5	4.7

Notes: Definitions of each occupation vary over the years. Figures in boldface identify the highest in each column.

Sources: U.S. Census (1983:22, 67, 73; 1993:60, 130–131, 148; 2000:PCT86).

Table 10.6a

Male Occupational Distributions in Hawai'i by Ethnic Group, 1896–1960 (in percent for each row)

Ethnic Group	Executive, Administrative, Managerial			Professionals					Sales, Technical, Admin.support, Clerical			Craft, Precision production, Repair			Operators			Service			Laborers				
	1940	1950	1960	1896	1910	1930	1950	1960	1940	1950	1960	1940	1950	1960	1940	1950	1960	1940	1950	1960	1896	1910	1930	1950	1960
Caucasian	20.0	18.5	19.4	4.9	5.5	5.5	4.5	16.9	16.3	14.1	13.3	17.4	21.3	19.2	14.4	12.7	11.7	3.4	6.7	5.5	9.3	na	4.4	5.1	8.4
Chinese	16.3	20.0	16.6	1.8	1.1	3.0	4.1	10.7	28.6	26.1	21.3	10.2	18.4	20.7	12.0	11.3	9.9	12.3	7.8	7.1	65.8	48.6	24.4	5.3	4.4
Filipino	1.4	3.0	2.7	na	.3	.5	.3	1.2	1.6	3.4	4.8	2.4	7.5	14.3	8.0	19.9	22.1	5.8	11.2	10.6	na	na	90.1	52.5	40.0
Hawaiian	5.8	7.9	na	1.4	3.2	5.2	2.8	5.7	8.3	9.9	na	15.4	2.9	na	19.8	20.1	na	8.9	10.0	na	30.0	44.8	38.8	22.9	na
Japanese	12.9	15.1	13.7	na	1.6	3.4	2.8	5.5	11.4	15.0	14.8	18.8	27.7	30.2	11.6	15.0	13.0	8.3	5.3	5.3	87.5	76.8	35.9	16.3	9.9
Korean	na	na	na	na	1.4	2.7	na	8.6	na	na	na	na	na	na	na	na	na	na	na	na	na	na	53.4	11.4	na
Puerto Rican	na	na	na	na	.2	1.1	na	.9	na	na	na	na	na	na	na	na	na	na	na	na	na	na	78.2	34.4	na
All Males	10.6	12.6	12.3	na	2.3	3.0	2.9	7.3	10.4	12.4	12.5	13.0	23.6	23.6	12.1	16.0	15.2	7.1	7.7	7.0	7.1	65.0	53.6	22.5	15.6

Table 10.6b

Male Occupational Distributions in Hawai'i by Ethnic Group, 1980–2000 (in percent for each column)

Ethnic Group	Executive, Administrative, Managerial			Professionals			Sales, Technical, Administrative support, Clerical			Craft, Precision production, Repair			Operators			Service			Laborers			Total		
	1980	1990	2000	1980	1990	2000	1980	1990	2000	1980	1990	2000	1980	1990	2000	1980	1990	2000	1980	1990	2000	1980	1990	2000
Black	.7	2.1	1.1	.6	1.0	1.4	.8	1.6	1.0	.4	.9	1.0	.7	.9	1.1	1.0	1.4	1.1	.6	1.0	1.5	.8	1.3	1.1
Caucasian	39.9	39.5	32.2	42.7	47.7	36.6	31.1	30.0	21.8	17.3	31.7	25.1	20.8	21.1	20.5	25.6	26.7	20.0	21.8	24.0	16.4	30.5	32.2	25.6
Chinese	8.5	7.8	6.5	8.5	8.0	6.1	7.6	7.4	5.2	3.1	5.0	3.0	4.5	5.6	4.9	6.8	7.1	4.6	3.7	3.5	2.0	3.1	6.9	5.1
Filipino	5.5	7.5	8.2	4.6	6.0	8.4	9.9	14.4	13.9	8.9	16.0	14.5	23.7	26.8	19.6	20.3	25.4	24.8	37.6	30.5	28.0	13.5	16.2	15.2
Guamanian	.1	.1	.1	.0	.1	.1	.1	.2	.1	.1	.3	.1	.1	.1	.1	.2	.1	.1	1.1	.2	.1	.1	.2	.1
Hawaiian	7.9	7.9	5.1	6.5	7.2	4.2	3.9	10.1	6.0	.7	12.3	7.3	19.4	17.0	10.1	13.9	12.8	6.9	15.2	15.5	8.7	10.8	10.8	6.2
Japanese	33.9	30.8	24.8	33.1	30.5	22.4	37.1	30.1	22.0	24.8	27.1	17.7	24.0	17.7	12.8	23.7	17.1	10.9	12.7	17.6	11.7	32.0	25.9	18.8
Korean	2.0	1.9	2.1	1.5	1.6	1.3	1.9	2.4	2.4	1.1	1.8	1.3	4.5	2.3	1.7	3.3	3.2	2.4	1.1	.6	.6	2.0	2.2	1.5
Mexican	.9	.8	1.1	.5	.7	1.0	.5	.4	1.3	.5	1.2	1.6	.4	.8	1.3	.7	1.3	1.7	.5	1.0	1.4	.5	.9	1.3
Puerto Rican	1.0	.7	1.1	.5	.7	1.2	.5	.7	1.8	1.3	2.1	2.0	2.9	2.9	2.5	1.9	2.2	2.5	2.8	2.8	3.3	1.4	1.6	1.9
Samoan	.3	.4	.5	.5	.5	.4	.9	.3	1.0	.5	.8	.9	1.9	1.7	1.6	1.3	1.5	1.4	1.1	1.7	1.4	.8	.9	.9
Vietnamese	.1	.2	.4	.2	.2	.3	.2	.1	.6	.1	.3	.2	.4	1.1	1.9	.6	.7	1.0	.2	.2	.9	.3	.4	.7
All Males	12.3	13.5	12.9	11.8	13.5	19.4	32.0	32.6	28.1	11.6	10.5	8.6	7.3	6.5	7.0	17.9	17.6	20.9	7.0	5.7	3.1			

Key: na = Figures not available.

Notes: Figures in each column do not always add up to 100 percent due to rounding errors and (for the 2000 census) mixed-race respondents that are not included in the figures. Definitions of each occupation vary over the years. From 1920 to 1930, figures report percentages of males aged 10 and over. From 1940 to 1950, males aged 14 and over. Figures in boldface identify the highest in each column.

Sources: Lind (1967:77, 80, 82;1980:87); U.S. Census (1923:1277–1278; 1932:88–89; 1943:20; 1952:115–116; 1983:22, 67, 73; 1993:60, 130–131, 148; 2000:PCT86).

jobs while gradually moving out of semiskilled to skilled positions. Japanese have enjoyed considerable social mobility from the time when the Democratic Party first occupied the governor's mansion.

Filipinos took over plantation work vacated by Chinese and Japanese after World War I. Ninety percent of Filipino males were manual laborers in 1930, but their numbers declined steadily, with only 7.8 percent in those jobs by 2000. What new jobs did they move into? By 1950, almost one-fifth were in semiskilled jobs and about one-tenth were in service occupations. Then from at least 1980, they increased in skilled labor and subordinate white-collar jobs. Increases in executive and professional positions did occur over the years, but only minimally. Filipino social mobility has been mostly from lower to higher blue-collar jobs.

Native Hawaiians, who held top positions in the days of the monarchy, were concentrated in unskilled and semiskilled labor jobs during the Territorial era. After statehood, they have been almost equally divided between the various blue-collar occupations, and they have not risen very much within white-collar jobs. Clearly, they have been passed by Chinese and Japanese, but have remained slightly above Filipinos. One reason is that many graduates of Kamehameha Schools, a top prep school in the Islands, have preferred to go to college outside Hawai'i (Wong 1975). Once there, they have decided to stay. Indeed, the census report that some 70 percent of mixed and pure Native Hawaiians now live on the Mainland (Grieco and Cassidy 2001:5, 9). The occupational data show that the indigenous population remaining in the Islands has clearly stagnated. Native Hawaiians, thus, may have been adversely affected by a "brain drain" of their talents from the Islands.

Another example of out-migration is Barack Obama. A major percentage of *African Americans* come and go on military assignments. Otherwise, they are concentrated in subordinate white-collar jobs and in the service industry. They doubled in professional jobs from 1990 to 2000, the decade when the military population (many with lower-status positions) was cut back.

Other ethnic groups evidently developed trends more from in-migration than from social mobility (Table 2.3). *Guamanians*, who increased in population from 2,000 to 7,000 from 1990 to 2000, included an influx of professionals to join a population previously concentrated in skilled labor. The 3,000 *Vietnamese* were primarily refugees in the 1980 census, but had become 8,000 immigrants by 2000, when nearly half were running their own businesses, as noted earlier. As employees, Vietnamese were concentrated in semiskilled occupations. *Koreans*, who were recruited to the plantations at the beginning of the 20th century, increased in white-collar jobs after 1980. Although concentrated in clerical/sales occupations, from 1980 to 2000 their population doubled from 12,000 to 24,000, parallel with a slight increase in executive and professional positions. *Mexicans*, the earliest ethnic group to migrate to the Islands, remained a small percentage of the population during most of the 19th and 20th centuries, but their numbers (20,000) were more numerous than Samoans (16,000) by the year 2000, and their increase from 14,000 in 1990 was due to in-migration from the U.S. Mainland, as more than 90 percent are American citizens. Clearly, they have been imported mostly to work as skilled laborers and secondarily in service jobs. As regards *Samoans*, the earliest data show 11,000 in 1980, an influx of 4,000 by 1990, but an increase of only 1,000 by 2000. They are concentrated in semiskilled jobs, with no signs of social mobility.

Puerto Ricans, who were recruited to the plantations after sovereign control of Puerto Rico was transferred from Spain to the United States, have had immense population increases since 1980 of at least 20 percent per decade (Table 2.1). Before those increases, Puerto Ricans gradually left agricultural labor, and by 1970 they had moved into skilled and semiskilled blue-collar jobs. The steady but slow increase in white-collar employment from 1980 may be attributable either to social mobility of long-time residents or to an influx from other parts of the United States.

In a broad brush, there are notable trends in occupational status. The most impressive social mobility has been among Chinese, who advanced before statehood, and Japanese, who rose into higher level jobs after statehood. Filipinos eventually moved out of unskilled labor jobs, but they have not gone much beyond mid-level positions. Native Hawaiians, however, declined after they lost political power, and they have not posted significant gains since then. Caucasians remain at the top throughout all the years studied.

EDUCATIONAL ATTAINMENTS

Readers may be surprised that African Americans have the highest rate of high school graduation among the major ethnic groups in Hawai'i (Table 10.7). There are two reasons. One is that few were recruited to work on the plantations. The other is that, until recently, 90 percent of the American volunteer army was required to have graduated from high school (Bender 2004). Both reasons explain why Caucasians and Mexican Americans rank second and third, respectively.

Table 10.7

High School Graduates Among Persons 25 Years and Over in Hawai'i by Ethnic Group, 1950, 1980–2000 (in percent)

Ethnic Group	Total				Females				Males			
	1950	1980	1990	2000	1950	1980	1990	2000	1950	1980	1990	2000
Black	na	**91.5**	**94.2**	**92.9**	na	86.0	92.7	**92.6**	na	**94.4**	**95.2**	**93.1**
Caucasian	26.6	85.7	89.3	92.7	27.2	84.7	88.4	92.6	26.0	86.7	90.1	92.7
Chinese	**28.9**	75.4	77.2	77.8	**27.9**	72.8	74.7	75.1	**29.7**	78.2	79.8	80.9
Filipino	3.7	51.3	63.2	71.4	7.7	55.1	64.2	71.1	3.0	48.0	63.2	71.7
Guamanian	na	69.0	82.3	89.7	na	54.1	78.9	87.3	na	82.1	85.1	91.8
Hawaiian	18.7	68.2	75.8	83.5	18.0	68.5	77.0	85.0	19.5	67.8	76.6	81.9
Japanese	20.8	72.6	80.3	86.3	18.7	70.0	77.9	84.7	23.2	75.4	83.0	88.1
Korean	na	72.4	73.4	78.4	na	66.5	68.2	74.0	na	81.7	81.4	86.4
Mexican	na	80.4	85.7	81.9	na	79.3	85.9	83.3	na	81.2	85.3	80.8
Puerto Rican	na	53.5	66.0	77.3	na	49.8	65.1	78.1	na	57.0	66.9	76.4
Samoan	na	51.0	65.3	74.5	na	44.3	59.4	75.1	na	58.4	71.1	77.3
Vietnamese	na	54.3	52.2	52.7	na	48.0	47.2	47.6	na	63.1	58.2	59.3
All Groups	20.2	73.8	80.1	84.6	20.9	72.5	78.4	83.6	19.3	75.2	81.7	85.6

Key: na = Figures not available.

Note: Figures in boldface identify the highest in each column.

Sources: U.S. Census (1953:76–77; 1983:21, 40, 64, 70; 1993:57, 122–123, 140; 2000:PCT64).

What also pops out from the numbers is the substantial increase in high school graduation for all groups after statehood. The slight decline in Vietnamese, the lowest in high school attainments, is attributable to the most recent influx of female immigrants from Vietnam.

High school graduates should at least qualify for clerical and skilled labor jobs. Indeed, for the year 2000, the rank-order correlation between secondary school graduation rates and percentages in the two categories plus executive and professional jobs is +.77. Chinese, Japanese, and Koreans have higher level positions than their educational qualifications would suggest, whereas Blacks and Native Hawaiians have much higher high school graduation rates than their relative standings in white-collar and skilled-labor jobs.

Turning to college graduates (Table 10.8), once again there has been a substantial increase in all groups since statehood. Caucasians and Chinese remain at the top, with Japanese and Koreans not far behind, while Blacks are slightly more than half the rate of the two top groups. One reason is that many Black males join the military immediately after graduating from high school on the Mainland and are posted to bases in the Islands, whereas Black females graduate from college at higher rates than females of most other ethnic groups. All other groups increased over time with the exception of Vietnamese, again reflecting the arrival of immigrants after 1990. The largest percentage gains (more than 10 percent) from 1980 are enjoyed by Guamanian males and Japanese of both sexes.

College graduates should qualify for managerial and professional positions. Before statehood, when most private-sector jobs at the largest businesses were controlled by Whites, even educated Japanese and Koreans were turned down for jobs (Kobayashi 2008). The rank-order correlation for the year 2000 is +.92, meaning that groups with higher rates of college graduation are also the ones landing higher status jobs, and vice versa. Today, college-educated Filipinos and Koreans are consistently underemployed in relation to their qualifications, whereas the most advantaged are Guamanians, filling more top-level positions than their college graduation rates indicate.

The future for each ethnic group should be ascertainable by examining those enrolled in college in the first six years after high school versus those who stop their education to find employment, so college enrollment figures may be important predictors (Table 10.9). More than half of Chinese and Japanese in recent years go to college, with Koreans and Guamanians not far behind. Vietnamese are rapidly catching up. The

Table 10.8

College Graduates Among Persons 25 Years and Over in Hawai'i by Ethnic Group, 1950, 1980–2000 (in percent)

Ethnic Group	Total				Females				Males			
	1950	1980	1990	2000	1950	1980	1990	2000	1950	1980	1990	2000
Black	na	14.0	15.2	21.9	na	14.8	19.1	25.1	na	13.5	12.8	18.8
Caucasian	14.8	28.2	30.2	36.5	**14.7**	23.0	27.1	35.0	**15.0**	33.0	33.0	37.8
Chinese	8.8	27.6	30.3	36.0	9.4	13.6	**28.5**	33.1	8.3	31.9	32.4	39.3
Filipino	.2	10.8	11.6	16.2	.7	13.6	13.9	18.2	.2	8.4	9.4	14.0
Guamanian	na	9.1	9.3	21.5	na	8.3	13.7	16.4	na	9.8	5.8	26.0
Hawaiian	2.4	7.7	9.1	12.6	2.8	6.9	8.7	12.5	1.9	8.5	9.6	12.8
Japanese	3.0	19.8	25.2	31.3	2.3	17.6	23.8	30.6	3.8	22.1	26.7	32.2
Korean	na	17.9	18.6	24.3	na	12.4	14.3	19.8	na	26.5	29.5	32.4
Mexican	na	9.8	12.0	16.3	na	9.9	11.9	17.3	na	9.7	12.0	15.6
Puerto Rican	na	3.5	5.1	8.6	na	3.3	4.7	9.0	na	3.6	5.5	8.2
Samoan	na	3.3	5.0	6.8	na	2.3	4.3	5.4	na	4.5	5.7	8.3
Vietnamese	na	9.8	14.0	10.6	na	4.2	12.5	10.0	na	17.8	15.9	11.4
All Groups	6.1	20.3	22.9	26.2	6.3	17.1	21.4	25.5	5.9	23.0	24.4	26.9

Key: na = Figures not available.

Note: Figures in boldface identify the highest in each column.

Sources: U.S. Census (1953:76–77; 1983:21, 40, 64, 70; 1993:57, 122–123, 140; 2000:PCT64).

Table 10.9

College Enrollment in Hawai'i by Ethnic Group (18–24 Years), 1950, 1990, 2000 (in percent)

Ethnic Group	1950	1990	2000
Black	na	13.4%	19.5%
Caucasian	1.5%	20.8	24.8
Chinese	4.7	**53.7**	**60.6**
Filipino	1.4	30.7	33.0
Guamanian	na	40.2	49.4
Hawaiian	2.2	22.2	26.3
Japanese	**7.1**	52.3	57.3
Korean	na	47.0	53.4
Mexican	na	18.4	19.8
Puerto Rican	na	16.6	20.0
Samoan	na	22.4	20.1
Vietnamese	na	35.3	48.7
All Groups	5.0	30.0	44.6

Notes: Figures may include out-of-state students but exclude students studying outside Hawai'i. Figures in boldface identify the highest in each column.

Source: U.S. Census (1953:39, 62–65; 1993:57, 122–123, 140; 2000:PCT63).

remaining groups made unimpressive gains from 1990 to 2000. Many Caucasians in the 18–24 age group are in the military in Hawai'i and thus are less likely to be enrolled in college than other groups, including Native Hawaiians.

The rank-order correlation between college enrollment in 1990 and college completion by 2000 is +.91. College dropout rates are a problem only for Samoans. The only other anomalies are that Black and White college graduates in Hawai'i appear to complete their degrees on the Mainland before arriving in Hawai'i.

CONCLUSION

In 1977, the judgment that Native Hawaiians were a disadvantaged ethnic minority was accepted by a judge in a Hawai'i court in which I served as expert witness (*Hawai'i v Dukelow*). The standard used was whether an ethnic group was substantially below attainments in income, occupation, and education than the top ethnic groups. That opinion, still applicable today, also applies to Filipinos, Puerto Ricans, Samoans, and Vietnamese.

Correspondingly, the nonminorities in Hawai'i are Caucasians, Chinese, and Japanese. Between the minorities and nonminorities are four groups—Blacks, Guamanians, Koreans, and Mexicans—who are doing well on some measures but poorly on others.

The data demonstrate substantial upward mobility for Chinese and Japanese over the years. Blacks, Guamanians, Koreans, and Vietnamese are the only groups with consistent income improvement relative to the top groups; except for Vietnamese, all three also improved in educational attainments and occupational status. Filipinos, Puerto Ricans, and Samoans experienced mobility to urban blue-collar jobs as they left the plantations, but they have not made inroads into white-collar occupations despite their consistent educational advances. Mexicans do not fit into any particular pattern, as their relative incomes have fluctuated without a trend. They have advanced in college attendance but not high school graduation rates, and their only occupational pattern is a shift from blue-collar skilled labor to white-collar clerical/sales jobs.

Several of the six possible explanations for social mobility are supported by census data. Caucasians and Japanese are excellent candidates for *politically driven mobility*, whereas eight years of a Native Hawaiian governor and a Filipino governor had minimal impact upon members of their own ethnic groups.

Chinese and Japanese social mobility fits the traditional model of *capital accumulation*, in which one generation invests in the education of the next, which then advances occupationally. That explanation evidently applies as well to rising incomes of Blacks, Guamanians, and Koreans, who have posted gains in executive and professional jobs.

Census data are insufficient to support the *institutional racism* scenario. Some evidence of barriers to the educational advancement of Filipinos and Native Hawaiians is presented in Chapters 11 and 12, but a stronger case appears elsewhere (Haas 1992). Anecdotally, the main beneficiaries of "affirmative action" are Japanese, who made inroads into upper-status jobs in corporations owned by Whites because they controlled governmental institutions that enforced nondiscrimination laws. There is some evidence that out-migration from the Islands may have been a response to institutional racism (see Chapter 9).

Economic transformation is perhaps the most seductive explanation for patterns of social mobility, as the sooner an ethnic group left the plantations, the more that group has prospered. As military spending tapered off, the remaining Blacks have advanced in incomes, occupational status, and education.

Migration to Hawai'i evidently has slowed overall progress for some affected groups—Chinese, Filipinos, Koreans, and Vietnamese. Recent immigrants have diluted gains by all four groups. Out-migration, however, has adversely affected the status of Native Hawaiians.

The *cultural* theory, which blames the victim for lack of progress (cf. Ryan 1976), is a throwback to long-discarded justifications for racism. There is not an iota of empirical support for the notion.

What do the data show about the impact of social mobility, or lack thereof, on relative ethnic harmony in Hawai'i? First, the most populous groups (Caucasians and Japanese) are content with their higher status positions. Most of the smaller groups have tasted a modicum of social mobility as well. Native Hawaiians have every basis for frustration on their declining status compared to the days of the monarchy, but they are the ones who have most loudly trumpeted the Spirit of Aloha. However, continuing racial intermarriage will make social mobility more difficult to measure in the future.

Although relative rankings of ethnic groups have remained roughly the same since Barack Obama left Honolulu in 1979, he was present while Japanese moved beyond working class status and other groups sought to do likewise. For Obama (2008:295), however, attitudes of complacency and resignation about inequality are unacceptable. Due to the multicultural ethos that pervades the Islands, there is an implicit insistence today that no group should be left behind.

Chapter 11

Multiculturalizing Elementary and Secondary Education

Nina K. Buchanan, Robert A. Fox, and Michael Haas

*Parents have the primary responsibility for instilling an ethic
of hard work and educational achievement in their children.
But parents rightly expect their government, through the
public schools, to serve as full partners in the educational
process—just as it has for earlier generations of Americans.*
(Obama 2008:190)

In 1967, five-year-old Barry Obama enrolled in kindergarten at Noelani
Elementary School, the only American public school that he ever
attended. He soon left for Indonesia, where he was in elementary schools
from grades 1–4. Had he stayed in Honolulu, Barry Obama could have
attended the public school to which he was geographically assigned
(unless parents presented a good case for a geographic exception). But
his mother insisted that he should go to the best school in the Islands,
and in 1971 Barry was accepted into the 5th grade at Punahou School,
the oldest private school west of the Mississippi. Punahou remains today
as one of the country's most elite, and one of the most expensive private
schools in Hawai'i (*Honolulu Advertiser* 2008).

Obama, as he later reflected, was fully aware at the time of the *"glaring differences between the facilities we enjoyed at Punahou and the crumbling public schools"* (Obama 1999). And he recalled: *"There was something about this place and this school that embraced me, gave me support, game me encouragement and allowed me to grow and prosper"* (Husein and Chang 2005).

As of 2010, some 178,189 students were enrolled in kindergarten, elementary, and secondary public education in Hawai'i. Some 37,155 students are served by Hawai'i's 147 private schools (EducationBug 2009; Hawai'i Association of Independent Schools 2009; *Hawaii Catholic Herald* 2009:14). While it is unfair to characterize all Hawai'i private schools as better than public schools, Obama's application to Punahou was doubtless based on the belief that the private school choice would produce a higher educational outcome. Indeed, the quality of Hawai'i public schools today ranks 49th out of the 50 states (American Legislative Exchange Council 2008:16).

Obama's choice of school was made in the context of a unique history of educational development in the Islands (Brieske 1961; Midkiff 1935; Stueber 1964; Wist 1940). That history can be described as a struggle of non-Whites to advance educationally—with unfortunate obstacles, remarkable successes, and uniquely Hawaiian solutions. Yet that history suggests how education on the Mainland can be transformed by the national leader who is eager to transform public education so that all can benefit.

SCHOOLING UNDER THE MONARCHY

Before the arrival of Captain Cook, a system of traditional education operated to prepare the nobility to rule, while the mass of the population engaged in food gathering and related activities. When Protestant missionaries from New England arrived in the 1820s, the nobility was eager to gain the knowledge of the foreigners (Haoles), who set up mission schools.

After a decade of educating adults of the Native Hawaiian nobility and royalty, the missionaries turned their attention to future generations, for whom they established two types of schools. *Common schools* enrolled Native Hawaiian children of the nonelite classes with instruction in the vernacular. *Select schools* were of three types: (1) boarding schools, designed to get children of the ali'i (nobility) away from the "corrupting" influence of parents; (2) the O'ahu Charity School (from

1833) for offspring of mixed Native Hawaiian-Caucasian parentage, as some were abandoned by seafaring fathers; and (3) various private schools for the Haoles.

In 1841, Punahou School opened as an English-language missionary school. Native Hawaiians, allowed to attend Punahou as early as 1848, increasingly began to enroll, but they had to be "wealthy and civilized" (Pennybacker 1991:121). The first Chinese student entered Punahou in 1867, and the first Japanese in 1885 (Forbes 1991:461). From 1896 to 1945, there was a ceiling of 10 percent for Asians, increased to 12 percent from 1945 to 1955. The quota was abolished one year after *Brown v Board of Education of Topeka* (347US483) ordered Mainland schools to desegregate, a ruling that was interpreted as placing Punahou's tax-exempt status in jeopardy (Newport 1991:157; Pennybacker 1991:120–121). In 2009, some 2,389 of Punahou students (64 percent) were classified as Asian and Pacific Islander and 1,240 as Caucasian (33 percent). The remaining 3 percent consisted of 90 Hispanics, 20 Blacks, and 4 Native Americans (Rucker 2009b). Punahou currently advertises that preferences in admission are given to qualified candidates who are "children of alumni, faculty or staff or of Hawaiian descent, descendants of Punahou's missionary founders, or siblings of enrolled students" (Rucker 2009b).

Other private schools, notably 'Iolani and St. Andrew's Priory, began in the last half of the 19th century primarily to accommodate Native Hawaiians. Since they had no racial quotas, they became multiethnic as soon as Asian parents could afford to send their children to private schools (Table 11.1).

In 1837, the Board of Missions began to cut aid to the Protestant mission schools in Hawai'i, and Horace Mann coincidentally became the head of the state educational system in Massachusetts. Responding to the new financial reality, under which all mission aid was to cease within a decade, the Kingdom of Hawai'i decided in 1841 to follow Mann's example by establishing a system of tuition-supported public education throughout the Islands, the first country in the world to do so.

Since Protestants in effect ran all the schools, Catholic and Mormon missionaries tried to compete by operating small tuition-free private schools on funds provided from their own missionary boards in the United States. The influence of the Protestant missionaries over the king was so considerable that after 1854 no sectarian schools were allowed to enroll more than 25 pupils.

Table 11.1

Private School Enrollment in Hawai'i by Ethnic Group, 1874–2000 (in percent for grades 1–12)

Year	Black	Caucasian	Chinese	Filipino	Guamanian	Hawaiian	Japanese	Korean	Mexican	PRican	Samoan	Vietnamese
1874	na	29.8%	na	na	na	**70.2%**	na	na	na	na	na	na
1896	na	75.1	7.7%	na	na	16.0	1.2%	na	na	na	na	na
1900	na	42.8	13.6	na	na	39.5	3.6	na	na	na	na	na
1910	na	35.6	12.6	na	na	34.1	12.9	na	na	8.4%	na	na
1920	na	34.4	14.6	1.2%	na	29.2	17.1	2.6%	na	.9	na	na
1930	na	36.0	10.4	2.7	na	25.2	23.1	2.1	na	.5	na	na
1946	na	30.6	11.6	6.5	na	28.9	16.7	1.2	na	1.0	na	na
1970	na	43.8	6.0	8.2	na	11.7	27.1	1.3	na	na	na	na
1980	.6%	40.8	10.0	8.9	.2%	14.9	19.4	1.6	.8%	2.2	.6%	1.2%
1990	1.0	33.7	10.3	12.8	.1	13.8	21.1	3.3	1.3	1.9	.6	.4
2000	.6	24.4	5.4	6.0	–	7.7	11.5	2.0	1.9	2.0	.3	.3

Key: na = Figures not available.

  – = Number is above 0 but below .1 percent.

Notes: Figures add to 100 percent horizontally when other ethnic groups are added, including "other". Figures in boldface identify the highest in each row. For 1970, data for Koreans applies only to Honolulu.

Sources: Gulick (1937:156); *Honolulu Advertiser* (1957); Hawai'i (1874:2; 1896:19; 1900:103; 1910:55; 1912:80; 1914:9; 1921:70; 1930:159); Kaser (1975b); U.S. Census (1972:211–212, 214–215; 1973:11, 70, 129, 178, 180; 1983:40, 64, 70; 1993:57, 122–123,140; 2000:TablePCT61). For more complete data, see Haas (1992:Table 11.1).

Parents were taxed $2 per child enrolled in common schools and $3 per child in select schools. Public funds raised in this manner defrayed all tuition costs of common schools and half the tuition costs at private schools. By 1857, more funds went to the select schools than to the common schools (Reinecke 1935). Tuition for elementary common schools ended in 1888. Public funds were denied to private schools after 1896.

Attendance in the English-language select schools gradually outstripped the vernacular common schools. In 1854, all select schools had authority to teach English to Native Hawaiians, a practice extended gradually to the common schools.

In 1878, Portuguese laborers arrived. As the first immigrant group recruited to work in the sugarcane fields allowed to bring wives and children in any quantity, Portuguese parents wanted their children to learn English, not Hawaiian, and school administrators saw the wisdom of having English as the vehicle to homogenize a population that already consisted of large numbers of Chinese and Japanese as well as Haoles (Whites) and Native Hawaiians.

Although a few Chinese, German, and Portuguese language schools opened in the 1880s, a flood of Japanese-language schools, financed largely by Buddhist missions in Hawai'i, opened in the last decade of the 19th century (Brieske 1961:305–308). Except for two brief shutdowns (see Chapters 2, 4), they have continued ever since.

There was one excellent school in Honolulu that Barry Obama's mother never considered. Back in 1887, the will of Princess Bernice Pauahi Bishop led to the establishment of Kamehameha Schools. Today, Kamehameha has a $7.2 billion endowment, on a par with Duke, Harvard, Princeton, Stanford, and Yale (Daysog 2009; cf. Ruibai 2004), and dwarfing Punahou (Table 11.2). Although nothing in the will specifically restricted attendance at Kamehameha to children of Native Hawaiian ancestry, the first students were children of Native Hawaiian parentage, and the practice has continued ever since despite various challenges (see Chapter 2).[1] Standard English was emphasized so that the education would be at the same level as at Punahou and in the common and select schools. Nowadays, Kamehameha Schools enroll about one-fourth of all Native Hawaiian children. Most of the rest attend public schools (Hannahs 1983:170).

SCHOOLING FROM 1893 TO 1959

The overthrow of the monarchy in 1893 changed the educational landscape. English became the official language of government in 1896 and

Table 11.2

A Comparison of Kamehameha Schools and Punahou School, 2009

Kamehameha Schools	Punahou
Founded in 1841	Founded in 1887
Preschool + K–12	K–12
Nondenominational Protestant	Nondenominational Protestant
Main campus on Oʻahu (Kapalama Heights)	Campus on Oʻahu (Makiki)
Smaller campuses on the islands of Hawaiʻi and Maui	No campuses elsewhere
Enrollment usually restricted to Native Hawaiians	Quota on Asians abandoned in 1955
Admission based in part on qualifying exam	Admission based in part on qualifying exam
Applicant-to-admission entry ratio = 8:1	Applicant-to-admission to high school ratio = 3.3:1
Current enrollment = 6,388	Current enrollment = 3,750
Yearly tuition = $17,800	Yearly tuition = $16,675
11% receive scholarships	14% of high school students receive scholarships
$7.2 billion endowment	$174 million endowment
More than 90% of graduates go to college	99% of graduates go to college
Once attended by former Governor John Waiheʻe	Once attended by current president Barack Obama

Notes: From 2008, Kamehameha Schools has awarded some scholarships to enable Native Hawaiians to attend other private schools. Kamehameha Schools also offers college scholarships.

Sources: *Honolulu Star-Bulletin* (2008b). Kamehameha Schools (www.ksbe.edu); *Peterson's Private Secondary Schools* (2004:478); Punahou (www.punahou.edu).

thereafter prevailed in the public schools. Monolingualism and monoculturalism became official policy. The decline of Hawaiian-language schools, according to the Republic of Hawaiʻi's school authorities, amounted to a "linguistic revolution" (Hawaiʻi 1896:22). By 1896, the government allowed only three vernacular Hawaiian schools, which were required to teach English. Native Hawaiian children then flooded the public schools (Table 11.3).

Table 11.3

Public School Enrollment in Hawai'i by Ethnic Group, 1874–2007 (in percent of grades 1–12)

Year	Black	Caucasian	Chinese	Filipino	Guamanian	Hawaiian	Japanese	Korean	Mexican	PRican	Samoan	Vietnamese
1874	na	70.1%	na	na	na	12.9%	na	na	na	na	na	na
1892	na	28.3	3.3%	na	na	67.4	.6%	na	na	na	na	na
1900	na	29.2	6.4	na	na	52.3	10.5	na	na	na	na	na
1912	na	24.6	10.4	na	na	26.2	35.2	1.2%	na	2.4%	na	na
1924	na	15.7	9.8	3.4%	na	16.9	51.0	1.8	na	1.9	na	na
1936	na	11.2	7.8	6.3	na	14.8	54.0	2.4	na	1.9	na	na
1946	na	28.6	4.8	10.1	na	21.3	47.0	1.1	na	2.0	na	na
1970	na	na	6.0	14.8	na	11.3	27.1	1.2	na	na	na	na
1980	1.5%	28.4	4.1	18.5	.2%	17.9	19.7	1.8	1.1%	3.4	3.0%	.6%
1990	2.7	26.9	4.6	19.8	.3	19.1	16.0	2.0	1.8	4.1	2.8	1.0
2000	1.7	14.0	2.7	15.5	.1	9.5	7.1	1.5	2.2	4.6	2.0	.9
2007	2.3	14.7	3.2	20.5	na	27.6	9.2	1.3	na	na	3.4	na

Key: na = Figures not available.

Notes: Figures add to 100 percent horizontally when other ethnic groups are added, including "other." Figures in boldface identify the highest in each row. Korean 1970 data are for Honolulu only. The census figures used for 2000 classify mixed-race people as "other," resulting in undercounts especially affecting Native Hawaiians and Japanese.

Sources: Hawai'i (1874:2; 1892:21; 1900:102; 1912:80; 1924:70); Hawai'i Department of Education, annual reports of the Superintendent; U.S. Census (1972:212–215; 1973:11, 70, 129, 178, 180; 1983:40, 64, 70; 1990:57, 122–123, 140; 2000:PCT61); U.S. Congress (1946:717). For more complete data, see Haas (1992:Table 11.3).

During its brief period as an independent Republic (1894–1898), a Board of Education (BOE) replaced the Ministry of Education with responsibility for all public education (Dotts and Sikkema 1994). Today, the Aloha State is the only one of the 50 states to have a statewide school system, with a statewide board of education and a single superintendent at the apex of a statewide educational bureaucracy, a legacy of the days when Whites dominated politics and dealt with non-Whites as colonized subjects. With 257 DOE schools and 31 charter schools on seven islands, top administrators in Honolulu have little ability to identify and address problems of their far-ranging school system.

Haole parents wanted to keep their children away from the so-called "contaminating" influence of the developing Creole (Pidgin) language, so nearly one-fourth of the schoolchildren attended private schools by the late 1890s. After Hawai'i became a Territory of the United States, an influx of Whites arrived from the Mainland to take over leadership of the public schools from Native Hawaiians.

Under the Territory of Hawai'i, Washington-appointed governors subscribed to the assimilationist stress on Americanization. In 1920, alarmed at reports of discrimination, federal investigators went to Hawai'i. The committee's report (U.S. Interior Department 1920) criticized the Territorial government for restricting upward mobility by having only four public high schools, accommodating a measly 3 percent of the population. In response, the Territory opened five new high schools and 15 intermediate schools.

Adopting a recommendation of Frank Bunker (1922), author of a federal survey of education in the Territory, a novel system of segregated education began in 1924. Children certified competent in oral Standard English were to enroll in "English Standard Schools" (ESSs), where Haole teachers prevailed. The remaining public schools were attended and taught increasingly by non-Haoles. Even when non-Haole students and teachers had exemplary English, a Pidgin accent was a sufficient ground to assign them to non-ESSs (Stueber 1964:254). School conversations in Hawaiian and Creole were actively discouraged except at the school on the small island of Ni'ihau, where Native Hawaiian is spoken almost exclusively.

Over the years, many non-Whites have regarded the use of Standard English as a form of snobbery, a tradition that continues to the present among members of working-class families. Creole-speaking children sometimes call better English speakers "fags" for using Standard English (Meredith 1965).

The new linguistically segregated system of public instruction, which disproportionately assigned non-White children to inferior schools but did not exclude them on basis of race per se, provided an opportunity for White parents to send their children to public schools of high quality. Haole support for the new system of segregation was also financial, as parents lobbied for more taxes to pay for public schools. Although Caucasians contributed some 80 percent of the tax revenues for public education, private schools spent twice as much per student as public schools (Stueber 1964:249, 302). The desired academic result, preparing Haoles for college while retarding the educational attainments of non-Whites, was achieved thereby (Stueber 1964:255–256). The social result was to foster a community of interest among yet another generation of non-Whites, who learned to despise those who were denying them an opportunity to receive the best education possible.

In 1931, the University of Hawai'i (UH) opened a Teacher College (called the College of Education from 1957). Prospective teachers enrolled at the university to be certified. Because former teaching credentials were no longer honored unless teachers were recertified at UH, the percentage of Native Hawaiian teachers dropped sharply (Table 11.4).

President Franklin Roosevelt's New Deal brought many educational reforms. In 1933, the Territorial legislature adopted a policy of "equal educational opportunity," the cornerstone of which was the requirement to equalize per-student expenditures for all schools. A second reform, adopted in 1936, was open enrollment, dropping the previous limit of allowing only 75 percent to 80 percent of all elementary school graduates to enroll in secondary schools. Inconsistent with the policy of equal educational opportunity, however, a disproportionate percentage of White students was still bused from their homes past non-ESSs to ESSs. Fees for books, courses in home economics and typing, kindergarten, and library cards were abolished in 1942.

After the attack on Pearl Harbor in 1941, private and public schools closed for eight weeks, and many school buildings were converted for war purposes. During the war, patriotism was stressed, and special classes in English began in the schools. Since many Caucasians left for the Mainland, the number of White children in ESSs fell from 4,024 in 1941 to 1,261 in 1942. To fill their places, many Chinese, Japanese, and Koreans were admitted, and by 1946 they outnumbered Caucasians in ESSs (Stueber 1964:342, 344). Standard English tracks for non-White students were even established in non-ESSs during the war.

Table 11.4

Public School teachers in Hawaiʻi by Ethnic Group, 1888–2007 (in percent)

Year	Black	Caucasian	Chinese	Filipino	Hawaiian	Japanese	Korean	Samoan
1888	.0%	42.4%	.0%	.0%	57.6%	.0%	.0%	.0%
1894	.0	47.6	.0	.0	52.4	.0	.0	.0
1900	.0	70.6	.0	.0	28.4	.0	.0	.0
1908	.0	54.6	1.6	.0	43.8	.0	.0	.0
1916	.0	56.6	6.1	.0	35.0	2.2	.0	.0
1924	na	54.5	11.1	na	14.2	5.1	na	na
1948	na	47.0	*	.8	5.7	46.4	*	na
1967	na	35.0	10.0	4.0	11.0	38.0	na	na
1974	.3	18.7	8.9	2.2	7.0	57.9	1.4	na
1980	.3	17.1	8.2	2.7	7.0	59.5	1.2	na
1990	.6	20.9	7.5	4.0	7.5	54.6	1.0	na
2002	.6	25.9	5.1	6.0	10.4	37.7	.9	.4
2007	.4	22.8	3.9	5.7	9.4	28.9	.8	.3

Key: na = Figures not available.

       * = counted with Japanese.

Notes: Figures add to 100 percent horizontally when other ethnic groups are added, including "other". Figures in boldface identify the highest in each row. For 1967, data are for Oʻahu only.

Sources: Hawaiʻi (1888:16; 1894:16; 1900:99; 1908:59; 1916:64); Hawaiʻi Department of Education, annual reports of the Superintendent; *Honolulu Star-Bulletin* (1971). For more complete data, see (Haas 1992:Table 11.2).

     In 1947, the Territorial legislature decided to phase out assignment to schools on the basis of language ability, starting in grade 1, a process of desegregation that was to last 12 years. The last class enrolled on the basis of de jure language segregation graduated in 1960. The social stigma associated with the division between the two types of schools was the primary motivation behind a campaign to abolish ESSs (Hormann 1947).

     Patterns of housing segregation, established as a result of the pattern of rural residential settlement into Filipino plantation camps, Hawaiian homestead lands, and White-dominated military bases were not remedied by a reversion to neighborhood patterns of enrollment, however. School attendance zones ensured de facto school segregation whenever they coincided with ethnic residential enclaves, especially in elementary rural schools. As a result, many non-Whites were isolated from the Honolulu mainstream. Military buses continued to take military dependents past schools with predominantly non-White enrollment to public schools operated on military bases in central Oʻahu, a practice that continued until 1968, when Congress prohibited the use of federal funds for busing students to schools.

Integrated schools enrolled students with diverse abilities. Whereas formerly the stress in non-ESSs was to prepare students vocationally, integrated schools offered new courses for students seeking to go to college. To satisfy competing demands for instruction, the school system established ability grouping, which, in turn, resegregated students so that darker-skinned ethnic groups (mostly Filipinos and Native Hawaiians) tended to be located in the lower tracks (Haas 1992:Table 6.3). The school dropout rate for Filipinos and Native Hawaiians, as reported in census statistics, reflected the differential treatment.

PUBLIC SCHOOL CONTROVERSIES AFTER STATEHOOD

When Hawaiʻi became a state, the Department of Public Instruction was renamed the Department of Education (DOE). A superintendent was kept as top administrator. While Barry attended Punahou, conflicts surfaced in public schools.

Language instruction. Japanese-language courses began in public schools in 1959 and grew rapidly among students of Japanese ancestry (Kaser 1975a), while courses in European and minority languages declined (Maier 1975), reflecting the changing language abilities within the composition of public schoolteachers. In 1963, the state legislature no longer permitted Native Hawaiian students the option of enrolling in courses in the Hawaiian language. Thereafter, courses in Hawaiiana, often taught largely by teachers of Japanese ancestry, replaced the former Hawaiian-language courses (Table 11.4). A largely Japanese teaching staff was, in effect, shutting down language teaching for other ethnic groups in a subtler manner than previous crackdowns on Japanese-language schools.

Segregation. After statehood, the economic level of the Japanese community rose to the plateau previously achieved by Chinese and Whites in Hawaiʻi. An increasing percentage of Japanese schoolchildren, accordingly, entered private schools from the 1970s (Tables 11.3 and 11.4). As a result, Japanese teachers in the public schools increasingly faced classes where the percentage of students of their own ethnicity was on the downswing in relation to students of other ethnic groups, especially Filipinos and Native Hawaiians. Despite racial diversity in Honolulu public schools, affluent Caucasian, Chinese, and Japanese were predominant in private schools other than Kamehameha.

The Civil Rights Act of 1964 (Title IV) authorized a study of barriers to equal education opportunity. The study, soon contracted to a team of sociologists (Coleman et al. 1966), did not analyze Hawai'i separately to ascertain whether national findings were applicable locally. Nevertheless, lower academic performance of Filipinos and Native Hawaiians was soon identified in several studies (Gallimore, Boggs, Jordan 1974; Hawaii Association for Asian and Pacific Peoples 1974:23–57; Werner, Bierman, and French 1971; Werner and Smith 1977) and attributed to such factors as a lack of cultural sensitivity toward the needs of educational minorities on the part of teachers and school administrators, the prevalence of the Creole tongue at home, and the monoculturalist destruction of the self-concept of the less-affluent groups, whose educational and occupational futures were dead-ended because of ability-group tracking. By the 1970s, many schools had as many as five tracks, and at least one school operated 17—more than any other school district in the United States.

In one study teachers were found to have marked down Native Hawaiians with lower aspirations about going to college (Melahn 1986:489). Minority student alienation was attributed primarily to a perception that teachers were unfair in giving them low grades (Mau 1986). Yet another study found that test scores of Filipinos and Native Hawaiians were not only far below those of Caucasians, Chinese, and Japanese (Morton, Stout, and Fischer 1976) but even declined from grades 2 to 6. The inference was that school experiences were responsible for lowering academic attainments of minority children.

DOE officials argued that Filipinos and Native Hawaiians scored poorly because of their lower socioeconomic standing (Port 1979; Savard and Araki 1965; Verploegen 1986). But a later study found that schools with the largest percentages of Filipino and Native Hawaiian students had the lowest test scores (Haas 1988), thereby confirming the national finding that segregation is associated with lower academic performance (Coleman et al. 1966).

The Civil Rights Act of 1964 (Title VI) mandated that all ethnic groups must derive equal opportunities from institutions financially supported by the federal government. To monitor compliance, all school districts in the United States were first required to provide annual counts of enrollment by ethnicity. Since the state's single school district did not fit the

Black/White racial categories common on the Mainland, members of Hawai'i's congressional delegation secured an exemption for the DOE from filling out federal forms on the ethnicity of students in each school (Gereben 1970a). As a result, the Aloha State was exempted from desegregation monitoring.

From 1965, when Congress reformed immigration policies, a flow of Chinese, Filipino, and Korean immigrants arrived in Hawai'i, bringing many children with limited or no English background into the public schools. Immigrant non-English-speaking children accounted for approximately 6.25 percent of DOE enrollment, three times the national average (Pablo, Ongteco, and Koki 2002).

Following familiar monoculturalist procedures, the DOE assigned new immigrant students to lower tracks. Accordingly, many intelligent immigrant students found themselves in classes with native English speakers of lesser academic aptitude. In some cases, immigrants of average intelligence were even assigned to classes for the mentally retarded. For others, there were limited Teaching English as a Second Language programs in some schools, but provided by teacher aides who were not always qualified.

In 1972, the Emergency School Aid Act (ESAA) provided funds to facilitate desegregation and language assistance. Although public schools in the Islands had the largest percentage of immigrant children among the 50 states, DOE personnel decided that ESAA funds were not relevant to Hawai'i, so they did not submit a grant application until Congresswoman Patsy Mink pressed the DOE to apply (Wilcox 1974). ESAA guidelines required that the DOE count students by ethnicity. Accordingly, annual ethnic counts of students resumed in 1974 (*Honolulu Advertiser* 1974a).

In *Adams v Richardson* (480F2d1159), a federal court during 1973 defined a "segregated" school statistically as one in which the percentage of any race at a particular school differs by 20 percent from that race's percentage in the school district as a whole. By that standard, about half of Hawai'i public schools in 1974 were determined to be segregated (Haas 1992:Table 6.6), mostly those near Filipino plantation camps, Hawaiian homestead lands, and military bases. Although no formal segregation complaint has ever been filed in the Fiftieth State, segregation had an adverse impact upon student safety, as noted in the following discussion.

School violence. Before World War II, in the recollection of onetime School Superintendent Techiro Hirata, the only school violence of any consequence consisted of organized gangs that roamed from school to school to cause mischief (Verploegen 1974). After the bombing of Pearl Harbor in 1941, Japanese American children became victims of "rap-a-Jap" attacks on frequent occasions, mostly involving Filipino, Korean, and Portuguese bullies (Lind 1946:59).

During the 1952/1953 school year, less than 1 percent of DOE students were referred to counselors for misconduct (Hawai'i 1953:6, 21). After statehood, as Mainland-born Whites increasingly enrolled in public schools, they were taunted by warnings of a mythical "kill-a-Haole day," not realizing that they were being perceived by their tormentors as failing to assimilate to more deferential Island ways. Upset parents then responded by routing their children to private schools, where they met students of other affluent groups. By 1974/1975, after passage of the Emergency School Aid Act, some 13.3 percent of all DOE students were cited for disciplinary infractions on three or more occasions (cf. Haas 1988), and there were 21.2 offenses of violence per thousand students, the highest rate in the nation (National Institute of Education 1978:I–B6).

A study of DOE schools found that violence was most intense in secondary schools that enrolled disparate streams of students from ethnically identifiable (segregated) elementary schools and in schools where immigrants were disproportionately classified as "mentally retarded" (Haas 1988). An attitude study of seniors within four O'ahu high schools in 1976 found that most students were fearful of violent incidents and that schools with higher percentages of college-bound students and fewer cross-ethnic friendships had the most ethnic tension (Wegner 1976:14–15, 54). Two other studies concluded that ethnicity, not social status, was correlated with the lower educational attainments of Filipinos and Native Hawaiians (Wegner 1977; Wegner, Sakihara, and Takeuchi 1976).

Situations that triggered school violence in Hawai'i varied considerably, but a pattern was evident. Children seeking to define their identities at schools, but not receiving relevant instruction, formed cliques based on ethnicity or language and laid territorial claims to trees and other portions of schoolyards. Little violence took place inside the classroom. Instead, students who found school unrewarding and boring were absent from class but present on the school grounds (Armstrong 1975; cf. Verploegen 1989a; Wegner, Sakihara, and Takeuchi 1976:20). Students who hung around bathrooms extorted money from students using the toilet facilities by threatening them with a beating.

At the end of the school day, students might emerge from classes divided into ability-grouped sections, whereupon those in the lower tracks would hurl verbal abuse, such as "dumb Haole," "Buddhaheads," and "here come the bago'ongs" (the name of a distinctive Filipino spice). Although those with the most cross-ethnic friends reported the least ethnic tension, children in more ethnically homogeneous upper-status tracks most feared violence (Wegner 1976:31, 36). Lower-track students, whose honor or pride was challenged by the apparently snobbish bearing of an upper-track or Mainland-born student, whom they doubtless did not know on a personal basis, might resort to fisticuffs (Wegner 1976:47).

Meanwhile, teachers observed acts of violence but cited their union contract as a reason for not trying to stop even the more brutal incidents, leaving crisis intervention to a disinterested school administration. Accordingly, the police would be called, an arrest made, and all students would be told to go home immediately. Although juvenile arrests skyrocketed in the 1970s (Haas 1988:731), Filipino immigrants were less likely to be arrested than Hawai'i-born students (Agbayani-Cahill et al. 1975), so the violence was predominantly blamed on local students who resented the attainments of upward-mobile groups.

CIVIL RIGHTS MOBILIZATION

The Filipino community, which sent its offspring to schools where they felt treated as outsiders, responded quickly when a Filipino died at a public school in 1974. Indeed, several studies noted that immigrant parents placed a higher value on education than local parents (Melahn 1986; Research Information Services 1977; Wegner 1977:7; Wegner Sakihara, and Takeuchi.1976:20).

The O'ahu Filipino Community Council (OFCC) formed a task force of Filipino educators, who prepared a report with 25 recommendations (OFCC 1975). Although they presented copies to public school officials, the governor, and the BOE, there was no response. Later that year, after a second Filipino died at another school, members of the OFCC task force identified 22 DOE policies and practices that adversely affected Filipinos, circulated a petition calling for a federal civil rights compliance review of the DOE, obtained some 750 signatures on the petition, and sent the petition to the BOE (*Honolulu Star-Bulletin* 1975).

Again, the OFCC was ignored. A high-ranking DOE official of Japanese ancestry even told a television reporter that he "didn't understand the need for special programs. After all, we made it without them" (quoted in Haas and Resurrection 1976:43). While he made that statement, which in effect vindicated the OFCC complaint that there was intentional discrimination, DOE personnel were sending a larger percentage of their children to private schools than the state average (Watanabe 2001).

Next, the petition was sent to the Office for Civil Rights (OCR) of the federal Department of Health, Education, and Welfare (HEW). Upon receipt of the class-action complaint, the federal agency contacted DOE Superintendent Charles Clark, who initially threatened not to cooperate. When civil rights officials pointed out that noncooperation would result in prompt termination of all federal funds to the DOE, Clark relented and received two investigators in May 1976. In June, the federal agency issued a report citing the DOE for violating Title VI of the Civil Rights Act of 1964 by failing to provide appropriate language assistance to Filipinos as well as to Koreans, Samoans, and other immigrants. The DOE was thus ineligible to renew its $2.5 million ESAA grant, pending negotiation of an agreement to establish better procedures for identifying students in need of English-language assistance, and to provide these students with special language programs (Verploegen 1976).

OFCC, in response to the noncompliance finding in 1976, renewed its call for a full review of all aspects of DOE operations covered in the original petition. Again, there was no BOE or DOE response to the Filipino community. Later in 1976, People's Party senatorial candidate Tony Hodges released to the press the list of segregated schools obtained from an ongoing school violence study, charged the DOE with racism, and backed OFCC's call for a full OCR compliance review.

Reacting to mounting pressure, Clark charged that OFCC was inciting violence by complaining, and he refused to meet with the Filipino educators to discuss their call for a federal compliance review. At this point, Governor George Ariyoshi intervened (Woo 1976). Clark reversed his stand and asked OCR to do a compliance review (*Honolulu Advertiser* 1976). Federal officials, busy with a full schedule of civil rights complaints in California, then replied that if the DOE wanted to exercise voluntary compliance with the law, it should review itself. Clark then signed an agreement to set up bilingual education programs with federal funding.

Subsequently, OCR officials cited the DOE for continued language discrimination from 1977 to 1990 (cf. Ong 1980). The DOE's programs for language-minority students were serving only half the eligible students by 1981. What was occurring initially was paper compliance without sufficient commitment of resources to equip immigrant students to enter the educational mainstream.

Many immigrant students, meanwhile, were dropping out of school without an educational experience that they regarded as useful for earning an income. When immigrants arrived home from school each day, adults were at work, so they lacked parental guidance. The limited campus violence of the mid-1970s gradually turned into organized gang violence during the late 1970s. Some immigrant students, aware that opportunities for upward mobility were blocked in the public schools, went into the business of selling small amounts of narcotic drugs (cf. Chesney-Lind et al. 1992). As rival gangs battled for control of the market, they attracted more young members, engaged in turf battles, and executions of gang members began to occur on and off the grounds of public schools. In time, there were an estimated 45 violent gangs on Oʻahu, mostly composed of Filipinos and Samoans (Infante 1991a).

AFFIRMATIVE ACTION RESPONSE

The struggle for equality in public education made frequent headlines while Barry Obama was at Punahou, insulated from the controversy. While African Americans on the Mainland were continuing to struggle for civil rights, the newspapers and television in Honolulu exposed Barry to a civil rights campaign for Filipinos.

In 1982, after Barry left for college on the Mainland, the Hawaiʻi State Advisory Committee to the U.S. Commission on Civil Rights held public hearings on a related issue—why the DOE was making no progress to hire schoolteachers from ethnic groups other than the dominant Japanese. The resulting report charged the DOE with deliberate discrimination, especially against Filipino applicants, who had risen from 2 percent to only 3 percent of the teachers during the previous decade (U.S. Commission on Civil Rights 1983).

In 1984, after the BOE appointed Francis Hatanaka as the new DOE superintendent, civil rights compliance increased. The BOE agreed that "preference" in hiring would thenceforth go to groups underrepresented in the jobs to be filled. The percentage of Japanese teachers then began a steady decline, and other groups, particularly Caucasians and Native Hawaiians, gradually increased (Table 11.4).

While Filipinos were struggling to succeed in a society whose norms they accepted, yet encountered discrimination, many Native Hawaiians were increasingly ambivalent about wanting to be a part of American society (Wegner 1976:44). Instead of equal treatment to take their place in the United States as yet another successful minority, Native Hawaiians were trying to save a culture in danger of extinction. In 1974, Congress recognized their quest, granting Native Hawaiians the same status as American Indians in the Native American Programs Act. A further breakthrough came in 1978, when the state legislature mandated that all DOE students take courses in Hawaiian Studies. Since there were insufficient qualified teachers for the new program, the DOE hired kūpuna (Native Hawaiian elders) on a part-time basis from 1980.

Meanwhile, Native Hawaiian leaders formed needs assessments task forces in several areas, including education (Hannahs 1983). As in the case of the earlier Filipino report, the DOE initially ignored recommendations from Native Hawaiians.

In the 1986 campaign for lieutenant governor, Republican candidate Vicky Bunye raised the issue of DOE discrimination against Filipinos, which had been documented in a comprehensive study of state employment patterns (cf. Haas 2010b:Ch. 3). Her main focus was on employment of Filipino teachers, with the aim of improving the quality of instruction by hiring more culturally sensitive schoolteachers. Although she lost the election, the issues at last received prominent statewide attention.

After the election, Charles Toguchi became DOE superintendent. He was eager to reverse any unequal educational opportunities in the public schools. The BOE, in turn, set up the Citizens' Task Force on Affirmative Action for Filipinos, the first response to matters raised by the OFCC in 1974 and 1975. After the task force presented its report in 1987, the BOE agreed to several new programs for equal opportunity in education and employment.

Teaching-as-a-Career clubs in high schools, one of the new programs, were designed to attract more Filipinos and other underrepresented groups to become schoolteachers. A Career Shadowing Program provided mentoring to help new minority hires to become successful teachers. Filipinos who formerly taught school in the Philippines were disproportionately flunking the National Teacher Examination (NTE) test upon arrival in the Islands, so the DOE set up NTE Preparation Workshops. In addition, several DOE-University of Hawai'i projects, were launched in the late 1980s to provide some college experience for minority high school students (see Chapter 12).

To assist speakers of Hawai'i Creole English, the DOE used federal funds to support a short-term Hawai'i Creole Project. Although not renewed, the project had possible relevance to Ebonics, a tongue based on

West African languages that was perpetuated by slavery, segregation, and substandard schools on the U.S. Mainland (*Honolulu Advertiser* 1997).

For immigrant children, a Bilingual Education Coordination Project was set up in 1978 to provide language assistance. By 1991, the federal government gave the DOE's bilingual educational program a clean bill of health, and the DOE resolved most of the 19 complaints dealing with language issues from 1991 to 2009. From 1975, federal funds supported 35 projects to assist the ongoing language programs benefiting more than 20,000 limited English proficient students (Pablo, Ongteco, and Koki 2002). Some are continuing.

In 1989, the Wai'anae Coast School Concerns Coalition protested unequal school facilities for Native Hawaiians on the Western side of O'ahu (Viotti 1989). After the group's leader, Michael Kahikina, threatened a lawsuit, the DOE responded in a few months with promises of increased funding to Wai'anae schools (Verploegen 1989b).

School violence persisted as schoolchildren increasingly joined gangs. In 1985/1986, an average of 18 cases of disorderly conduct occurred per day in Island public schools (Glauberman 1988). In 1988, Hawai'i ranked highest among the 50 states in teacher concerns over absenteeism, disruptive behavior, parental and student apathy, racial discord, theft, vandalism, and violence (Verploegen 1988). An educational task force reported (Verploegen 1989a) that the most unruly students (Native Hawaiians) were those who perceived that they were rejected by school personnel (mostly Japanese). During 2006/2007 there were 19.7 violent incidents per thousand students and about 50 disorderly conduct cases per day (Hawai'i 2008c:Table 9). Unlike problems of assault on teachers reported on the Mainland, fellow students have been the main targets of violence in Hawai'i public schools (Infante 1991c), particularly Whites (Todd 1999).

When DOE administrators failed to remedy the situation, victims again complained to the federal government (*Honolulu Star-Bulletin* 1999; Kobayashi 2008; Thompson 2009). In 1999, OCR, now within the U.S. Department of Education, required the DOE to develop a statewide plan to cope with racial harassment after problems were documented at public schools on Maui.

But no such plan was in place for a decade, and further complaints were filed, resulting in a major federal investigation in 2008. Whites, according to the investigation, remained the principal victims of hostile school environments, though Japanese were among the estimated 50 percent of students who reported that they had been bullied. In one case, a White girl's jaw was dislocated when a student repeatedly slammed her head against a concrete wall.

In each incident, recommendations for corrective action were adopted by the DOE, but there was no monitoring of the lack of implementation at the school level, and parents were denied access to grievance procedures. On the last day of 2008, OCR set strict deadlines for step-by-step development of procedures for schools to deal with harassment complaints. The ultimate sanction for further noncompliance is termination of millions of dollars of federal financial assistance to Hawai'i public schools.

Meanwhile, disabled students were left by the wayside in Hawai'i public schools. Numerous complaints to OCR yielded little progress. In 1993, a disabled Maui student named Jennifer Felix went to federal court claiming that the DOE failed to provide services required by the federal Individuals with Disabilities Education Act. In 1994, due to overwhelming evidence of neglect, the state settled, and the entire program of dealing with disabled students was to be modified over the next decade at an estimated cost of $1 billion (Nakaso 2009). That same year, the DOE agreed to provide appropriate education for two autistic students, but specialists were never assigned to them, so their parents sued in 1999, and a federal appeals court finally agreed in 2010 on the merits of their case, though the best ages to advance their learning capabilities had long passed (Honolulu Star-Advertiser 2010e).

Due to the Felix case, the upper administration was required to certify that teachers assigned to classes were trained appropriately. The same was true of administrators, who formerly had been part of the problem. Disciplinary procedures were also to be standardized, though differing between regular and special needs students. It is too soon to tell whether needed reforms have been adopted.

Today, approximately half of those at DOE schools are "special needs" students. Some 29 percent are considered to be economically disadvantaged. Special education students constitute 5 percent; English-language learners, 4 percent; and multiple needs students, 12 percent. Clearly, the DOE invests a lot with little expectation of stellar results.

Of the 279 civil rights complaints filed with the U.S. Department of Education's Office for Civil Rights from 1991–2009, disability issues have been the most numerous, accounting for 112 (40 percent). Race discrimination occupied 60 cases (about 22 percent), mostly involving complaints from Blacks and Whites. Only 30 complaints (11 percent) were resolved amicably.

INNOVATIVE PROGRAMS

During the 1980s, after Obama left for college on the Mainland, efforts to improve equal educational opportunity competed for attention with innovations aimed at advancing the overall quality of education, particularly after publication of the National Commission on Excellence in Education's *A Nation at Risk* (1983), a nationwide critique of public schooling. In Hawai'i, automatic "social promotions" ended, and promotion from one grade to another was limited to students with passing grades. A passing score on competency tests became a requirement for a diploma, and course requirements increased.

Perhaps the most innovative idea emerged in 1984, when Native Hawaiian instructors at the University of Hawai'i's main campus organized a pilot program of total instruction in the Hawaiian language at a private school. In 1987, the BOE approved a trial of this "immersion program" at the kindergarten and first grades on the campuses of two public elementary schools. The program expanded to five schools by 1991. By 1992, the program included all grades, with one hour of English language instruction for grades 5–12. Known as the Hawaiian Language Immersion Program (HLIP), Anuenue Elementary School was established as the first fully operational HLIP school in 1995. Later, the concept was incorporated into the charter school movement (Table 11.5). Some 1,500 students are currently enrolled in the HLIP program.

In 1988, Congress authorized the establishment of the Native Hawaiian Education Council, a body charged with the responsibility to assess needs and to work toward meeting those needs. One element of the program, as further mandated by Congress in 1994, was to promote literacy, either in English or Hawaiian.

In 1989, the Board of Education established a program of special learning centers in most high schools. Serving as "magnet schools," the aim was to provide specialized career-oriented curricula articulated to particular professions. There are now 30 learning centers in such subjects as business, communications, health, international studies, math and the sciences, and vocational programs.

"Academies," with even more intensive training than in the magnet schools, were developed next. In 1991, a High School Health Academy opened with 54 sophomore aspiring health care workers, a field of employment with a serious labor shortage (Infante 1991b:A1). The program was designed to prepare students for entry to a professional

Table 11.5

Native Hawaiian-Oriented Schooling in the State of Hawai'i

Year Established	Name of Program	Features	Schools Involved
1887	Kamehameha Schools	Preschool + K–12 instruction in English and Hawaiian	3
1904	Ni'ihau Elementary School	K-8 Hawaiian-language instruction	1
1963	Hawaiiana curriculum in Department of Education schools	K-12 Hawaiiana courses	All
1987	Hawaiian Language Immersion Program (HLIP), otherwise known as Ka Papahana Kaiapuni Hawai'i	K-12 Hawaiian-language instruction 5-12 English-language instruction	19
1999	Ni'ihau High & Elementary School	K-12 Hawaiian-language instruction 5-12 English-language instruction	1
2000	Hawaiian Culture Focused Charter Schools	K-12 Hawaiiana courses, including some language instruction K-12 English-language instruction	7
2001	Immersion Charter Schools	K-12 Hawaiian-language instruction 5-12 English-language instruction	5
2008	Kako'o Ho'ona'auao	Expenses for private school students	All[a]

[a]Scholarships could potentially be provided to all private schools, though the actual number of recipient schools is unknown.

degree in nursing by graduating nurse's aides. An Academy of Travel and Tourism opened in 1992. The programs, which depended on outside funding, are not currently operating.

The DOE also undertook several programs to identify and to prepare students with college potential. Compared to a national average of 60 percent, some 51 percent of all graduates from public high schools in

Hawai'i go to college—18 percent to community colleges and 33 percent to four-year institutions of higher learning (Moreno 2009b), though an undetermined percentage are later dropouts.

In 1991, the BOE adopted a form of decentralization known as School/Community-Based Management (SCBM) that involved incorporating parents, community leaders, and teachers into educational decision making. SCBM differed from Mainland counterparts in that the management councils were instructed to incorporate traditional Native Hawaiian values, such as lōkahi (harmony), kōkua (helpfulness), and laulima (cooperativeness), but were given little authority over the school curricula or budget. Community-based decision making required consensus, often a nearly impossible impediment, and emphasized avoiding embarrassment over substance. Generating as much disharmony as satisfaction (Cotton 1992; Fox and Buchanan 2004; Koki 1998), SCBM neither met the public's desire for greater local control of centrally run schools nor conformed to the legislature's expectations. The legislature responded with a succession of statutes designed to loosen the reins of control exercised by the BOE on all aspects of Hawai'i public education, but the DOE resisted loss of control. Although SCBM was eventually adopted at about half the public schools, dissatisfaction cried out for a new approach, and SCBMs were abolished in 2006.

In 1995, the state legislature, recognizing that the BOE was unable or unwilling to bring about genuine school reform, passed laws empowering local groups under strict limitations to form two Student-Centered Schools that were allowed limited local autonomy under a local school advisory board.

In 1999, the legislature followed the lead of 35 other states by identifying charter schools as the mechanism to make community-run schools possible, similar to the Hawai'i School for the Deaf and the Blind, which began under a different name in 1914. The legislation authorized New Century Public Charter Schools, including start-ups, school-within-school programs, and entire school conversions from DOE control to charter schools. In 2006, the legislature assigned overall responsibility for charter schools to a Charter School Review Panel, but the BOE continues a turf battle by sponsoring legislation almost every year to "clarify" jurisdiction (Fox and Buchanan 2007). All charter schools have their own school boards.

Today, most of the 31 charter schools either are on Neighbor Islands or serve the Native Hawaiian communities—or both. Serving diverse populations, the primary reason for starting charter schools was to gain autonomy from a distant center of control, the DOE headquarters in Honolulu. With the encouragement of the Federal Charter School Program, community groups applied for grants to fund planning and implementation of entirely new schools. Some 8,202 students were enrolled in charter schools during 2010, compared to 169,187 in the remaining public schools (Goya 2011). Additional charter schools were approved in 2010, anticipating funding from the Obama administration's Race to the Top program, which later granted the DOE $75 million (Vorsino 2010a).

Five charter schools for Native Hawaiians have adopted the Hawaiian language immersion program, in which more than 80 percent of those enrolled are Native Hawaiians. Seven Hawaiian Culture charter schools focus more on culture than immersion in the language. Both view culture and an emerging Hawaiian epistemology as a vehicle to move disadvantaged Native Hawaiian students to higher achievement and improved confidence in their ability to flourish (Buchanan and Fox 2005).

Of the 65,000 Native Hawaiian students in Hawai'i public schools today, some 2,000 are in Hawaiian-language charter schools (Gionson 2009). Thus, what began as a law to empower the creation of a limited number of charter schools became a strong force for even more Native Hawaiian-focused education in the state (Table 11.5).

Several problems have resulted from increased instruction in the Hawaiian language. One is that teacher training programs had to be developed due to a lack of qualified teachers in the Hawaiian language. Because many parents of children enrolled in Hawaiian Immersion schools do not speak the language, parents are expected to attend evening classes. A more vexing problem is that the DOE requires all public schools to meet the same performance standards. In 2010, Hawai'i became the second state to adopt Common Core State Standards for knowledge and abilities adopted by the National Association of School Boards of Education, though such questions as alleged cultural and linguistic bias in standardized tests have yet to be resolved.

The DOE has long offered night schools, otherwise known as "community schools." In 1996, the various adult schools were brought under a single framework. In addition to facilitating literacy and high school graduation for dropouts or those from other countries, the traditional curriculum has involved citizenship classes. Currently, courses also serve to broaden cultural, recreational, and social interests.

The DOE also operates E-School, that is, distance-learning courses utilizing websites, e-mail, threaded discussion, chatrooms, streaming video, and online textbooks. E-School, the modern equivalent of correspondence courses, is offered by 30 to 48 secondary schools and typically serves from 200 to 400 students per semester. Students may take a maximum of two courses per term.

In 2000, Running Start began as a pilot program between high schools in Honolulu and Honolulu Community College so that students could take college courses and earn credit. In 2003, some 338 students completed the program, which expanded statewide, but 149 finished in 2004.

With the advent of the No Child Left Behind Act of 2001, testing for competency has challenged Hawai'i public schools. The sanction of shutting down schools that do not perform at national standards meant more attention to quantitative scores on math and reading than to ethnic or language issues. Few of the state's public schools are unconditionally "in good standing" under the Adequate Yearly Progress standards (Moreno 2009a). Currently, the DOE claims that 62 percent of students meet or exceed standards in reading but 21 percent are well below, whereas for math only 34 percent meet or exceed standards and 42 percent are well below (Hawai'i 2008c). About one-sixth of DOE students drop out before graduation. After DOE graduates matriculate at the University of Hawai'i, well over half need remediation in math and reading (Roth 2009).

In 2003, a program originally developed on the Mainland began at two high schools. Known as Freshman Success Academy, the program is a school within a school, fenced off from the main high school. Meanwhile, one-third of entering ninth grade students, who are identified as likely dropouts or flunkouts, take intensive courses so that they can complete at the 10th grade level with their peers (Essoyan 2004).

Step Up, a new college-bound program, emerged in 2009. Students having at least a "B" average are awarded a special diploma for taking algebra and geometry; biology, chemistry, or physics; expository writing; and a senior project.

From 2009, Kako'o Ho'ona'auao (to support enlightenment through education) provides private school funding for children of about 175 parents or primary caregivers eligible for Hawaiian homelands. Some $500,000 is allotted each year (*Honolulu Star-Bulletin* 2010b).

The alternative to private and public schools is homeschooling, which Obama experienced while in Indonesia. About 6,000 students are homeschooled in Hawai'i compared with 178,000 in public schools and 38,000 in private schools. Parents do not require advance approval to educate their children at home. They only need to file a "notice of intent to home educate the child," a "record of planned curriculum," and either an annual report of progress using nationally normed standardized tests or a written narrative. However, it is difficult for the DOE to monitor and enforce the required tests and reports, so homeschooled students do not earn credits toward high school graduation.

By the beginning of the 21st century, the public schools had a serious teaching shortage. With too few available to be hired locally, DOE recruiters went to the Mainland to recruit about one-fourth of the new teachers. Increasingly, White teachers from monoethnic and monocultural parts of the Mainland have entered Hawai'i public schools, often unprepared for a multiethnic student body and a multicultural curriculum but destined to learn about important multicultural innovations and traditions while pressured and frustrated in working toward improved test scores (cf. Ravitch 2010). On average, more than half of those recruited from outside the Islands quit within five years (Vorsino 2010d), so new recruitment efforts are re-launched each year. A more comprehensive approach, scholarships to train more local students as schoolteachers, remains unfunded.

CONCLUSION

Barack Obama's education at Punahou was, in retrospect, the best possible choice for a future president. Hawai'i has notoriously ranked last among the 50 states in the percentage of state funding for K–12 education, and many deficiencies remain (Donnelly 1996; Schooland 2007).

The political succession from ruling Native Hawaiians to Territorial White governors to the ruling majority of Democrats, mostly Japanese, clearly has impacted the public school system in peculiar ways. After statehood, White children increasingly exited from public schools to attend private schools, joined in due course by affluent Chinese and Japanese classmates, leaving public schools as the last resort. Upward-mobile public school students, whose ethnicity most closely matched the staff, were able to attend college-bound classes in public schools, while darker-skinned pupils encountered low teacher expectations, and their overall test scores declined.

Due to community protest, followed by professional program development and BOE acceptance of innovations, public education in Hawai'i has become more responsive to the needs of its multiethnic population. Rather than a backlash to multicultural education, as on the Mainland

(Santa Cruz 2010), the new educational multiculturalism enjoys wide acceptance and lacks vocal critics in the Islands. Multicultural education promotes mutual respect, not resentment, while also treating students as individuals.

The severe economic downturn in 2009, accounting for a budget shortfall of more than $1 billion, presented Governor Linda Lingle with a dilemma—lay off hundreds of teachers or cut their pay by reducing the school year. The choice of furloughs has rankled everyone. Nevertheless, the Reinventing Education Act of 2004 provides that 70 percent of school budgets is controlled by principals, who can save programs developed at individual schools (Moreno 2010a).

Barack Obama experienced a multicultural curriculum at Punahou (Remnick 2010:76), while Filipinos and Native Hawaiians sought to overcome discrimination in public schools. By 2005, he chaired the Annenberg Challenge, a foundation dedicated to reform public schools to plug the "*achievement gap*" for poor students (Broder 2005). Hawai'i offers such a model, albeit a work in progress.

NOTE

1. Presumably, any child can apply for admission to Kamehameha and might be accepted if space is available. Indeed, one was accepted on that basis recently. Children of Kamehameha teachers, regardless of ethnic background, can attend the school. In a recent court case, however, an orphan or abandoned child, for whom there is no information on ancestry, was denied admission to Kamehameha, and others without Native Hawaiian ancestry have sued for admission. The schools receive federal funds and tax-exempt status despite an overwhelming enrollment of students of Native Hawaiian ancestry, according to Internal Revenue Service rulings, because of the undeniable benefits for a minority community (cf. Jones 1967).

Chapter 12

A University Searching
for Identity

Michael Haas

> Our investment in education can't end with an improved ele-
> mentary and secondary school system. In a knowledge-based
> economy where eight of the nine fastest-growing occupations
> this decade require scientific or technological skills, most
> workers are going to need some form of higher education to
> fill the jobs of the future. And just as our government insti-
> tuted free and mandatory public high schools at the dawn of
> the twentieth century to provide workers the skills needed for
> the industrial age, our government has to help today's work-
> force adjust to twenty-first-century realities.
>
> (Obama 2008:194)

In September 1959, Ann Dunham enrolled at the main campus of the
University of Hawai'i in Mānoa Valley (UHM). An anthropology major,
she took a class in Russian, as did some college students across the country after the Soviet Union launched the satellite Sputnik the previous
year. Another student in the class, Barack Hussein Obama, was an economics major from Kenya and the first UHM student from Africa. Fascinated with the articulate, intelligent Kenyan, Ann dated him, eventually
became pregnant, and bore a son, the future president.

After Barack Senior left for a graduate degree at Harvard, Ann took Barry to Seattle, enrolled at the University of Washington, but in 1963 returned to live with her parents in Honolulu while again attending UHM. In 1996, she went with her second husband, Lolo Soetero, to Indonesia, where she eventually completed field work in anthropology and received a PhD in 1992.

While Barry attended Punahou, he often attended basketball games at UHM, where he enjoyed seeing African Americans play on the university's basketball team. In 1979, when Barry was about to graduate from Punahou, he shocked his mom by intimating that he would go to a local community college. His mom strongly disagreed. Instead of suggesting that he follow in her footsteps by enrolling at UHM, she recommended that he should go to a better school on the Mainland, as was customary for Punahou grads. After applying to several schools, he chose Occidental College, subsequently Columbia University, and later Harvard University. Law professor Laurence Tribe, now employed in the Obama administration, found him to be his best student ever (Schoenberg 2007).

Why did his mother recommend against attending the University of Hawai'i? She probably made the right choice, as quite a struggle to multiculturalize the University of Hawai'i was underway when he went off to college. She was doubtless unaware that the University of Hawai'i was about to live up to its promise in multicultural education regarding African Americans, as that fall the first African American female (Kathryn Takara) was hired to teach courses in Black studies with the UHM Ethnic Studies Program.

Years later, his sister Maya received a PhD in education at UHM. She and her husband Konrad Ng are now on the UHM faculty.

Today, the University of Hawai'i has an identity problem. Local students, mostly non-White, are overwhelmed by UHM White administrators and faculty, who sometimes make local students uncomfortable because they have not sufficiently assimilated to Hawai'i's multicultural ethos, a tension that continues to play out at UHM, though much less so at community colleges.

THE EMERGENCE OF HIGHER EDUCATION IN HAWAI'I

Higher education came to Hawai'i in 1857, when Punahou School, a prep school originally set up to educate Haoles, instituted a private two-year institution known as O'ahu College. The two-year private college continued until 1934.

The impetus for a public four-year institution of higher learning came from Honolulu postmaster William Kwai Fong Yap, who wanted his daughter and son to go to a four-year college. Unable to afford to send them to the Mainland, he launched a petition. In 1907, the Territorial government agreed, and the College of Agriculture and Mechanic Arts opened its doors in 1908. After a retitling in 1912 as the "College of Hawaii," the institution was renamed the "University of Hawaii" in 1920 at its campus in Mānoa Valley (UHM), east of downtown Honolulu.

By the latter third of the century, UHM was joined on Oʻahu by two four-year campuses (at Hilo and West Oʻahu) and four two-year community colleges (Honolulu Community College, Kapiʻolani Community College, Leeward Community College, Windward Community College). There are three community colleges on Neighbor Islands (Hawaiʻi Community College, Kauaʻi Community College, Maui Community College). In 2003, Maui Community College first offered baccalaureate degrees.

A few other institutions of higher learning exist in Hawaiʻi. A Catholic institution, St. Louis Junior College, started in 1955, becoming four-year Chaminade College in 1957 and Chaminade University of Honolulu in 1977. Church College of Hawaiʻi, operated by the Mormon Church on the North Shore of Oʻahu from 1955 as a junior college, was upgraded to a four-year institution in 1958, and became a branch of Brigham Young University in 1974. Nondenominational Hawaiʻi Pacific College opened in downtown Honolulu in 1965, became Hawaiʻi Pacific University in 1990, and in 1992 absorbed nondenominational Hawaiʻi Loa College, which from 1965 had been operating independently at Kailua, Oʻahu. Although these universities fill important needs in the community, the rest of the chapter discusses developments within the largest institution of higher learning in the Islands, the multicampus University of Hawaiʻi (UH).

ADMISSION AND ENROLLMENT

Initially, UH enrollment was not diverse (Wist 1940:168, 210). More than two-thirds of the students were Caucasian, and Chinese constituted the largest minority (Table 12.1a). More students of Japanese ancestry began to attend from the mid-1920s. Filipino students remained largely outside until the 1960s. Compared with modest enrollment figures in the early years, Native Hawaiians nearly disappeared in the 1960s and have never returned to the same percentages that they maintained in the 1920s and 1930s. Japanese were the most numerous students by the

Table 12.1

Enrollment at the University of Hawai'i by Ethnic Group, 1915–2008 (in percent)

(a) Mānoa Campus

Year	Black	Caucasian	Chinese	Filipino	Guamanian	Hawaiian	Japanese	Korean	PRican	Samoan	Vietnamese
1915	na	**84.7%**	8.3%	.7%	na	1.4%	3.5%	1.4%	na	na	na
1921	.0%	**50.0**	22.6	.9	na	7.8	16.1	2.6	na	na	na
1930	.0	23.0	23.0	1.0	na	14.0	**37.0**	2.0	na	na	na
1939	na	22.0	23.0	.4	na	10.0	**40.0**	4.0	na	na	na
1961	na	22.1	14.3	2.4	na	1.4	**53.5**	1.9	na	na	na
1971	.6	31.9	11.2	2.1	na	3.2	**40.7**	1.6	na	na	na
1981	.6	24.8	11.7	4.1	na	3.9	**35.8**	2.1	na	na	na
1990	.8	23.0	11.4	7.9	na	6.0	**29.8**	2.8	na	na	na
2000	.8	22.7	10.0	8.6	na	8.6	**23.0**	4.3	.3%	na	na
2008	1.2	**25.5**	7.4	7.9	.5%	9.8	16.8	4.0	.1	1.6%	1.2%

(b) Community Colleges

Year	Black	Caucasian	Chinese	Filipino	Guamanian	Hawaiian	Japanese	Korean	PRican	Samoan	Vietnamese
1978	1.1%	22.4%	6.5%	12.2%	na	5.0%	**30.0%**	1.6%	na	na	na
1988	1.2	22.5	6.3	16.2	na	11.2	**23.3**	2.5	na	na	na
1998	1.1	16.6	5.4	**18.9**	na	16.7	16.5	2.4	.6%	na	na
2008	1.1	14.9	4.1	17.4	.3%	**21.0**	11.8	2.1	.1	.8%	.9%

Key: na = Figures not available.

Notes: Figures add to 100 percent horizontally when other ethnic groups are added. After spring 1978, figures refer to fall enrollment. "Caucasian" figures include Portuguese and other Caucasians but not Puerto Ricans. Only undergraduates are counted from 1929 to 1939. Figures in boldface identify the highest in each row.

Sources: Dannemiller (1973); Gereben (1970b); Gulick (1937:78); Hawai'i (1915:60); Martorana and Hollis (1962:71); Institutional Research Office, *University of Hawaii Quarterly Bulletin,* 3 (December 1924:5, 11); UH, Institutional Research Office *Fall Enrollment Report* (1996–2008). For more complete data, see Haas (1992:Table 12.1).

1930s as well as when community colleges opened in the 1970s (Table 12.1b). Caucasians have been more numerous than other ethnic groups in the last decade. Today, Filipino and Native Hawaiian enrollment percentages are greater at community colleges than at UHM.

In 1959, Congress established the Center for Cultural and Technical Interchange between East and West, known colloquially as the East-West Center, as an autonomous UHM unit. The goal is to bring students and scholars together from East and West in ethnically diverse Hawai'i.

The addition of the East-West Center brought UHM within the rank of the top 10 universities in amounts of federal funds received. Soon, hundreds of students from Asian and Pacific countries, many with important academic and political connections, were attending. Barack Obama Senior was not on an East-West Center fellowship, though Ann Dunham later became a grantee while a candidate for a doctorate in anthropology. In 1975, after the United States left Vietnam, the East-West Center became independent of UH, Congressional funding plummeted, and the focus shifted to research conducted by various specialized centers, sometimes even competing for grants with UHM faculty.

With the election of John Burns as governor of Hawai'i in 1962, when the post-war "baby boom" was graduating record numbers of high school students, the state legislature dramatically increased the university's budget, and the Board of Regents authorized an increase in enrollment at the Mānoa campus to 25,000. After reaching a peak attendance during the 1970s, enrollment fell somewhat and has leveled off.

The enrollment for fall 2010 was an unprecedented 60,231 for all campuses—20,137 for Mānoa, 4,085 for the Hilo campus, 1,494 for West O'ahu, and 34,515 for all seven community colleges combined. Women outnumber men, about 16 percent come from outside Hawai'i, and graduate students account for about 13 percent. Some 28,000 are in non-credit courses.

PROGRAMS TO INCREASE STUDENT DIVERSITY

Many UH students attend classes in the daytime, work in the afternoons, and study at home in the evening, so campus events are not well attended. Student activism is infrequent but effective whenever leaders either are sons and daughters of influential legislators and state government administrators or are Native Hawaiian activists who deservedly call out for justice. Activism skyrocketed in the late 1960s due to opposition to the American involvement in Vietnam's civil war. Later, ethnic diversity issues arose, as noted in the following discussion.

Table 12.2

College-Age Persons and University of Hawai'i Enrollment, 1980–2000 (in percent)

Year	Campus	Cohort	Black	Caucasian	Chinese	Filipino	Hawaiian	Japanese	Korean	PRican
1980		20–24	5.1%	**43.6%**	4.8%	10.2%	10.9%	19.3%	1.6%	2.2%
	UHM		.6	24.8	11.7	4.1	3.9	**35.8**	2.1	na
	CCs		1.2	22.4	6.8	13.1	10.0	**27.8**	2.3	na
1990		18–24	4.9	**35.4**	5.4	16.5	12.6	15.7	2.0	2.5
	UHM		.8	23.0	11.4	7.9	6.0	**29.8**	2.8	na
	CCs		1.2	**22.3**	6.0	17.0	12.2	20.5	2.7	na
2000		18–24	3.1	**23.1**	2.9	14.2	7.2	8.5	1.6	3.5
	UHM		.8	22.7	10.0	8.6	8.6	**23.0**	4.3	.3
	CCs		1.4	16.9	5.1	**18.1**	17.0	15.9	2.4	.6

Key: UHM = percentages refer to enrollment at the University of Hawai'i Mānoa campus.

CCs = percentages refer to enrollment in all UH community colleges.

Figures for Blacks and Caucasians, are not comparable because they include military personnel.

Notes: The first row in each triplet comes from the nearest census report of persons under 25. For 1980, the census figures are for persons 20–24. For 1990 and 2000, the figures are for persons 18–24. Figures may not add to 100 percent in each row due to rounding errors and unavailability of enrollment data for other ethnic groups. Figures in boldface identify the highest in each row.

Sources: Table 12.1; US Census (1983:64–65, 70; 1993:122–123, 156; 2000:PCT63).

Using those of college age as benchmarks to assess representation, Filipinos and Native Hawaiians are clearly underrepresented at UHM but made up the deficit at community colleges from 1980 to 2000 (Table 12.2). Filipino and Native Hawaiian percentages have consistently improved at UH over the years, but Puerto Ricans have been consistently underrepresented. Community colleges have attracted more of a cross section of recent high school graduates around the state than UHM. Accordingly, diversity programs have focused primarily on admission to UHM, using two methods (Table 12.3)—outreach (going off campus to recruit) and financial aid (tuition waivers and scholarships).

In the late 1990s, separate diversity programs were consolidated into the Student Equity, Excellence, and Diversity Office (SEED) at the Office of Student Services under the UHM Vice Chancellor for Students. SEED, now an umbrella for several programs (Table 12.3), also provides support to the Commission on Diversity, a body composed of administrators, faculty, and students that was formed in 1992 to bring issues of diversity related to curriculum as well as faculty, staff, and student recruitment to the attention of UHM administrators. The Commission, in turn, has representation from similar bodies, notably the Commission on Disability Access and the Commission on the Status of Gay, Lesbians, Bisexuals, Transgendered and Intersex Equality.

A few Caucasian students have grumbled about diversity programs over the years (cf. Conklin 2003). Recently coming from the Mainland, they may not have understood UH's approach to diversity issues.

In 2004, the University paid a student $52,000 to settle a discrimination case involving a Native Hawaiian who was part Black. The case involved a Kamehameha Schools graduate who applied for admission to the medical school just before receiving his baccalaureate degree from UHM. Applying as a "disadvantaged student," he was surprised when his application was denied because of his 3.38 grade point average (GPA), though the school's average was then 3.46. Students with 2.3 GPAs had previously been admitted, and only one Black male had ever been admitted before. The student then attended the University of Missouri medical school instead (Vorsino 2004).

Several explanations account for why some minorities enroll at community colleges more than at Mānoa:

1. Public school counselors tend to steer Caucasian, Chinese, Japanese, and Koreans into UHM, while either discouraging other ethnic groups from taking college-preparatory courses or encourage them to go to community colleges (Agbayani 1994:9; Campos 1991).

Table 12.3
Programs of the UHM Student Equity, Excellence and Diversity (SEED) Office

Program	Students Served
Bridge to Hope (BTH)	Low-income student parents
Children's Center	Day care for students
College Opportunities Program (COP)	Ethnically disadvantaged students denied admission because of low SAT despite academic potential
Diversity and Equity Initiative	Applicants for innovative diversity research, workshops, etc.
Gaining Early Awareness and Readiness for Undergraduate Programs (GEAR UP)	Mentoring college prep program at an intermediate school
Gay, Lesbian, Bisexual, Transgender, and Intersex (GLBTI) Student Services	Counseling sexual minorities
Graduate/Professional Access Program	Undergraduates from disadvantaged backgrounds seeking graduate degrees ethnically disadvantaged students
Health Careers Opportunities Program (HCOP)	Disabled students
KŌKUA Program	Native Hawaiian Students
Kua'ana – Native Hawaiian Student Development Services	Students in two high schools attended Primarily by Native Hawaiians
Mānoa Educational Talent Search (METS)	Underrepresented minorities in high schools and at UHM
Office of Multicultural Student Services (OMSS)	Increase awareness of multicultural issues; informal academic advising and advocacy
Osher Reentry Scholarships	Students who want to return after 5 or more years of absence from college to finish degrees
Senior Citizen Visitor Program	Course auditors 60 and over
Women's Center	Female students seeking support

2. Community colleges do not stress preparation of students for Mānoa (Astin 1982:192; Junasa 1982; Okamura 1991:19–22).
3. A principal requirement for admission to UHM is a minimum score on the Scholastic Aptitude Test (SAT), which is often blamed for skewing ethnic enrollment patterns (Hanford 1982) and has been banned

as a screening device by the University of California. Evidence that Filipinos enrolled at UHM have below-average SATs but respectable grade-point averages (Cablas 1991; Ikeda, Pun, and Torro 1984:3; Wegner 1978:37) suggests that greater weight in admission could be assigned to high school grades. Nevertheless, in 1984, a UHM faculty review committee on admission standards obstinately insisted on maintaining SAT scores as the principal screening criterion.

4. Those living far from Mānoa Valley find commuting difficult and rental housing expensive near campus (Agbayani 1994:9), so they attend community colleges in larger numbers. Inexpensive student housing is available for only 16 percent of students, compared to an average of 47 percent at comparable Mainland universities (Sherman 1984).

5. Most special programs for minorities have been financed too modestly to produce an increase in representation, reflecting lesser administrative support than needed to achieve greater parity. Most department heads as well as college and professional school deans, primarily Caucasians, have paid little attention to the need for greater student diversity (D'Andrea and Daniels 2008).

STUDENT RETENTION AND GRADUATION

UHM campuses graduate lower percentages of baccalaureate degrees compared to other public research state universities in the United States (Kelly and Jones 2005). However, UH community college graduation rates are closer to the national norms, and UHM graduate degrees are awarded above the national average. The top UHM undergraduate students are very bright and exceed their counterparts at the better California State University campuses, where I have taught. Course completion rates are high (Table 12.4a).

Dropout rates are higher for Filipinos and Native Hawaiian students, who disproportionately receive lower grades (Table 12.4b, c; Ikeda et al. 1984:7; Okamura 1991:8). Lower grades of Blacks and Caucasians may be due to competing demands among those in the armed services. The most common remedy for low grades is tutoring.

Accordingly, several task forces have been formed to prepare reports outlining problems to be addressed in order to determine how to increase graduation rates (University of Hawai'i 1986a, b). One recommendation was to establish the Hawaiian Studies Center. Other task

Table 12.4

Student Performance at the University of Hawai'i at Mānoa by Ethnic Group, 1988–2006 (in percent)

(a) Course Completion Rate (in percent)

Year	Black	Caucasian	Chinese	Filipino	Hawaiian	Japanese	Korean
1988	93%	92%	**95%**	91%	87%	94%	89%
1989	87	93	95	94	92	95	94

(b) Grade Point Average

Year	Black	Caucasian	Chinese	Filipino	Hawaiian	Japanese	Korean
1988	2.56	2.86	**2.92**	2.64	2.58	2.81	2.56
1989	2.54	2.89	**2.90**	2.74	2.70	2.87	2.85

(c) Freshmen Completing Degrees within Five Years (in percent)

Cohort Years	Caucasian	Chinese	Filipino	Hawaiian	Japanese	Korean
1987-1993	40.4%	**62.8%**	51.0%	40.3%	57.3%	na
1987–1995	42.4	52.9	56.6	37.6	**57.7**	na
1990–2006	33.2	**57.0**	37.1	29.8	45.9	39.3%

Key: na = Figures not available.

Notes: Figures add to 100 percent horizontally when other ethnic groups are included. Figures in boldface identify the highest in each row.

Sources: National Center for Higher Education Management Systems (1991); UH (2009a).

forces identified problems of Filipinos (UH 1988), Indochinese (Sananikone 1991), African Americans (Takara 1992), and Samoans (Agbayani 1994). However, no studies have focused on Mexicans, Native Americans, or Puerto Ricans.

The main factor accounting for college dropouts is inadequate high school preparation. A second factor is lack of finances (UH 1988; Okamura 1992:6). Other factors are harassment of students, institutional neglect, and instructional insensitivity.

A grotesque example of harassment occurred in 1999. After a Faculty Senate meeting one day, a student said something to a professor who had shouted strong words during the discussion. As the two left the auditorium, the professor so pestered the student that he quickened his pace and ultimately told the faculty stalker "Fuck off!" The professor then took off his belt and threatened to rape him while 50 faculty members looked on, doing nothing. While the student was screaming, two students attempted to intervene, but the faculty member persisted until the arrival of campus police, who in turn called the Honolulu Police Department, although no charges were filed (Chan 1999). As a result, a study of gay and lesbian students was undertaken. In 2002, the report successfully recommended the formation of a Lesbian, Gay, Bisexual, Transgendered, Intersex Student Services office, with a safe zone inside its office. Nevertheless, two homophobic incidents occurred later: In 2007, UHM refused to let two gays live together in a campus dorm, and in 2009 a coach uttered "faggot" on national television (Bernardo 2008; Humphrey 2009).

More subtle problems have been identified in various reports. Caucasian professors often give extra weight in grading to articulate class participation, thereby penalizing non-White students who might excel in written work yet believe that it would be rude to express an unusual opinion in class (Chattergy 1992:5). Some innovative instructors have discovered that Native Hawaiian students do better when the classroom environment is aligned with values of peer cooperation and teacher-learner apprenticeship rather than competition (Sing 1986).

SOCIETAL RESULTS OF DIVERSITY PROGRAMS

One measure of the success of various diversity programs is increased minority enrollment. Another is the graduation of more qualified minority professionals. Although some graduates might leave the state, and members of professions might move to Hawai'i from the Mainland, census data can be used to assess progress (Table 12.5).

As regards engineers, Japanese are the most numerous by far, Chinese are above parity, and Whites are slightly below for the year 2000. Filipinos and Native Hawaiians are far below parity. The other ethnic groups have been left behind.

Whites dominate the legal profession, Chinese are more than twice their numbers among the total employed, and Japanese are above par. Filipinos and Native Hawaiians are greatly underrepresented. Blacks and Puerto Ricans are the only other groups at or above par. There are no Guamanian or Samoan attorneys.

Physicians predominately wear white coats over white skin. Chinese doctors are more than twice their share of the workforce, and Japanese are slightly below parity. While Filipinos have steadily gained, they

Table 12.5
Composition of Selected Professions in Hawai'i by Ethnic Group, 1920–2000 (in percent)

Year	Black	Caucasian	Chinese	Filipino	Guamanian	Hawaiian	Japanese	Korean	Mexican	PRican	Samoan	Vietnamese
(a) Engineers, 1980–2000												
1980	.8%	31.9%	15.2%	1.5%	.1%	4.8%	41.1%	1.5%	.1%	.3%	.2%	.2%
1990	.7	32.5	11.7	4.7	–	4.0	42.0	.9	.2	–	–	.7
2000	.3	23.8	11.5	7.6	–	1.8	39.3	1.0	.2	.0	.1	.4
(b) Lawyers, 1970–2000												
1970	.1%	58.0%	14.4%	1.3%	na	1.3%	23.0%	2.0%	na	na	na	na
1974	1.0	55.0	15.0	1.0	na	1.0	24.0	2.0	na	na	na	na
1991	.3	49.5	14.9	2.6	na	2.9	27.9	1.7	na	na	na	na
2000	1.2	44.4	12.0	1.2	.0%	2.9	20.0	.6	.6%	1.7%	0%	.1%
(c) Physicians, 1920–2000												
1920	na	64.7%	2.6%	.0%	na	1.3%	30.7%	na	na	na	na	na
1965	.0%	49.4	19.9	2.5	na	1.4	24.5	2.2%	na	na	na	na
1970	.0	51.2	19.0	2.6	na	1.3	23.0	2.0	na	na	na	na
1978	.0	33.6	12.4	3.1	na	.8	14.2	1.6	na	na	na	na
1989	–	49.7	18.6	4.2	na	1.3	23.9	1.2	na	na	na	na
2000	.3	50.5	12.7	5.7	.2%	.8	15.3	1.0	1.1%	0%	.1%	.8%
(d) Benchmark: All Employed Persons, 2000												
2000	1.1%	25.6%	5.1%	15.2%	.1%	6.2%	18.8%	1.9%	1.3%	1.9%	.9%	.7%

Key: na = Figures not available.
– = more than 0 percent but less than 1 percent.

Notes: Figures report percentages of persons employed in each profession by ethnic group and add to 100 percent horizontally when other ethnic groups are included. Census data in 1980, 1990, and 2000 are for persons 16 and over in each ethnic group. Figures in boldface identify the highest in each row. Some Caucasians decline to state an ethnic identification when asked by informal sources.

Sources: Haas (1992:103); Hirata (1971:54); Hawai'i (1965:1; 1970b:4; 1978:7); Hawai'i State Bar Association (1991); Hawaii Medical Association (1990); U.S. Census (1923:1278; 1983:44, 67, 71; 1993:60, 130–131; 2000:PCT86). For more data, see Haas (1992:Table 12.2).

must triple their percentage of physicians to catch up. Native Hawaiians have declined percentagewise and have far to go. Guamanians, Koreans, Mexicans, and Vietnamese are close to their percentages of the employed population. Blacks and Samoans are below parity. There are no Puerto Rican physicians.

Public schoolteacher statistics, as reviewed in the previous chapter (Table 11.4), show that Japanese are still the most numerous, some 10 percentage points above their share of the workforce. There is a slow if unsteady increase in Filipinos, but they are still far below their population in the workforce. The other groups mostly fall below their percentages of the workforce.

Both the law and medical schools appear to lack credible records in advancing the percentage of minority graduates. The irony is that the William S. Richardson School of Law is named after the famous Native Hawaiian Supreme Court Chief Justice, and the longtime dean of the School of Medicine was lauded for his efforts at minority recruitment (Altonn 2008).

Caucasian graduates of Mainland professional schools account for their larger numbers in the statistics. UHM diversity programs show more results for Filipinos than for other groups.

CURRICULUM AND RESEARCH

The University of Hawai'i rightly considers itself to be the premier academic institution in the mid-Pacific, with unrivaled strength in Asian and Pacific studies, astronomy, and tropical biology. In addition to graduate degrees awarded in the various departments of humanities, natural sciences, and social sciences, there are professional degrees in many fields (accounting, architecture, Asian and Pacific studies, business administration, education, engineering, law, medicine, nursing, ocean and earth sciences, pharmacy, social work, travel industry management, and tropical agriculture).

Research funding per faculty is above the national average (Kelly and Jones 2005). Whereas the budget for UHM was $386 million in 2009, and cut to $320 million in 2010, research grants to the campus total approximately $400 million (Vorsino 2010e).

Multicultural instruction has existed at the University of Hawai'i for some time, with many courses on Asia and the Pacific. A year of world history, a requirement for many years, was premised on 40 percent of coverage on African, Asian, Hispanic, Native American, and Polynesian civilizations. In 1999, when the actual content was exposed as Euro-history (Kreifels 1999), the requirement was dropped to a semester and a required Hawaiian Studies course was instituted.

Research on ethnic relations in Hawai'i was an important focus in the early years of the Department of Sociology. In 1920, sociologist Romanzo Adams established the Social Research Laboratory, promoting the image of the Islands as a living laboratory of ethnic and social relations (UH 2005). Renowned University of Chicago sociologist Robert Ezra Park visited and taught at the university in the 1920s. From his experience in the Islands, Park (1938:196) developed the concept of an integrated society that swept the imagination of leading thinkers in the United States, ultimately resulting in the landmark Supreme Court decision in 1954, *Brown v Board of Education of Topeka* (347SpCt483), which declared an end to segregated schooling.

Adams renamed his unit the Sociology Laboratory in the 1930s. When Adams retired in 1934, the new director was Andrew Lind, who had a University of Chicago doctorate in sociology. The following year he launched a journal, *Social Process in Hawaii*, which is still published.

In 1959, the Committee for the Preservation and Study of Hawaiian Language, Art and Culture was established. The Committee's most famous project was the publication of the Hawaiian-English and English-Hawaiian dictionaries (Pukui and Elbert 1964,1965).

Because many Hawai'i residents never leave the state or even their home island, psychology professor Abe Arkoff shortly after statehood launched a program to offer students an opportunity to spend their junior year at a Mainland college or university. From 1978, Arkoff's program was superseded by UH participation in the National Student Exchange program, which promotes two-way exchanges with 190 Mainland colleges and universities.

In the 1970s, a faculty member at the Hilo campus organized a semester for students in Sweden, and a few faculty soon followed suit. The efforts were consolidated during 1988 into a single Study Abroad unit that today offers opportunities to study in more than 40 countries within Africa, Asia, Europe, the Middle East, and the Pacific.

By the late 1960s, Ethnic Studies departments sprouted at universities around the United States, often after protests and confrontations. In 1970, implementing a resolution passed by the state legislature, UH President Harlan Cleveland (grandson of President Grover Cleveland) appointed a committee of all-White faculty to plan such a program (Gladwin 1972). Since the composition of the committee occasioned a student protest, a temporary faculty hire, African American English Bradshaw, was named director of the new Ethnic Studies Program in 1971. New courses offered opportunities to learn about the American experiences of Chinese, Filipinos, Native Hawaiians, Japanese, and Koreans. Initially, there was even a Haole Studies course.

Among the faculty hired part-time was James Anthony, a Fijian who was outspoken in condemning colonialism and racism. When the program's faculty asked to appoint Anthony full-time for the following year, Cleveland blocked his appointment. Then Bradshaw was fired for insisting on Anthony.

Next, Dennis Ogawa, an instructor in the program, was named the new director. When Ogawa backed Anthony's discharge, he came under attack from faculty and students, and the future of the program itself appeared in doubt. The dean then appointed an all-White committee to make recommendations on the future of the program. The result was a student sit-in, a campus petition calling for Ogawa's resignation, successful administrative pressure on White faculty to withdraw their names from the petition, and Ogawa's eventual resignation to teach in the Department of American Studies.

Ethnic Studies faculty members were all untenured. The Board of Regents had not approved the program on a permanent basis. In the mid-1970s, the program lost about half its positions and barely survived during budgetary cutbacks due to the economic effects of the dramatic increase in energy prices. For many years, the program lacked sufficient numbers to develop a coherent baccalaureate program despite high enrollment.

In 1974, meanwhile, a UHM administration-appointed faculty committee recommended naming the newly constructed social science building after Stanley Porteus, a psychology professor hired in the 1920s who accepted stereotypes of plantation supervisors as evidence of the inferiority of most non-Haoles (Porteus and Babcock 1926). When the Board of Regents accepted the recommendation, faculty and students protested. In 1975, the Board of Regents held a public hearing on the matter (Steinberg, Johnson, and Cahill 1975), but announced that the naming of the building was irrevocable, presumably sending a message that they believed that activists were disrespectful of established authority. Campus protests on the matter then petered out, but resurged from time to time.

Thus, in 1979, when Barack Obama was considering where he might go to college, headlines discouragingly reported struggles regarding

Porteus Hall and Ethnic Studies. And the University of Hawai'i offered little in African American Studies.

Seven years later, after the election of Governor John Waihe'e in 1986, support for multiculturalism returned. Faculty positions were gradually restored to the Ethnic Studies Program, which was finally granted departmental status in 1995.

Meanwhile, an emphasis on Asian studies began very early at the University of Hawai'i. A short-lived Oriental Institute, which began in 1935, was abolished during World War II. After the war, scholars specializing in various regions in Asia and the Pacific gradually formed study committees for China, Japan, Korea, Southeast Asia, South Asia, and Pacific Island studies. In 1987, the study committees were promoted to the status of centers within the new School of Hawaiian, Asian, and Pacific Studies (SHAPS). One SHAPS unit was the degree-granting Center for Hawaiian Studies. Another was the Committee for the Preservation and Study of Hawaiian Language, Art and Culture, which had been formed in 1959.

In 1987, the Center for Studies of Multicultural Higher Education was launched as a locus for institutional research on problems of ethnic relations at the university but was abolished in 1995. In 1991, the Social Science Research Institute sponsored a Center for Research on Ethnic Relations, which ultimately shepherded *Multicultural Hawai'i* (Haas 1998). Mainland foundations, however, were uninterested in state-of-the-art research proposals about multicultural Hawai'i, and the Center languished without a major grant until abolished in 1998.

However, SEED soon filled the gap through its Diversity and Equity Initiative. Offering small grants for teaching, research, performance, training programs, workshops, visiting speakers, and outreach and recruitment activities, the Initiative has focused on issues of culture, ethnicity, gender, race, and sexual orientation, with grants up to $5,000 available to all UH campuses, not just UHM.

In 1997, the University of Hawai'i at Hilo launched the first master's program in an indigenous language by launching the Ka Haka 'Ula O Ke'elikōlani College of Hawaiian Language, which grew to offer a doctorate in 2006. In 2009, UHM began a program to train teachers to handle instruction at the public school on Ni'ihau, where residents speak a unique dialect of Native Hawaiian.

In 1998, Ah Quon McElrath was among members on the UH Board of Regents originally appointed by Governor Waihe'e. Receptive to complaints that the social science building was still named after Porteus, she persuaded the Regents to rename the building, which changed to Saunders Hall after both Allan Saunders, retired political science professor, and his wife Marion, an innovative educator, who together founded Hawai'i chapters of the League of Women Voters in 1948 and the American Civil Liberties Union in 1965. Allan was perhaps best known for leading a protest against the Territorial governor in 1953, when UH faculty sported Aloha shirts with tails out instead of the required neckties. The tradition that Friday is "Aloha Shirt Day" prevailed throughout the Islands thereafter.

Among recent developments is the establishment of an administrator-faculty-student Commission on Disability Access in 1998 to identify resources needed for handicapped students. In 2003, the Center for Disability Studies launched the *Review of Disability Studies*. The Center also offers small grants on disability and diversity studies.

In 2007, the various programs devoted to Hawaiian studies were consolidated into the degree-granting Hawai'inuiākea School of Hawaiian Knowledge. With the withdrawal of the Hawaiian Studies Center from SHAPS to form the research-oriented Kamakakūolani Center for Hawaiian Studies, SHAPS was renamed the School of Pacific and Asian Studies.

Every five years, degree programs are reviewed by a faculty committee, but they rarely focus on multiculturalizing the curriculum. Proposals to advance multiculturalism often go to the state legislature for support, since existing faculty usually oppose innovations that might eclipse them. As Frank Marshall Davis warned Barack Obama, the focus of White faculty is often on training non-Whites to think White (Obama 1995:97).

UNIVERSITY GOVERNANCE

The Board of Regents, appointed by the governor to be the supreme authority of the University of Hawai'i system, sets general policy, presumably leaving the university administration to operate daily affairs without undue overt interference. However, former Vice President David Yount (1996:118) once accused a majority of politically connected Japanese appointees of interfering with the autonomy of the university.

The Regents have never established a committee or task force to deal with minority affairs. Instead, Yount (1996:Ch. 5) accused the Regents of privately intervening to insist upon the employment of aging well-connected "old boys" from earlier political eras. Occupants of patronage jobs, in turn, have ensured that construction contracts have been signed with firms providing campaign contributions. Sometimes, the construction is shoddy (Stauffer 2001).

Patterns of governance change with management styles of UH presidents. Many have preferred a closed management style in which there is little consultation with subordinates while working primarily on one issue at a time (Yount 1996:349–60). Progress in diversity is generally associated with those who have a more open management style.

There has been much turnover of presidents, who are largely recruited from the Mainland. Foreign to the local power structure, some have brought in cronies and try to impose Mainland-centric ideas, thereby upsetting the downtown political establishment, existing tenured administrators (who are sometimes politically connected), faculty, and students. Some recent presidents have been let go because they tried in exasperation to divert funds to their own priorities (cf. Stauffer 2001). Then a new president comes from the Mainland, and the scenario is replayed.

UHM top administrators, who are predominantly but decreasingly Caucasian (Table 12.6), have never developed a comprehensive plan to achieve equal educational opportunity for minorities. The higher administration leaves the task of promoting ethnic equality largely to deans, many of whom ignore the plight of less advantaged groups.

Presidents from the Mainland complacently consider UH more diverse than any university they have previously encountered. Yet they fail to recruit from the large number of administrators at traditionally Black colleges who form part of the labor pool from which UH selects top administrators.

The burden of addressing problems of minority students, therefore, has fallen on SEED. From 1988, new faculty received an orientation from the Center for Studies of Multicultural Higher Education, but that unit was terminated in 1995.

In 1992, Susan Hippensteele, hired to handle student complaints about discrimination, dealt with about 100 complaints each year, sometimes also assisting faculty. But her role as complaint advocate was abolished in 2000, one among many signs of lack of administrative support for correcting problems.

The Office for Civil Rights of the U.S. Department of Education reports handling 166 discrimination complaints from 1991 to 2008, of which about one-third are disability issues, another third deal with sex discrimination, and one-fourth focus on race discrimination (about half from Native Hawaiians and half from Whites). Only 11 have been resolved amicably. Using complaints as a method of problem identification leading to solutions has not been the accepted model by the upper administration or the Board of Regents. Management instead has mostly

Table 12.6

University of Hawai'i Administrators by Ethnic Group, 1908–2003 (in percent)

(a) Mānoa Campus

Year	Black	Caucasian	Chinese	Filipino	Hawaiian	Japanese	Korean
1908	.0%	100.0%	.0%	.0%	.0%	.0%	.0%
1950	.0	100.0	.0	.0	.0	.0	.0
1958	.0	88.5	.0	.0	.0	11.5	.0
1975	na	70.9	8.7	.4	.0	17.8	*
1987	1.1	70.7	9.0	1.2	.6	15.6	*
1995	.8	48.0	10.4	1.6	4.0	34.4	*

(b) Community Colleges

Year	Black	Caucasian	Chinese	Filipino	Hawaiian	Japanese	Korean
1975	na	37.9%	9.1%	.0%	6.1%	43.9%	*
1984	2.0%	32.7	4.1	2.0	6.1	57.1	*
1995	na	39.6	na	na	na	na	na

(c) Mānoa Campus + Community Colleges

Year	Black	Caucasian	Chinese	Filipino	Hawaiian	Japanese	Korean	PRican	Samoan
2001	.9%	44.3%	7.1%	1.9%	3.3%	40.6%	1.4%	.0%	.0%
2002	2.0	45.9	7.1	3.1	2.6	36.2	2.0	.0	.0
2003	2.1	46.9	7.2	3.6	3.6	35.1	2.1	.0	.0

Key: na = Figures not available.

        * = included with Chinese this year to fit a 12-column punch card.

Notes: Figures add to 100 percent horizontally when other ethnic groups are included. Figures in boldface identify the highest in each row. UHM figures for 1995 include the UH system offices. For more data, see Haas (1992: Table 12.4).

Sources: University of Hawai'i affirmative action plans and catalogs.

looked upon university governance as a top-down enforcement of one-size-fits-all exercise of power that must never be challenged.

Members of the Hawai'i State Legislature, hoping for athletes that will bring national talent to win sporting events, have generously allocated funds to the university's athletic programs. As a result, many African Americans have been recruited. Barry Obama attended many UHM basketball games to see Blacks play. However, some White coaches have discriminated against them (Afro-American Association of Hawaii 1991; Associated Press 1991; Barayuga 2003; Takara 1992; Tsai 1992).

In 2003, a substantial tuition increase was proposed. A week-long student strike resulted, attracting some 500 students and faculty, which culminated in a sleep-in by 50 of those involved at the administration building on the eve of a Board of Regents meeting to rule on the proposal. Although President Kenneth Mortimer promised not to call the police during the peaceful demonstration, they showed up anyway. After the Board of Regents rejected the tuition increase, faculty and students protested Mortimer's apparent perfidy. A fact-finding committee was formed, and Mortimer resigned. When the committee's report lambasted racism and sexism on campus, the conclusion was pooh-poohed by the upper administration.

In 2006, Interim Mānoa Chancellor Denise Konan established an ombudsman office, which was designed to help, sometimes through conciliation, those seeking direction on where to go in the bureaucracy to solve problems. Students primarily took advantage. Some 10 percent of the cases involved discrimination. The office was closed three years later due to budget cuts, leaving a maze of impotent bodies—the Alternative Dispute Resolution Program, Mānoa Mediation and Peace Club, the Advocacy Office, Gender Equity Office, Counseling and Student Development Center, an Office of Judicial Affairs for student complaints, and the EEO Officer for faculty discrimination issues.

In short, UH presidents begin their tenure with a Mainland orientation that inevitably runs afoul of stakeholders. Complaints emerge. They respond with an atmosphere of intimidation and a failure to take truly corrective action. Then mass protests or sit-ins drive them out.

FACULTY

Whereas SEED is a multicultural effort by lower administrative personnel, faculty initiatives lag far behind. UH instructors, on the front line of the mission of the university, primarily come from the Mainland (Table 12.7a, c).

When new faculty positions emerge, academic departments seek the best qualified from a pool of applicants after recruitment through professional association contacts, though equal employment opportunity (EEO) guidelines require that new hires must reflect the nationwide pool of applicants (Table 12.7b, d). When Hawai'i-born applicants lack nationwide reputations through extensive publications in professional journals, their qualifications are evaluated negatively. State legislators and others in town are disappointed when UHM fills openings either with Mainland Whites or Asians from Asia rather than those born in Hawai'i.

Local students find themselves enrolled in an institution with so many Whites that they feel intimidated by representatives of Mainland culture. Some even sense racism in encounters with faculty (Chan 1999; Shapiro 2001). Most White faculty, however, believe that UHM, with more than 25 percent Asian professors, has the most diverse faculty in the United States (Kaser 1990).

Caucasian faculty transplanted from the Mainland who feel isolated tend to form all-Caucasian cliques, which operate similar to British clubs in foreign countries. Instances of White racial harassment of local students sometimes occur (Hippensteele and Chesney-Lind 1995). Meanwhile, those who are more open-minded learn about the multicultural ethos primarily though a kind of cultural osmosis or, more commonly, marry local spouses.

Chinese and Japanese faculty are the principal non-White faculty, but federal guidelines require hiring Blacks and Hispanics in the same percentages as on the Mainland. The failure of departments to recruit and retain more Blacks is a persistent problem, specifically noted by the EEO office, which each year receives only a dozen complaints—more about sex than race discrimination.

In 1979, an official newly assigned to the U.S. Department of Labor (USDOL) in Honolulu ruled that the UHM affirmative action plan was negligent in several respects. The statistical analysis was judged inadequate because it was not being updated annually and was not disseminated to deans, who, in turn, were not informing department heads of EEO requirements. UHM was the only campus with an affirmative action plan, so USDOL mandated affirmative action plans for all UH campuses and then undertook regular monitoring for the first time.

Table 12.7

University of Hawai'i Faculty by Ethnic Group, 1908–2003 (in percent)

(a) Mānoa Campus

Year	Black	Caucasian	Chinese	Filipino	Hawaiian	Japanese	Korean	Samoan	PRican
1908	.0%	100.0%	.0%	.0%	.0%	.0%	.0%	.0%	.0%
1920	.0	100.0	.0	.0	.0	.0	.0	.0	.0
1930	.0	91.8	4.8	.0	.0	4.8	.0	na	na
1940	.0	89.3	6.1	.0	.0	3.1	1.5	na	na
1950	.0	88.0	4.7	.0	1.9	5.1	.3	na	na
1960	.1	82.7	4.6	.1	1.2	1.0	.3	na	na
1975	na	72.1	9.3	1.0	1.4	14.7	*	na	na
1985	.3	70.8	9.6	1.0	1.6	14.4	*	na	na
1995	.3	69.3	10.5	1.0	1.8	12.6	*	na	na
2003	.6	61.9	9.1	1.7	4.0	12.3	2.3	.3	.3

(b) University Faculty Benchmark (USA average)

Year	Black	Caucasian	Chinese	Filipino	Hawaiian	Japanese	Korean	Samoan	Hispanic
2003	4.9%	78.8%			Asian/Pacific: 7.7%				3.0%

(c) Community Colleges

Year	Black	Caucasian	Chinese	Filipino	Hawaiian	Japanese	Korean	Samoan	PRican
1975	na	50.5%	8.7%	2.0%	3.8%	32.0%	*	na	na
1984	.0%	51.9	8.9	3.6	5.0	30.1	*	na	na
1995	4.5	63.6	na	na	na	na	na	na	na
2003	.6	46.4	6.4	4.4	8.4	27.5	1.4%	.2%	.2%

(d) Community College Faculty Benchmark (USA average)

Year	Black	Caucasian	Chinese	Filipino	Hawaiian	Japanese	Korean	Samoan	Hispanic
2003	6.6%	83.3%			Asian/Pacific: 3.4%				4.7%

Key: na = not available.

* = included with Chinese this year to fit a 12-column punch card.

Notes: Figures add to 100 percent horizontally when other ethnic groups are included. Figures in boldface are the highest in each row.

Sources: University of Hawai'i affirmative action plans and catalogs; UH Institutional Research Office (2002–2004); National Center for Education Statistics, Data Analysis System, Table 14. For more data, see Haas (1992:Table 12.5).

Nevertheless, matters of UHM ethnic and gender balance were relegated to paper compliance. For example, a form was designed in 1983 for all departments requesting to fill vacant positions, and the newly created EEO officer alerted all hiring units before screening applicants that they would be monitored for conformity to the affirmative action plan. When more Caucasian females were hired but not more minorities, the 1984 affirmative action plan identified the source of the problem as the failure of African Americans and Filipinos to apply. Thus, the plan appeared to blame minorities for their own underrepresentation, contrary to the spirit of affirmative action, which puts the burden of outreach to underutilized minorities on the employer.

Under USDOL pressure, the university then amended its affirmative action plan to provide that preference would go to underrepresented groups whenever qualifications for applicants were otherwise equal. Rather than an aggressive effort to hire African Americans and Hispanics, the most underrepresented ethnic groups, the directive was instead interpreted to mandate an effort to find some basis, however vague, for claiming that nonminorities were better than minorities. Students, as before, were deprived of an exposure to the intellectual vitality of African American and Hispanic scholars.

In 1985, comprehensive guidelines for nondiscrimination in recruitment were disseminated throughout UHM, and forms to monitor how well each job applicant satisfied stated criteria were disseminated to hiring units for the first time. At the same time, the campus EEO officer, who previously held a temporary appointment, was then given a permanent assignment with civil service protection. But the task of monitoring employment decisions was transferred from the EEO officer to deans and directors, who in turn lacked resources to carry out EEO responsibilities. Although some deans were progressive, others ignored the need to hire minority faculty. When some minority faculty were hired, as outspoken instructor Haunani-Kay Trask (1992) reports in her chilling experience as an assistant professor in American Studies, mistreatment often resulted. She later left American Studies to join the new Center for Hawaiian Studies. Meanwhile, more timid female and minority faculty continued to suffer from discrimination.

In 1990, the U.S. Department of Education cited inadequacies in the university's complaint procedures regarding the handicapped and victims of sexual harassment. And in the following year, an accreditation team from the Western Association of Schools and Colleges (1991) noted a lack of standardization in personnel selection procedures as well as a failure in affirmative action. Asked to study UHM employment patterns, the state legislative auditor's office noted that the proportion of minorities on the UHM payroll had declined from 29 to 28 percent from 1979 to 1989. Filipinos and Native Hawaiians were considered the most under-utilized, and staff EEO resources were deemed inadequate (Sue 1991).

In 1990, a Caucasian student from Louisiana wrote a letter to the editor of the UHM newspaper, expressing outrage that he was slurred as a "Haole," which he incorrectly perceived to be a cussword in a state that he believed to be excessively race conscious (Carter 1990). Subsequently, the Director of the Center for Hawaiian Studies, Haunani-Kay Trask (1990; cf. 1992:48), replied in the letters column that Haoles encounter hostility in the Islands because Native Hawaiians have never accepted their colonization and marginalization. Moreover, she said, if Carter did not like Hawai'i, he could always return to the Mainland.

Next, faculty from the UHM Philosophy Department called upon Trask to resign as head of Hawaiian Studies, alleging that her letter constituted "racial harassment" (Laudan et al. 1990). The three missives led to more letters to the editor, a rally attended principally by students opposed to the temerity of the Philosophy Department, sound bites on evening television news programs, newspaper editorials, and invitations for Trask to speak. She then made the case that Native Hawaiians awaited justice and that UHM was a hotbed of "institutional racism." In due course, Trask was cleared of charges filed by the Philosophy Department, and the furor died down.

With employment issues in the forefront, the university administration decided to study problems of discrimination more systematically. Three studies revealed that minorities and women were disproportionately denied tenure, received lower pay, and got promotions a few years later on the average than Caucasian males (Hauser and Mason 1993; Ikeda and Johnsrud 1991, 1993). The chief reason cited for discrimination was intellectual and social isolation, that is, the tendency for White male departmental in-groups to snub ethnic out-groups and females, professionally and socially, and then to discount their academic performance. Only partial salary adjustments were made as a result.

One Japanese-born faculty, for example, was twice denied promotion by his own department in the 1970s because his colleagues felt he acted like a "Japanese professor." As a result, he retained a lower pay grade during his several decades of service until his retirement The same department later refused to apply for a grant to host Philippine scholars for a summer of collaborative and independent research. The university could be a better institution if pointless faculty rivalry ceased.

In 1995, Governor Ben Cayetano asked all agencies of state government to cut costs by about 20 percent in light of budget shortfalls. Part-time instructors, including Asian and Pacific language faculty, were pink-slipped, though a social science dean allowed a department to hire a Kurdish faculty member with ancestry from Turkey. Native Hawaiian students and supporters mobilized in the spring to have funds restored so that they could learn Hawaiian, and the university administration caved in after a half-day sit-in.

Some 2,000 faculty and students led a march that same year to the state capitol to demand fewer budget cuts. Governor Cayetano responded by characterizing leaders of the rally as ill mannered. He doubtless knew that Islanders would understand the remark to mean that Haoles, as if still on the plantations, were trying to dictate state priorities. Later, his press secretary publicly identified a particular White faculty member who hurled obscenities during the rally. Faculty, Cayetano (2009:341) later noted, had no plan to share the burden created by falling state revenues and no interest in the fact that the alternative was more budget cuts to the neediest and poorest. However, faculty perceived an undercurrent of anti-Haole prejudice, a repetition of occasional derisive statements by state government officials over the years.

Increasing pressure for UH to achieve greater autonomy from the governor and legislature led to a constitutional amendment in 2000 allowing UH to retain its tuition revenue rather than first surrendering that amount to the state's general fund and later begging for equivalent legislative appropriations. However, the tuition revenue became a slush fund for future university presidents rather than an opportunity for needed reforms and programs (Stauffer 2001). In 2001, aware of the misuse of the tuition, faculty struck for more pay, staying on the picket line 13 days until demands were met. The chasm between administrators and faculty remains.

CONCLUSION

Had Barack Obama attended the University of Hawai'i, he would have majored in political science, one of the very strongest UHM instructional departments. He would have tried out for the basketball team. But he would have had very few Black professors and Black student colleagues. Controversies during the 1970s, when he was at Punahou, severely marred the reputation of UHM.

Showing dignity on behalf of just causes, UHM multiethnic students have won several victories from the university administration by making specific demands. The issues that mobilize students have been clear and narrow, and student demonstrators have been well behaved.

Multiculturalism advances within progressive units of the university, though systematic coordination and monitoring are absent. The multiethnic student body, some able administrators, and interculturalized faculty have done what they could to enable the university to increase multiculturalism.

Barack Obama's sister and brother-in-law and the memory of his parents link the president to the University of Hawai'i today. But the university's identity crisis continues.

Chapter 13

Crime and Justice without Profiling

A. Didrick Castberg

*We consider these rights to be universal[:] . . . the right not
to be detained by the state without due process; the right to a
fair and speedy trial.*

(Obama 2008:103)

Barack Obama appears to have had no brush with the law during his
years in Hawai'i. Although he admits to smoking joints, Honolulu police
rarely consider that a problem. He experienced some minor social discrimination, which served to raise his consciousness that he was being
perceived as an African American. He was doubtless aware of high-pro-
file sit-ins and demonstrations by Native Hawaiians who were being
evicted from their longtime residences in the 1970s so that property
owners could profit by turning subsistence agriculture and housing into
expensive real estate developments. And he presumably watched the
cops-and-robbers television series *Hawaii Five-O* (1968–1980).

  After working as a community organizer in New York and Chicago,
Obama attended Harvard Law School. Upon graduation, he joined a
law firm in Chicago, and he taught civil rights and constitutional law at
the University of Chicago. As an Illinois legislator, he sponsored a law to
curb racial profiling, which does not exist in Hawai'i, as noted herein.

THE LEGAL SYSTEM IN HAWAIʻI

Crime and justice are handled quite differently in Hawaiʻi for a variety of reasons. The first is that the state is geographically isolated, some 2,500 miles from the Mainland United States and 3,800 miles from Asia. The Transportation Security Administration agency screens people traveling to and from the state, and the U.S. Department of Agriculture inspects plants and animals coming into and leaving the state. As a result, interstate transportation of illegal goods and criminals is more tightly controlled than in any other state.

Another important fact is that there are only two levels of government—state and county (Table 13.1). Although there is an incorporated City and County of Honolulu, there are no cities independent of counties. The City and County of Honolulu includes the most populous island, Oʻahu, as well as several islands stretching from northwest of Kauaʻi toward but not including Midway Island (which is administered by the U.S. Fish and Wildlife Service). Kauaʻi County includes the islands of Kauaʻi and Niʻihau. Maui County covers most of three populated islands—Lānaʻi, Maui, and most of Molokaʻi. The County of Kalawao, the site of the former leper colony, is separated from the rest of Molokaʻi by high cliffs, and is run by the Hawaiʻi Department of Health. The County of Hawaiʻi consists of a single populated island. There are also many unpopulated small islands.

The four main counties have their own law enforcement agencies, while the court and corrections systems are under state control. Criminal law (dealing with felonies and misdemeanors) is made by the state legislature, while county councils define local petty offenses. There is no state police department, that is, no "Hawaiʻi Five-O."

Although each county but Kalawao runs its own police academy, there are no uniform state standards for selection and training of police

Table 13.1
Basic Statistics of Counties of Hawaiʻi, 2000

Counties	Hawaiʻi	Honolulu	Kauaʻi	Kalawao	Maui	Total
Population	148,677	876,156	58,463	147	128,094	1,211,537
Square miles	4,028	600	622	13	1,159	6,423
Density (pop. per sq. mi.)	37	1,460	94	11	111	189

Source: U.S. Census (2000:Quickfacts;TableDP-1)

officers. In the four main counties, police chiefs are appointed by county police commissions, but prosecutors are elected by voters in each county. Judges are appointed by the governor, on the recommendation of the Judicial Selection Commission, and confirmed by the State Senate. Residents of the three settlements in Kalawao elect their own sheriff but otherwise have no official governance structure.

The state sheriff has limited functions, such as transporting detainees, serving court orders, and protecting state facilities, the governor, lieutenant governor, and foreign dignitaries. County sheriffs have comparable responsibilities.

The crime rate in Hawai'i is relatively low. Honolulu is the safest major city in the United States, as violent crime is well below the national average (Boylan 2008b; Home Security Guru 2009).

ETHNICITY AND CRIME

The various ethnic groups making up the Islands' population are not proportionately represented in the state's criminal justice system, ranging from police officers to convicted felons. There is little evidence to suggest that any discrimination in hiring, arrest, conviction, and sentencing occurs.

On the Mainland, Caucasians constitute a majority of the population and a majority of those employed in most criminal justice systems, while minorities are disproportionately represented among those arrested, convicted, and sentenced. In Hawai'i, there is no majority racial or ethnic group. The ethnic makeup of personnel in the criminal justice system does not reflect that of the population as a whole, but there is no evidence of any adverse effect on the administration of justice.

Nevertheless, one historical example reminds Islanders of past ethnic and racial bias in Hawai'i's criminal justice system, namely, the Massie case (see Chapter 2). The wife of a naval officer claimed that she had been raped by five non-Whites. Taking justice into their own hands, the mother of the alleged victim and several U.S. Navy personnel kidnapped and killed one of the defendants. Many, if not most, Caucasians both in Hawai'i and on the Mainland believed at the time that the murder was justified. After a jury found the defendants guilty of manslaughter, they were sentenced to 10 years at hard labor. However, Governor Lawrence Judd commuted their sentences to one hour in the custody of the State Sheriff. Shortly afterward, they were taken to Pearl Harbor, put on a naval vessel, and left for the Mainland.

The criminal justice process often begins with arrest decisions by a police officer who observes a crime being committed or who has probable cause to believe a crime has been committed. Alternatively, a grand jury may issue an indictment if convinced of the evidence presented by a prosecutor. While some data suggest that arrest decisions by police officers on the Mainland may be based to some extent on ethnic or racial factors (Kappeler et al. 1994), no studies to date have documented such discrimination in Hawai'i.

Ethnicity may play a role in arrest decisions in the Islands, as the disproportionate crime rate of certain ethnic groups is well known by police officers, and that knowledge is likely to result in increased attention to such groups due to their perceived criminality. Grand juries, on the other hand, are much less likely to take ethnicity into account when seeking an indictment. Because many persons are of mixed-race ancestry, surnames alone do not give a definitive clue of the ethnicity of persons under investigation, so grand juries may not know the ethnicity of the defendant.

Should plea bargaining occur (when prosecutor and defense attorney on behalf of a defendant agree on a reduced offense and a guilty plea), ethnicity might affect a prosecutor's willingness to be generous, either with respect to the defendant or the defense attorney. But no evidence supports such a proposition to date. Instead, personal factors are most likely to affect plea decisions, notably the attitude of the defendant and prior working relationships between a defense counsel and a prosecutor. In the unlikely event that a case goes to trial, a judge's ethnic bias could affect legal decisions, including rulings on motions, findings of guilt in bench trials, and sentencing, but there is no suspicion of any such discrimination in Hawai'i.

ARRESTS

Analyzing crime statistics for two time periods, 1994 and 2008, there are some consistent patterns (Tables 13.2 and 13.3). For 1994, Samoans and Others are the most likely to be arrested in relation to their share of the total state population, whereas Japanese are the least likely. Chinese and Koreans are close to Japanese in avoiding arrest. Blacks are arrested at nearly twice their share of the population. Although Filipinos do not have disproportionately high arrest rates in general, they constitute 70.6 percent of those arrested for manufacture or sale and 43.5 percent of those arrested for possession of synthetic narcotics (usually crystal methamphetamine, or "ice"). Filipinos constitute 58.2 percent of those arrested for gambling (primarily cockfighting). Caucasians are disproportionately arrested for negligent manslaughter (66.7 percent), arson (55.2 percent), and prostitution (50.9 percent). African Americans and Koreans also have disproportionately high numbers of arrests for prostitution. Since a substantial percentage of Blacks and Whites are stationed on military bases, the statistics are skewed in accordance with their larger percentages among those aged 18–24 (Table 13.2).

In 2008, Blacks and Samoans were the most likely to be arrested, whereas Chinese and Japanese were the least likely (Table 13.3). Although Caucasians, Chinese, Filipinos, Japanese, and Native Hawaiians are the most numerous groups in Hawai'i, other groups are represented in the criminal justice system, notably Mexicans, Native Americans, Puerto Ricans, Tongans, and Vietnamese. State but not federal figures on arrests and dispositions often lump some persons into the "Other" category.

Ethnically based youth gangs in Honolulu have been involved in numerous acts of violence as well. Two decades ago, Filipino gangs accounted for 44 percent; Samoans gangs, 26 percent; and Native Hawaiian gangs, 13 percent (Chesney-Lind et al. 1992:17). More recent data are unavailable.

Table 13.2
Arrests in Hawai'i by Ethnic Group, 1994 (in percent)

Major Crimes	Black	Caucasian	Chinese	Filipino	Hawaiian	Japanese	Korean	Samoan	Other
Murder	3.7%	25.9%	3.7%	13.0%	**27.8%**	5.6%	1.9%	9.3%	9.3%
Rape	10.6	**33.3**	.8	6.5	22.8	5.7	.0	4.1	16.3
Robbery	5.7	27.0	2.9	4.8	**30.8**	4.1	2.2	9.2	13.3
Assault	9.3	**31.9**	1.6	14.1	21.0	3.2	2.8	7.3	8.9
Burglary	2.6	**32.6**	2.1	11.8	27.4	7.4	1.2	3.8	11.0
Larceny	5.1	**43.0**	2.6	9.0	18.5	6.6	1.2	2.8	10.9
Auto Theft	3.8	22.5	2.5	14.3	**32.3**	5.6	.9	6.3	11.9
Arson	3.4	**55.2**	.0	6.9	20.7	10.3	.0	.0	3.4
Total	4.9	**37.1**	2.4	10.3	22.4	6.3	1.3	4.0	11.1
Population	2.5	33.4	6.2	15.2	12.5	22.3	2.2	1.4	4.3
Ratio	1.96	1.11	.39	.68	1.79	.28	.59	2.86	2.58

Key: Ratio = percentages of total arrests divided by population percentages.

Notes: Except for rounding errors, percentages sum to 100% in each row. Figures in boldface identify the highest in each row.

Sources: Hawai'i (1994:39; 1995:104, 106).

Table 13.3

Arrests in Hawai'i by Ethnic Group, 2008 (in percent)

Major Crimes	Black	Caucasian	Chinese	Filipino	Hawaiian	Japanese	Korean	Samoan
Murder	7.7%	**38.5%**	0%	7.7%	7.7%	3.8%	.0%	.0%
Rape	13.4	**32.0**	1.0	19.6	22.7	8.2	.0	3.1
Robbery	8.6	30.0	.5	9.1	**35.5**	3.6	.0	12.7
Assault	4.6	**37.1**	1.0	15.5	30.4	4.9	1.1	5.4
Burglary	2.2	**39.6**	1.3	18.4	29.9	4.4	.9	3.3
Auto theft	2.4	34.4	.6	14.2	**40.2**	3.9	.4	4.1
Other theft	3.6	**46.0**	4.2	12.7	26.4	6.4	1.2	2.4
Arson	3.7	37.0	7.4	3.7	**44.4**	3.7	.0	.0
Total	3.8	**39.0**	1.1	12.9	27.5	5.3	.9	3.4
Population	1.7	**24.1**	4.7	14.2	20.0	16.5	2.0	1.2
Ratio	2.24	1.62	.23	.91	1.38	.32	.45	2.83

Key: Ratio = percentage of total arrests for major crimes divided by total population percentage.
Note: Figures in boldface identify the highest in each row.
Sources: Hawai'i (2008d); Table 1.2.

VICTIMS OF CRIME

According to a random sample of 3,000 Hawai'i residents, conducted in 1994, there is a wide variation in victimization by ethnicity. Native Americans, who constitute less than 1 percent of the population, reported the highest victimization rate, followed by Native Hawaiians (Table 13.4a). Blacks and Japanese were the least likely to be crime victims. Higher socioeconomic status increases the likelihood of being a victim of property crime (Table 13.4b). Violent crime is most common at lower income levels.

Focusing on murder in more recent years (Table 13.5), there is a tendency for the murderers and victims to be of the same race. Whites are the most likely to be murderers as well as the victims, but at the same share of the population. Comparing victims with population, American Indians should be the most fearful of being murdered, but their offenders are at par with their victims. Blacks and to a lesser extent Filipinos are much more likely to be offenders than victims. In relation to their share of the population, Chinese, Japanese, and Koreans are least likely to be homicide victims. Income differences do not account for rates of homicide or victims of homicide, as the rank-order correlations are nearly zero.

Another window into crime in Hawai'i is that there are relatively few hate crimes (Table 13.6). Clearly, anti-Haole crime stands out in the

Table 13.4

Victimization in Hawai'i by Ethnic Group and Income, 1994 (in percent)

(a) Race/Ethnicity

Ethnic Group	All Crimes	Violent Crime	Property Crime
American Indian	71.4%	57.1%	71.4%
Black	35.3	5.9	29.4
Caucasian	39.0	12.7	34.6
Chinese	41.8	16.5	35.2
Filipino	43.8	11.5	38.5
Hawaiian	50.8	17.7	43.8
Japanese	33.2	6.1	30.5
Korean	40.0	15.0	40.0
Mixed Asian	36.8	15.8	36.8
Other	43.2	10.8	40.5

(b) Income

Income Group	All Crimes	Violent Crime	Property Crime
Under $15,000	31.9%	14.3%	26.9%
$15,000 – $24,999	34.7	9.8	29.9
$25,000 – $34,999	37.1	9.3	32.5
$35,000 – $49,999	42.1	13.4	38.9
$50,000 – $74,999	43.6	12.2	39.9
$75,000 – $99,999	42.4	11.2	39.2
$100,000 +	45.5	13.6	40.0

Notes: Figures do not sum to 100 percent because not everyone in each category was a crime victim.

Figures in boldface identity the highest in each column.

Source: Hawai'i (1994:4–5).

statistics. Chief Justice Ronald Moon recently reminded an audience of a case when a local teenager yelled "fucking Haole" as he and his father beat a Caucasian couple in a parking lot (Kobayashi 2008). The verbal assault by a Caucasian faculty member of a gay Caucasian student, as reported in Chapter 12, is a much milder case.

POLICE AND PROSECUTION

Possible bias on the Mainland on the part of White police who profile Blacks for arrest has long been noted (Hermann and Cassack 2003). In

Table 13.5

Murder Victims and Offenders in Hawaiʻi by Ethnic Group, 2008

Ethnic Group	Median Income of Males	Victims		Offenders		State Population
		Number	Percent	Number	Percent	Percent
American Indian	$20,371	1	4.0%	1	4.2%	0.3%
Black	29,017	0	.0	2	8.3	1.7
Caucasian	38,431	6	**24.0**	6	25.0	**24.1**
Chinese	43,777	1	4.0	0	.0	4.7
Filipino	29,061	3	12.0	4	16.7	14.2
Hawaiian	34,801	5	20.0	5	20.8	20.0
Japanese	**46,653**	2	8.0	0	.0	16.5
Korean	40,563	0	.0	0	.0	2.0
Samoan	26,984	1	4.0	1	4.2	1.2
Other	na	6	24.0	5	20.8	13.3
All Groups	36,808	25	100.0	24	100.0	100.0

Key: na = Figures not available.

Notes: "AmericanIndian"includesAlaskanNatives."Hawaiians"includepart-Hawaiians. The "Other" population includes mixed-race persons other than part-Hawaiians. Except for rounding errors, figure sum to 100 percent in each column. Figures in boldface identify the highest in each column.

Sources: Tables 1.2 and 10.2; Hawaiʻi (2008a, d).

Table 13.6

Hate Crimes in Hawaiʻi, 2002–2008

Type of Crime	Victims	Incidents	Percent
Race/Ethnicity	White	9	45%
	Black	2	10
	Japanese	2	10
	Arab	1	5
Sexual Orientation	Homosexual	4	10
Religion	Jewish	1	5
	Muslim	1	5
All Incidents		20	100

Note: Figures in boldface identify the highest in each column.

Source: Hawaiʻi (2008e).

Hawai'i, police departments 50 years ago were made up primarily of Native Hawaiian and Portuguese officers, though the higher administrative positions tended to be held by Caucasians, Chinese, or Japanese. Today, however, one finds much greater diversity at all levels of police work. Combining military and civilian police departments, nevertheless, the percentages are still not representative of Hawai'i's population as a whole (Table 13.7). Nearly half of the police in Hawai'i are Native Hawaiian, and there is some overrepresentation as well for Blacks and Samoans. Asian groups (Chinese, Filipinos, Japanese, Korean, and Vietnamese) are underrepresented. However, ethnic occupational self-selection may be occurring, as the occupation is often perceived as a "Hawaiian job." Discrimination cannot altogether be discounted, as a Filipino police officer won a discrimination case against his former department in 1993 (Kobayashi 1993). Prosecutors, however, have sought greater diversity in their offices (Haas 1992:116).

One study found a relationship between ethnicity and arrests for some offenses, but none with respect to the charging decision by the prosecutor or the sentence by the judge (Hawai'i 1982:16–17, 55). But 99 percent of all cases referred to the prosecutor's office by the police result in charges, so any discrimination at the arrest stage could well be continued at the charging stage.

Table 13.7
Law Enforcement Workers, 2000 (in percent)

Ethnic Group	Percent	Population
Black	2.7%	1.7%
Caucasian	22.6	**24.1**
Chinese	2.7	4.7
Filipino	8.1	14.2
Guamanian	.2	.1
Hawaiian	**43.9**	20.0
Japanese	12.5	16.5
Korean	.9	2.0
Mexican	1.8	1.6
Puerto Rican	2.6	2.5
Samoan	2.0	1.2
Vietnamese	.0	.7

Notes: The mixed-race population has been reallocated to Hawaiians.
Figures in boldface identify the highest in each column.
Source: U.S. Census (2000:PCT1, 86).

Given virtually unchecked power of prosecutors to charge (or not charge), there is certainly an opportunity for decisions to be made on the basis of extralegal criteria. But one study found no relationship between prior convictions and age, employment, and marital status, and gender. Instead, the data showed that a person's prior criminal history is a much better predictor of being charged than personal characteristics, even though personal characteristics other than race and ethnicity do have an effect on the charging decision (Hawai'i 1982:55). Similar studies of the criminal process on the Mainland have found that race is not a factor in prosecutorial decision making (Eisenstein and Jacob 1977:284).

Comparing the diversity of the arrestee population and prosecutors' offices, the likelihood of systematic discrimination against any one ethnic group is quite small. While a Caucasian prosecutor might seek more serious charges against Filipino defendants, for example, a Filipino prosecutor might be less lenient with Caucasian defendants. For such discriminatory charging to have any effect, the defense attorney either would have to be incompetent or equally prejudiced, as overcharging can be easily dealt with by opting for trial.

Another factor that might tilt the scales of justice to disfavor those charged with crimes is the defense attorney's ethnic group. Although there are more Caucasian lawyers than any other ethnic group, their percentage has gradually declined over the years (Table 12.5b). At the same time, the complete absence of Samoan attorneys must surely be a factor in that group's higher rates of arrest and conviction.

According to the state's *Access to Justice* report for 2007, only 20 percent of low- and moderate-income Hawai'i residents have civil legal needs met, and legal service providers are able to serve 33 percent of those who seek assistance (Hawai'i 2007). Accordingly, in 2008 the Access to Justice Commission was launched to work toward filling the gap.

THE JUDICIARY

There are two levels of trial courts in Hawai'i—District Courts and Circuit Courts. District Courts hear nonjury traffic, landlord-tenant, small claims, civil cases involving claims of $25,000 or less, temporary restraining orders, and misdemeanor criminal cases. Circuit Courts have concurrent jurisdiction with District Courts over nonjury civil cases involving claims between $10,000 and $25,000, and exclusive jurisdiction over jury and nonjury cases involving felony offenses and civil matters involving more than $25,000. There are also Family Courts, which deal with juvenile and domestic matters, though both District and Circuit Court judges may hear Family Court cases. Appeals from lower courts go to the Hawai'i Supreme Court.

Judges serve 10-year terms, and may be reappointed. District and Circuit Court judges are first nominated by the nine-member Judicial Selection Commission. The commissioners, who hold staggered 6-year terms, no more than four of whom may be lawyers, are appointed by the governor, the State House of Representatives, State Senate, the Bar Association, and the Chief Justice of the State Supreme Court. The Commission recommends names to the Governor for vacancies on the Supreme Court, Intermediate Court of Appeals, and Circuit Courts, while names for District Court vacancies are sent to the Chief Justice. The State Senate votes to confirm those nominated by the Governor. Per diem judges (in effect, part-time judges) are appointed by the Chief Justice.

Although no comprehensive study has been undertaken in many years, it appears that judges in Hawai'i are fairly representative of the Hawai'i Bar Association in terms of ethnicity (Tables 12.5b and 13.8) and gender.

Table 13.8

Judges in Hawai'i by Ethnic Group, 1971–2009 (in percent)

(a) Supreme Court

Year	Caucasian	Chinese	Filipino	Hawaiian	Japanese	Korean
1971	1 (20.0%)			1 (20.0%)	**3 (60.0%)**	
1996	1 (20.0)		1 (20.0%)	1 (20.0)	1 (20.0)	1 (20.0%)
2009	**2 (40.0)**		1 (20.0)		1 (20.0)	1 (20.0)

(b) Circuit Court

Year	Caucasian	Chinese	Filipino	Hawaiian	Japanese	Korean
1971	2 (14.3%)	2 (14.3%)	2 (14.3%)	2 (14.3%)	**6 (42.9%)**	
1996	**10 (45.5)**	3 (13.4)	2 (9.1)	1 (4.5)	5 (22.7)	1 (4.5%)
2009	**14 (43.8)**	4 (12.5)	3 (9.4)	2 (6.3)	7 (21.9)	2 (6.3)

(c) All Judges

Year	Caucasian	Chinese	Filipino	Hawaiian	Japanese	Korean
2000	**51 (27.0%)**	50 (26.5%)	3 (1.6%)	3 (1.6%)	44 (23.3%)	15 (7.9%)

Notes: Figures in parentheses are percentages of the total and sum to 100 percent in each row.
Figures in boldface identify the highest in each row.

Sources: Office of the Administrative Director, Hawai'i Department of the Judiciary; U.S. Census (2000:PCT86).

No judges have been impeached in Hawai'i. The most controversial issue is whether to reappoint sitting judges who want to stay on the bench.

Historically, judges in the Islands have been Caucasian, Chinese, and Japanese, constituting more than three-fourths of those on the bench (Table 13.8c). The Judicial Selection Commission as well as past and present governors have made a concerted effort to appoint judges from underrepresented groups (Haas 1992:116). Nevertheless, there is an absence of Guamanian, Mexican, Puerto Rican, and Samoan judges. The only female judges are Caucasian, Chinese, and Japanese.

The Hawai'i Supreme Court in 1971, for example, was composed of five males, including one Caucasian, three Japanese, and one Native Hawaiian (Table 13.8a). In 1996, the Court was composed of one woman of Japanese ancestry, and one man each of Caucasian, Filipino, Korean, and Native Hawaiian ancestry. In 2009, Governor Linda Lingle's appointment of a Caucasian replaced a seat formerly held by another Caucasian, who retired. All justices in Hawai'i must retire by their 70th birthday.

In 1971, nearly half of Circuit Court judges were Japanese men (Table 13.8b). In 1996 and 2009, nearly half were Caucasians, and Japanese were the second most numerous. In 1971, the only woman was Caucasian, but by 1996 eight female judges had joined the bench. Whereas about one-fourth of District Court judges are Caucasian, Chinese, and Japanese, one-seventh are Korean, but there is only one Native Hawaiian and not a single Filipino.

Aside from the Massie case, the most famous civil cases involve Barack Obama. Several petitions have been filed to obtain a release of his birth certificate. The litigation has proved unnecessary because the Obama presidential campaign posted the appropriate document, Certificate of Live Birth, on the Internet. Newspaper stories announcing his birth have also been cited in support of the fact that he was born in Honolulu and therefore is a citizen of the United States. The Hawai'i Department of Health has affirmed that his original birth certificate is on file, but the expense of responding to so many requests resulted in a law in 2010 that bars further responses.

INCARCERATION

After arrest, prosecution, and conviction, a judge issues a sentence that may include a fine or a prison term. The disparity between ethnicity of the general population of Hawai'i and those incarcerated is well known (Table 13.9). Proportionately, Samoans are the most likely to be imprisoned in relation both to arrest rates and their share of the Hawai'i population. Although census figures tend to underreport Native Hawaiians, they also constitute a greater percentage of the inmate population compared with those arrested for offenses. Caucasians are least likely to serve time after being arrested.

One hypothesis to explain why Whites are less likely to be imprisoned is that they may have better legal representation (Table 12.5b) before White judges (Table 13.8), as they are often arrested for very serious offenses (Tables 13.2, 13.3 and 13.5). An alternative hypothesis is that mandatory sentences are imposed on serious crimes. Another possible reason is that a disproportionate number of Whites are sent out of state because overcrowding at the adult facility (O'ahu Community Correctional Center) resulted in federal supervision under a consent decree from 1985 to 1999, when the state sent prisoners to facilities in Kentucky, Texas, and other states (Magin 2006).

Table 13.9
Prison Population in Hawai'i by Ethnic Group, 2008 (in percent)

Ethnic Group	Inmate Population	Arrest Rates	Ratio	State Population
Black	4%	4%	1.0	2%
Caucasian	23	38	.6	24
Chinese	1	1	1.0	5
Filipino	12	13	.9	14
Hawaiian	39	27	1.4	20
Hispanic	4	na	na	7
Japanese	5	5	1.0	17
Korean	1	1	1.0	2
Samoan	5	3	1.7	1
Other Pacific Islander	2	na	na	1
Other and not reported	4	9	.44	7

Key: The ratio is calculated by dividing the inmate population by arrest rates.
na = Figures not available.

Notes: Figures sum to 100 percent in each column.
Figures in boldface identify the highest in each column.

Sources: Hawai'i (2008b:43); Table 13.3; U.S. Census (2000:Table PCT1).

Once incarcerated, prisoners are often abused. Recently, some women were sent back from a Kentucky prison because of sexual assaults. In 2006, a federal judge found in *R.G. v Koller* that the Hawai'i Youth Correctional Facility in Kailua, O'ahu, violated the civil rights of bisexual, gay, lesbian, and transgendered (BGLT) youth, whom prison guards abused and harassed without an appropriate response from prison authorities, even though incidents were recorded in written reports. Attending physicians and psychologists repeatedly urged more safety for the prisoners, but their pleas went unheeded. Verbal slurs and physical assaults were common. The case is the first in the nation to address the mistreatment of BGLT youth in correctional facilities (Magin 2006).

. After inmates are released, recidivism can be a problem. In 2004, Circuit Judge Steven Alm had such concern that he created a project called Hawai'i's Opportunity for Probation with Enforcement (HOPE) to oversee 34 "high-risk" probationers, that is, those most like to re-offend. Today, of the 8,000 probationers, some 1,500 are in the program. Results of a controlled study show positive results: Missed appointments dropped 80 percent, drug use declined 86 percent, and less than half committed a subsequent offense (Dooley 2009a). The HOPE program has gained nationwide attention, yet another example of how compassionate, multicultural methods work in Hawai'i.

CONCLUSION

Hawai'i's criminal justice system reflects its differences in many ways. Race and ethnicity are only part of the reason why Hawai'i is so different. Indigenous Polynesians are disproportionately found in the court rooms and prisons, but the reason is their socioeconomic status, not their race (Honolulu Star-Advertiser 2010b).

Isolation from the other states, history, and other factors make Hawai'i unique. While the legal and political systems are quite similar to those in other states, culturally Hawai'i has elements of Asia, Polynesia, Europe, as well as the United States.

Perhaps an American president who is both White and African American and whose first name is "Barack" could only come from a place like Hawai'i, where during his youth had no fear that he would be mistreated by police or the courts. Racial profiling and other indignities suffered by Blacks on the Mainland shocked him into conceiving of multicultural improvements, from anti-profiling legislation in Illinois to support for job training programs for former felons (Obama 2008:305–307).

Chapter 14

Political Economy and Contemporary Social Struggles

Ibrahim Aoudé

> *To stay competitive and keep investors happy in the global marketplace, U.S.-based companies have automated, downsized, outsourced, and offshored. They've held the line on wage increases. . . . But a sizable chunk of . . . blue-collar union workers . . . has resisted this agenda. As far as they're concerned, free trade has served the interests of Wall Street but has done little to stop the hemorrhaging of good-paying American jobs.*
>
> (Obama 2008:172, 173)

In Hawai'i's multiethnic and multicultural population, recent political decisions have provoked social struggles, which go back as far as the 1970s, when Barry Obama was a teenager. That history gives considerable insight into how Obama views economic reality, which has shaped his presidency.

ECONOMIC HISTORY OF HAWAI'I

The destruction of the communal, self-sufficient Native Hawaiian system, including its feudal social stratification between nobility and commoners, is an example of the violence by which capitalism was historically established through the colonization of native peoples. The development of a plantation system from the 1830s brought capitalism. By the 1850s, Haoles had significant control, which developed into effective and then full control by the time of the "Bayonet Constitution" of 1887 and the overthrow of the monarchy in 1893 with the aid of members of the American military.

Curiously, the Haole oligarchy developed its political and economic control through its dependency on the outside world. Plantations became viable economically through American markets for sugar. Ultimately, plantation society was stabilized through annexation in 1898, which gave the Haole oligarchy full economic and political control over a caste-like system with ethnic minorities on the plantations. In the early 20th century, the Haole oligarchy was also able to drive a political wedge between Native Hawaiians and other non-Whites (see Chapter 8).

After World War II, workers of all nationalities, but primarily Japanese, wanted to rid themselves of the oppressive plantation-oriented system. Allied with liberal Whites, the workers brought about the so-called "Democratic Revolution" by first gaining control of the Democratic Party and then capturing power from the Republican Haole oligarchy as a result of the 1954 election, when Democrats promised to effect land reform and to restructure the political economy.

The 1954 Democratic Party "revolution" had its social base in the plantation workers, who sought to wrest control from the Haole oligarchy. In fact, however, the reins of power were transferred from one set of capitalists to another without undermining the economic power of the Haole elites (Kent 1983:Ch. 10; Stauffer 2001). In 1954, several Japanese Americans, including the future Senator Daniel Inouye, started Central Pacific Bank, which was chartered by the State of Hawai'i and made loans that might have been denied by Haole-owned banks that had long dominated the Island economy.

However, the role of the "revolutionary" Democrats was no different from that of Republican William Quinn, the first governor after statehood. Both Quinn and his successor, Democrat John Burns, were successful in attracting American capital from the Mainland, notably Congressionally-approved funding for such infrastructure development as the H-1 Freeway, Honolulu International Airport, the expansion of Ala Moana Beach Park to include Magic Island, and roads in Volcanoes National Park. Many "pork barrel" projects have tried to help Hawai'i's economy, but jobs created thereby are always temporary.

To marginalize Haole Republican economic power, the Democratic Party sought to attract outside investment (Stauffer 2001). That investment came quickly when, in 1955, Henry J. Kaiser became the biggest landowner in Waikīkī, just one year after he had established his residence in the Islands. He built the Hilton Hawaiian Village hotel, developed a 6,000-acre residential project known as Hawai'i Kai, and established a cement plant (Fuchs 1961; Kent 1983:105).

An infusion of outside capital began in the 1950s as the Cold War heated up. Military spending in Hawai'i increased, exceeding income from pineapple and sugarcane production. After statehood, delegates to Congress from the Islands gravitated toward committees dealing with military spending, and they made sure that "pork barrel" expenditures would also provide jobs in other areas.

In 1959, the Tokyu Corporation invested $1 million to open Shirokiya Department Store at the Ala Moana Shopping Center. Next, Kenji Osano purchased the Princess Ka'iulani and Moana Surfrider hotels in 1963. Ten years later, Japanese investors purchased eight hotels in the state, in part to alleviate discrimination against Japanese tourists in other hotels (Haas 1992:247). After purchasing the Royal Hawaiian and Sheraton Waikiki, in 1974, Osano owned all Sheraton hotels in Waikīkī, and he bought the Sheraton Maui for $105 million in that year as well.

Hawai'i pineapple and sugar were gradually priced above foreign producers, so plantations began to shut down from the 1970s, and the Haole economic interests abandoned the plantations for real estate and later became subsidiaries of multinational corporations. Military spending declined after the end of the Vietnam War and later the Cold War (Table 2.4), so tourism became the major source of income to Hawai'i. Whereas the military provided employment from outside, personnel demands for labor-intensive tourism were substantially met by workers leaving the plantations and their immigrant families. A depiction of structural economic changes may be seen in the changing profile of employment since statehood (Table 14.1).

As Barry Obama grew up, Hawai'i's economy was on an upswing. His grandmother rose to become a vice president of a local bank. His grandfather managed a furniture store far from the center of the new Honolulu retail boom. When the store went out of business, he switched to sell insurance, albeit not very successfully in an Island where longtime residency improves one's chances of getting clients.

Hawai'i's boom years (1959–1990), when growth averaged 5 percent annually (Smith 1995), were partly the result of global capitalist transformation that consisted of increased corporate investment and jet airplane travel, essential ingredients for transforming the Islands into a major tourist attraction, with such supportive economic activities as

Table 14.1

Employment Structure in Hawai'i, 1960–2000 (in percent)

Job Category	1960	1970	1980	1990	2000
Professional, Managerial and Technical	21%	25%	23%	30%	32%
Farming, Skilled Craft, Operator, Laborer	42	35	27	23	19
Sales, Clerical, Service	32	40	50	47	49
Other	5	1	0	0	0
Total	100	101	100	100	100

Note: Figures in boldface identify the highest in each column.

Sources: U.S. Census (1962:185–188; 1972:295–301; 1983:152–161; 1993:35; 2000:PCT86).

construction, finance, and real estate development. However, the enviable economic performance did not trickle down to the lower rungs of the multiethnic working class, especially Filipinos and Native Hawaiians (Aoudé 1994, 1995), a fact of little concern to the ruling circles who oversaw a fast-growing economy.

Hawai'i has been characterized by uneven development, not only through its heavy dependence upon tourism, but also due to an increasing dependency upon offshore capital. Although most of the capital influx came from the American Mainland, a large chunk came from Japan and foreign sources (Table 14.2). When the world economy boomed, so did Hawai'i, but downturns throughout the global economy hit Hawai'i hard. The Islands, in short, have lost control in a more profound way due to what economist George Pai (1986:7) calls the "increased vulnerability of the economy to external economic conditions."

Economists in Hawai'i were concerned about the increased dependency of the economy on foreign speculative investment. Economic planners began to contrast *speculative investment*, especially in tourism, which creates low-quality jobs (low wages with little or no fringe benefits), from high-quality jobs from *productive investment*. According to Pai (1989:11–12):

> [The] overall position of state policy toward investment, in general, and foreign investment, in particular, is to encourage the growth of investments that help to diversify Hawaii's economy and contribute to the overall social welfare of the people, while at the same

Table 14.2

Foreign Investment in Hawai'i by Country of Origin, 1970–1989 (in million U.S. dollars)

Source	Amount
Australia	$ 193
Canada	167
Hong Kong	231
Japan	6,800
United Kingdom	163
Other	846
Total	8,400

Sources: Jokiel (1988); Kim (1994:42).

> time taking steps to control those investments that are known to generate negative social impacts . . . . [F]oreign investment needs to respond to the larger social and cultural needs of the community, rather than simply the private profit-maximization motives of individual businesses.

Although foreign investment was actively sought to decrease the Islands' dependency on tourism through diversification of the economic base, most investments instead maintained growth within the tourist industry. As Laura Brown and Walter Cohen (1975:3) have observed, "multinationalization has led either to outright acquisition by outside interests or to a greater dependence on more dominant centers of international trade and investment."

The state's economy was doing very well at the macrolevel during the 1980s. From 1987 to 1990, the gross state product (GSP) increased from about $20 to $27 billion (Aoudé 1995:227). Visitor expenditures increased from $5.5 billion to $10.4 billion in the same period. But in the 1990s, the Gulf War and the recessions in both California and Japan lowered tourism's contribution to the GSP (Kent 1994:183–184). In 1982 dollars, the GSP for 1992 and 1993 was $19 billion and $18.6 billion, respectively. But real growth was -0.03 percent in 1994 (Bank of Hawaii 1996:7).

From 1985 to 1987, some 11.1 percent of families earned less than $10,000, while 32.3 percent of families earned under $20,000. About one-third of Hawai'i's families hover around the poverty line (Hammes, Oliveira, and Sakai 1992:39, 40, 45). Most distressing is the fact that 80 percent of pre tax income expended by individuals in the Islands goes to the purchase of necessities (Crane and Okinaka 1992:60). In 1988, the cost of living in Hawai'i averaged 17 percent higher than that of the continental United States, while per-capita disposable income was only 2 percent higher. Trade, services, and state and local government sectors have been traditionally known for low wages and low productivity.

From 1988 to 1992, the cost of living for a family of four on O'ahu jumped to 39.6 percent higher than that of the continental United States. Hawai'i's average wage was 1.1 percent lower than the U.S. average—40 percent lower, adjusting for cost-of-living differences (Hawai'i 1993:301, 339).

Were it not for the wave of Japanese foreign investment in the 1980s, Hawai'i's economy would have been in the doldrums much earlier than the 1990s. From 1990 to 1995, the GSP grew at a compound annual rate of 0.03 percent but improved slightly in 1996 (0.9 percent) and 1997 (1.5 percent), and climbed in 1998 (2.2 percent) and 1999 (2.5 percent) (Bank of Hawaii 1999:6–7). Japan's sluggish economy in the 1990s had a negative impact.

The events of September 11, 2001, also had an adverse effect. In Hawai'i, where the best GSP performance had been no more than 2.5 percent in the previous two years (First Hawaiian Bank 1999:3), tourism nosedived. A further plunge occurred due to the Great Recession that began in 2008.

The financial and economic crisis that emerged during 2008 made matters worse across the globe. In Hawai'i, the civilian unemployment rate deteriorated from 2.6 percent to 7 percent from 2007 to early 2009 (UH 2009b). Unemployment for all 2009 was projected to reach 7.4 percent.

During 2009, the expectation was for a 6.8 percent decrease in visitor arrivals. When the H1N1 flu epidemic emerged, Japanese visitors stayed away in droves. Tax revenues were down more than 10 percent (Borreca 2009). By 2010, the income needed to afford a modest two-bedroom rental in Hawai'i was $64,396 annually, $26,000 more than the national average (Vorsino 2010b).

Social inequality exists in Hawai'i (see Chapter 10) and worsens whenever the economy declines. Whereas the state government estimated the number of homeless at about 8,000, the number in the mid-1990s was actually closer to 12,000 (Aoudé 1994:71–84). During the 1990s, the percentage of the population below the poverty line increased

(Table 10.3; cf. Witeck 1995:17). Filipinos, Native Hawaiians, Samoans, and Vietnamese are overconcentrated in service occupations (Table 10.6). Guamanian, Native Hawaiian, Puerto Rican, Samoan, and Vietnamese families have high poverty levels, compared with other ethnic groups (Table 10.3; cf. Barringer 1995). Ethnicity and class are strongly correlated (Okamura 2008).

Meanwhile, global changes in production have propelled the capitalist economy into crisis. Several economists argue that qualitative shifts (from electromechanics to electronics) in the means of production require qualitative shifts (private to communal) in the relations of production (Peery 1993; Reich 1991; Rifkin 1995).

In the age of transnational capital, the "New Economy" hype about global business, diversification, and "free markets" did not benefit Hawai'i. The Islands have lost control over their own destiny, perhaps forever.

DIVERSIFICATION AS AN ILLUSION

Soon after statehood, Hawai'i's economic development was praised by both mainstream writers (Fuchs 1961) and decision makers in the private and public sectors (Hitch 1992). From 1962, planners began to talk about "economic diversification" as an alternative to dependence on a single economic sector. But how could the Islands create new economic sectors to become significantly less dependent upon tourism? The concept soon became "a problematic for all seasons" (Aoudé 1995).

Productive economic diversification, long a goal of government economists and others in Hawai'i, has not taken place thus far to any significant degree. Economic planners have tried to make constructive suggestions, but in vain.

After World War II, policy makers were convinced that Hawai'i had a major role to play in a Pacific Rim strategy. The establishment of the East-West Center in 1960 seemed auspicious, and the once-powerful sugar corporations branched out to become multinationals.

In 1961, the state legislature set up a task force to draw up a Hawai'i State Plan, one goal of which was to achieve "balanced" development in order to benefit the people. Revisions have been adopted over the years, including one for 2010. State intervention is needed, some argue, so that the vagaries of the "free" market will not impede the desired goal of economic diversification. Such noble intentions and exhortations, however desirable, run counter to the inherent dynamic of the profit motive in capitalism.

From the 1970s, economic and political elites began to envision a new role for the Islands as the "hub of the Pacific," imagining that, by the year 2000, Hawai'i would have a great role to play both in commerce and finance, serving as a Singapore for the Pacific. For example, bonds were issued by Hawai'i state government to raise capital:

> In October 1963 . . . , a Bank of America consortium purchased $39.6 million worth of state bonds, while a Chase Manhattan syndicate snapped up $15 million of a subsequent issue. From 1958 to 1968, the state's outstanding public bonds increased sharply from $212 million to $528.9 million, while an average of $48 million in bonds was sold annually between 1960 and 1967. (Kent 1983:142)

But the purchasers of bonds were speculators, seeking a return on their investment in the form of interest rates that added to the state debt.

After years of economic growth, the Fiftieth State was nowhere near becoming the "hub of the Pacific." For example, airplanes that once stopped en route from Asia and the Pacific to the Mainland United States now mostly fly nonstop, bypassing Honolulu.

The next idea, to attract the growing electronics industry to manufacture parts for new products, was the concept of "high-tech" Hawai'i. However, the Islands could not hope to compete with such low-wage countries as México and Singapore. Furthermore, there soon was a glut of electronic commodities in the global market. And environmental pollution from an electronics industry would endanger the well-being of the number one industry, tourism.

Hawai'i's policy makers next tried to find a niche that would emphasize research and development in biotechnology, electronics, geothermal, and space industries. But such projects require long periods of development before they actually go online (Herbig and Kramer 1994). Even if, for some reason, venture capital were to finance such projects on a grand scale, they are not labor intensive and would not be able to generate sufficient employment to decrease dependency on tourism. Since advanced technology industries require the employment of specializations unavailable in the state, skilled labor would have to be imported. An increase in affluent residents would also put pressure on such scarce Island resources as housing, land, and water. Finally, the comparative advantage of such projects in Hawai'i is dubious in the context of global competition in the fields of biotechnology, electronics, and space.

CAMPAIGN 1994, CAYETANO, AND LINGLE

The economy has always played a central role in Hawai'i politics. The gubernatorial campaign of 1994 was a true watershed, with three candidates vying.

Pat Saiki (1994a, b), the Republican candidate for governor, concentrated on two main points in her campaign: (1) Yes, John Burns had a vision for Hawai'i, but outgoing incumbent Governor John Waihe'e and the rest of the Democrats were unimaginative non-leaders who mishandled big on the economy and were extremely corrupt. (2) The time had come to restore Burns's vision by kicking the rascals out. Saiki blamed the Democrats for everything that went wrong in the state while dismissing economic and political global influences that are so clearly crucial to the state's economic health. In short, she underestimated the intelligence and knowledge of the electorate by providing advertising without substance.

Due to the lethargic performance of the Island economy, Saiki concentrated on the theme of Hawai'i becoming a "Pacific Partner." But that theme was hollow because the Islands had been trying to become the center of the Pacific in investment, technology, and trade since before the days of Burns, and all such efforts came to naught for reasons having to do with transnational corporate strategies, including the global division of labor and the dearth of capital and natural resources in the state (Aoudé 1995; Kent 1983).

Ben Cayetano, a self-styled "New Democrat," ran as the Democratic Party candidate for governor that year. Although he articulated the same economic problems as Saiki, his message was more concrete. He hoped to stimulate economic growth in order to cut the "paradise tax," that is, the differential between Hawai'i's cost of living and that of the continental United States.

Whereas Saiki concentrated on Hawai'i's international role, Cayetano (1994) linked that role with issues near and dear to the people, such as attracting investment, cleaning up government, educating children, helping small business, reforming the land use planning process, and reforming worker's compensation and health insurance. Cayetano clearly understood the politicoeconomic context. He believed that a solution to the economic crisis was within reach by creating niches for Hawai'i in various international markets.

A third candidate, longtime Honolulu Mayor Frank Fasi, promised to clean up corruption, help small business, and look out for the interests of the less affluent. A political maverick, Fasi ran as the gubernatorial candidate of his new Best Party.

When votes were tallied, Cayetano won. His 134,978 votes exceeded 113,158 for independent candidate Fasi, and 107,908 for Saiki. After the election, the Best Party was dissolved. Thus, before taking office, Governor Cayetano knew that his election by a plurality meant that he lacked a clear mandate and would have to appeal to diverse interests.

The campaign promises of 1994, however, soon gave way to the economic realities of 1995. A higher cost of living and unemployment in Hawai'i's tourist markets negatively impacted state revenues. One of Governor Cayetano's first acts was to declare that the state's financial picture was grimmer than he originally believed. The projected deficit for the state budget 1995–1997 biennium, first estimated at $250 million (Kresnak and Botticelli 1995), was later revised upward. It was not possible to institute programs in everyone's interest. Nor was it possible to eliminate the budget deficit without raising taxes. Cayetano responded by severely cutting the state budget. Consequently, employee health care costs and worker's compensation were on the chopping block. His critics perceived that he was balancing the budget on the backs of the working class, especially those at the lower rungs, whereas he believed that he was exercising leadership in hard economic times (Cayetano 1995:20). Cayetano had promised to create programs that would be in everyone's interest in order to convince voters that current sacrifices were for their future benefit. A chorus echoed that "Hawai'i's easy days are over" (Griffin 1994).

Whereas in 1995 Governor Cayetano was consumed with attending to deficit-spending problems, his program in 1996 was to pay attention to "diversifying" the economy, a goal that for decades had failed to materialize to any significant degree. Cayetano was more realistic about diversification than most political leaders. While he gave lip service to the diversification narrative, he pursued public policies that bolstered such critical economic sectors as tourism and construction, in part to revive the lagging construction industry (*Honolulu Advertiser* 1996).

Big-ticket development (such as the Waikīkī Convention Center) and niche tourism (expecting that some visitors might convalesce in the Islands) were Cayetano's way of recognizing that there are limits to diversification in the global economy. As tourism declined, jobs had to be found somewhere to avoid large-scale unemployment.

For Governor Cayetano, reforming the government meant downsizing, facilitating the way for business, especially small business, and creating jobs. One economic truism is that businesses create jobs. Businesses, of course, like incentives. Due to insufficient tax revenue and state income, the costs of doing business had to be cut. Proposed incentives for business included tax breaks and enterprise zones.

In his master plan, *Restoring Hawaii's Economic Momentum* (1996), Cayetano asserted that the economic crisis in Hawai'i was essentially due to structural problems and was not merely cyclical. True to mainstream economic wisdom, he contended that there were three pillars for economic recovery: (1) correcting fiscal balances, (2) encouraging production in the business sector, and (3) reducing barriers to doing business. All three steps were then directly or indirectly related to privatization and "free enterprise." To implement his policies, he identified six imperatives:

1. promote a positive business environment,
2. encourage new investment to reinvigorate the economy,
3. find new areas of economic growth,
4. focus on Asia and the Pacific,
5. reinforce Neighbor Island economic growth, and
6. invest in education and human resources.

Cayetano, thus, sought measures that responded to structural changes in the economy.

The plan involved short-term capital improvement projects, using bonds and public funds, to encourage business expansion. The long-term approach called for more investment and privatization. Coupled with more cuts in the state budget, the hope was that the economy would begin to grow at a healthy rate.

Cayetano had limited options. As governor, he promised success in expanding health services, the finance, insurance, real estate, and tourism sectors. Incentives to business, a cornerstone of the plan, were translated into more cuts in health care for many indigent families, who could no longer access free non-emergency dental services, while the legislature slashed welfare benefits (*Honolulu Advertiser* 1996). To attract business, enterprise zones were to be free from union contracts, tax holidays were instituted, and the worker's compensation law was watered down.

To his credit, Cayetano recognized structural problems in the economy, but the source of the economic crisis was within the global economy. Local solutions could only yield limited results. Social problems, meanwhile, worsened, including crime, drugs, and poor educational attainments. The crisis could not be overcome by addressing symptoms, no matter how sophisticated the plan.

Cayetano also had to struggle with the economic effects of 9/11 on the Island economy. He became increasingly unpopular, especially because he appeared to blame the victims—working-class people—for their plight by telling them that they had not been creative enough to change with the new demands of the global economy (Petranek 2001:3–4). He privatized government functions and provided more state subsidies for tourism interests, but the economy remained in the doldrums.

Cayetano was not able to curtail corruption and patronage. It was difficult to rid the state of its entrenched political culture, especially since many Democrats are tied to corporate business interests and had become more conservative over the years, privileging capital to the detriment of workers, a reality decried by Cayetano (2009), who always remembered growing up in the poorest section of Honolulu.

When Republican Linda Lingle was elected in 2002, she presided over an even deeper recession, particularly from 2008, when the world economy tanked. Her policies differed little from those of Cayetano. The deteriorating performance of Hawai'i's economy as a consequence of the global crisis could only have negative social effects. Devastating cuts in the state budget adversely impacted economic indicators, furloughs began, layoffs followed, and more cuts were expected.

Energy costs have continued to soar. In 2007, Hawai'i adopted a law requiring electric utilities to provide 10 percent of their electricity from renewable sources and energy efficiency by 2010 and 70 percent by 2030 (Wiles 2010). In 2010, a Korean motor vehicle manufacturer signed an agreement with the State of Hawai'i to establish a manufacturing assembly plant in Honolulu for producing electric vehicles that might employ 1,000 (Wiles 2010). Operations will ideally begin in 2012.

RECENT PROGRESSIVE SOCIAL STRUGGLES

Since the arrival of Haole traders and missionaries, Hawai'i's history has been a chronicle of disenfranchisement and oppression of the indigenous people as well as exploitation and oppression of plantation workers. The majority of the Islands' people have never enjoyed political and economic control over Hawai'i's resources.

Hawai'i's history is rich with examples of progressive social struggles. The first plantation strike occurred in July 1841, when indigenous

Hawaiian workers struck at Kōloa, Kaua'i (Beechert 1985). Other strikes occurred in the 1890s and repeatedly thereafter (see Chapter 9).

The change in the power structure from Haole Republican to Japanese Democrats at the ballot box in 1954 was peacefully accepted. During the Republican era, workers on the plantations mobilized in the form of strikes because normal political channels would not listen to them. The Territory and later State of Hawai'i was thus perceived to have graduated to normal politics in 1954, without further need for mass mobilization to achieve redress. The internal and external economic and political forces that brought about the 1954 Democratic "revolution" soon dissipated, however. Organized labor, a pillar of the "revolution," eventually lost much of its steam.

The radical discourse of the 1950s died in later decades. True, Democrat Tom Gill challenged mainstream Governor John Burns, a Democrat, in the 1970 primary election for governor, articulating his message as that of assisting the disenchanted and dispossessed, the very rhetoric that mobilized voters to vote Democratic in 1954 (Coffman 1973:39). But he was the exception, and he lost despite having a long-term view of the ongoing economic transformation of the Islands.

In the mid-1970s, while Obama was a teenager, a few demonstrations protested the massive infusion of Japanese capital but died down. Also in the mid-1970s, women and Filipinos worked within the system for certain goals (see Chapter 11). They formed organizations, held meetings, and presented grievances to state government officials. Although they operated independently of each other, they came together to confront the Department of Education. Overwhelmingly employed as librarians and teachers, women of all ethnicities wanted to break through glass ceilings to become administrators (Table 11.4; Haas 1992:Table 5.9). Local Filipinos, meanwhile, were being denied entry-level teaching jobs, and the need of immigrant Filipino children to learn English was ignored. When coalitions of both groups achieved no progress in direct discussions with officeholders, civil rights complaints were filed, and the federal government investigated.

As a result, a modicum of success was achieved, but only after replacement of two superintendents by the Board of Education. The first articulated sexist remarks at a large meeting on women's issues, whereupon the audience visibly moaned. Humiliated, he resigned, admitting inadequacy in dealing with new issues. The second resignation occurred after federal civil rights officials issued a finding that Hawai'i's

Department of Education was violating the language needs of Filipino immigrants. The superintendent tried to defend discriminatory policies during the investigation, and a public hearing on the subject pointed out his expendability.

The Board of Education then responded by appointing Donnis Thompson, an African American woman, as superintendent. The two movements appeared appeased, but she soon confided that she was being defied by Japanese officials entrenched in the higher administrative ranks. She realized that she had been hired as a figurehead. Nevertheless, the federal government monitored progress to address language minority needs over the next decade (see Chapter 11).

While women and Filipinos were using normal channels to redress grievances, more basic issues about the political economy of Hawai'i arose. From about 1969, progressive social struggles have developed through six stages in which the indigenous Native Hawaiian movement has been linked to the multiethnic, multinational worker's movement in the belief that they can only be successful if they work together. In addition, a strategic linkage has been forged between progressive people's movements in Hawai'i and the continental United States. The strategy is to look beyond ethnicity to class interests, as in the historic struggle to establish labor unions. The Haole oligarchs who once ruled the Islands were no longer a target of protest, as they had already decided to merge with the much more formidable external capital and left the Islands. Instead, grassroots social movements emerged in opposition to the consequences of economic growth in their daily lives (Aoudé 1999b).

First stage. Leading activists in the initial stage of protest consisted primarily of Filipinos, Native Hawaiians, and, to a lesser extent, Japanese, who joined to stop malicious efforts to evict poor people from their homes. The tactics consisted of demonstrations, visits to legislative bodies and offices of developers, pickets, and sit-ins. Police were forced to make arrests on occasion, as when a cordon of demonstrators held hands to block bulldozers.

Several movements opposed the conversion of farmland into real estate developments. However, Native Hawaiians evicted from their lands lost in both the struggles of Makua Valley in 1969 and Kalama Valley in 1971.

Among successes in the early 1970s, Chinatown and Ota Camp were sites of anti-eviction struggles, primarily of Filipino workers. Waiāhole-Waikāne was the site of a struggle against evictions of Japanese and Native Hawaiians by real estate developers who owned agricultural

land and wanted windfall profits through residential rezoning (Gesh-
wender 1980–1981). The first stage of the social struggle was primarily
defensive, fighting evictions, and was based primarily in working-class
communities that had been inspired by the civil rights and anti-war
movements.

The emergence of ethnic studies at the University of Hawai'i at Mānoa
was an integral part of the social struggle, playing a key role in the development of grassroots movements (Aoudé 1999a). That proactive dimen-
sion continued in the second stage, enabling the Ethnic Studies Program
to gain permanence as the Department of Ethnic Studies by 1995.

Second stage. The mid-1970s witnessed the beginnings of the second
stage of protest—the grassroots Native Hawaiian social movement for
land. The first action stopped the bombing of the island of Kaho'olawe
(see Chapter 2). But the movement soon galvanized around the issue
of ceded lands, that is, land taken over by governments after 1893 that
had been held in common for the people by the monarchs. In the second
stage, the social struggle took the offensive.

Regaining a measure of Native Hawaiian sovereignty became central
to the discourse. Native Hawaiians have been the most exploited and
oppressed nationality by the multiethnic capitalist class. Land is power in
Hawai'i (Cooper and Daws 1985). Most Native Hawaiians own no land,
so some are organizing to reclaim what they consider to be their nation.
Native Hawaiians, mostly members of the working class (see Chapter
10), have much in common with the rest of the multiethnic working class,
which has been hit hard by economic downturns in the state.

Linkage between the land and social ills, such as discrimination,
employment, homelessness, and a shortage of low-cost housing (Vorsino
2010b), is logical for three reasons: (1) The Native Hawaiian movement
links the fight to regain ancestral lands with the broader quest for better
health care, housing, and jobs. (2) Progressives are increasingly working
alongside Native Hawaiians for the broader quest, realizing that resolution of the Native Hawaiian land issue is central to the alleviation of
misery and poverty for the multiethnic working class. (3) Ruling circles
are trying to find ways to co-opt, derail, or divide the movement.

Third stage. When Governor Cayetano proposed legislative cuts from
social programs for the poor in 1995, the multiethnic core from the first
stage joined Native Hawaiians and their supporters from the second
stage. A huge rally was held at the State Capitol. Cayetano's unpopular-
ity resulted in Linda Lingle's near victory in the gubernatorial elections
of 1998.

Protests from the mid-1990s also focused on the "Hawaiian vote" of 1996. Elites of other ethnic groups feared that they might lose economic control if Native Hawaiians succeeded in getting back land taken by government that had been held in trust for the Native Hawaiian people by the former monarchs. Accordingly, in 1996, the legislature authorized a "Hawaiian vote," that is, a referendum asking whether Native Hawaiians truly wanted to begin a process of setting up Hā Hawai'i, a new political structure that would negotiate with the State of Hawai'i on such issues as education, health, and land. The vote was engineered because the state elite wanted to refocus from the land ownership issue to the creation of a new political entity (Aoudé 1999a:291–292). Hā Hawai'i was to be in charge of elections for delegates at a constitutional convention that would establish some sort of Native Hawaiian government. Although many Native Hawaiians boycotted the vote, the proposal gained majority support, thereby assuring that the most fundamental question—the illegal appropriation of ancestral land by state government—would be deferred.

A division within the Native Hawaiian movement also emerged in 2000, when Senator Dan Akaka sponsored the Native Hawaiian Government Reorganization Act. Ostensibly designed to give the indigenous movement more control over its affairs, Native Hawaiian opponents pointed out that the bill would have the effect of containing that movement by creating a bureaucratic process that might—or might not—get to the central issue, namely, who will control ancestral lands of the Native Hawaiian people. Supporters of the bill in the Islands include some Democrats and Republicans, but the "Akaka Bill" has been steadfastly opposed by conservatives in Congress.

Meanwhile, the ideology of globalization had been promoted during the past decade as a cure for Hawai'i's economic problems (Steger 2002), though the Islands failed to diversify and "catch up" with the "New Economy." Instead, there have been buyouts of local businesses by giant corporations headquartered elsewhere. The effect of globalization is manifold, including the continuing decapitalization of Hawai'i as multinational firms take profits made in the Fiftieth State outside the state rather than investing inside (cf. Petranek 2001:1–6).

Businesses and property in Hawai'i are in a very real sense up for auction in the world economy. The only concerted effort to hold back the capital outflow has been the persistent desire of Native Hawaiians to regain control of their ancestral lands. Otherwise, the capital outflow will never end.

Challenges to globalism occurred primarily at the grassroots level. Numerous rallies, demonstrations, and forums have been held to protest the adverse effects of globalization. The most important demonstration took place in May 2001, when the Asian Development Bank met in Honolulu (Aoudé 2004:249).

Fourth stage. The invasion of Afghanistan during 2001 added the new anti-war peace movement to the social struggles, notably a section of the labor movement. Other grassroots organizations and individuals followed suit. Co-optation of a large section of the Native Hawaiian movement contributed to the temporary marginalization of the land issue.

The main feature of the fourth stage was defensive. In addition to protesting the war, the new social forces were also opposed to the attack on civil liberties, led by President George W. Bush, which was supported by Republicans as well as likeminded or intimidated Democratic members of Congress.

In Hawai'i, the Hotel Employees and Restaurant Employees Union, Local 5, took the lead in the labor movement against the war and in defense of civil liberties. A significant section of the Hawai'i State Democratic Party also threw itself into the anti-war struggle, and a main section of the indigenous movement took an anti-war position. A further intensification of the anti-war movement resulted from the Anglo-American invasion of Iraq during 2003. The protest movement, accordingly, was energized to defeat President George W. Bush's bid for a second term. His opponent, John Kerry, won in Hawai'i but lost in a close national election. As was true of the three previous stages, the fourth confirmed the integral relationship among the international, national, and local situations.

The gubernatorial election in 2002 might have provided an opportunity for progressive forces within the Democratic Party to pull together in opposition to Republican Linda Lingle's bid for governor. But they did not do so. Lingle's election as the first Republican governor in 40 years could have been a wake-up call to continue the social struggles that long energized Hawai'i politics, but her landslide re-election in 2006 proved the opposite.

Observers sympathetically oriented toward the mass movements attributed the Democratic defeats in 2002 and 2006 to four factors: (1) The Democratic Party moved to the right, especially under Cayetano, yielding to the neoliberal ideology of globalization as the supposed solution to the state's financial problems. (2) Demographic changes had occurred in the Islands over the previous 25 years due to in-migration from the continental United States of conservatives, both religious and secular, who traditionally vote Republican. (3) A considerable number of members of ethnic groups that traditionally voted Democratic had become more conservative. (4) Many Native Hawaiians switched allegiance to the Republican Party (see Chapter 9).

Meanwhile, religious and secular right-wing groups mobilized, attacking indigenous rights in the language of anti-discrimination, civil rights, and constitutionalism. In *Rice v Cayetano* (528US495), the Supreme Court of the United States rendered a decision in 2000 that nullified the state practice of permitting only Native Hawaiians to vote for members on the governing board of the Office of Hawaiian Affairs, a state government department.

Fifth stage. The progressive people's movement saw a clear linkage between the wars in Afghanistan and Iraq, on the one hand, and privatization and budget cuts, on the other. Nationally, the link was that money for the wars was taken out of social programs. Locally, one link was that funds were pumped into a military research project at the University of Hawaiʻi, while tuition increased.

In regard to the military project, UH President David McClain sought to affiliate a U.S. Navy research unit with the Mānoa campus. When the proposal leaked out in 2005, faculty and students were strongly opposed and not only testified against the move but also occupied his office for six days. During spring 2006, Interim Mānoa Chancellor Denise Konan presented a negative recommendation on the matter to the Board of Regents. McClain then shifted gears, getting Board of Regents approval during the summer to affiliate the research center with the UH system as a whole rather than with the Mānoa campus. An unpopular decision was made while faculty and students were on summer break.

Sixth stage. During 2008, Barack Obama was running in Democratic Party primaries as a presidential candidate. He won big in both the Democratic Party caucuses and in the November general election in Hawaiʻi. The mobilization effort for Obama was unprecedented in the history of Hawaiʻi, affecting all ethnic groups and social classes.

The population was tired of war, the consequences of the economic crisis, and a Republican governor who had been completely supportive of Bush's domestic and foreign policies. Indigenous rights were also a significant part of the mix, and Obama had declared his support of a modified Akaka Bill.

But the sixth stage is already proving to be more intractable than any previous stages because the unprecedented global economic crisis determines much of what the Hawai'i elite must do to maintain its economic interests and social privilege. With a $1 billion deficit projected for 2009/2011, Governor Lingle played hardball with the public employee labor unions—demanding pay cuts, furloughs, and reduced fringe benefits. Some 650 state employees not covered by union contracts, meanwhile, were laid off (De Pledge 2009). Labor unions have attempted to negotiate for the best deal for their members.

The indigenous struggle is more complicated than before. Splits within the Native Hawaiian movement are primarily on the lines of support or opposition to the Akaka Bill. Meanwhile, local right-wing forces, supported by counterparts in the continental United States, continue to attack the Akaka Bill.

Despite overwhelming support for Obama's candidacy, grassroots political activists, even in the state's Democratic Party, later expressed disappointment with President Obama's escalation of the war in Afghanistan and his compromise positions on health reform and other issues.

But the ongoing social struggle has not lost its bearings. Senator Dan Inouye, who became chair of the Senate Appropriations Committee, has long taken advantage of his position to help the Islands, calling himself the "No. 1 earmarks guy in the U.S. Congress," though with suspicions sometimes that he has been influenced by campaign contributions (Sample 2009). One of his pork barrel deals, which was made with Republican Majority Leader Trent Lott of Mississippi, resulted in having two "superferries" constructed by an Australian firm in Mississippi for passenger and auto travel between the islands of Hawai'i.

When the first superferry arrived in 2007, Governor Lingle waived the requirement for an environmental impact statement (EIS), which greatly displeased environmentalists concerned about the effects on local fishing as well as seasonal arrivals of whales. After the inaugural service to Maui was greeted by a few protesters, a local judge banned another trip until an EIS was filed with the court, whereupon Lingle called the legislature into special session to pass a law to make the waiver a matter of law. The judge then lifted the restraining order, whereupon environmentalists appealed his decision.

Meanwhile, surfers on surfboards blocked the entrance to the harbor on the superferry service's first trip to Kaua'i. So many protesters greeted the second superferry to Kaua'i that all future trips there were cancelled. In 2009, after the Hawai'i Supreme Court ruled that the law exempting the service from an EIS was illegal, the company soon declared bankruptcy, and the superferry sailed from the Islands. That same year a proposal to convert farms into homesites was turned down by the Land Use Commission (Essoyan 2009), a mini-victory for small-scale farmers.

CONCLUSION

The worldwide recession that began in late 2008 has devastated Hawai'i's economy. Budget cuts are only part of the story.

In late 2008, when only 16 percent of all failing banks were awarded funds from the Temporary Asset Relief Program, the denial of funds for the Central Pacific Bank was reversed after a telephone call from Inouye (Kiel and Applebaum 2009). The Senator was indeed continuing to look after Hawai'i, albeit microeconomically, and the bank received $135 million (Segal 2009).

Meanwhile, the indigenous movement can be positioned to play a central role in the larger progressive people's movement in the Islands. The social struggles can only intensify, given the impact of the global economy on national and local arenas.

What the protest movements demonstrate is that Hawai'i's political system exemplifies a truly multiethnic democracy in which all ethnic groups join together to stop political elites from high-handed action. However, the fact that protesters must go to the streets today is an indication of the existence of a mass society (Kornhauser 1959), namely, that political parties are not operating in an intermediate role between government and the masses. The political party leadership, in other words, is in bed with the economic establishment. Courts, therefore, fill the gap by playing an intermediate role between the executive and legislative branches, on the one hand, and sometimes side with the masses who have sought a redress of grievances in the streets, just as they have done in times past.

Today, the Haku Alliance, a small business lobbying group supported by big business, strongly opposes the gains won through hard struggle by labor—minimum wage, unemployment insurance, and worker's compensation. But sometimes the elites win. Sometimes they lose.

Hawai'i politics is similar to current Mainland mass society politics with one important exception—mass demonstrations have been effective on many occasions. In addition, the various ethnic groups work together rather than at cross purposes when protest issues are class based. Observing principles of Hawai'i's multicultural ethos, they often gain the respect of the political elites, who are often forced to capitulate in order to save face.

Barack Obama's model of grassroots democracy, as demonstrated by his 2008 election campaign, is similar to the first stage described previously. His friends and relatives have doubtless updated him on succeeding mobilization movements. His election victory would have been impossible without that model.

Chapter 15

The Communitarian
Pragmatist President

Michael Haas

*I think that there's the possibility—not the certainty, but the
possibility—that I can't just win an election but can also
transform the country in the process, that the language and
the approach I take to politics is sufficiently different that I
could bring diverse parts of this country together in a way
that hasn't been done in some time, and that bridging those
divisions is a critical element in solving problems like health
care or energy or education.*

(Robinson 2007)

Barack Obama's inauguration on January 20, 2009, was historic. The
press insisted that he was the first Black president and was from Illinois. The conventional thinking, that one drop of Black blood makes a
person Black, had still not been transcended into his acceptance as the
first biracial, mulatto, multicultural—and Black—president. That he was
born in Honolulu was not celebrated. Indeed, some extremist detractors
continue to doubt whether he was born in the United States of America
and is part of some sort of conspiracy hatched by a secret power elite.

Yet Obama was reared primarily by a White mother and two White
grandparents. And he lived in a multiethnic, multicultural environment
for most of the first 18 years of his life. To experience African American

culture first hand, he had to leave Hawai'i. Although he would have encountered culture shock after arriving on the Mainland, he clearly retains multicultural perspectives and values that were wired into him during his youth.

During his first year in office, President Obama puzzled many observers. Pundits repeatedly asked, "Why is he like that?" and then relied on explanations that revealed much about themselves. Some biographers suggest that his parents and grandparents shaped him (cf. Wolffe 2009). Even though his mother lived in Kansas only four years, she is described as a "Kansan" by many biographers because her parents lived and married there. Another perspective is that he matured at a very early age (Alter 2010; O'Reilly 2009; Weisberg 2010). Some, including Hillary Clinton during the nomination campaign, have claimed that academic elitism is his main influence (cf. Gerson 2010; Meacham 2009c; Plouffe 2009:226). Others believe that he was largely shaped by his experience as an African American (Remnick 2010) or in Chicago (McClelland 2010; Mendell 2007). Fareed Zakaria (2009) believes the influences to be his mother and his Indonesian experience (cf. Remnick 2010:430). Kathleen Parker (2010a), who believes Obama has feminine traits, clearly is unaware that strict male/female roles are a Western fixation, and that he did not spend his childhood in the West. The most extraordinary claim is that he has a "Kansas-Indonesia-Kenya background" (Lelyveld 2010:6)! Stranger still, he is accused of being Kenyan (cf. D'Souza 2010). His campaign manager described how he learned to campaign better, and some pundits have sought to explain changes since he became president as a political maturation (Baker 2010; Plouffe 2009:203; Thomas and Connolly 2010).

His multifaceted life permits him to be viewed from a variety of perspectives, telling much about the biographers' biases. With the exception of a couple of thin Honolulu-based publications (Glauberman and Burris 2008; Jacobs 2009), and the insights of Chicagoans Edward McClelland (2010) and Eric Whitaker (Alter 2010:144), systematic and dismissive exclusion of his Hawai'i background from serious consideration by Mainland biographers is not only Cyclopsian myopia but also may embolden those who believe that Obama was not born in Hawai'i.

Although there may be some truth to all these views about such an extraordinary politician, *Dreams from My Father* provides testimony for the view that he grew up in Honolulu and was exposed to an "Aloha Zen" culture quite different from that prevailing on the Mainland. Ever since, he has been observing principles of Hawai'i's multicultural ethos.

Most Mainland observers deliberately choose to ignore Obama's many admissions that his values are rooted in his Hawai'i experience, where communitarianism prevails and Social Darwinism is rejected.

Anyone who adapts to the multicultural ethos of Hawai'i and then moves to the Mainland will have adjustment problems. The biculturalized values of his Mainland-born mother and grandparents helped him a lot to make that adjustment. His high school classmates remember his early maturity, which served him well when he went off to college. To be successful in rough-and-tumble Chicago politics, he had to learn how to be effective in a manner that would not work in Hawai'i. But his belief in how multiethnic societies can be harmonious is based on personal experience, and that is in part why his wife has said that nobody can understand Barack Obama until they first understand Hawai'i (Mendell 2007:20).

HOW HAWAI'I INFLUENCES PRESIDENT OBAMA

Each chapter thus far has identified how Hawai'i developed multiculturalism, resulting in interethnic peace despite confronting its normal share of political conflicts. Barack Obama lived in Hawai'i during the 1960s and 1970s, when a multicultural transformation enriched the language, media, literature, music, politics, organized labor, the social structure, public and higher education, criminal justice, and the economy.

After a brief biographical sketch, Chapter 1 defined the 12 components of the multicultural ethos to which President Obama is an exemplary representative. What is baffling to observers on the Mainland about his personality and values is obvious to anyone who has lived in Hawai'i. Voters in 2010 remained puzzled, and his party suffered losses.

A history of Hawai'i appeared in Chapter 2. Most tourists know little about the tragic loss of sovereignty of the Hawaiian people and their patient efforts to achieve redress through peaceful protest despite adverse legal opinions and political chicanery. Obama learned a lot from that history, and declared June 11, 2010, as national Kamehameha Day to coincide with Hawai'i's state holiday commemorating the leader who unified the Hawaiian Islands in 1810, calling upon *"all Americans to celebrate the rich heritage of Hawaii with appropriate ceremonies and activities"* (*Honolulu Star-Advertiser* 2010d).

Differences between residents of Honolulu and the Mainland, as measured in polls presented in Chapter 3, prove that the multicultural ethos is unique to Hawai'i. What is most salient is the stress on group harmony over the individualism of the Mainland. Obama's experience in

Hawai'i informs him that multiethnic diversity does not result in attitudinal balkanization. Those moving to the Islands from the Mainland, can adapt their views, and the rest of Hawai'i rewards them accordingly. But those who leave the Islands for the Mainland are shocked almost daily in situations that would never happen in the land of Aloha.

Chapter 4 explained the rise of a special language in Hawai'i, a state where bilingualism is officially approved. Words in the official languages, English and Hawaiian, in turn, are embedded with other languages in a Creole tongue, a language with its own grammar, syntax, and other elements, which is spoken by most local-born residents of the Aloha State. Obama's occasional use of that tongue proves that he is a populist and not a language snob. Although he spoke English with a Kansas accent at home and at school, many languages are spoken in homes and at cultural events in the Islands. Meanwhile, Native Hawaiians are reviving their language. The idea that a language might be disdained or suppressed is unthinkable in Hawai'i today.

In the media, as Chapter 5 reported, newspapers emerged from the various ethnic groups, and multilingual programming on radio and television is common. Rather than tearing apart the social fabric, multicultural media have brought everyone together into a mutual cultural admiration society. When Barry Obama watched *Star Trek*, he saw a fictional paradigm of the real-life experience that he encountered in Hawai'i—representatives of several cultures working together and respecting one another.

Literature in Hawai'i today, as described in Chapter 6, has gone beyond mischaracterizations by monocultural outsiders to involve a multicultural conversation among local writers with varying perspectives. Obama's *Dreams from My Father* is an embodiment of that special vision. He appears to have particularly doted on readings at the feet of African American poet Frank Marshall Davis on visits to his pad in Waikīkī. The poet Shelley (1840), who once said, "Poets are the unacknowledged legislators of the world," doubtless had in mind individuals with the literary and political talents of Barack Obama, as his poetic *Dreams* morphed into his manifesto *Audacity*. Indeed, he felt that "*the whole election* [of 2008] *was a novel*" (Balz and Johnson 2009:376). However, as Mario Cuomo (1990:584) once said, "We often campaign in poetry, but then we're always required to govern in prose."

The music of Hawai'i, according to Chapter 7, has offered to the world three new musical instruments—the slack key guitar, the steel guitar, and the 'ukulele. Residents of Hawai'i indulge themselves, either as performers or as listeners, with a wide variety of musical offerings without the sharp dichotomy between "Western versus ethnic" that often prevails on the Mainland. Whereas Obama has gravitated to the music of African Americans during his life, he celebrated a variety of musical forms at his inauguration and continues to have broad musical tastes.

Onetime polarization between Haole Republicans and Japanese Democrats has been transcended by a multicultural politics in Hawai'i, according to the description in Chapter 8. The significance of a Japanese American elected and reelected as governor of Hawai'i, the first non-White chief executive of any state, must have caught the imagination of a young Barack Obama, who from an early age expressed an ambition to be president. His view of politics as bringing diverse people together in a common quest was inspired by the Aloha State, where negative campaigning is abhorrent and opposing candidates disagree without being disagreeable.

According to Chapter 9, multiethnic plantation workers in Hawai'i joined forces through organized labor against White business elites, who were forced to make concessions because of a continuing labor shortage. Obama's mother and grandparents were not union members, but young Barry sold ice cream to help his family of middle class renters in a modest high-rise apartment. Union mobilization of pressure to better the lives of the working class, notably through universal health care legislation in 1974, serves as a paradigm for his later pursuit for public office, not the Social Darwinist belief that government exists only to help those who are productive.

Social mobility, as documented in Chapter 10, was something tangible for Barack Obama while attending Punahou, his prep school. Upward mobile Japanese studied as equals alongside Whites of established wealth. Although Black students felt isolated, he was spurred to success by rubbing elbows with the upper crust.

Obama's experience in private schools, first chosen by his mother and now exhibited in his selection of schooling for his two daughters in the nation's capitol, suggests that he has reason to believe that public schools need considerable improvement in quality of education, particularly teachers who go beyond the minimum to bring out the best in their students. As described in Chapter 11, he lived in Honolulu when the major civil rights protests affecting public schools involved Filipinos, a very different perspective from the struggle of African Americans on the Mainland. Subsequently, thanks in part to that Filipino struggle but in large measure to pressure from Native Hawaiians, public schools in Hawai'i have done much to move from monoculturalism to multiculturalism.

Barry Obama would have benefited from courses taught by passionate political scientists at the nearby Mānoa campus of the University of Hawai'i, and he may have heard of the struggle to establish Ethnic Studies as well as the dearth of African American faculty. However, his mother wisely persuaded him to expand his horizons by going to college on the Mainland. Multicultural perspectives at the University of Hawai'i, as described in Chapter 12, lag behind the rest of the state because administrators and faculty are among the least acculturated to Hawai'i's multicultural ethos. The prodding for multiculturalism has come primarily from local students and cosmopolitan faculty.

Crime statistics in the Aloha State, as presented in Chapter 13, offer the paradox that Native Hawaiians constitute half of the police force yet a quarter of those arrested and nearly half of those imprisoned. Ethnic diversity has not set one group against another. Obama's very different experience on the Mainland led him to champion a law in Illinois to deter racial profiling and to nominate empathetic Supreme Court justices.

Regarding the political economy of Hawai'i, Chapter 14 argues that prospects for Island prosperity are bleak because the private and public sectors in Hawai'i have lost control of the economy. Obama was present when grassroots mobilizations emerged to stop greedy landowners. Indeed, his experiences in Hawai'i, Indonesia, and Kenya give him a wider vision of the need to balance local control with globalization.

The first 14 chapters, in short, provide some context for the thinking of a candidate who became president. It should therefore be no surprise that he felt that the popular mandate was to revitalize America culturally, economically, politically, and socially—"*to create a society, not just individual families, based on [the] values . . . of looking out for one another, of sharing, of sacrificing for each other*" (Remnick 2010:294). And he had a working model in mind for his philosophy—Hawai'i.

After Obama's election in November 2008, he enjoyed the holidays in Honolulu while drawing up plans for his presidency. He promised not only to take bold action on many fronts, but also to change the mindset in Washington. Although his reforms were formulated in practical terms, he clearly wanted to confront and transform the monoculturalism of national politics because he did not approve of bickering, confrontationalism, and narrowmindedness in Washington. As the first two years of his presidency played out, he brought to bear the principles of the multicultural ethos (friendliness, humility, joviality, respectfulness, nonconfrontationalism,

communitarianism, harmony, serenity, piety, humanism) in the way he
governed, as noted in the following discussion. Communitarianism is his
philosophy; the other principles describe his style of governing.

Whereas others have assessed policy successes and failures of the
Obama presidency, the aim of this chapter is to demonstrate how his
reliance on precepts of the multicultural ethos that he assimilated as a
boy in Honolulu has directly impacted his key decisions. What follows
may amaze those who have inappropriately tried to analyze Obama.

INAUGURATION

Barack Obama gave a clear indication of his communitarianism and
his piety by arranging for prayers to be delivered by three persons
with very different views—openly gay Episcopal Bishop Gene Robert-
son, the Reverend Joseph Lowery of the Southern Christian Leadership
Conference, and the Reverend Rick Warren of Saddleback Church,
Orange Country, California. The latter's views on abortion and gay
rights were anathema to many of Obama's supporters. When asked
to justify Warren's selection, Obama's press office made the following
statement:

> *This is going to be the most inclusive, open, accessible inaugura-
> tion in American history. . . . The president-elect certainly disagrees
> with him on [lesbian, gay, bisexual, transgender] issues. . . . But it
> has always been his goal to find common ground with people with
> whom you may disagree on some issues.* (Mooney 2009)

In Hawai'i, different cultural perspectives mean different opinions,
and Obama wanted the full range of views to be recognized. His method
of finding "*common ground*" was thus identified as bringing persons
with contrary views together socially before dealing with contentious
issues, thereby ensuring that differences would be expressed without rancor because a foundation of mutual respect had first been laid.
President Obama, thus, began by putting Hawai'i's multicultural ethos
into practice.

The inaugural address stressed many themes from the presidential
campaign. After respectfully complimenting President George W. Bush's
"*generosity and cooperation,*" he stressed longtime American ideals.
While identifying hardworking and innovative people as heroes, he also
tried to establish an ethical boundary line to separate those with greed

and irresponsibility as culprits. To approach the problems, he indicated that he would pursue "*hope over fear, unity of purpose over conflict and discord* [and] . . . *an end to the petty grievances and false promises, the recriminations and worn-out dogmas . . .*"

Regarding inclusiveness, he stressed that

> *our patchwork heritage is a strength, not a weakness. We are a nation of Christians and Muslims, Jews and Hindus—and nonbelievers. We are shaped by every language and culture, drawn from every end of this Earth; and because we have tasted the bitter swill of civil war and segregation, and emerged from that dark chapter stronger and more united, we cannot help but believe that the old hatreds shall someday pass; that the lines of tribe shall soon dissolve; that as the world grows smaller, our common humanity shall reveal itself.*

The words he spoke were not just platitudes but rooted in a reality that he experienced during the formative years of his life in Honolulu. Rather than pontificating with hyperbole, he preferred a humbler rhetoric.

Mindful of Martin Luther King, Jr.'s, "I Have a Dream" speech, the theme of Obama's inaugural address is summed up by a sentence that many have ignored: "*I have a dream about America.*" The America he knew as a boy was a dream compared to the nightmare that was keeping the country on edge when he was sworn in—an economy on the verge of depression, difficult foreign wars, international terrorists plotting against the United States, health care unaffordable for one-sixth of Americans, and endless partisan wrangling that had been preventing the political system from solving problems for ordinary Americans while the rich complacently showed no corporate or national responsibility.

He was quite serious on inauguration day, showing very little joviality. The fun began in the evening when inaugural balls began. He was soon to learn that a post-partisan America was a long way off. Vested interests would try to stymie his agenda.

APPOINTMENTS AND NOMINATIONS

Barack Obama's first appointment, Joe Biden as his Vice President, was accepted by the Democratic Party in mid-2008 and by the public on Election Day. Biden's principal virtue, according to Obama, is that he is people oriented (Plouffe 2009:295).

Prior to becoming president, Barack Obama began to select members of his cabinet and White House staff. Some 7,000 federal government employees are personally selected by the president of the United States. As someone relatively new to Washington and thrust onto the national scene in his mid-40s, he had not accumulated sufficient acquaintances and friendships so that the task would be easy, and he had no major management experience other than running a series of well-disciplined, successful political campaigns. He wanted diversity of opinions to facilitate logical deliberation.

Obama's selection of transition director John Podesta, onetime White House official under President Bill Clinton, assured that a large number of members of the former Clinton administration would be appointed, including Hillary Clinton, with whom he made peace by offering her the job of Secretary of State. More than 50 staff members of Podesta's Center for American Progress were chosen (Alter 2010:47), including his codirector, part-Japanese Pete Rouse, who became Senior Adviser to the President, a title shared with Chicagoans Valerie Jarrett and David Axelrod. Rahm Emmanuel, another Chicagoan, became Chief of Staff.

The president was also loyal to those with Harvard degrees or faculty positions, the only other sizeable group represented in the White House. Later, he hired his former Harvard mentor Laurence Tribe to develop a program to guarantee indigents access to counsel, something available in Hawai'i but not nationwide.

Although Obama managed to get his Cabinet appointed, the vetting process was unusually slow, both in the White House and in Congress. As a result, there was a serious lack of personnel at middle levels to work on details for major policy initiatives. For example, fewer than half of appointive State Department officials were confirmed by midsummer 2009 (Alter 2010:124). By the end of April 2010, moreover, Senate Republicans only allowed confirmation of 71 percent of the top 500 policymaking positions, impairing Obama's ability to get things done (*Washington Post* 2010).

Obama followed precedent by appointing nearly 40 advisors, dubbed by the media as "czars," to coordinate policy on specific subjects within the White House. Such officials did not require Senate approval. But the advisors could not direct implementation within administrative departments that Obama had not yet staffed, so the task was left to civil servants, who notoriously favor the status quo. The number of "czars" was about as many as Bush had.

Three Republicans joined Obama's Cabinet, an almost unprecedented inclusiveness. He retained Thomas Gates as Secretary of Defense, a man who has kept any partisan leanings to himself in order to work for the common good of several administrations. The second Republican was Transportation Secretary Ray LaHood, who had decided not to run for reelection to Congress from his district in Peoria, Illinois. LaHood, who demonstrated fairness while chairing impeachment proceedings against Bill Clinton, had been noted for years as a quintessential bipartisan, working with his colleagues in the House of Representatives on both sides of the aisle. Obama sought to nominate Republican Senator Judd Gregg as Commerce Secretary, but Gregg pulled out when Republicans pressured him to avoid capitulating to a Democratic President (Alter 2010:119). His Army Secretary appointment was held up by Republican Senators from Kansas who feared that Guantánamo prisoners might be sent to a facility in their state, Fort Leavenworth. John McHugh, a Republican member of Congress from upstate New York, finally became Secretary of the Army in September 2009.

Most striking about Obama's key choices is that many lived abroad as children (Baratholet and Stone 2009). Treasury Secretary Timothy Geithner spent most of his childhood outside the United States, as his father worked for the Ford Foundation's program in Asia, including in India, Indonesia, and Thailand. While in Indonesia, Geithner's father oversaw the microfinance programs developed by Obama's mother and met her. Valery Jarrett was born in Iran, where her father ran a children's hospital, and then lived in London from the age of 5 to 6. High-ranking military officers, of course, are likely to have had overseas assignments, and indeed retired General Jim Jones, National Security Adviser, spent most of his childhood in France, where his father, a Marine, was stationed. Retired Major General J. Scott Gration, a senior military adviser and special envoy to Sudan, had early experience in the Congo, where his parents were missionaries, and he had been flight instructor in Kenya from 1980 to 1982.

President Obama's inclusive Cabinet-level appointments include two Blacks (Eric Holder, Jr., UN Ambassador Susan Rice), two Hispanics (Kenneth Salazar, Hilda Solis), and three Asians (Steven Chu, Gary Locke, Eric Shinseki). Nine Cabinet Secretaries are Caucasian (Clinton, Shaun Donovan, Gates, Geithner, Arne Duncan, LaHood, Janet Napolitano, Kathleen Sebelius, Thomas Vilsak). There are five women and 11 men.

Shinseki, born in Lihue, Kaua'i, left for military service in Vietnam in 1965, when Obama was only four years old on the island of O'ahu.

Other Hawai'i-born appointments are Raymond Jefferson as Assistant Secretary of Labor and Andy Winer as External Affairs Director of the National Oceanic and Atmospheric Administration.

At full Cabinet meetings, seven (including Obama but excluding Rice) are minorities and 10 (including Vice President Joe Biden) are nonminorities, something unusual in Washington but almost resembling the more diverse Cabinets of Hawai'i governors. The Cabinet Secretary, Chinese American Chris Lu, is a Harvard Law classmate. Yet there is no Black from the South and no political scientist to provide a wider perspective.

Possibly the most crucial appointment was Chief of Staff Rahm Emanuel, sometimes known as Rahmbo (Alter 2010:Ch. 10). A multitasker who does not mind showing his testosterone, Emanuel was hired to corral support for the president's agenda (Baker and Zeleny 2009). A former Clintonite, he evidently made sure that corporate America would continue to bankroll the Democratic Party, even if that meant some compromising of Obama's agenda (Moyers 2009).

One-third of the White House staff are minorities, and 44 percent are women (Light 2008). Perhaps due to Rahm Emmanuel's profanity, the early nucleus was perceived as a "boys club" (Draper 2009). Giving him a truly different perspective from the various meetings during the day is Valery Jarrett, whose onetime multimillion-dollar real estate firm provides some contacts with the business community (and fund-raising sources) as well as the perspective of a minority woman with international experience. Obama considers her *"family"* because of long-time shrewd counsel and loyal friendship (Draper 2009). Indeed, both were onetime community organizers in Chicago, but she is the only one in the White House with both solid business experience and an ability to converse empathetically with a president who is deeply touched by difficult personal experiences among his constituents and has not forgotten his own challenges at a time when he was selling ice cream at Baskin-Robbins in Honolulu. However, the new faces did not include a social psychologist, that is, someone who could develop a strategy to change the culture in Washington. And by 2012 several were gone—Axelrod, Emmanuel, Gates, Jones, and two economic advisers (Christina Romer and Larry Summers).

Later, President Obama nominated Sonia Sotomayor to be an Associate Justice of the Supreme Court after surprising Senators that one of his humanistic criteria for a judge was someone who would show *"empathy,"* a characteristic of most judges in Hawai'i, who have a reputation for fairness and sensitivity to problems faced by ordinary citizens. Obama wanted to diversify the composition of the Supreme Court, and he was loyal to her while she endured a verbal onslaught during confirmation hearings. During his search for a second Supreme Court nominee, he looked for a "*consensus builder*" and nominated Elena Kagan, a moderate liberal (Parsons and Savage 2010).

Two prominent nominees had tax problems and paid fines, testing President Obama's ethical standards. He accepted supporter Tom Daschle's withdrawal from the nomination for Secretary of Health and Human Services over a tax issue, saying "*I screwed up.*" But he lowered the bar to accept Tim Geithner, who also had a tax problem in the past. Geithner had special knowledge about how to deal with Wall Street, having worked with former Treasury Secretary Henry Paulson on the bank bailouts.

However, by the end of 2009, Republican obstruction meant that fewer than half of his 65 nominees to the federal bench were confirmed (4 of 26 at the appellate level), and many more positions remained vacant without nominations from Obama, mostly due to the lengthy vetting process (*New York Times* 2009). By mid-2010, more than three dozen were being held up by Republican Senators by various legislative maneuvers (O'Keefe 2010; Williams 2010), and Obama did not press the issue. He continued to show respect to Republicans, even when they failed to reciprocate and blocked his agenda. He refused to abandon his nonconfrontational style until on the campaign trail in 2010.

Traditionally, big donors receive ambassadorial and other key appointments. But Obama has nominated only 30 of his 324 top fund-raisers (those bundling $100,000 or more). Few have been invited to social functions at the White House (Shear and Eggen 2009), giving the distinct appearance that Obama will not let big money influence his decisions.

His decision to honor 16 individuals with the Presidential Medal of Freedom in mid-August 2009 provided considerable insight into his values. The common virtue he stressed was each person's humanism in doing something significant to improve human rights.

GETTING DOWN TO BUSINESS

A president is not only head of government but ceremonial head of state. Journalists, who can turn presidents into celebrities or role models, have reported what Barack likes to drink, eat, and wear as well as his entertainment preferences, thereby humanizing him. For example, President Obama one day walked in the rain without a raincoat or umbrella (Fiore and Barabak 2009), astonishing observers who were unaware that

Honoluluans customarily walk through gentle "pineapple showers" on
Oʻahu in a similar manner. According to David Gergen, he "has brought
a more relaxed sensibility to his public appearances, an Aloha Zen, a
comfortable calm that reflects a man who seems easy going, not so full
of himself" (Stolberg 2009). Journalist Jonathan Alter (2010:Ch. 9),
similarly, refers to Obama as having a "Zen temperament."

Obama reportedly begins the day at 7, when he goes to the White
House gym. Afterward, he breakfasts with the family and reads the
morning newspapers. He walks downstairs to the Oval Office each day
at 9 or 9:30. He then receives economic and security briefings as well as
mail from about 10 ordinary citizens among thousands received daily.
He quickly handles paperwork, as he delegates and is not a microman-
ager. When he has time, he reads the 10 letters, even routing some to his
staff. He then alternates between restless pursuit of his agenda and quiet
time to reflect.

He enjoys diverse perspectives, as is common at multiethnic gatherings
in Honolulu. On one occasion, he enjoyed bringing together Michael
Bloomberg, Newt Gingrich, and Al Sharpton for a friendly chat in the
White House. But he failed to build consensus among them.

Compared to the campaign, he is more serious but, as before, leaves
time for jovial banter (Drew 2009). He still talks to close friends by
Blackberry to keep in touch (K. Walsh 2009). He attends as few staff
meetings as possible, preferring to drop in on aides collegially in order
to goad them into completing their tasks while donning big smiles as he
passes others in the hallway en route.

As he demonstrated throughout the campaign, Barack Obama has
extraordinary executive ability. He often disarms his critics by demonstrating competence with humility and decisiveness after consensus
building. One writer found a pattern to how he operates:

> the announcement of a lofty goal, the delegation of implementa-
> tion to second-rank officials, a missed deadline or two, last-minute
> intervention by the president to rescue the effort from collapse, and,
> finally mixed results—followed by a statement claiming victory.
> (McManus 2009)

Another observer characterizes his decision-making style as "method-
ical, thoughtful, cerebral, a believer in consensus and process. . . . Barack
Obama is an incremental man" (Quindlen 2009). He rarely has second
thoughts about decisions made but unhesitatingly admits mistakes.

He is very much in control at meetings, which sometimes finish late, showing his orientation to nonpunctual "Hawaiian time." He can give a "disappointed parent look" but usually makes others feel respected (Drew 2009). Whereas he elicits as many perspectives as possible at meetings, he avoids the development of factions by summarizing what has been said and then identifying the next steps required before he will be ready to make a decision. He handles differences of opinion by maintaining a businesslike focus in a charming manner (Alter 2010:199, 322–323). When an individual seems a bit intemperate, Obama characteristically asks that person to stay behind for a one-to-one chat, hoping to help that individual to calm down, gain perspective, and reclaim serenity (Draper 2009).

He also makes public appearances throughout the day, appearing humble, jovial, and placid. Lunches sometimes consist of a cheeseburger, chicken or fish, and waffle fries, occasionally dining out in working-class neighborhoods, consuming food that his wife Michelle undoubtedly disapproves of. His favorite drinks are chilled black forest berry and green dragon teas. A smoker since Honolulu days, Obama has claimed that he is 95 percent cured (Akers 2009).

He concludes the working day at 6:30. Dinners are with his family, and he stays with his daughters until they are put to bed at 8:30. He then works alone until 11:30, and reads himself to sleep by midnight from folders prepared by his staff (Fiore and Barabak 2009; Meacham 2009a).

He and his wife, Michelle, have shown little interest in redecorating the White House, though they arranged for the transfer of 47 art works from national art galleries, including art by African Americans and pop-art painter Ed Ruscha (Muchnic 2009). They were eager to adopt Bo, a hypoallergenic dog, to fulfill an election promise to their two daughters.

Obama has taken his family to sporting events, a dance concert, a stage play, and school events, as if completely at home in a Honolulu on the Potomac. He broke years of tradition when he sneaked out without the press one night to attend a soccer game with one of his daughters. He opened the White House for trick-or-treaters on his first Halloween night. No other president in memory has shown so much respect for the people of Washington and their environs. As a president guarded by security personnel, he most misses "*taking walks*" (Feller 2010).

Inside the White House, the Obamas hosted a poetry jam during May 2009 featuring novelist Michael Chabon, actor James Earl Jones, and others, with the Obama daughters in attendance. He discussed the novels of Argentinean Jorge Luis Borges during a White House meeting that same month with Chilean President Michele Bachelet.

President Obama's first Washington party was held in conjunction with Super Bowl 2009, when he invited 75 guests of both political parties to a meal of beer and hotdogs. Rather than sitting in the plush chairs in front of the screen, he humbly joined the rest in the "cheap seats" (Fiore and Barabak 2009).

At the annual White House picnic in 2009, he flew in Hawai'i chef Alan Wong, who prepared a lū'au for 2,300, including the traditional kālua pig and poi as well such fusion dishes as coconut-and-macadamia-nut-encrusted lamb chops and tilapia with wasabi potato salad amid palm trees and tiki torches (Gross 2009; Pace and Simmons 2009). But more traditional fare prevailed in 2010.

One of the first journalistic reports dealt with his informality in matters of clothing—how frequently he wears suits without the jacket, rolling up the shirtsleeves, and his "business casual" extends to his staff on weekends. He does not observe Aloha Shirt Fridays, however. During the winter he turns the temperature of the White House way up to Hawai'i springtime temperatures. He shows respect for those who work in the White House by bringing them birthday cakes.

During Congress' August 2009 recess, President Obama visited the Grand Canyon and Yellowstone Park with his family. During the rest of the vacation, however, they roamed about the 28.5 acres of a $20 million estate on Martha's Vineyard Island (Nicholas 2009), where he sometimes vacationed before becoming president. Park visits, including Acadia in 2010, may look populist but not the Island retreat, which he pays for out of his own pocket. In 2010, he briefly vacationed in Panama City, Florida. His port of call at the end of 2009 was Honolulu, where he feels most at home with family and friends.

Obama is the first sitting American president to appear on Jay Leno's *Tonight Show*, David Letterman's *Late Show, Sixty Minutes* and *The View*. His readiness to be interviewed and frequent press conferences and speeches communicate a friendly, humble, and relaxed presence. Fully aware that others think of him as Spock, he watched the latest *Star Trek* film in the White House (Meacham 2009a).

President Obama does not engage in much small talk, does not try to curry favor with others by flattery, and dislikes repeating himself as he does on the campaign trail. He refuses to follow Bush's example of talking down to the American people through the press, preferring to treat the public with respect by presenting proposals rationally.

Some observers have commented unfavorably on his Island-style joviality, calling his sense of humor inappropriate or sarcastic (McNamara 2009; cf. Plouffe 2009:146; Parker 2010b). They presumably prefer him to be more strait-laced and serious, but laughter at his jokes during annual White House Correspondents dinners has drowned them out.

Nevertheless, he is privately angry whenever his family is attacked. Tears have fallen from his eyes when leaders in the civil rights come to mind (Pace 2010). The word *"furious"* first emerged to characterize Obama's reaction to the failure of agencies to integrate and act on information before a Nigerian student boarded an airplane with the intention to ignite a bomb over Detroit on Christmas Day 2009 (Hosenball, Isikoff, and Thomas 2010). He also indicated exasperation toward British Petroleum (BP), which stonewalled its incompetence in dealing with a catastrophic oil leak in the Gulf of México during 2010, but he maintained a dignified bearing while critics wanted him to show disrespect. He then effected a communitarian solution—to have BP set up an escrow account for tort claims, managed by the same person who handled damages for World Trade Center victims. Meanwhile, conservatives wanted BP alone to handle the matter, and some liberals recommended direct lawsuits.

One particular reporter, 11-year-old Damon Weaver, asked President Obama if he would be his "homeboy." The president then smiled broadly and jovially responded, *"Absolutely!"* (*Boston Globe* 2009).

He often nods his head in respect on greeting others. But when Obama bowed to the Japanese emperor and the Saudi king, monocultural American critics saw his sign of protocol and respect quite differently. He remains personally popular due to his earthy demeanor, a quality learned easily in Hawai'i, but he flashes fewer smiles as president than he did during the campaign. His Aloha seems more reserved now that the weight of the world is upon him.

BIPARTISANSHIP

A serious assessment must focus on issues. Obama's analysis in *The Audacity of Hope* is mainstream political science—that serious domestic and international problems had not been addressed effectively for more than a decade because of divisive partisanship due to the rise of a politics of mass society. He found some areas of possible agreement among conservatives and liberals on several issues, but communitarianism was the real antidote—to forge community. He wanted to replace the anomic culture bred by Social Darwinism in American politics, a belief that everyone should fend for oneself, leaving the rich in control. But, due to Island diffidence, he failed to do so.

According to Senior Adviser David Axelrod, Obama's most important "change" message was to unite the country, bring about true bipartisanship, and solve problems while keeping lobbyists at bay (Alter 2010:428). In contrast with the communitarian politics in Hawai'i, Washington's bitter wrangling clouds reasonable, middle-of-the road solutions. Observing how partisanship was trumping problem solving, Obama's September 2009 address to Congress on the need for health insurance legislation stressed his humanistic perspective:

> *When we can no longer even engage in civil conversation with each other over the things that truly matter, we don't merely lose our capacity to solve big challenges. We lose something essential about ourselves.*

Obama's communitarian philosophy meshed well with voters. To get anything done in Washington, of course, he would have to be a pragmatist. A major theme of Obama's candidacy and presidency has been the need to change the tone in Washington into a more bipartisan direction. He had cooperated with Republicans in the Illinois Senate, tried to do so in Congress as a freshman Senator, and now hoped to show leadership as president. Yet he failed to reconstitute the bipartisan "Gang of 14" of 2005 or recognize Senator Ron Wyden's bipartisan health plan in forming a moderate core to forge major legislative proposals.

Congress and the two political parties were very set in their ways when he took up residence in the White House (Balz 2010). Democrats had an agenda that had been frustrated while George W. Bush was president. Republicans were frightened that they would become irrelevant if they jettisoned their preference for small government by going along with bold new successful government initiatives from President Obama. Yet Obama was never for big government: "*We don't want government to solve our problems but what we do expect is that government can help*" (Remnick 2010:448). Both Democrats and Republicans overlooked his middle-of-the-road communitarian philosophy—that government should be a catalyst in bringing people together to solve their own problems (Pollan 2010).

Columnist David Brooks (2010d) acutely notes that perceptions of Obama depend upon ideological perspectives:

If you ask a conservative Republican, you are likely to hear that Obama is a skilled politician who campaigned as a centrist but is governing as a big-government liberal. He plays by ruthless, Chicago politics rules. He is arrogant toward foes, condescending toward allies and runs a partisan political machine. If you ask a liberal Democrat, you are likely to hear that Obama is an inspiring but overly intellectual leader who has trouble making up his mind and fighting for his positions. He has not defined a clear mission. He has allowed the Republicans to dominate debate. He is too quick to compromise and too cerebral to push things through.

Brooks characterizes Obama as a "pragmatic progressive" who has tenaciously pursued fulfillment of his campaign promises. Yet, Brooks goes on:

He has tried to find this balance in a town without an organized center—in a town in which liberals chair the main committees and small-government conservatives lead the opposition. He has tried to do it in a context maximally inhospitable to his aims.

Another writer oxymoronically characterizes him as a "pragmatic ideologue" (Douthat 2009). Yet his pragmatism involves a propensity to compromise within a communitarian context:

[M]y values are deeply rooted in the progressive tradition, the values of equal opportunity, civil rights, fighting for working families, a foreign policy that is mindful of human rights, a strong belief in civil liberties, wanting to be a good steward for the environment, a sense that the government has an important role to play, that opportunity is open to all people and that the powerful don't trample on the less powerful. . . . But I'm much more agnostic, much more flexible on how we achieve these ends (Remnick 2010:437).

President Obama continued to seek bipartisanship long after Republicans made clear their desire to block him. Although his visits with House and Senate Republicans were viewed as failures, he did not give up trying.

Early in 2009, he offered $300 million in tax cuts to entice Republicans to support his economic stimulus plan. But they were unimpressed, later felt slighted by the majority Democrats for asking them to sign on after details had been hammered down without them, and said so, thereby postponing his bipartisan gambit until Republicans won in 2010.

Nevertheless, the unappreciated evidence of his earnest bipartisanship is the extent of his continuity with the previous administration (Bacevich 2010). For example when Obama backed John McCain's cap-and-trade energy policy, Republicans opposed the idea, thereby frustrating bipartisanship. While Republicans control one or both houses of Congress during his presidency, bipartisan cooperation will be necessary. However, a party that has departed from normal discourse, using a rhetoric of civil war, bodes ill for future cooperation with Barack Obama.

What critics and supporters miss is that the tenets of the multicultural ethos are ingrained in President Obama's personality. He is sincere about wanting to bring everyone together to solve long-postponed major problems of the country as a whole, as clearly laid down in his *Audacity of Hope* manifesto and his uncelebrated "five pillars" speech at Georgetown University in 2009 (new rules for Wall Street, deficit reduction, and investments in education, health care, and renewable energy). Beneficiaries of the pillars are identified humanistically as homeowners, innovators, students, the uninsured, and jobseekers. For the first time, he attacked Republicans as *"enemies"* during a 2010 rally (Allen 2010). His rational discourse was too mild to answer the fearmongers, however.

When Barack Obama tries to persuade someone, he patiently listens to the other person, and then states his point of view within a larger perspective—but without pressure. His relaxed, sensible bearing of Aloha often carries the day, but not with Social Darwinist Republicans who believe that governmental power should trample on those who are poor, unproductive, and weak (cf. Hofstadter 1955). Examples are easily identified in foreign and domestic policy.

FOREIGN POLICY

Barack Obama's speech in Berlin during mid-2008 at the end of an eight-country visit to establish his foreign policy credentials marked the first time a candidate carried a presidential campaign outside the United States, viewing the world as one multicultural family (Fineman 2009). Indeed, he has also referred to himself as *"the first Pacific president"* (Higgins and Kornblut 2009). Many expected that he would open a new chapter in American world leadership. As president, Obama has embodied that quest in keeping with a long American tradition:

> [I]n times of tragedy, the United States of America steps forward and helps. That is who we are. That is what we do. For decades, America's leadership has been founded in part on the fact that we do not use our power to subjugate others, we use it to lift them up—whether it was rebuilding our former adversaries after World War II, dropping food and water to the people of Berlin, or helping the people of Bosnia and Kosovo rebuild their lives and their nations. . . . When we show not just our power, but also our compassion, the world looks to us with a mixture of awe and admiration. That advances our leadership. That shows [that] the character of our country. . . . is acting on behalf of our common humanity. (Obama 2010c)

These remarks might appear to have been delivered in acceptance of the Nobel Peace Prize in 2009 but were instead used to describe the American humanitarian effort in Haïti, wherein he forged cooperation between former presidents Bill Clinton and George W. Bush. Nevertheless, the contrast with the latter's response to New Orleans' Katrina was obvious.

Pundits and scholars are always eager to identify a president's "foreign policy doctrine." During the presidential campaign, Obama pointed out that the reputation of the United States had suffered badly during the Bush administration, so he offered to resolve problems nonconfrontationally—by cooperation and negotiation rather than by bullying, lecturing other countries, or unilateral action, just as the politics of the Aloha State involves wide discussions among ethnic and interest groups, leaving nobody out deliberately. One journalist has referred to his foreign policy as "unafraid to deploy American power but mindful that its use must be tempered by practical limits and a dose of self-awareness" (Dionne 2009), based on such remarks as his speech to Congress on February 22, 2009:

> [A] new era of engagement has begun. For we know that America cannot meet the threats of this century alone, but the world cannot meet them without America. We cannot shun the negotiating table, nor ignore the foes or forces that could do us harm. We are instead

called to move forward with the sense of confidence and candor that serious times demand.

In accepting the Nobel Peace Prize while commander-in-chief of a war in Afghanistan, he articulated the theory of "just peace," that is, the view that lasting peace requires an end to both human rights repression and to structural violence, that is, poverty for the masses amid plenty for elites (cf. Galtung 1964; Thistlethwaite 2009). That theme was stressed in a more specific set of goals outlined in a speech to the West Point graduating class in 2010:

Countering violent extremism and insurgency; stopping the spread of nuclear weapons and securing nuclear materials; combating a changing climate and sustaining global growth; helping countries feed themselves and care for their sick. (Shear 2010)

The same goals were embedded later that year in Obama's National Security Strategy paper, which went beyond military pursuits and counterterrorism to include democratic, economic, and social rights.

Obama rejects both the Scylla of a purely idealist foreign policy that enforces American goals on the world and the Charybdis of conservative unilateral realpolitik, which advances national interest regardless of consequences. Instead, his communitarian foreign policy involves motivating other countries and working through international institutions to achieve goals together in the world interest, thereby moving from the cowboy era of unilateralism to a "post-imperial" era of multilateralism in which all countries have *"rights and responsibilities"* (Zakaria 2009). As Senator Daniel Akaka has often said, those from Hawai'i have a special responsibility of "extending Aloha to the world" (Senate speech, September 20, 1997). Obama not only projects Aloha to win hearts and minds around the world but also encourages other countries to follow suit.

Barack Obama's approach is to find common ground respectfully with other countries before moving the agenda to more sensitive matters, both with allies and enemies, an approach that works in Hawai'i. His aim is to restore American credibility by having foreign policy live up to the ideals of the country, avoiding arrogance, bluster, narcissistic moralism, and unilateralism.

Accordingly President Obama's first bold action was to announce an intention to close Guantánamo in the *"interest of justice."* He told the world that the United States would no longer be a gross violator of international law in dealing with terrorists at home or abroad. In essence, he declared that the "war on terrorism" was over, and he would treat lawbreaking terrorists in accordance with the rule of law. Although he ordered compliance with the Geneva Conventions, the following month the military reported that they would only comply with one article out of hundreds of provisions. A victim of amateur waterboarding (drowning) while a child in Indonesia, something unthinkable in Hawai'i, Obama explicitly banned torture and later exposed Bush-era memos that justified torture. When he decided not to prosecute Bush for war crimes, as many urged, he showed respect to a duly elected former president, just as Bush impressively extended courtesy toward president-elect Obama. Acknowledging that prosecutions might eventually occur (Johnston and Savage 2009), many illegalities nevertheless rolled over to his presidency and were not halted when he entered the Oval Office (Haas 2009, 2010a), notably at Guantánamo.

Implementing the closure of Guantánamo, which requires Congressional cooperation, is just one of several unfulfilled goals. When he tried to obtain appropriations to shut down Guantánamo, Republicans characterized all prisoners as terrorists, even those whom Bush cleared for resettlement as innocent. A wedge was driven between Obama and Congressional Democrats, who went along by blocking resettlement of innocent prisoners in the United States. When Republicans demanded trials in military commissions that would violate the Geneva Conventions, Obama had Congress amend the Military Commissions Act to provide more compliance with the Geneva Conventions. But defense attorneys are expected to challenge procedures, ensuring that trials will be challenged and possibly take years to conclude instead of the more obvious methods—criminal prosecutions and military courts-martial (cf. Haas 2010a:Ch. 31, 42).

Obama has refrained from using the words "Islamic extremism" and "jihad" to reach out to moderate Muslims (Elliott 2010). Rather than identifying the enemy as "terrorism," his National Security Strategy declares that "Our enemy is not terror because terror is a state of mind" and that "terrorism is but a tactic." Instead, the "enemy is Al Qaeda and its terrorists affiliates." Rather than trying to cow Americans over fear of terrorism, as prominent Republicans prefer, Obama reassures that "*as Americans, we refuse to live in fear*" (Gearan and Apuzzo 2010). The candidate of hope is the antidote to those who try to cultivate a nation of cowards, fearful of everything, for partisan advantage (Haas 2010a:Ch. 43).

Obama has announced major changes in American foreign policy through interviews and speeches. His first press interview was with Al Arabiya, to reassure the Arabic-speaking world that the United States was after Al Qaeda and did not demonize the Islamic faith. Subsequently, he delivered major speeches in Ankara, Prague, Strasbourg, and Cairo, humbly stressing that he wanted to listen to the leaders of the world before acting, and for the first time the United States joined the UN Human Rights Council. His preference for quiet diplomacy with gross violators of human rights, however, deprived subordinates of leverage to press for changes in repressive policies. He infuriated conservatives by admitting that America had "*shown arrogance and been dismissive, even derisive*," but he also criticized some Europeans for "*casual*" if "*insidious . . . anti-Americanism*" As always, he seeks a middle way.

Balance, engagement, diplomacy, evenhandedness, multilateralism, and pragmatism may indeed characterize the style of President Obama's foreign policy. But that leaves substance.

To jump-start diplomacy with leaders that Bush eschewed as enemies, Obama sent two letters to Iran's supreme cleric Ayatollah Ali Khamenei, dispatched several high-level envoys to meet Syrian President Bashar Al Assad, sent a special representative to North Korea, pushed the "reset button" with Russian President Dmitry Medvedev and Prime Minister Vladimir Putin by scrapping Bush's proposed missile defense installations in the Czech Republic and Poland, and after receiving Venezuelan President Hugo Chávez's anti-American book sent an ambassador to Caracas (cf. Diehl 2010). Restrictions were lifted on travel of relatives to Cuba, and full normalization was offered if all political prisoners were released (Rowe 2009b). Direct dialog with Burma (Myanmar), the first in more than a decade, began on several issues, and the Burmese military regime promised to cut ties with North Korea. President Obama also appointed a special envoy, retired Air Force Maj. Gen. J. Scott Gration, to normalize relations with Sudan. He urged the Israeli government to freeze construction within settlements.

But what were the results?

Although open to dialog (Plan A), he met resistance from several countries (Iran, Israel, North Korea, Sudan, Syria). Plan B, reflecting his early experience in Jakarta and later political training in Chicago, consisted of sanctions of various sorts. An increase on tariffs on Chinese tires, which were deemed to be deliberately underpriced to drive out competition, was among the earliest examples of the latter, though China began to assert considerable independence. Plan A, of course, reveals his communitarian preferences. Plan B is his pragmatism. The economic crisis within the United States precludes a Plan C, that is, offering large amounts of foreign aid or other economic largesse as tools of persuasion.

Regarding military sanctions, he once confided, "*I don't take [violent] options off the table when it comes to U.S. security, period*" (Meacham 2009b). The earliest example of his toughness came when he dispatched Navy SEALs to intercept Somali pirates in order to rescue an American captain in April 2009. More quietly, he ordered the Central Intelligence Agency to increase drone attacks on presumed residences of Al Qaeda leaders inside Pakistan, but the associated civilian casualties in Pakistan prompted a Pakistan-born American citizen to plant a bomb in Times Square on May Day 2010 (Bates, Crilly, and Freeman 2010).

Obama thinks humanistically of people rather than just as cannon fodder for goals of high politics. His unprecedented visit to coffins of slain American soldiers during mid-2009 made clear that Plan B's would be last resorts. He appointed a new commander in Afghanistan, who in turn conducted an unwelcome publicity campaign to compel him to agree to a major increase in troops (Alter 2010:Ch. 21). In agreeing to a more modest escalation in Afghanistan during his West Point speech, many observers considered his speech cold and detached, but it is a clue to his personality that he felt that his remarks were his "*most emotional speech*" (Rotella 2009). He then obtained UN Security Council approval, not Congressional reauthorization, to continue the mission to stabilize Afghanistan on the pretext that otherwise Al Qaeda might return.

One clear success of the new quiet diplomacy is closer cooperation with Russia, which has led to assistance in fighting the Afghan military campaign, some support for sanctions against Iran, and a 30 percent nuclear arms reduction agreement. And the United States is gaining support for war crimes trials of Burmese leaders (Lynch 2010).

During 2009, Obama incrementally developed a comprehensive plan to extricate the United States from the excesses of two wars (Haas 2010a: Ch. 42), and he began to withdraw the American military presence in Iraq under a 2010 deadline that was first proposed by Prime Minister Nouri Al Maliki during mid-2008. But extraordinary rendition, extrajudicial executions, and indefinite detention remain in the arsenal as tools for combating terrorism, contrary to campaign promises.

Perhaps the biggest accomplishments are unprecedented pledges at multilateral conferences. In matters of international economics, a world depression was evidently avoided after Obama sold Keynesian policies to fellow industrial nations in 2009 (though not in 2010), when he also persuaded the richest countries to support a $1 trillion bailout of developing economies, an almost unparalleled example of successful inclusiveness. In 2009, at Copenhagen representatives of 183 countries agreed to reduce more greenhouse gasses than at the Kyoto accord of 1997 (Tannersley 2010), albeit not in the form of a treaty. In April 2010, heads of state and government from 47 countries agreed in a conference at Washington to secure weapons-grade materials from falling into the hands of terrorists. The latter meeting was the largest gathering of world leaders since 1944, when government heads met in San Francisco to adopt the United Nations Charter. And Israeli-Palestinian talks resumed.

Obama has repeatedly sought to return American foreign policy to its *"moral bearings"* (Gardner 2009). According to counterterrorism expert Richard Clarke (2010), the United States is now "winning the war of ideas" with Al Qaeda because his outreach to the Islamic world has enabled moderate Muslims to attack terrorism, something impossible during the previous administration. Massive demonstrations in Iran took place only days after Obama's Cairo speech, but his approval ratings in the Muslim world sank one year later when deeds did not follow up his words (Richter 2010). He was delighted that the American military occupation of Iraq ended on schedule in mid-2010. President Obama has not solved every world problem, but he generated some optimism about the future. There are no quick fixes in most world problems.

DOMESTIC POLICY

Presidents have much latitude to operate foreign policy, but voters are more critical of domestic policy. President Barack Obama's communitarian philosophy means that he rejects the Social Darwinist right-wing philosophy of leaving everyone on their own socioeconomically as well as a left-wing penchant to erect European social democracy. He instead supports ways of having the government assist private citizens and groups to help one another. According to economist Harry Oshima (1970), the more equal a country's distribution of income, the more economic growth, an empirical finding that may motivate Obama's quest for a more equitable American economy.

On taking office, Obama soon realized that his record as president would be judged by whether the economy improves (K. Walsh 2009; Wilson 2009a). In almost every policy area, the cost of his policies has far exceeded what he expected in his manifesto *The Audacity of Hope.*

Most observers have castigated Wall Street for the economic crisis, and Obama has agreed that it

> *is simply not sustainable ... to have an economy where, in one year, 40% of our corporate profits came from a financial sector that was based on inflated home prices, maxed-out credit cards, over-leveraged banks and overvalued assets.* (Klein 2009)

Obama shared his more balanced communitarian analysis of the source of the economic crisis with Congress on February 24, 2009, as follows:

> *[W]e have lived through an era where too often, short-term gains were prized over long-term prosperity; where we failed to look beyond the next payment, the next quarter, or the next election. A surplus became an excuse to transfer wealth to the wealthy instead of an opportunity to invest in our future. Regulations were gutted for the sake of a quick profit at the expense of a healthy market. People bought homes they knew they couldn't afford from banks and lenders who pushed those bad loans anyway. And all the while, critical debates and difficult decisions were put off for some other time on some other day.*

For President Obama, everyone was to blame. His overall goal was to change the country's mind-set so that everyone would play a more constructive part together rather than yielding to customary Mainland-style American individualistic Social Darwinism. However, Wall Street perceived that Obama made them villains.

Under the Troubled Assets Relief Program (TARP), first passed under Bush as well as a second installment that Congress quickly passed a few days before Obama took office, he soon set rules for handling AIG, Bank of America, Chrysler, Chrysler Financial, Citigroup, GMAC, and General Motors rather than nationalizing them. Ford's president congratulated Obama on his action to rescue Chrysler and General Motors (Hyde 2009).

Some Republicans maliciously accused him of "socialism," a term that refers to government ownership and operation of the means of pro-duction, which clearly did not apply. Whereas some conservatives were prepared to let auto companies and banks fail, and leftists might have preferred takeovers, Obama's nuanced support of Chrysler and General Motors was primarily focused on the humanistic goal of saving jobs while rescuing the automakers only after they came up with a plan to restructure themselves, whereupon they could manage their companies without government interference. Auto sales then rebounded when Congress authorized and reauthorized the "cash for clunkers" program. Obama chided financial institutions for allocating enormous bonuses, presumably with bailout funds, although little could be done to realign executive salaries after most TARP money was repaid.

In mid-February 2009, Congress passed a $787 billion stimulus bill, the American Recovery and Reinvestment Act, which was simultaneously the biggest tax cut, the biggest infrastructure investment, and the biggest spending bill for education, energy, health care, and science in American history. Job creation was the aim. His advocacy was phrased humanistically:

> *It's not about helping banks—it's about helping people. Because when credit is available again, that young family can finally buy a new home. And then some company will hire workers to build it. And then those workers will have money to spend, and if they can get a loan too, maybe they'll finally buy that car, or open their own business. Investors will return to the market, and American families will see their retirement secured once more. Slowly, but surely, confidence will return, and our economy will recover.*

Although the stimulus bill was barnacled with job-producing earmarks, the resulting 10,000 small-scale projects did not perk up the economy. Economists agree that Obama's actions halted the onset of Great Depression 2.0, creating or saving about three million of eight million jobs lost (O'Brien 2010). But that left millions more of unemployed wondering when their turn would come, as businesses recapitalized and consumers paid off debts rather than making new purchases. Nevertheless, the fact is that a president can do very little to manage the economy (Samuelson 2008). Today, America has to import skilled workers because insufficient engineers, mechanics, and nurses are graduating in the United States and far too many go into "law, finance, consulting and nonprofit activism" (Brooks 2010c).

New financial regulations to prevent another Great Recession passed in mid-2010 after Obama made clear that the people wanted significant changes; otherwise, Wall Street lobbyists would be seen as owning Congress. Even though George W. Bush supported taxpayer bailouts of banks while president, Republicans now opposed any bailouts of financial institutions. The communitarian alternative, supported by Obama but opposed by Republicans, was to require "too big to fail" institutions to set up their own fund to assist in an orderly shutdown of giant banks in the future. Requiring derivatives of banks to be posted on the open market and establishing a bipartisan commission to find solutions to the budget deficit was also communitarian. But Congressional Republicans opposed both reforms.

In his communitarian *The Audacity of Hope* he had drawn from his experience, analyzed problems, and offered practical solutions. Whether in the arts, education, the environment, or health care,, many of candidate Obama's proposals were rooted in his life in Hawai'i.

A onetime poet with literary talent, widely recognized in his *Dreams from My Father*, he is the only president to enter office with an arts policy promising to increase funding to the National Endowment for the Arts (Goodale 2009). Among his priorities are expanding public/private partnerships between schools and arts organizations, creating an Artists Corps, and publicly championing the value of arts education.

Barack Obama went to the very best schools in America and benefited, but much public education on the Mainland is no better than in Hawai'i. After becoming president, he articulated his communitarian philosophy toward education in the following terms:

> *Too many supporters of my party have resisted the idea of rewarding excellence in teaching with extra pay, even though it can make a difference in the classroom. Too many in the Republican Party have opposed new investments in early education, despite compelling evidence of its importance. . . . But there is one more ingredient I want to talk about. The bottom line is that no government policies will make any difference unless we also hold ourselves more accountable as parents.* (Wilson 2009b)

The latter point recalls how his mother read to him early in the morning before going to work and how his father insisted that he should study rather than watch a favorite television program. Obama reminded the nation of his upbringing in his address to Congress on February 2, 2009:

> [My proposed] *education policies will open the doors of opportunity for our children. But it is up to us to ensure they walk through them. In the end, there is no program or policy that can substitute for a mother or father who will attend those parent/teacher conferences, or help with homework after dinner, or turn off the TV, put away the video games, and read to their child.*

President Obama's communitarian encouragement of parents to take more of a role in the education of their children clearly differs from both the conservative preference for private school vouchers and liberals who pour money into failing schools.

The federal stimulus package had the largest educational innovation fund—$115 billion—in decades (Alter 2009). Some funds were for updating school libraries and laboratories and expanding broadband access for schools. Other funds saved some but not all teachers' jobs, though he supported a Rhode Island school superintendent who fired all teachers at a failing school (Brooks 2010f). Some $4 billion of the fund is available for state-run merit pay programs, thereby leaning more toward the Republican approach to public education than to the traditional perspectives of teacher's unions. His criterion for public programs in education is simple—whatever is *"good for kids"* (Alter 2010:90).

In his address to Congress on February 22, 2009, Obama judged that *"dropping out of high school is no longer an option. It's not just quitting on yourself, it's quitting on your country—and this country needs and values the talents of every American."* Accordingly, the Race to the Top program aims at rewarding innovative reforms, including more support for charter schools, by providing competition among states to apply for $4.5 billion in assistance aimed to turn around "dropout factories." Seeking to *"guarantee a shot at opportunity for every American [schoolchild] who's willing to work hard,"* as he said at the University of Michigan commencement address in May 2010, one focus is to narrow the gap with lower-performing students. Another is to enhance college preparation (Obama 2010b).

As for educational standards, Obama has left that task to the National Governors Conference and the National Association of School Boards of Education, yet another example of communitarian pragmatism—stimulating reliance on cooperation in the private sector for the public good. Doubtless based on his mother's community work in Indonesia, he also stresses the value of service learning, and he signed into law a tripling in the size of AmeriCorps (Isensee 2009).

Regarding college, he had only recently paid off his student loans before first running for office. Obama still remembered and greatly valued the financial assistance that made his rise possible from a humble beginning. His goal is for the United States to have the highest proportion of college graduates in the world by 2020. Having made his way through college with scholarships, similar to his mom's postgraduate education, he asked Congress to allocate some federal stimulus dollars for $77 billion for college student assistance. In 2010, he also signed legislation to break up the Sallie Mae program, in which the government squandered money by subsidizing banks to provide student loans, even if not repaid, and then hounded students in default to amass more profits. Similarly, significant changes were made under the Credit Card Accountability Responsibility and Disclosure Act of 2009.

Contrasting his adopted Chicago with pristine elements of the natural beauty of Hawai'i from his youth and during annual trips back to Honolulu, he extend federal protection to two million acres of wilderness lands by signing a law at the end of March 2009. Having lived in a Hawai'i with largely unharnessed, if ample, wind and solar power resources, he promised during his campaign to provide leadership in increasing the share of American energy from renewable sources. As President Obama doubtless knew, Hawai'i in 2007 mandated electric utilities to provide 10 percent of their electricity from renewable sources and energy efficiency by 2010 and 70 percent by 2030 (Wiles 2010). In 2009, California passed a law setting a goal of 33 percent of energy to come from renewable sources by 2020, and soon after taking office he granted a waiver to California to enforce higher fuel-efficiency standards than the rest of the country. He also he set a national goal of 17 percent renewables by 2020 and 80 percent by 2050. Whereas right-wingers pooh-poohed the need to mitigate greenhouse gas emissions, and many on the left wanted more government subsidies for alternative energy development, the communitarian approach was to help the industry cooperate through a cap-and-trade system that John McCain had once supported (and later opposed). Obama's economic stimulus package included funds for mass transit and high-speed trains. When Senate Republicans did not want to burden businesses by agreeing to a comprehensive energy bill, Obama was blamed for not pushing hard enough.

Under presidential authority created by Clean Air Act, President Obama announced in May 2009 the first national limit on greenhouse gas emissions in the form of automobile emission standards. By 2016, all new cars and trucks manufactured in the United States must average 35.5 miles per gallon or better, a standard equal to European limits as of 2009 (B. Walsh 2009). With Chrysler and General Motors then dependent upon government support, both companies adopted the new standards.

Noting that Native Hawaiians consider the ocean around Hawai'i as "*sacred*," Obama was frustrated over the environmental catastrophe in the Gulf of México that arose during the spring of 2010. Having been incorrectly informed a few weeks earlier that deep-sea drilling was safe, he appointed a commission to undertake a thorough review of offshore drilling while urging Congress to get serious about supporting alternative energy initiatives. Two weeks after escaping oil began to pollute Southern states, he visited fishing communities and others in the affected communities and continued to do so, showing empathy for their plight but he largely left the problem to the polluting company and the Coast Guard instead of using a heavy hand from the White House.

President Obama's top domestic priority was reform in health insurance. As a boy, he lived in Hawai'i, the state that in 1974 adopted a universal health insurance plan mandating all employers to provide coverage for their employees. Thanks to his grandmother's job at a bank, she and his grandfather were covered by that plan, which has long provided the lowest premium rates, highest percent insured, and healthiest people in the country (Altonn 2009). Indeed, Michael Dukakis, during 1991, became my colleague in the Political Science Department at the University of Hawai'i at Mānoa to study the plan, which he took back to Massachusetts. President Bill Clinton later asked Governor John Waihe'e to be his Secretary of Health and Human Services to sell the plan. But Waihe'e turned down the offer, and Clinton's complicated plan was defeated. Now Obama wanted again to protect millions of uninsured and underinsured in the United States, though he made no public mention of the Hawai'i plan. As with his goals and his proposals from arts to education to energy to the environment, he respectfully ceded leadership to Congress to write the details of health care legislation, hoping for bipartisanship.

On February 4, 2009, Obama signed an extension of the Children's Health Insurance Program, which had twice been vetoed by President George W. Bush, so four million more children and pregnant women were covered. Prospects for universal coverage appeared likely on March 5, 2009, when C-SPAN covered discussions involving all the major stakeholders, in accordance with Obama's communitarian playbook. But some attended only for show.

Then the fireworks began. When lobbyists tried to discredit Obama's proposals he commented:

> *They're doing what they always do, descending on Congress, using every bit of influence they have to maintain the status quo that has maximized their profits at the expense of American consumers despite the fact that recently a whole bunch of those same American consumers bailed them out.* (Puzzanghera 2009)

Despite Obama's bipartisan outreach, Republican Party loyalists launched harsh and often false, malicious propaganda against health care legislation at a level never before experienced in recent American history. Democrats claimed that there was a right to health and that the richest country should join all other industrial democracies in providing universal health care. Republicans frightened 95 percent of American people already with health insurance that their benefits would be cut to cover the 5 percent to be insured. After Georgia Republican Senator Johnny Isakson amended the bill in committee to provide for advance care planning for seniors, Sarah Palin attacked the bill for offering Democratic-sponsored "death panels" (Byrne 2009).

Obama reacted to the authors of hyperbole and lies about health care proposals as would anyone in Hawai'i: He would not get in the gutter with them. Hotheads who shout in the Islands, unaware of the pervasive multicultural ethos, will be economically boycotted, socially ostracized, and will eventually return to the Mainland. Although he considered *"wild accusations"* as *"troublesome"* (Associated Press 2010b), and once said, *"We all make mistakes"* (*Washington Post* 2009), he maintained his dignity by calmly identifying misinformation, but his stress on logic and reason failed to counter fear and suspicion. Although he could not restrain himself from criticizing FOX network pundits and commentator Rush Limbaugh for crossing the line of decency (contrary to Benjamin Franklin's standards, let alone Hawai'i's multicultural ethos) with their fulminations, he did not present a convincing message of his own because for months there was no single Congressional bill to back, and some Democratic Senators crudely insisted on pork barrel amendments before providing support. Yet he continued to urge Congress to pass health care legislation, lest his presidency would be judged a failure, reflecting on one occasion that *"I'd rather be a really good one-term president than a mediocre two-term president."*

Reluctantly, Obama accepted a Plan B approach, allowing Democrats to bulldoze legislation over Republicans. After the complex health insurance reform vote, some officeholders even received death threats, presumably goaded by talk-show rhetoric. Yet he never provided a "fireside chat" to explain the new law before or after passage.

What emerged did not please left-wingers who insisted on a public option to ensure that insurance companies would have stiff competition. Libertarians disliked the requirement for everyone to buy health insurance, with a hefty fine for those who refused, though they never objected as loudly about mandatory auto insurance. Instead, at the center of the communitarian health care bill was a communitarian employer mandate—a partnership in which employees and employees would share the cost of insurance premiums. Hawaiʻi's health care plan was indeed the centerpiece. Conservatives refused to understand Obama's communitarian logic—that overall health care costs are higher when some refuse affordable health insurance, get sick, do not seek medical care, spread disease, and ultimately end up in hospital emergency rooms, expecting the public to foot the bill through higher private health care premiums. Costs might now be contained, thanks to the new health care legislation, though major provisions would not go into effect until 2014.

Other issues were back-burnered to avoid distractions as Obama pursued his top priority. The president met with various groups to assure them that their interests had not been forgotten—including gays, immigration reformers, civil rights advocates, trade unions, and African Americans. Then their turnout on election day 2010 reportedly slumped. Blacks wondered whether he was ignoring them because he was truly "post-racial."

POST-RACIAL?

On the eve of his inauguration, just as he had said in 2006 (Heilemann and Halperin 2010:71–72), Barack Obama envisioned that the following might be the effect of being the first African American president of the United States:

> *There is an entire generation that will grow up taking for granted that the highest office in the land is filled by an African American.... I mean, that's a radical thing. It changes how [B]lack children look at themselves. It also changes how [W]hite children look at [B]lack children. And I wouldn't underestimate the force of that.* (Fletcher 2009)

Thus, President Obama basked in the spotlight as a historic president whose election fulfilled the dream of Martin Luther King, Jr. Regarding the historic nature of his election, President Obama remarked with characteristic humility:

> *[A]t the inauguration, I think that there was justifiable pride on the part of the country that we had taken a step to move us beyond some of the searing legacies of racial discrimination in this country, but that lasted about a day.* (Ewers 2009)

Then, doubtless recalling the way in which people of various racial backgrounds mingle together smoothly in Hawai'i compared to the U.S. Mainland, he hoped that his presidency, including his relations with Congress and Wall Street, would forge a spirit of greater harmony and communitarian 'ohana:

> *What I hope to model is a way of interacting with people who aren't like you and don't agree with you that changes the temper of our politics. . . . And then part of that changes how we think about moving forward on race relations. Race relations becomes a subset of a larger problem in our society, which is we have a diverse, complicated society where people have a lot of different viewpoints.* (Fletcher 2009)

Whereas pundits tried to debate whether Barack Obama's election would mean the dawning of a "post-racial" color-blind America, candidate Obama refuted that notion in his election manifesto *The Audacity of Hope* (Ch. 7) by calling attention to festering problems as well as the mindset change needed before a serious debate on what should be done. Later, during the campaign, when he gave his Philadelphia speech on race, he asked Whites to reflect on the Black experience as well as for Blacks to feel some sympathy for the way Whites approach racial problems. His purpose appeared to be to disavow the role of "angry Black" and to assume that of "honest broker." He approaches racial issues without a sense of embitterment, of grievances over past slights, viewing such problems in a wider economic and social context. He was unprepared when Shirley Sherrod, the wife of a famous slain Freedom Rider, was peremptorily fired in mid-2010 (Dowd 2010), but he viewed the resulting controversy contextually as media hyperbole.

Today, there is an opportunity for careful assessment. For some in the public, his serene presidential posture may have had a calming effect. But others in the United States grew up believing that Blacks were inferior, and a president whose complexion is dark threatens their conception of how America had been governed for more than 200 years.

One way to determine whether the country is "post-racial" is to look at scientific studies. In June 2008, a poll reported that 50 percent of registered voters believed race relations to be very or extremely important, whereas 29 percent felt the issue to be of lesser importance and 23 percent unimportant (Fiorina 2010:9). Although polls during the campaign demonstrated that his support was weakest among older White men, 95 percent of the electorate professed a willingness to vote for an African American as president (Balz and Johnson 2009:379; Remnick 2010:450).

A poll conducted at the end of President Obama's first hundred days in office found that two-thirds of Americans characterized race relations as "good" (Stolberg and Connelly 2009). Twice as many Blacks thought so compared to their view in July 2008. But by November, 53 percent (65 percent among Blacks) still decried ethnic and racial divisions in the country, with 83 percent of Democrats praising Obama for uniting the country while 77 percent of Republicans said the opposite while their leaders where sowing distrust and fear about Obama (Barr 2009).

Obama set a poor example by jumping to a conclusion that a Cambridge police officer acted "*stupidly in arresting somebody [for disorderly conduct] when there was already proof that they were in their own home.*" The "somebody" was Harvard professor Henry Louis Gates, Jr. Later details of the encounter suggested that Gates may have provoked the police officer. However, Glen Beck of FOX News then accused Obama of being a "racist" with a "deep-seated hatred of White people." Humbly admitting his mistake, President Obama tried to calm the situation by inviting both Gates and his arresting officer, James Crowley, for a beer at the White House, yet another use of nonconfrontational conflict resolution, and the press frenzy blew over. He wriggled out of the corner into which he had painted himself by being a gentleman, stating that the conversation proved the communitarian axiom that "*what brings us together is stronger than what pulls us apart*" (Wallsten and Dorning 2009), and moved on (cf. McManus 2010b).

In a poll taken after the Gates kerfuffle, the American people, particularly Whites, expressed the view that Obama handled the situation badly, and for the first time his approval rating as president fell below 50 percent (Wallsten and Dorning 2009). In August 2009, rage about health insurance reform proposals expressed at town hall meetings convened by members of Congress served to hint that President Obama's popularity among Whites was slipping. By November, Obama's approval rating among Whites was 39 percent, though 90 percent among Blacks (Blow 2009). Much of the subtext of White disenchantment is based on fear that Whites are losing control as the percentage of minorities increases.

Many factors could account for changes in attitudes before and after Obama became president. Four studies by psychologists yielded contradictory results, using controlled experiments to determine whether he has had an impact on race relations (Aronson, Jannone, McGlone, and

Johnson-Campbell 2009; Effron, Cameron, and Monin 2009; Friedman 2009; Plant et al. 2009).

Elected on a landslide to bring about significant change, with a long-range view of the country in mind, Republicans feared that Obama would usher in decades of Democratic Party rule through the change in mind-set that he proposed. Believing that they had to do anything to stop him in order to keep their party alive by articulating criticism, their rhetoric has in part fueled the rise of anti-Black Internet traffic and an increase in hate groups (Blow 2009; Southern Poverty Law Center 2009), including the launching of at least 50 new militia training groups. Several "citizen's courts" and "grand juries" have even issued indictments against President Obama for treason. "Sovereign citizens" have appeared, claiming that Whites have more rights than non-Whites. Some even question whether he was born in Honolulu. The fear that Blacks may discriminate against Whites (cf. Serrano 2010) suggests the need for a nationwide report on employment patterns (cf. Coleman et al. 1966).

President Obama, meanwhile, has insisted that policy differences drive those who are dissatisfied, not race (Silva 2009). He claims to understand their anxieties better than they realize and has given support to their exercise of free speech.

A post-racial Hawai'i would be impossible, as multicultural persons proudly celebrate their many ancestral origins. The same is true in many part of the Mainland. The idea of a post-racial America, in other words, is an illusion.

CONCLUSION

Hawai'i's number one export, Ed Beechert (author of Chapter 8) has often said, is its people. Those imbued with the Aloha Spirit have quietly been spreading friendliness, joviality, and the other qualities of Hawai'i's multicultural ethos to the rest of the United States and the world. Now that Barack Obama has arrived on the national and global stage, there is an opportunity for all Americans to learn how to become more positive in human relationships—by following his example of inclusive bridge building and respectful discourse. Obama is a role model for a philosophy that could bring the country and the world together. According to academic Kathleen Hall Jamieson, Obama personifies what America might ideally become (East-West Center 2009).

Those who have previously missed the link between Hawai'i and Obama may still remain skeptical after reading preceding chapters by careful scholars who have not sought to exaggerate the special qualities of the Aloha State. By ignoring such an important element of the Obama presidency, the pundits have failed to inform the American people of his most important asset—the multicultural basis for his popularity.

Moderate conservative columnist David Brooks and coauthor Gail Collins opine that Western-focused modes of thinking may not be adapted to the complex problems of the 21st century, and they believe that Asians are more context oriented (Brooks and Collins 2009). Their insight is obviously applicable to President Obama, who was exposed in his youth not only to Asians in Honolulu, but also Indonesians in Jakarta.

What Obama's election signified was that voters were ready to embrace something very different from the past. According to social psychologists, a fundamental shift in thinking begins when frozen attitudes thaw because they do not work. Some of the thawing among Americans may have occurred prior to Obama's election when President George W. Bush changed course during 2007 and 2008, facing a Democratic Congress and a Supreme Court that repeatedly ruled that his administration was engaging in unconstitutional acts (Haas 2009:Table1.2). But new values have to be understood for a fundamental change to occur.

The United States of America is not an ordinary country with just people, buildings, economic transactions, and scenery. The United States became the first idealist nation in 1776, when a group of eminent people from 13 colonies decided to subscribe to principles of equality and freedom. In time, America allowed millions of immigrants to prosper by establishing the legal and moral framework of democracy and became the richest nation in the world.

But the institution of slavery poisoned that framework from the beginning. After slavery was abolished, a caste system arose in which a few mainstream Whites maintained privilege over the rest of the people. In so doing, according to Swedish sociologist Gunnar Myrdal (1944), the country became encumbered by what he called the "American dilemma," namely, a tension between American ideals and American reality.

Whereas American reality has brought much prosperity to a complacent White middle class, who take constitutional principles for granted, minorities are the most fervent advocates of American ideals. For many centuries, American leaders have articulated American ideals in their speeches but abandoned them in practice. When Barack Obama won a landslide election, his supporters found his belief in American ideals to be truly authentic, not platitudinous. They believed that he was seeking to benefit ordinary people, not entrenched interests.

Precisely because Barack Hussein Obama II is the son of a father of one nationality who married an American of a different skin color and grew up in a state where non-Whites constitute a majority, he is different from ordinary politicians. He is a humbly born idealist with exemplary personal qualities and a philosophy based on the Aloha Spirit. And he has achieved success as an "*eternal optimist*" (Drew 2009).

However, there is a fundamental contradiction between President Obama's cultural and political agendas. On the one hand, he stands for communitarian ideals, seeking to be inclusive by bringing together those with differing perspectives to find "*common ground*." That's how life proceeds and politics works in the Aloha State, where mutual respect is a crucial norm, and incremental progress is achieved through consensus building. But on the U.S. Mainland, politics commonly operates by pragmatism—cutting deals that betray high principles because of strong opposition from a variety of interests that refuse to give up their power, their profits, and their prejudices.

In other words, Plan A is communitarian bipartisanship. But Plan B has been to allow a Democratic Congress to pursue an agenda without Republican support. Therein lies the contradiction. He abandoned his transformational goal of Aloha (Ganz 2010).

The most difficult objective proclaimed by Barack Obama has been Plan A—to transform America so that once again ideals can overshadow interests. When he was once asked in 2007 why he was running for president, he said:

I am in this race because I don't want to see us spend the next year re-fighting the Washington battles of the 1990s. I don't want to pit Blue American against Red America: I want to lead a United States of America. (Krugman 2009)

One man cannot change the culture of a nation. Were he to have his priorities passed more quickly, he would have to employ Plan B hardball politics. But for Obama, culture should trump politics. He would rather be true to his core values than to achieve his campaign promises disrespectfully. He is a compromiser. He wants America to be united again, seeking democracy, justice, progress, and prosperity. But to carry out his agenda, he must favor new policies, and anything new is likely to be opposed. His communitarian agenda involves "using government to help set a context for private sector risk-taking and community initiative" (Brooks 2010b, e).

Unlike presidents who dominated the radio waves (Franklin Roosevelt) and television (Ronald Reagan), Obama became president in an era when the multiplicity of cable television channels means that presidential interviews and speeches reach a very narrow audience on traditional media. They have been also broadcast through media that young people are most likely to access, notably Facebook and YouTube. His messages have been scattered to the winds, fodder for FOX News and MSNBC to do battle, ignoring his accomplishments and his nuances.

Because the media have not been helpful, President Obama has often fallen into the trap identified by former White House press secretary Scott McLellan (2008) in running a "permanent campaign" as a way to goad Congress into translating his campaign promises into legislation. But in a campaign, the rule is to answer opponents quickly so that their charges will not stick. As president, Obama evidently lacked the time to counter opposition narratives, such as Republican Senator Mitch McConnell's constant drumbeat about "reckless spending and debt, the burdensome red-tape and job-killing taxes" (Parsons 2010). In response, Obama stuck to a quiet but visionary mantra but gave no "fireside chats" to explain his objectives in enough detail to prove that constant Republican carping was empty rhetoric. Instead, the Republican message got through.

In world affairs he has been patient with leaders of various countries, allowing them either to support his policies or otherwise without bullying them. In domestic matters, he has been trying to keep to the middle of the road while alienating rightists and disappointing leftists. Coming after a president who tried to stretch the limits of executive power to the maximum, his perception of his role as president understandably appears much weaker. Although humility is required of a leader in Hawai'i, for Mainlanders he appears less than a leader because he is not boldly pretentious. Yet his accomplishments have been monumental–health care universality, Wall Street regulation, environmental progress, educational reform, and improved American respect around the world.

His rhetoric while in Washington has often been arcane—that of a college professor. Many Americans appreciate simpler statements and are confused about what he wants done and why, a mistake that he has admitted (McManus 2010a; Stephanopoulos 2010). Initially, he failed to communicate his theory of governance, namely, that he is engaging in communitarian nation building—rebuilding the strength of the United States by spending more on education, energy, health, infrastructure, and jobs to achieve an "American renewal" (Remnick 2010:441). Later, he took up the phrase "nation building" from perceptive journalist Thomas Friedman (2009) to explain his goals. Then he dropped that narrative.

An important test that Obama sets for himself is whether the tenor of the country's politics will improve. Although seeking bipartisanship,

Republican opposition has been fierce. Partisanship might have been reduced if Obama's proposals were on simple matters, but he set his highest priorities on the very issues that most divide Democrats from Republicans. That he is not a post-partisan president disappoints millions of Americans who heard his idealistic rhetoric during the campaign, and hoped for a change in Washington. For the political culture to change, recalcitrant incumbents would have to be defeated by members of a younger generation, who were the core of his most enthusiastic supporters in his election campaign but too young to run for office.

Accordingly, President Obama has not yet fulfilled his promise. America is still not united despite his communitarian penchant for compromise and middle-of-the-road or left-of-center politics. Although seeking transformation, he was aware that "*With change comes risk . . . which takes some time for people to process*" (Balz and Johnson 2009:292).

He has impressed former president George H. W. Bush, who has praised the humanism of Obama as "genuinely concerned about helping others" (Parsons 2009). Despite many successes, he has been checkmated by Congress, the media, military leaders assigned to Afghanistan and Guantánamo, Wall Street, banks that would not make loans to small businesses, employers who would not rehire, British Petroleum, rogue countries abroad, terrorists, hyperpartisan Republicans, and even by some in his own political party who do not appreciate his multicultural outlook. And biographers have missed his essence by ignoring his roots in Hawai'i.

But without a more coherent statement of his middle-of the-road communitarianism, he cannot persuade others. Absent have been epigrammatic speeches in "*teachable moments*," such as the address on race from Philadelphia on March 18, 2008. His first Oval Office speech, which came in mid-June 2010 over the oil catastrophe in the Gulf of México, disappointingly dealt nonconfrontationally with the theme of responsibility more than a specific action program. By losing control of the initiative, wild accusations and legitimate complaints have echoed, never definitively answered. With Democrats on the verge of losing control of Congress in November 2010, he operated without memorable slogans and a clear vision for his next two years in office that might mobilize supporters. Republicans could then look good by promising to cut spending and taxes.

What has been overlooked by most observers is the reason for the idealism within the movement that elected America's first multicultural president. The tenets of Hawai'i's multicultural ethos to which President Barack Obama subscribes are not just about etiquette and values but are at the core of the intercultural Aloha Spirit that is fervently believed and practiced in Hawai'i. For Obama, living up to one's responsibilities is more important than quarterbacking, catchphrases, or sound bites. But in 2010 was too laid back to impress voters.

President Obama has brought a profound philosophy into the very center of power. He hopes that America will become more multicultural, that is, more like Hawai'i. All 15 chapters herein prove that an understanding of Hawai'i and each of the 12 principles of the Islands' multicultural ethos explain Obama's unusual characteristics: (1) He reaches out to foreign enemies, hoping to win them over with his seductive friendliness. (2) He extends his hand to Republicans, despite their contrary behavior, because of his inclusiveness. (3) In contrast with his predecessor's unwillingness to admit a mistake, he freely does so in a humble yet charismatic manner. (4) While some are taken aback by his efforts to chuckle and make light comments, he is a true representative of the joviality that pervades the Islands. (5) Although supporters have been disappointed that he has refrained from attacking his opponents, he is unwilling to do so because being respectful is central to his personality; he expects others to disagree without being disagreeable. (6) Rather than getting his way by strong-arming those who have stood in his way, such as by denying funds to Congressional districts or states where his most bitter opponents live, he prefers a nonconfrontational approach to bridge differences. (7) Although he could go along with the public desire for retribution against bankers and torturers, he projects a more conciliatory view. (8) His bipartisanship is based on a view that government should both provide harmony for the people and be conducted in a harmonious manner. (9) There is nothing more baffling about Obama than his seeming inability to show emotion, yet those on the Mainland need to realize that his serenity is based on the view that showing anger is viewed as childish and immature in Hawai'i. Nevertheless, behind the scenes he lost his temper to rein in General Stanley McChrystal, who used media leaks to end-run Obama on Afghanistan policy until he received a dressing down in the White House (Alter 2010:Ch. 21) and later was fired. (10) According to Obama, what sustains his belief in a better America is his *"faith"* (Banks 2010). His sincerely religious piety nourishes his pragmatic optimism. (11) Many observers wonder why he took so long to design a new strategy for Afghanistan, not realizing that he was engaging in rational deliberation while he visited dead soldiers returning home. What they missed is his that his humanism is paramount, his belief that people come before principles, his repeated reference to the suffering yet resilience of ordinary Americans.

In his State of the Union address on January 27, 2010, he more explic-itly laid down some ethical boundaries, the 12th tenet of Hawai'i's multicultural ethos: (1) He says *no* to unilateralism in foreign policy, believing that his friendliness remains a seductive asset. (2) He says *no* to freezing Republicans out of the policy process, preferring inclusive-ness. (3) He says *no* to arrogance, asking for more accountability, hon-esty, and humility on the part of those elected to serve the people as well as those in corporate boardrooms who impact ordinary Americans. (4) He says *no* to frantic discourse, insisting on being jovial, smiling, and truthful. (5) Although he says *no* to those who are disrespectful and invent falsehoods to oppose policies, he scolded the Supreme Court right in front of them for empowering corporations to bankroll elections with unlimited funds, thereby potentially threatening democracy. (6) He says *no* to confrontational Senate Republicans who require 60 votes to pass almost anything, instead preferring more dialogue. (7) He says *no* to anti-communitarian Wall Street. (8) He says *no* to torture and those who would use terroristic methods to fight terrorism as counterproduc-tive and disharmonious. (9) He says *no* to emotional appeals, insisting that calm logic prevail in public discourse. (10) He says *no* to ignoring religious principles that take seriously the responsibility to care for the disadvantaged and the poor. (11) He says *no* to self-interested ideolo-gies that ignore the problems of ordinary people, preferring humanistic policies. (12) And there are inevitable exceptions to the ethical principles whenever he confronts forces larger than the presidency.

According to one accounting, President Barack Obama has fulfilled most of his major campaign promises (Alter 2010:425–427). But he has not changed the tone in Washington to become more like that in Hawai'i. Cultural change takes time and cannot be effected with just smiles and speeches. A centrist third party is perhaps needed. For success in his multicultural goals, more Obama-like presidents would have to be elected, and bitter partisanship would have to erode as the voters see the light and vote out politicians who are arrogant, disrespectful, con-frontational, exclusivist, conflict-oriented, greedy, volatile, unprincipled, and seek to impose their ideologies on others. In other words, Hawai'i's multicultural ethos would have to be embraced.

Some day politicians in Washington may change their mind-set into working together in a spirit of communitarian pragmatism despite fun-damental differences. Meanwhile, we have more years to get better acquainted with President Barack Obama, The Aloha Zen president.

Appendix: The Aloha Spirit Law

[§§ 5-7.5] The Aloha Spirit.

a. **The Aloha Spirit** is the coordination of mind and heart within each person. It brings each person to the Self. Each person must think and emote good feelings to others. In the contemplation and presence of the life force, **Aloha**, the following **unuhi laulā loa** (free translation) may be used:

- Akahai, meaning kindness to be expressed with tenderness;
- Lōkahi, meaning unity, to be expressed with harmony;
- 'Olu'olu, meaning agreeable, to be expressed with pleasantness;
- Ha'aha'a, meaning humility, to be expressed with modesty;
- Ahonui, meaning patience, to be expressed with perseverance.

These are traits of character that express the charm, warmth, and sincerity of Hawai'i's people. It was the working philosophy of native Hawaiians and was presented as a gift to the people of Hawai'i.

- **Aloha** is more than a word of greeting or farewell or a salutation.
- **Aloha** means mutual regard and affection and extends warmth in caring with no obligation in return.
- **Aloha** is the essence of relationships in which each person is important to every other person for collective existence.
- **Aloha** means to hear what is not said, to see what cannot be seen, and to know the unknowable.

b. In exercising their power on behalf of the people and in fulfillment of their responsibilities, obligations and service to the people, the legislature, governor, lieutenant governor, executive officers of each department, the chief justice, associate justices, and judges of the appellate, circuit, and district courts may contemplate and reside with the life force and give consideration to **The Aloha Spirit**. [L 1986, c 202, §1]

References

Abercrombie, Neil (2008). "Foreword." In Stu Glauberman and Jerry Burris, eds., *The Dream Begins: How Hawai'i Shaped Barack Obama*, pp. vi–viii. Honolulu: Watermark.

Adams, Romanzo C. (1926). "Hawaii as a Racial Melting Pot," *Mid-Pacific Magazine*, 32 (3): 213–216.

Adams, Romanzo C. (1933). "The Unorthodox Race Doctrine of Hawaii." In E. B. Reuter, ed., *Race and Culture Contacts*, pp. 143–160. New York: McGraw-Hill.

Afro-American Association of Hawaii (1991). "Report on the University of Hawaii and the African-American Athlete." Reprinted in Honolulu: Center for Research on Ethnic Relations, University of Hawai'i at Mānoa, *Document Series*, #8.

Agbayani, Amefil (1994). *O Le Sulufa'iga: Report of the University of Hawai'i Task Force on Samoans and Pacific Islanders in Higher Education*. Honolulu: Office of Student Equity, Excellence and Diversity, University of Hawai'i at Mānoa.

Agbayani-Cahill, Amefil, et al. (1975). "A Study of Immigrant and Non-Immigrant Youth on Oahu." Honolulu: unpublished manuscript, Behavioral Research Group, Office of Human Resources, City and County of Honolulu.

Agence France Press (2007). "Obama Touts Life in Asia, Kenyan Background," *Agence France Press*, November 19.

Akaka, Moanike'ah (2009). "Re-Examining Post-Statehood Identity," *Honolulu Star-Bulletin*, August 21.

Akers, Mary Ann (2009). "Obama on Smoking: '95 Percent Cured'," *Washington Post*, June 23.

Allen, Mike (2010). "John Boehner to Hit President Obama on 'Enemies'," *Politico*, November 1.

Alter, Jonathan (2009). "Scoring Obama's First 100 Days," *Newsweek*, May 4.

Alter, Jonathan (2010). *The Promise: President Obama, Year One*. New York: Simon & Schuster.

Altonn, Helen (2008). "UH Dean Opened Medical Field to Minorities," *Honolulu Star-Bulletin*, July 19.

Altonn, Helen (2009). "National Health Reform Bills Would Exempt Hawaii," *Honolulu Star-Bulletin*, October 31.

American Legislative Exchange Council. (2008). *Report Card on American Education,* 15th Edition. Washington, DC: American Legislative Exchange Council.

Anthony, J. Garner (1955). *Hawaii under Army Rule*. Stanford, CA: Stanford University Press.

Aoudé, Ibrahim (1994). "Hawai'i: The Housing Crisis and the State's Development Strategy," *Social Process in Hawaii, 35*: 71–84.

Aoudé, Ibrahim (1995). "Tourist Attraction: Hawai'i's Locked-in Economy." In Peter Manicas, ed., *Social Process in Hawai'i: A Reader*, pp. 226–242. New York: McGraw Hill.

Aoudé, Ibrahim G., ed. (1999a). *The Ethnic Studies Story: Politics and Social Movements in Hawai'i*. Honolulu: Department of Sociology, University of Hawai'i at Mānoa.

Aoudé, Ibrahim (1999b). "Strategic Consideration for Social Struggles." *Social Process in Hawai'i, 39*: 284–300.

Aoudé, Ibrahim G., ed. (2001). *Public Policy and Globalization in Hawai'i*. Honolulu: University of Hawai'i Press.

Aoudé, Ibrahim G. (2004). "Globalization in Hawai'i: The Promise of Globalism and the Reality of Capitalism." In Manfred Steger, ed., *Rethinking Capitalism,* pp. 243–53. Lanham, MD: Rowman & Littlefield.

Apio, Alani (2003). "Kāmau." In Alani Apio, Tammy Haili'ōpua Baker, Lee Cataluna, and Victoria Nalani Kneubuhl, eds., *He Leo Hou—A New Voice—Hawaiian Playwrights*, pp. 17–81. Honolulu: Bamboo Ridge Press.

Arcayna, Nancy (2002). "Dances of Life," *Honolulu Star-Bulletin*, June 10.

Ariyoshi, Rita (2004). "Mean Old Mr. Sun Cho Lee and the Role of Ethnic Human in Hawai'i," *spirit of hawaii.com*, December.

Armstrong, Diane (1975). "Police Report on Student Crime: 669 Arrests Here in 7 Months," *Honolulu Star-Bulletin*, September 26.

Aronson, Joshua, Sheana Jannone, Matthew McGlone, and Tanisha Johnson-Campbell (2009). "The 'Obama Effect': An Experimental Test," *Journal of Experimental Social Psychology*, 45 (July): 957–960.

Associated Press (1991). "UH's Treatment of Blacks Questioned: Black Athletes Have Been Involved in a Series of Incidents," *Honolulu Star-Bulletin*, October 4.

Associated Press (2010a). "New Obama Book Coming," *Los Angeles Times*, September 15.

Associated Press (2010b). "Obama on Presidency: One Needs 'Pretty Thick Skin'," *Washington Post*, April 2.

Astin, Alexander W. (1982). *Minorities in American Higher Education*. San Francisco: Jossey-Bass.

Avila, Oscar (2010). "Obama's Census Choice: 'Black'," *Los Angeles Times*, April 4.

Bacevich, Andrew J. (2010). *Washington Rules: America's Permanent Path to Power*. New York: Metropolitan Books.

Baker, Peter (2010). "Steep Learning Curve as Chief in Time of War," *New York Times*, August 28.

Baker, Peter, and Jeff Zeleny (2009). "Emanuel Wields Power Freely, and Faces the Risks," *New York Times*, August 15.

Balz, Dan (2010). "The Polarizing President," *Washington Post*, September 5.

Balz, Dan, and Haynes Johnson (2009). *The Battle for America 2008*. New York: Viking.

Bank of Hawaii (1996). "Selected Economic Indicators," *Business Trends*, 41 (January/February): 7.

Bank of Hawaii (1999). *Hawaii 1999: Annual Economic Report*. Honolulu: Bank of Hawaii.

Banks, Adelle M. (2010). "Obama Tells Church Faith 'Keeps Me Calm'," *Christianity Today*, January 18.

Barabak, Mark Z., and Richard Fausset (2009). "On Race Issue, Obama Is Staying Firmly Low-Key," *Los Angeles Times*, September 20.

Baratholet, Jeffrey, and Daniel Stone (2009). "A Team of Expatriates," *Newsweek*, January 26.

Barayuga, Debra (2003). "State Supreme Court Upholds '98 Ruling Against UH in Speech Case," *Honolulu Star-Bulletin*, September 13.

Barr, Andy (2009). "Poll: U.S. Too Politically Divided," *USA Today*, December 1.

Barringer, Herbert (1995). "The Educational, Occupational and Economic Status of Native Hawaiians." Paper presented at the Ethnic Studies Community Conference, Honolulu, May 20–21.

Bates, Daniel, Rob Crilly, and Colin Freeman (2010). "Did Hard Times Create the Times Square Bomber?," *Daily Telegraph*, May 8.

Bayuni, Endy M. (2009). "Obama's Indonesian Classroom," *New York Times*, January 17.

Beechert, Edward D. (1985). *Working in Hawai'i: A Labor History*. Honolulu: University of Hawai'i Press.

Beechert, Edward D. (1988). "Technology and the Plantation Labour Supply: The Case of Queensland, Hawai'i, Cuba, and Louisiana." In Bill Albert and Adrian Graves, eds., *The World Sugar Economy in War and Depression, 1914–1950*, pp. 131–142. London: Routledge.

Beechert, Edward D. (1993). *Aupuni i La'au: A History of Hawai'i's Carpenters Union, Local 745*. Honolulu: Center for Labor Education and Research, University of Hawai'i at Mānoa.

Bender, Bryan (2004). "Army Recruits with Diplomas Hit 25-Year Low," *Boston Globe*, January 23.

Benn, Denis M. (1974). "The Theory of Plantation Economy and Society: A Methodological Critique," *Journal of Commonwealth and Comparative Politics*, 12 (November): 249–260.

Bennett, Milton J. (1998) *Basic Concepts of Intercultural Communication*. Boston: Intercultural Press.

Bernardo, Rosemarie (2001). "Pearl Harbor Peninsula Residents Recall Wartime Discrimination," *Honolulu Star-Bulletin*, December 8.

Bernardo, Rosemarie (2008). "UH Reaches Settlement in Gay Pair's Housing Suit," *Honolulu Star-Bulletin*, August 30.

Bickerton, Derek (1983). "Creole Languages," *Scientific American*, 249 (1): 116–122.

Bickerton, Derek (1998). "Language and Language Content." In Michael Haas, ed., *Multicultural Hawai'i: The Fabric of a Multiethnic Society*, Ch. 3. New York: Garland.

Black, Cobey (2002). *Hawaii Scandal*. Waipahu, HI: Island Heritage Publishing.

Blond, Phillip (2010). *Red Tory*. London: Faber & Faber.

Blount, James (1893). *Papers Relating to the Mission of James Blount*. Washington, DC: Government Printing Office.

Blow, Charles M. (2009). "Black in the Age of Obama," *New York Times*, December 4.

Boehlert, Eric, and Jamison Foser (2008). "Cokie Roberts on Obama's Vacation: 'I Know His Grandmother Lives in Hawaii and I Know Hawaii Is a State,' But It Looks 'Foreign, Exotic'," *Media Matters*, *http://mediamatters.org/items/200808100001*, August 10.

Borreca, Richard (1985). "Wooing the Filipino Vote," *Honolulu*, 20 (November): 24

Borreca, Richard (1990). "Mednick Says 'Balanced Ticket' Are Actually Words of Racism," *Honolulu Star-Bulletin*, July 13.

Borreca, Richard (1991). "Dec. 7: Military Replaces Civilian Rule," *Honolulu Star-Bulletin*, December 2.

Borreca, Richard (2005). "Legislature Overturns a Dozen Lingle Vetoes, Tying a Record," *Honolulu Star-Bulletin*, July 14.

Borreca, Richard (2009). "State Tax Revenue Declines by 10.9%," *Honolulu Star-Bulletin*, November 10.

Borreca, Richard (2010a). "Abercrombie in Slight Lead for Governor," *Honolulu Star-Bulletin*, January 18.

Borreca, Richard (2010b). "'Culture War' Engulfs Hawaii Democrats," *Honolulu Star-Advertiser*, August 1.

Borreca, Richard (2010c). "The Race Is on and Already Negative Adds Are Out Front," *Honolulu Star-Advertiser*, August 20.

Boston Globe (2009). "Cub Reporter, 11, Aces Presidential Interview," *globe.com*, August 15.

Boucher, Geoff (2009). "One More Trek as the Logical Spock," *Los Angeles Times*, May 11.

Boylan, Dan (1992). "Blood Runs Thick: Ethnicity as a Factor in Hawai'i's Politics." In Zachary A. Smith and Richard C. Pratt, eds., *Politics and Public Policy in Hawai'i*, Ch. 4. Albany: State University of New York Press.

Boylan, Dan (2000). *John A. Burns: The Man and His Times*. Honolulu: Sinclair Library, University of Hawai'i at Mānoa (video recording).

Boylan, Dan (2009). "25 Years Later," *MidWeek*, July 22.

Boylan, Peter (2008a). "Hannemann Shows Hefty Lead in Honolulu Mayor's Race Poll," *Honolulu Advertiser*, October 23.

Boylan, Peter (2008b). "Thefts Have Pushed up Crime Rate in Hawaii," *Honolulu Advertiser*, January 8.

Brannon, Johnny (2004). "Bainum Retains Lead over Hannemann," *Honolulu Advertiser*, October 24.

Brieske, Phillip R. (1961). *A Study of the Development of Public Elementary and Secondary Education in the Territory of Hawaii*. Seattle: PhD dissertation, University of Washington.

Broder, David S. (2010). "Obama and the Challenge of Slow Change," *Washington Post*, April 15.

Broder, John M. (2005). "After Hurricane Katrina," *New York Times*, September 5.

Brooks, David (2010a). "The Broken Society," *New York Times*, March 18.

Brooks, David (2010b). "The Day after Tomorrow," *New York Times*, September 15.

Brooks, David (2010c). "The Genteel Nation," *New York Times*, September 12.

Brooks, David (2010d). "Getting Obama Right," *New York Times*, March 12.

Brooks, David (2010e). "The Long Strategy," *New York Times*, July 27.

Brooks, David (2010f). "Race to Sanity," *New York Times*, June 3.

Brooks, David, and Gail Collins (2009). "Western Men Are Doomed," *New York Times*, November 19.

Brown, Laura, and Walter Cohen (1975). *Hawaii Faces the Pacific*. Palo Alto, CA: Pacific Studies Center.

Buchanan, Nina K., and Robert A. Fox (2005). "Back to the Future: Ethnocentric Charter Schools in Hawaii." In Eric Rofes and Lisa M. Stulberg, eds., *The Emancipatory Promise of Charter Schools: Towards a Progressive Politics of School Choice*, pp. 77–106. Albany, NY: State University of New York Press.

Bunker, Frank F. (1922). "The Education of the Child of the American-Born Parent in Hawaii," *Hawaii Educational Review*, 11 (September): 1–2.

Burris, Jerry (1974). "If He Weren't Running . . . McClung Would Back Gill over 2," *Honolulu Advertiser*, October 2.

Burris, Jerry (1990). "Undecided Voters Hold Key to Senate Victory," *Honolulu Advertiser*, October 31.

Burris, Jerry (1994a). "The Battle for Your Vote for Governor—and Some Clues as to Who Will Win It: Ethnicity, Party Do Matter, But Issues May Matter in '94 . . . ," *Honolulu Advertiser*, October 23.

Burris, Jerry (1994b). "Who's Seen as Most Caring, Honest, Able? Opinion Poll Gives Saiki Best Marks," *Honolulu Advertiser*, February 20.

Burris, Jerry (2008). "Obama's Chicago Roots Tangled in Hawaiian Soil," *Honolulu Advertiser*, October 30.

Bushnell, O. A. (1971). *The Return of Lono: A Novel of Captain Cook's Last Voyage.* Honolulu: University of Hawai'i Press.

Bushnell, O. A. (1972). *Ka'a'awa: A Novel about Hawaii in the 1850s.* Honolulu: University Press of Hawaii.

Byrne, John (2009). "GOP Senator Calls Sarah Palin's 'Death Panel' Remarks 'Nuts'," *AlterNet.org*, August 11.

Cablas, Armando (1991). "Pilipino Americans and the Scholastic Aptitude Test at the University of Hawai'i at Mānoa: A Review of the Literature," *Social Process in Hawaii*, 22: 91–106.

Cable News Network (2006). "America Votes 2006." *http://www.cnn.com/ELECTION/2006/pages/results/states/HI/S/01/epolls.0.html.*

Campos, Danilo (1991). "Operation Manong Program for Minority Students." Paper presented at the annual convention of the Association for Asian-American Studies, Honolulu, May 30.

Canada, Royal Commission on Bilingualism and Biculturalism (1965). *Report.* Ottawa: Royal Commission on Bilingualism and Biculturalism.

Caplan, Jeremy, and Kristina Dell (2008). "The Six Degrees of Obama," *Time*, December 29.

Carnevale, Mary Lu (2008). "Live-Blogging Obama's News Conference—Day Three," *Wall Street Journal: Washington Wire, http://blogs.wsj.com/washwire/2008/11/26/live-blogging-obamas-news-conference-day-three/,* November 28.

Carter, Joey (1990). "Being Haole in Hawaii," *Ka Leo o Hawai'i*, September 5.

Castberg, A. Didrick (1966). *The Ethnic Factor in Criminal Sentencing.* Evanston, IL: PhD dissertation, Northwestern University.

Castberg, A. Didrick (1990). *Japanese Criminal Justice.* New York: Praeger.

Cataluna, Lee (2003). "Da Mayah." In Alani Apio, Tammy Haili˜opua Baker, and Lee Cataluna, eds., *He Leo Hou—A New Voice—Hawaiian Playwrights*, pp. 147–202. Honolulu: Bamboo Ridge Press.

Cataluna, Lee (2005). *Folks You Meet in Longs.* Honolulu: Bamboo Ridge Press.

Cataluna, Lee (2009). "Few Will Celebrate 50 Years of Statehood," *Honolulu Advertiser*, August 21.

Cayetano, Ben (1994). *This Is What I Believe; This Is What I'll Do*. Honolulu: Cayetano for Governor Campaign.

Cayetano, Ben (1995). "Better for Business?," *Hawaii Business*, 40 (January): 15–21.

Cayetano, Ben (1996). *Restoring Hawaii's Economic Momentum*. Honolulu: Department of Business, Economic Development, and Tourism, State of Hawai'i.

Cayetano, Benjamin J. (2009). *Ben: A Memoir, from Street Kid to Governor*. Honolulu: Watermark.

Chan, Gaye M. G. (1999). "Faculty Member Assaults Student Leader While Other Faculty Watch." *http://www.qrd.org/qrd/usa/hawaii/1999/faculty. member.assaults.student.leader-11.16.99*.

Chang, Heidi (2008). "Hawaii Helped Shape Barack Obama," *VOAnews.com*, August 12.

Chapin, Helen Geracimos (1996). *Shaping History: The Role of Newspapers in Hawai'i*. Honolulu: University of Hawai'i Press.

Charlton, Brian (2007). "Obama Had Multiethnic Existence in Hawaii," *Associated Press*, February 6.

Chattergy, Virgie (1992). "Complexity and Challenge: Asian Americans in Higher Education," *Teaching & Learning*, 5 (Spring): 4–5.

Chawkins, Steve (2009). "A Princely Link to Fame," *Los Angeles Times*, November 9.

Chesney-Lind, Meda, et al. (1992). *Gangs and Delinquency in Hawaii*. Honolulu: Center for Youth Research, Social Science Research Institute, University of Hawai'i at Mānoa.

Chock, Eric (1986a). "Poem for George Helm." In Eric Chock and Darrell H. Y. Lum, eds., *The Best of Bamboo Ridge: The Hawai'i Writers' Quarterly*, p. 21–23. Honolulu: Bamboo Ridge Press.

Chock, Eric (1986b). "Tūtū on the Curb." In Eric Chock and Darrell H. Y. Lum, eds., *The Best of Bamboo Ridge: The Hawai'i Writers' Quarterly*, p. 6. Honolulu: Bamboo Ridge Press.

Chock, Eric, James Harstad, Darrell Lum, and Bill Teter, eds. (1998). *Growing up Local: An Anthology of Poetry and Prose from Hawai'i*. Honolulu: Bamboo Ridge Press.

Chun, Gary C. W. (2009). "Exhibit Shows the Harsh Life of Honouliuli Internment Camp," *Honolulu Star-Bulletin*, December 7.

Clarke, Richard (2010). Interview on Hardball with Chris Matthews, MSNBC, April 20.

Clement, Russell (1980). "From Cook to the 1840 Constitution: The Name Change from Sandwich to Hawaiian Islands," *Hawaiian Journal of History*, 14: 50–57.

Coffman, Tom (1970). "Burns' Best Support from Women, AJAs," *Honolulu Star-Bulletin*, January 15.

Coffman, Tom (1973). *Catch a Wave: A Case Study of Hawaii's New Politics.* Honolulu: University Press of Hawai'i.

Coleman, James Samuel, et al. (1966). *On Equality of Educational Opportunity.* Washington, DC: Government Printing Office.

Coleman, Stuart (2008). "Tea with Barack Obama's Sister," *salon.com*, October 23.

Conan, Katherine (1946). *The History of Contract Labor in the Hawaiian Islands.* Princeton, NJ: Princeton University Press.

Conklin, Kenneth R. (2003). "Ethnic Diversity at University of Hawaii Is Harmed by Race-Based Tuition Waivers," *Hawaii Reporter*, July 14.

Cooper, George, and Gavan Daws (1985). *Land and Power in Hawaii: The Democratic Years.* Honolulu: Benchmark Press.

Corsi, Jerome R. (2009). "Obama's Parents Didn't Live at Newspaper Birth Address: Barack's Dad Had Bachelor Pad, Mother Left Hawaii with Baby," *WorldNetDaily.com*, August 18.

Cotton, Kathleen (1992). "School-Based Management." *Northwest Regional Laboratory School Improvement Research Series* [On-line]. *http://www.nwrwel.org/scpd/sirs/7/topsyn6.html*.

Crane, Jeffrey L., and Alton M. Okinaka (1992). "Social Dynamics of the Aloha State: The Population of Hawai'i." In Zachary A. Smith and Richard C. Pratt, eds., *Politics and Public Policy in Hawai'i*, Ch. 3. Albany: State University of New York Press.

Cuomo, Mario Matthew (1990). *Public Papers of Mario Cuomo, 1987.* Albany, NY: State of New York.

D'Andrea, Michael, and Judy Daniels (2008). "Promoting Multiculturalism, Democracy, and Social Justice in Organizational Settings: The University of Hawaii Case Study," unpublished manuscript.

D'Souza, Dinesh (2010). "How Obama Thinks," *Forbes*, September 9.

Dana, Richard Henry, Jr. (1840). *Two Years before the Mast: A Personal Narrative of Life at Sea.* New York: New American Library, 2009.

Dannemiller, James E. (1973). "Ethnicity at the University of Hawaii." Honolulu: Survey Research Office, Social Science Research Institute, University of Hawai'i at Mānoa, unpublished manuscript.

Davenport, Kiana (1994). *Shark Dialogues.* New York: Atheneum.

Davis, William Michael (2008). *Barack Obama: The Politics of Hope.* Stockton, NJ: OTTN Publishing.

Daws, Gavan (1968). *Shoal of Time.* New York: Macmillan.

Daws, Gavan, and Bennett Hymer, eds. (2008). *Honolulu Stories: Voices of the Town through the Years, Two Centuries of Writing.* Honolulu: Mutual Publishing.

Day, A. Grove, and Carl Stroven, eds. (1959). *A Hawaiian Reader.* New York: Appleton-Century-Crofts.

Day, Richard R. (1985). "The Ultimate Inequality: Linguistic Genocide." In Nessa Wolfson and Joan Manes, eds., *Language of Inequality*, pp. 163–181. New York: Mouton.

Daysog, Rick (2009). "Downturn Hit [*sic*] Kamehameha Schools with $2.2 Billion Loss," *Honolulu Advertiser*, December 16.

Dayton, Kevin (1998). "Abercrombie Enjoys Significant Lead," *Honolulu Advertiser*, September 11.

de Crèvecœur, Michel Guillaume Jean (1782). *Letters from an American Farmer*. London: Davies.

De Pledge, Derrick (2009). "Hawaii State Worker Layoffs Cut Back to 650 Instead of 1,100," *Honolulu Advertiser*, November 13.

de Tocqueville, Alexis (1835). *Democracy in America*. New York: Vintage, 1945.

Diehl, Jason (2010). "Where Are Obama's Foreign Confidants?" *Washington Post*, March 8.

Digman, John, and Daniel W. Tuttle (1959). "An Analysis of Oahu's 1956 City-County Election." Honolulu: Center for Research on Ethnic Relations, Social Science Research Institute, University of Hawai'i at Mānoa, *Working Paper #6* [reprint].

Digman, John, and Daniel W. Tuttle (1961). "An Interpretation of an Election by Means of Obverse Factor Analysis," *Journal of Social Psychology*, 53 (April): 183–194.

Dingeman, Robbie (1997). "Aloha Spirit Important to Hawaii, Residents Say," *Honolulu Advertiser*, October 26.

Dionne, E. J., Jr. (2009). "The Obama Doctrine," *Washington Post*, April 16.

Donnelly, Christine (1996). "Report Flunks Hawai'i on School Funding," *Honolulu Star-Bulletin*, April 4.

Dooley, Jim (2009a). "Failures Tarnish Hawaii Program to Rehabilitate Offenders," *Honolulu Advertiser*, November 8.

Dooley, Jim (2009b). "Palace Charges Dropped for 6," *Honolulu Advertiser*, March 31.

Dorning, Mike, and Christi Parsons (2007). "Carefully Crafting the Obama 'Brand'," *Chicago Tribune*, June 12.

Dotts, Cecil K., and Mildred Sikkema (1994). *Challenging the Status Quo: Public Education in Hawaii 1840–1980*. Honolulu: Hawaii Education Association.

Dougherty, Michael (1992). *To Steal a Kingdom: Probing Hawaiian History*. Waimanalo, HI: Island Style Press.

Douthat, Ross (2009). "The Obama Way," *New York Times*, December 25.

Dowd, Maureen (2009). "Spock at the Bridge," *New York Times*, March 1.

Dowd, Maureen (2010). "You'll Never Believe What This White House Is Missing," *New York Times*, July 24.

Draper, Robert (2009). "The Ultimate Insider," *New York Times*, July 21.

Drew, Joan (2009). "The Thirty Days of Barack Obama," *New York Review of Books*, March 26.

du Puy, William Atherton (1932). *Hawaii and Its Race Problem*. Washington, DC: Government Printing Office.

Dudley, Michael Kioni, and Keoni Kealoha Agard (1990*). A Call for Hawaiian Sovereignty*. Honolulu: Na Kane o Ka Malo Press.

East-West Center (2009). "Kathleen Hall Jamieson: On the Media, Politics and a President Named Obama," *Observer & EWCA Update* (East-West Center), Spring 2009.

EducationBug (2009). *Hawaii Private School Statistics*. Retrieved 19 February 2009 from *http://hawaii.educationbug.org/private-schools/*.

Edwards, Joella (2009). "Buff 'N Blue & Black." In Ron Jacobs, ed., *Obamaland: Who is Barack Obama?*, pp. 60–63. Honolulu: Trade Publishing.

Effron, Daniel. A., Jessica S. Cameron, and Benoît Monin. (2009). "Endorsing Obama Licenses Favoring Whites," *Journal of Experimental Social Psychology*, 45 (May): 590–593.

Eisenstein, James, and Herbert Jacob (1977). *Felony Justice: An Organizational Analysis of Criminal Courts*. Boston: Little, Brown.

Elliott, Andrea (2010). "White House Quietly Courts Muslims in U.S.," *New York Times*, April 19.

Engels, Friedrich (1884). *The Origin of the Family, Private Property and the State*. New York: Pathfinder, 1972.

Engle, Erika (2009). "KSSK Maintains Its Grip on Top of Radio Ratings," *Honolulu Star-Bulletin*, October 17.

Epstein, Henry (1975). "Interview." In *History of the United Public Workers Union in Hawai'i*. Honolulu: Hamilton Library, University of Hawai'i at Mānoa, microfiche.

Essoyan, Susan (2004). "Waianae Helps Freshmen Focus," *Honolulu Star-Bulletin*, June 1.

Essoyan, Susan (2009). "State Land Use Panel Rejects Plan for 12,000 Homes on Ewa Farms," *Honolulu Star-Bulletin*, August 29.

Etzioni, Amitai (1993). *The Spirit of Community: Rights, Responsibilities, and the Communitarian Agenda*. New York: Crown Publishers.

Etzioni, Amitai (2009). *New Common Ground: A New America, A New World*. Washington, DC: Potomac.

Ewers, Justin (2009). "Obama and Race Relations: Civil Rights Leaders Aren't Satisfied," *U.S. News & World Report*, April 30.

Faludi, Susan C. (1991a). "Homeland History: Plan of a Prince Is Co-opted," *Star-Bulletin & Advertiser*, September 15 [reprinted from *Wall Street Journal*, September 9].

Faludi, Susan C. (1991b). "How Everyone Got Hawaii Homelands Except Hawaiians: Federal Mandate Is Abused as Natives Wait Decades for Small Plots of Land; State Gives VIPs Huge Tracts," *Star-Bulletin & Advertiser*, September 15.

Fernandez, Yvette (1993). "KIKI Exec Apologizes to Hawaiians," *Honolulu Advertiser*, June 19.

Feller, Ben (2010). "For Obama, Selling an Agenda Can Get Personal," *Associated Press*, July 20.

Fineman, Howard (2009). "President of Planet Earth," *Newsweek*, October 19.

Finin, Gerard A. (2008). "Polynesia's First US President?," *Pacific Magazine.net*, July 14.

Fiore, Faye, and Mark Z. Barabak (2009). "Leading America in a New Direction," *Los Angeles Times*, April 19.

Fiorina, Morris P. (2010). "Culture War? The Road to and from 2008." In Thomas R. Dye, ed., *Obama: Year One*, Ch. 1. New York: Longman.

First Hawaiian Bank (1999). *Annual Economic Forecast: 1999–2000*. Honolulu: First Hawaiian Bank.

Fletcher, Michael A. (2009). President-Elect Sees His Race as an Opportunity," *Washington Post*, January 19.

Forbes, David W. (1991). "Look the Rock Whence Ye Are Hewn: A Reappraisal of Punahou's Early History." In Nelson Foster, ed., *Punahou: The History and Promise of a School of the Islands*, pp. 119–149. Honolulu: Punahou School.

Fornander, Abraham (1880). *An Account of the Polynesian Race*. 3 vols London: Trübner.

Fox, Robert A., and Nina K. Buchanan (2004). *The Impact of Collective Bargaining on Charter Schools in Hawaii: One State's Story*. Honolulu, HI: Hawai'i Educational Policy Center.

Fox, Robert A., and Nina K. Buchanan (2007). "A Charter School Law in Transition," *Journal of School Choice*, 1 (3): 145–175.

Franklin, Benjamin (1793). *The Autobiography of Benjamin Franklin*. London: Parsons.

Friedman, Ray (2009). "'The Obama Effect': Test-Taking Performance Gap Virtually Eliminated during Key Moments of Obama's Presidential Run." *http://sitemason.vanderbilt.edu/news/releases/2009/01/21/the-obama-effect-test-taking-performance-gap-virtually-eliminated-during-key-moments-of-obamas-presidential-run.71208*

Friedman, Thomas (2009). "More Poetry, Please," *New York Times*, November 1.

Friend, The (1887). "Anglo-Saxonizing Machines," *The Friend*, 45 (August): 63–64.

Fuchs, Lawrence H. (1961). *Hawaii Pono: A Social History*. New York: Harcourt, Brace & World.

Fujikane, Candice (1994). "Between Nationalisms: Hawai'i's Local Nation and Its Troubled Racial Paradise," *Critical Mass*, 1 (2): 23–58.

Fujikane, Candice, and Jonathan Okamura, eds. (2008). *Asian Settler Colonialism: From Local Governance to the Habits of Everyday Life in Hawai'i*. Honolulu: University of Hawai'i Press.

Fujiyama, Rodney M. (1967). *The Social Backgrounds of Hawaii's Legislators, 1945–1967*. Honolulu: Senior Honors Thesis, University of Hawai'i at Mānoa.

Gallimore, Ronald, Joan Whitehorn Boggs, and Cathie Jordan (1974*). Culture, Behavior and Education: A Study of Hawaiian-Americans*. Beverly Hills: Sage.

Ganz, Marshall (2010). "How Obama Lost His Voice . . . ," *Los Angeles Times*, November 3.

Galtung, Johan (1964). "A Structural Theory of Aggressive," *Journal of Conflict Resolution*, 1 (2): 95–119.

Gardner, David (2009). "U.S. Lost Its Moral Bearings over Torture, Says Obama—and Warns Bush Officials Could Be Charged," *Daily Mail*, April 21.

Gearan, Anne, and Matt Apuzzo (2010). "Security Strategy Seeks Non-Military Moves," *Associated Press*, May 26

Gereben, Janos (1970a). "Request for Racial Survey at UH an Error, HEW Says," *Honolulu Star-Bulletin*, October 19.

Gereben, Janos (1970b). "UH Integrated, U.S. Study Shows," *Honolulu Star-Bulletin*, November 10.

Gerson, Michael (2010). "Obama the Snob," *Washington Post*, October 19.

Geschwender, James A. (1980–1981). "Lessons from Waiahole-Waikane," *Social Process in Hawaii*, 28: 121–135.

Geschwender, James A. (1982). "The Hawaiian Transformation: Class, Submerged Nation, and National Minorities." In Edward Friendman, ed., *Ascent and Decline in the World-System*, Ch. 8. Beverly Hills, CA: Sage.

Geschwender, James A., Rita Carroll-Seguin, and Howard Brill (1988). "The Portuguese and Haoles of Hawaii: Implications for the Origin of Ethnicity," *American Sociological Review*, 53 (August): 515–527.

Gima, Craig (2004). "Dobelle Fired," *Honolulu Star-Bulletin*, June 16.

Gionson, T. Lihia (2009). "OHA Announces New Strategic Plan," *Ka Wai Ola*, 26 (October): 3.

Gladwin, Thomas (1972). "Institutional Racism at the University of Hawaii: The Ethnic Studies Program." Honolulu: Center for Research on Ethnic Relations, University of Hawai'i at Mānoa, *Working Paper* #7 [reprint].

Glauberman, Stu (1988). "Misconduct at Schools Seems to Be Declining," *Honolulu Advertiser*, May 21.

Glauberman, Stu, and Jerry Burris (2008). *The Dream Begins: How Hawai'i Shaped Barack Obama*. Honolulu: Watermark.

Glazer, Nathan (1975). *Affirmative Discrimination: Ethnic Inequality and Public Policy*. New York: Basic Books.

Glazer, Nathan (1997). *We Are All Multiculturalists Now*. Cambridge, MA: Harvard University Press.

Glick, Clarence E. (1980). *Sojourners and Settlers: Chinese Migrants in Hawaii*. Honolulu: University Press of Hawai'i.

Goldberg, Jonah (2010). "Obama's Ego and Our Mess," *Los Angeles Times*, October 12.

Gomes, Kerry (2002). "OHA's Roots Born of Controversy: History," *Ka Leo o Hawai'i*, October 28.

Goodale, Gloria (2009). "Obama's Call to Arts," *Christian Science Monitor*, January 16.

Gordon, Mike (2006). "Hawaii Land Reform Act," *Honolulu Advertiser*, July 2.

Goya, Sandy (2010). "Official 2010–11 Public and Charter School Enrollment," News Release, Department of Education, State of Hawai'i, October 18.

Grant, Glen (2005). *Obake: Ghost Stories in Hawaii*. Honolulu: Mutual Publishing Company.

Grant, Glen, and Dennis Ogawa (1993). "Living Proof: Is Hawaii the Answer?" *Annals of the American Academy of Political and Social Science*, 530: 137–154.

Grieco, Elizabeth, and Rachel Cassidy (2001). *Overview of Race and Hispanic Origin*. Washington, DC: U.S. Department of Commerce.

Griffin, John (1994). "Hawaii Easy Days Are Over: All Goals Will Take More Effort," *Honolulu Advertiser*, November 13.

Gross, Daniel (2009). "The Bailout Bonanza: TARP's Early Returns Are Impressive," *Newsweek*, September 7.

Gulick, Sidney L. (1937). *Mixing the Races in Hawaii: A Study of the Coming Neo-Hawaiian American Race*. Honolulu: Porter.

Haas, Michael (1988). "Violent Schools—Unsafe Schools: The Case of Hawaii," *Journal of Conflict Resolution*, 32 (December): 727–758.

Haas, Michael (1991). "Discoverers' Day, 1555: Gaetano Beat Capt. Cook by More than 2 Centuries," *Star-Bulletin & Advertiser* (Honolulu), June 16.

Haas, Michael (1992). *Institutional Racism: The Case of Hawai'i*. Westport, CT: Praeger.

Haas, Michael (2008). *International Human Rights: A Comprehensive Introduction* (2008). New York: Routledge.

Haas, Michael (2009). *George W. Bush, War Criminal? The Bush Administration's Liability for 269 War Crimes*. Westport, CT: Praeger.

Haas, Michael (2010a). *America's War Crimes Quagmire, From Bush to Obama*. Los Angeles: Publishinghouse for Scholars.

Haas, Michael (2010b). *Looking for the Aloha Spirit: Promoting Ethnic Harmony*. Los Angeles: Publishinghouse for Scholars.

Haas, Michael, and Peter P. Resurrection, eds. (1976). *Politics and Prejudice in Contemporary Hawaii*. Honolulu: Coventry.

Hall, Jack (1968). "Speech at Western Jurisdictional Conference of the United Methodist Church, Honolulu, July 25, 1968." San Francisco: ILWU International Library and Archives.

Hamasaki, Richard (1993). "Mountains in the Sea: The Emergence of Contemporary Hawaiian Poetry in English." In Paul Sharrad, ed., *Readings in Pacific Literature*, pp. 190–207. Woolongang, Australia: University of Woolongang New Literatures Research Center.

Hamasaki, Richard, and Mei-Li M. Siy, eds. (2009). *Westlake*. Honolulu: University of Hawai'i Press.

Hammes, David L., Ronald A. Oliveira, and Marcia Sakai (1992). "The State Economy." In Zachary A. Smith and Richard C. Pratt, eds., *Politics and Public Policy in Hawai'i*, Ch. 2. Albany: State University of New York Press.

Hammons, Steve (2008). "Obama's Scottish, Cherokee Ancestry Has Meaning," *American Chronicle*, October 8.

Hanford, George H. (1982). *Minority Programs and Activities of the College Board: An Updated Report*. New York: College Entrance Examination Board.

Hannahs, Neil J. (1983). *Native Hawaiian Educational Assessment Project Final Report*. Honolulu: Native Hawaiian Educational Assessment Project.

Harada, Wayne (1996). "Hawaii's Changing Face of Radio," *Honolulu Advertiser*, March 17.

Harris, Marvin (1968). *The Rise of Anthropological Theory: A History of Theories of Culture*. New York: Crowell.

Hartwell, Jay (1987). "Sometimes Waves in 'Melting Pot' Swamp the Aloha," *Star-Bulletin & Advertiser*, February 15.

Hauser, Robert M., and Karen Mason (1993). *The University of Hawai'i at Manoa Faculty Pay Equity Study: Gender and Ethnicity Pay Equity Analysis*. Honolulu: University of Hawai'i at Mānoa.

Hawai'i (1874). *Palapala Hoike aka Peresidena o Ka Papa Hoonaauao*. Honolulu: Board of Education, Kingdom of Hawai'i.

Hawai'i (1888). *Biennial Report of the President of the Board of Education*. Honolulu: Board of Education, Kingdom of Hawai'i.

Hawai'i (1892). *Biennial Report of the President of the Board of Education*. Honolulu: Board of Education, Kingdom of Hawai'i.

Hawai'i (1894). *Biennial Report of the Board of Education*. Honolulu: Board of Education, Republic of Hawai'i.

Hawai'i (1896). *Biennial Report of the Board of Education*. Honolulu: Board of Education, Republic of Hawai'i.

Hawai'i (1900). *Report of the Superintendent of Public Instruction*. Honolulu: Department of Public Instruction, Territory of Hawai'i.

Hawai'i (1901). *Report of the Governor of Hawaii to the Secretary of the Interior*. Honolulu: Governor of Hawai'i, Territory of Hawai'i.

Hawai'i (1902). *Report of the Governor of Hawaii to the Secretary of the Interior*. Honolulu: Governor of Hawai'i, Territory of Hawai'i.

Hawai'i (1908). *Report of the Governor of Hawaii to the Secretary of the Interior*. Honolulu: Governor of Hawai'i.

Hawai'i (1910). *Report of the Governor of Hawaii to the Secretary of the Interior*. Honolulu: Governor of Hawai'i.

Hawai'i (1912). *Report of the Governor of Hawaii to the Secretary of the Interior*. Honolulu: Governor of Hawai'i, Territory of Hawai'i.

Hawai'i (1914). *Report of the Governor of Hawaii to the Secretary of the Interior*. Honolulu: Governor of Hawai'i.

Hawai'i (1915). *Report of the Governor of Hawaii to the Secretary of the Interior*. Honolulu: Governor of Hawai'i.

Hawai'i (1916). *Report of the Governor of Hawaii to the Secretary of the Interior*. Honolulu: Governor of Hawai'i.

Hawai'i (1920). *Report of the Governor of Hawaii to the Secretary of the Interior*. Honolulu: Governor of Hawai'i, Territory of Hawai'i.

Hawai'i (1921). *Report of the Governor of Hawaii to the Secretary of the Interior*. Honolulu: Governor of Hawai'i.

Hawai'i (1922). *Report of the Governor of Hawaii to the Secretary of the Interior*. Honolulu: Governor of Hawai'i, Territory of Hawai'i.

Hawai'i (1924). *Report of the Governor of Hawaii to the Secretary of the Interior*. Honolulu: Governor of Hawai'i, Territory of Hawai'i.

Hawai'i (1928). *Annual Report of the Governor of Hawaii to the Secretary of the Interior*. Honolulu: Governor of Hawai'i, Territory of Hawai'i.

Hawai'i (1930). *Annual Report of the Governor of Hawaii to the Secretary of the Interior*. Honolulu: Governor of Hawai'i, Territory of Hawai'i.

Hawai'i (1931). *Annual Report of the Governor of Hawaii to the Secretary of the Interior*. Honolulu: Governor of Hawai'i.

Hawai'i (1932). *Annual Report of the Governor of Hawaii to the Secretary of the Interior*. Honolulu: Governor of Hawai'i, Territory of Hawai'i.

Hawai'i (1934). *Annual Report of the Governor of Hawaii to the Secretary of the Interior*. Honolulu: Governor of Hawai'i, Territory of Hawai'i.

Hawai'i (1940). *Annual Report of the Governor of Hawaii to the Secretary of the Interior*. Honolulu: Governor of Hawai'i, Territory of Hawai'i.

Hawai'i (1953). *Annual Report*. Honolulu: Department of Public Instruction, Territory of Hawai'i.

Hawai'i (1965). *Annual Report: Statistical Supplement*. Honolulu: Department of Health, State of Hawai'i.

Hawai'i (1970a). *Data Book: A Statistical Abstract*. Honolulu: Department of Planning and Economic Development, State of Hawai'i.

Hawai'i (1970b). *Statistical Report*. Honolulu: Department of Health, State of Hawai'i.

Hawai'i (1976). *Statistical Supplement*. Honolulu: Department of Health, State of Hawai'i.

Hawai'i (1977). *Data Book: A Statistical Abstract*. Honolulu: Department of Planning and Economic Development, State of Hawai'i.

Hawai'i (1978). *Statistical Supplement*. Honolulu: Department of Health, State of Hawai'i.

Hawai'i (1979). *Data Book: A Statistical Abstract*. Honolulu: Department of Planning and Economic Development, State of Hawai'i.

Hawai'i (1980a). *Legislative Report Relating to the Needs of Students with Limited English Speaking Ability in the Public Schools of Hawaii*. Honolulu: Department of Education, State of Hawai'i.

Hawai'i (1980b). *Statistical Supplement*. Honolulu: Department of Health, State of Hawai'i.

Hawai'i (1981). *Data Book: A Statistical Abstract*. Honolulu: Department of Planning and Economic Development, State of Hawai'i.

Hawai'i (1982). *Final Report: Socio-Economic and Demographic Characteristics of Offender Population*. Honolulu: Department of the Attorney General, State of Hawai'i.

Hawai'i (1983). *Data Book: A Statistical Abstract*. Honolulu: Department of Planning and Economic Development, State of Hawai'i.

Hawai'i (1985). *Statistical Supplement*. Honolulu: Department of Health, State of Hawai'i.

Hawai'i (1986a). *Data Book: A Statistical Abstract*. Honolulu: Department of Planning and Economic Development, State of Hawai'i.

Hawai'i (1986b). *Hawaiian Studies Program Guide*. Honolulu: Department of Education, State of Hawai'i.

Hawai'i (1987). *Data Book: A Statistical Abstract*. Honolulu: Department of Planning and Economic Development, State of Hawai'i.

Hawai'i (1990). *Data Book: A Statistical Abstract*. Honolulu: Department of Business and Economic Development, State of Hawai'i.

Hawai'i (1992). *State of Hawai'i Data Book: A Statistical Abstract*. Honolulu: Department of Business, Economic Development, and Tourism, State of Hawai'i.

Hawai'i (1993). *Data Book: A Statistical Abstract*. Honolulu: Department of Business, Economic Development, and Tourism, State of Hawai'i.

Hawai'i (1994). *Crime and Justice in Hawai'i*. Honolulu: Department of the Attorney General, State of Hawai'i.

Hawai'i (1995). *Crime in Hawaii, 1994*. Honolulu: Department of the Attorney General, State of Hawai'i.

Hawai'i (1998). *Native Hawaiian Data Book*. Honolulu: Office of Hawaiian Affairs, State of Hawai'i.

Hawai'i (2000). *2000 Vital Statistics*. Honolulu: Department of Health, State of Hawai'i.

Hawai'i (2005). *Data Book: A Statistical Abstract*. Honolulu: Department of Business, Economic Development, and Tourism, State of Hawai'i.

Hawai'i (2006). *Data Book: A Statistical Abstract*. Honolulu: Department of Business, Economic Development, and Tourism, State of Hawai'i.

Hawai'i (2007). *Access to Justice*. Honolulu: Department of the Judiciary, State of Hawai'i.

Hawai'i (2008a). *2008 Annual Report*. Honolulu: Department of Public Safety, State of Hawai'i.

Hawai'i (2008b). *Access to Justice*. Honolulu: Department of the Judiciary, State of Hawai'i.

Hawai'i (2008c). *Annual Report of the Superintendent.* Honolulu: Department of Education, State of Hawai'i.

Hawai'i (2008d). *Crime in Hawai'i.* Honolulu: Department of the Attorney General.

Hawai'i (2008e). *Hate Crimes in Hawai'i 2008.* Honolulu: Department of the Attorney General, State of Hawai'i.

Hawaii Association of Independent Schools (2009). *HAIS Family Guide to Private Schools.* Retrieved January 27, 2009 from *http://209.235.217.235/resources/30.pdf.*

Hawaii Catholic Herald (2009). "Back to School,", August 7.

Hawaii Medical Association (1990). *Directory of Hawaii Physicians.* Honolulu: Hawaii Medical Association.

Hawaii State Bar Association (1991). *Annual Directory.* Honolulu: Hawaii State Bar Association.

Hawaiian Sugar Planters' Association, Bureau of Labor and Statistics (1926). *Report of Montague Lord on the Filipino Contract, July 27, 1916.* Ai'ea, HI: Hawaiian Sugar Planters' Association Archives.

Heen, Walter M. (2009). "He We Go Again," *Ka Wai Ola,* 26 (October): 12.

Heilemann, John, and Mark Halperin (2010). *Game Change: Obama and the Clintons, McCain and Palin, and the Race of a Lifetime.* New York: HarperCollins.

Helm, Raiatea (2008). "Stars over Kahala." In Ron Jacobs, ed., *Obamaland: Who Is Barack Obama?,* pp. 118–119. Honolulu: Trade Publishing.

Herberg, William (1955). *Protestant, Catholic, Jew: An Essay in American Religious Sociology.* Chicago: University of Chicago Press.

Herbig, Paul A., and Hugh E. Kramer (1994). "The Potential for High Tech in Hawai'i," *Social Process in Hawaii,* 35: 56–70.

Hermann, Milton, and Lance Cassak (2003). *Good Cop, Bad Cop: Racial Profiling and Competing Views of Justice.* New York: Lang.

Higgins, Andrew, and Anne E. Kornblut (2009). "On Trip to Seal Ties with Asia, Trade Policy Threatens Rift," *Washington Post,* November 15.

Hippensteele, Susan K., and Meda Chesney-Lind (1995). "Race and Sex Discrimination in the Academy," *Thought & Action,* 11 (Fall): 43–66.

Hirata, Lucie Cheng (1971). *Immigrant Integration in a Polyethnic Society.* Honolulu: PhD dissertation, University of Hawai'i at Mānoa.

Hitch, Thomas (1992). *Islands in Transition: The Past, Present, and Future of Hawaii's Economy.* Honolulu: First Hawaiian Bank.

Hiura, Arnold, Stephen Sumida, and Martha Web, eds. (1979). *Talk Story: Big Island Anthology.* Honolulu: Bamboo Ridge Press.

Hofstadter, Richard (1955). *Social Darwinism in American Thought.* Boston: Beacon.

Home Security Guru (2009). "Home Security – Crime Data at a Glance (2008)." *http://www.homesecurityguru.com/hawaii-alarm-system.*

Hongo, Garrett, ed. (1995). *Under Western Eyes: Personal Essays from Asian America*. New York: Anchor.

Honolulu Advertiser (1957). "Segregated Kam?," December 20.

Honolulu Advertiser (1974a). "Cultural Deprivation in Schools Debated," October 30.

Honolulu Advertiser (1974b). "Pro-Ariyoshi Speech Sparks Controversy," September 21.

Honolulu Advertiser (1976). "Civil Rights Review OKd," October 22.

Honolulu Advertiser (1986). "Fasi Says Bunye 'Most Qualified' Candidate," July 24.

Honolulu Advertiser (1994a). "Assessing the Candidates," November 4.

Honolulu Advertiser (1994b). "How the Electorate Lines Up," November 6.

Honolulu Advertiser (1996). "Union Impasse: Time for Swift Arbitration, 'The State Is out of Money'," January 11 [editorial].

Honolulu Advertiser (1997). "Expert Says Pidgin Classes Support Ebonics Effort," January 5.

Honolulu Advertiser (1998). "Election: Poll Shows Lingle Gaining in Most Ethnic Groups," August 2.

Honolulu Advertiser (2008). "Hawaii Private Schools Raising Tuition Fees," February 22.

Honolulu Advertiser (2009). "Native Hawaiian Protesters End March, Burn 50th Star on U.S. Flag in Protest," August 21.

Honolulu Advertiser (2010). "Hawaii Still Leads U.S. with Highest Rate of Mixed Marriages," May 27.

Honolulu Star-Advertiser (2010a). "Aloha, Star-Bulletin," June 6.

Honolulu Star-Advertiser (2010b). "Economics at Root of 'Bias'," October 2.

Honolulu Star-Advertiser (2010c). "Local-Hire Law Needs Clarification," October 1.

Honolulu Star-Advertiser (2010d). "Obama Proclaims Friday Kamehameha Day," June 11.

Honolulu Star-Advertiser (2010e). "Settle DOE Autism Case Now," August 31.

Honolulu Star-Bulletin (1954). "7,000 New Citizens Took Oath under McCarran Act; 2nd Anniversary Today," December 23.

Honolulu Star-Bulletin (1971). "AJAs Had 45% of State Jobs in '64–67," December 22.

Honolulu Star-Bulletin (1972). *The Men and Women of Hawaii*. Honolulu: Star-Bulletin.

Honolulu Star-Bulletin (1975). "Filipinos Petition for Probe of DOE," November 19.

Honolulu Star-Bulletin (1978). "Professor Critiques Newspaper's Poll," November 3.

Honolulu Star-Bulletin (1999). "BOE Urges Isle Schools to Fight Discrimination," February 23.

Honolulu Star-Bulletin (2008a). "Obama Greets Supporters at Keehi Lagoon Park," August 8.

Honolulu Star-Bulletin (2008b). "School to Widen Its Tuition Options," May 9.

Honolulu Star-Bulletin (2010a). "'Local Jobs' Bill Might Backfire," April 21.

Honolulu Star-Bulletin (2010b). "OHA Education Grants Could Yield Useful Data," May 22.

Hoʻomanawanui, Kuʻualoha (2008). "This Land Is Your Land, This Land Was My Land." In Candace Fujikane and Jonathan Y. Okamura, eds., *Asian Settler Colonialism: From Local Governance to the Habits of Everyday Life in Hawaiʻi*, pp. 116–154. Honolulu: University of Hawaiʻi Press.

Hopkins, Jerry (1982). *The Hula*. Hong Kong: Apa.

Hormann, Bernhard (1947). "Speech, Prejudice, and the School in Hawaii," *Social Process in Hawaii*, 11: 74–80.

Hosenball, Mark, Michael Isikoff, and Evan Thomas (2010). "The Radicalization of Umar Farouk Abdulmutallab," *Newsweek*, January 11.

Howes, Craig, and Jon Osorio, eds. (2010). *The Value of Hawaii: Knowing the Past, Shaping the Future*. Honolulu: University of Hawaiʻi Press.

Huang, Yunte (2010). *Charlie Chan: The Untold Story of the Honorable Detective and His Rendezvous with American History*. New York: Norton.

Humphrey, Matt (2009). "Homosexual Slur of Notre Dame Dance Has Hawaii Football Coach Greg McMackin in Hot Water," *Orlando Sentinel*, July 30.

Husain, Laurel Bowers, and Laurie Uemoto Chang (2005). "Obama Encourages Students to 'Dream Big'," *Punahou Bulletin*, Spring issue.

Hyde, Justin (2009). "Ford Lauds Obama for Industry Rescue," *Detroit Free Press*, December 15.

Ifill, Gwen (2009). *The Breakthrough: Politics and Race in the Age of Obama*. New York: Doubleday.

Ikeda, Kiyoshi, and Linda K. Johnsrud (1991). *Preliminary Faculty Pay Equity Analysis, University of Hawaiʻi at Manoa*. Honolulu: University of Hawaiʻi at Mānoa.

Ikeda, Kiyoshi, and Linda K. Johnsrud (1993). *Faculty Pay Equity Study: Gender and Ethnicity Pay Analysis*. Honolulu: University of Hawaiʻi at Mānoa.

Ikeda, Kiyoshi, Shuk Han Pun, and Lisa Torro (1984). "The Relationship between Admission Variables and Academic Performance: A First-Year Analysis of First-Time Freshmen Registered in Fall 1983." Honolulu: University of Hawaiʻi at Mānoa, unpublished manuscript.

Infante, Esme J. (1991a). "HPD Urges Anti-Gang Program: Want Police Talks Required in Every School," *Honolulu Advertiser*, August 31.

Infante, Esme (1991b). "Farrington Opens Health Academy: School-Within-a-School Is a First for Hawaii," *Honolulu Advertiser*, September 4.

Infante, Esme (1991c). "Measuring Hawaii's Progress toward Bush's Education Goals," *Honolulu Advertiser*, October 1.

International Longshoremen's Association (1912). "Annual Meeting, Pacific District," *ILA Proceedings*, May.

Isensee, Laura (2009). "Obama Signs Legislation Tripling AmeriCorps National Service Program," *Dallas Morning News*, April 21.

Jackson, Miles, ed. (2004). "They Followed the Trade Winds: African Americans in Hawai'i," *Social Process in Hawai'i*, Vol. 43.

Jacobs, Ron, ed. (2009). *Obamaland*. Honolulu: Trade Publishing.

James, Henry (1907). *The American Scene*. London: Chapman & Hall.

Jarman, Robert (1838). *Journal of a Voyage to the South Seas, in the "Japan" Employed in the Sperm Whale Fishery, under the Command of Capt. John May*. London: Longman.

Johnston, David, and Charlie Savage (2009). "Obama Reluctant to Look into Bush Programs," *New York Times*, January 11.

Jokiel, Lucy (1988). "The New Big Five?," *Hawaii Business*, 33 (January): 19–26.

Jones, Larry (1967). "Negroes Here & Discrimination," *Star-Bulletin & Advertiser*, June 11.

Junasa, Bienvenido D. (1982). *A Study of the Relationship between Selected Variables and Levels of Academic Performance Among Filipino Full-Time Freshmen Students*. Ft. Lauderdale, FL: PhD dissertation, Nova University.

Kakesako, Gregg K. (1974). "No Place for Racism, Fasi Says," *Honolulu Star-Bulletin*, August 20.

Kakesako, Gregg K. (1977). "Ariyoshi: Limit Population," *Honolulu Star-Bulletin*, January 25.

Kallen, Horace (1915). "Democracy versus the Melting Pot," *The Nation*, 100 (February 18, 25): 190–194, 217–222.

Kallen, Horace (1924). *Culture and Democracy in the United States*. New York: Liveright.

Kamakau, Samuel M. (1976). *The Works of the People of Old*. Honolulu: Bishop Museum Special Publication # 61.

Kanae, Lisa Linn (2009). *Islands Linked by Ocean*. Honolulu: Bamboo Ridge Press.

Kanahele, George S., ed. (1979). *Hawaiian Music and Musicians: An Illustrated History*. Honolulu: University Press of Hawai'i.

Kane, Herb Kawainui (1997). *Ancient Hawai'i*. Honolulu: Kawaihui Press.

Kaplan, Eric Aubry (2010). "Race Matters," *Los Angeles Times*, August 27.

Kappeler, Victor E., et al. (1994). *Forces of Deviance: Understanding the Dark Side of Policing*. Prospect Heights, IL: Waveland.

Kaser, Tom (1975a). "Classes in Japanese on Decline," *Honolulu Advertiser*, April 28.

Kaser, Tom (1975b). "U.S. Probing Charges of Hiring Bias in Schools," *Honolulu Advertiser*, October 23.

Kaser, Tom (1990). "UH Will Seek Funds to Add Women, Minority Faculty," *Honolulu Advertiser*, October 6.

Kawaharada, Dennis (1994). "Towards an Authentic Local Literature of Hawai'i." In Lorna Hershinow, ed., *Hawai'i Literature Conference Reader's Guide*, pp. 56–60. Honolulu: Hawai'i Literary Arts Council.

Kawaharada, Dennis (1999). *Storied Landscapes: Hawaiian Literature and Place*. Honolulu: Kalamakū Press.

Keil, Paul, and Binyamin Appelbaum (2009). "After Call from Senator's Office, Small Hawaii Bank Got U.S. Aid," *Washington Post*, July 1.

Keir, Gerry (1974a). "In Demo Primary For Governor: It's Still a Tight, Three-Way Race," *Star-Bulletin & Advertiser*, September 29.

Keir, Gerry (1974b). "State Race Doesn't Look Close," *Honolulu Advertiser*, October 29.

Keir, Gerry (1974c). "A Tight Race for Governor," *Honolulu Advertiser*, September 3.

Keir, Gerry (1978a). "Fasi, Ariyoshi in Dead Heat, First Primary Survey Reveals," *Honolulu Advertiser*, August 25.

Keir, Gerry (1978b). "Fasi Surge into Strong Lead; Impact of Kohala Uncertain," *Honolulu Advertiser*, September 30.

Keir, Gerry (1982a). "Ariyoshi Has Sizable Lead; Anderson Gains over Fasi," *Honolulu Advertiser*, October 28.

Keir, Gerry (1982b). "Ariyoshi Maintains Wide Lead over King," *Honolulu Advertiser*, September 12.

Keir, Gerry (1986a). "Cec Heftel Way Ahead in Democratic Governor's Race," *Honolulu Advertiser*, August 4.

Keir, Gerry (1986b). "Governor's Race a Toss-Up with 20% Still Undecided," *Honolulu Advertiser*, October 28.

Kelly, Marion (1956). *Changes in Land Tenure in Hawai'i, 1778–1850*. Honolulu: MA thesis, University of Hawai'i.

Kelly, Patrick J., and Dennis P. Jones (2005). *A New Look at the Institutional Component of Higher Education Finance: A Guide for Evaluating Performance Relative to Financial Resources*. Boulder, CO: National Center for Higher Education Management Systems.

Kent, Noel J. (1983). *Hawaii: Islands under the Influence*. New York: Monthly Review Press.

Kent, Noel J. (1994). "The End of the American Age of Abundance: Whither Hawai'i?," *Social Process in Hawaii*, 35: 179–194.

Key, V. O. (1949). *Southern Politics in State and Nation*. New York: Knopf.

Kim, Karl (1994). "The Political Economy of Foreign Investment in Hawai'i," *Social Process in Hawaii*, 35: 40–55.

Kimura, Larry L. (1985). "Language." In *Native Hawaiian Study Commission Report: Report on the Culture, Needs and Concerns of Native Hawaiians*, vol. 1. Washington, DC: Government Printing Office.

Kingston, Maxine Hong (1976). *The Woman Warrior: Memoirs of a Girlhood among Ghosts*. New York: Knopf.

Kirch, Patrick Vinton (1985). *Feathered Gods and Fishhooks: An Introduction to Hawaiian Archaeology and Prehistory*. Honolulu: University of Hawai'i Press.

Kirkpatrick, John (1987). "Ethnic Antagonism and Innovation in Hawaii." In Jerry Boucher, Dan Landis, and Karen Arnold Clark, eds., *Ethnic Conflict: International Perspectives*, pp. 298–319. Newbury Park, CA: Sage.

Klein, Joe (2009). "The Rock Builder," *Time*, May 4.

Knowlton, Edgar (1991). "Sailor Juan Gaetano Was Probably Spanish," *Honolulu Star-Bulletin*, July 29 [letter].

Kobayashi, Ken (1993). "Fired Kauai Police Officer Harry J. Victorino Wins Bias Case: Awarded $80,700," *Honolulu Advertiser*, September 23.

Kobayashi, Ken (2008). "Racism and Prejudice Linger in Hawaii, Says Chief Justice," *Honolulu Star-Bulletin*, October 25.

Koki, Stanley (1998). *School/Community-Based Management Revisited in the Pacific*. Honolulu: Pacific Resources in Education and Learning (ERIC Document Reproduction Services ED415589).

Kornhauser, William (1959). *The Politics of Mass Society*. New York: Free Press.

Kotani, Roland (1978). *Palaka Power*. Honolulu, pamphlet.

Kotani, Roland (1985). *The Japanese in Hawaii: A Century of Struggle*. Honolulu: Hawai'i Hochi.

Kreifels, Susan (1999). "UH Faculty Approves Cuts in Core Requisites," *Honolulu Star-Bulletin*, December 9.

Kresnak, William (1990). "Political Parties Wooing Islands' Filipino Vote," *Honolulu Advertiser*, September 30.

Kresnak, William (1994). "Lewin Factor Enlivens Race for Governor," *Honolulu Advertiser*, September 11.

Kresnak, William, and Ann Botticelli (1995). "Gov. Makes First Budget Cuts: Two-Year Plan Has More Trims to Come," *Honolulu Advertiser*, February 7.

Krugman, Paul (2009). "Obama's Trust Problem," *New York Times*, August 21.

Kuroda, Yasumasa (1993). "Sociology of Paradise: Hawaii Today and Tomorrow," *Kansai University Review of Law and Politics*, 14 (March): 1–19.

Kuroda, Yasumasa (1998). "Public Opinion and Cultural Values." In Michael Haas, ed., *Multicultural Hawai'i: The Fabric of a Multiethnic Society*, Chap. 7. New York: Garland.

Kuroda, Yasumasa, and Chikio Hayashi (1995). "Rashomonesque Yamazakura." Paper presented at the Conference on Japanese Identity: Cultural Analysis, Teikyô Loretto Heights University, Denver.

Kuroda, Yasumasa, and Tatsuzô Suzuki (1991). "A Comparative Analysis of Arab Culture: Arabic, English and Japanese Languages and Values," *Behaviormetrika*, 30 (1): 35–53.

Kuykendall, Ralph S. (1938). *The Hawaiian Kingdom, 1778–1854*. Honolulu: University of Hawai'i Press.

Kuykendall, Ralph S. (1967). *The Hawaiian Kingdom: The Kalakaua Dynasty*. Honolulu: University of Hawai'i Press.

Lal, Brij, Doug Munro, and Edward Beechert, eds. (1993). *Plantation Workers: Resistance and Accommodation*. Honolulu: University of Hawai'i Press.

Landgraf, Kapulani (1994). *Nā wahi pana 'o Ko'olau Poko: Legendary Places of Ko'olau Poko*. Honolulu: University of Hawai'i Press.

Langer, Elinor (2008). "Famous Are the Flowers: Hawaiian Resistance Then— and Now," *The Nation*, April 8.

Laudan, Lawrence, et al. (1990). "Racism Does Not Belong Here," *Ka Leo o Hawai'i*, October 26.

Lelyveld, Joseph (2010). "Who Is Barack Obama?," *New York Review of Books*, May 13.

Light, Paul C. (2008). "No So Elite After All," *Washington Post*, December 12.

Lili'uokalani, Lydia (1898). *Hawaii's Story by Hawaii's Queen*. Tokyo: Tuttle, 1964.

Lind, Andrew W. (1938). *An Island Community: Ecological Succession in Hawaii*. Chicago: University of Chicago Press.

Lind, Andrew W. (1946). *Hawaii's Japanese: An Experiment in Democracy*. Princeton, NJ: Princeton University Press.

Lind, Andrew W. (1957). "Racial Bloc Voting in Hawaii," *Social Process in Hawaii*, 21: 16–19.

Lind, Andrew W. (1967). *Hawaii's People*, 3rd ed. Honolulu: University of Hawai'i Press.

Lind, Andrew W. (1969). *Hawaii: The Last of the Magic Isles*. New York: Oxford University Press.

Lind, Andrew W. (1980). *Hawaii's People*, 4th ed. Honolulu: University of Hawai'i Press.

Lind, Andrew W. (1982). "Immigration to Hawaii," *Social Process in Hawaii*, 29: 9–20.

Linmark, R. Zamora (1995). *Rolling the Rs*. New York: Distributed Art Publishers.

London, Jack (1909). "Koolau the Leper." In A. Grove Day and Carl Stroven, eds., *A Hawaiian Reader*, pp. 160–176. New York: Appleton-Century-Crofts.

Lum, Darrell H. Y. (1986). "Beer Can Hat." In Eric Chock and Darrell H. Y. Lum, eds., *The Best of Bamboo Ridge: The Hawai'i Writers' Quarterly*, pp. 175–183. Honolulu: Bamboo Ridge Press.

Lum, Darrell H. Y. (1998). "Local Genealogy: What School You Went?," In Eric Chock, James Harstad, Darrell Lum, and Bill Teter, eds., *Growing up Local: An Anthology of Poetry and Prose from Hawai'i*, pp. 11–12. Honolulu: Bamboo Ridge Press.

Lynch, Colum (2010). "China Campaigning Against International Probe of Possible War Crimes in Burma," *Washington Post*, October 25.

Lyons, Paul (2006). *American Pacifism: Oceania in the U.S. Imagination*. New York: Routledge.

MacFarquhar, Larissa (2007). "The Conciliator," *The New Yorker*, May 7.

MacMillan, Ian (2009). *Bone Hook: A Novel*. Honolulu: Mutual Publishing.

Magin, Janis L. (2006). "Hawaii Agrees to Change Policies for Incarcerated Gay Youths," *New York Times*, February 13.

Maier, John (1975). "Yucky-You-Live-Hawaii?" *Impulse* (Summer): 28–29.

Manicas, Peter T. (1997). "Deculturation, Assimilation, Accommodation and Ethnic Reconstruction: Lessons from Hawai'i." Paper presented at the Second International Conference on Globalism and Diaspora at Tsukuba University, Japan, March 10–12.

Maraniss, David (2008). "Trying to Find His Way at Punahou School," *Honolulu Advertiser*, August 31.

Martin, Jonathan (2008). "Obama's Mother Known Here as 'Uncommon'," *Seattle Times*, April 8.

Martin, Lynn J., ed. (1994). *Musics of Hawai'i; "It All Comes from the Heart": An Anthology of Musical Traditions in Hawai'i*. Honolulu: State Foundation on Culture and the Arts.

Martorana, S. V., and Ernest V. Hollis (1962). *The University of Hawaii and Higher Education in Hawaii*. Honolulu: Department of Budget and Finance, State of Hawai'i.

Marumoto, Masaji (1983). "The Ala Moana Case and the Massie-Fortescue Case, Revisited," *University of Hawaii Law Review*, 5 (Winter): 271–287.

Matsunaga, Mark (1987). "Some AJAs Fear a Dimmer Future," *Honolulu Advertiser*, February 16.

Mau, Rosalind Y. (1986). *Sources of Alienation in the Secondary School Setting of Hawaii*. Honolulu: PhD dissertation, University of Hawai'i at Mānoa.

Maugham, W. Somerset (1921). "Honolulu." In A. Grove Day and Carl Stroven, eds., *A Hawaiian Reader*, pp. 218–244. New York: Appleton-Century-Crofts, 1959.

McClelland, Edward (2010). *Young Mr. Obama: Chicago and the Making of a Black President*. New York: Bloomsbury.

McGregor, Davianna P. (1991). "Providing Redress for *Ka Po'e Hawai'i*: The Hawaiian People." Paper presented at the Spark M. Matsunaga Institute for Peace Conference on Restructuring for Peace: Challenges for the 21st Century, Honolulu, June 3.

McGregor, Davianna P. (2009). "Setting the Record Straight," *Honolulu Weekly*, May 13.

McLaughlin, Sean (1989). "Cable TV Is Hawaii's Channel to the Future," *Honolulu Star-Bulletin*, February 16.

McLellan, Scott (2008). *What Happened: Inside the Bush White House and What's Wrong with Washington.* New York: Public Affairs.

McManus, Doyle (2009). "There's More to the Job than Outsized Ambition," *Los Angeles Times,* December 27.

McManus, Doyle (2010a). "Obama's Change Came Too Late," *Los Angeles Times,* January 21.

McManus, Doyle (2010b). "Obama's Racial Allergy," *Los Angeles Times,* August 1.

McNamara, Mary (2009). "Ready or Not, He's in Prime-Time Mode," *Los Angeles Times,* March 25.

McPherson, Michael (n.d.). "A. J. W. MacKenzie & Son, 29 Miles Volcano," *Exquisite Course.*

Meacham, Jon (2009a). "Getting to Know Obama: The Sides We're Just Starting to See," *Newsweek,* May 25.

Meacham, Jon (2009b). "Let Loose the (Blue) Dogs of War," *Newsweek,* August 1.

Meacham, Jon (2009c). "Realism We Can Believe in," *Newsweek,* December 14.

Melahn, Christopher Lee (1986). *An Application of an Ecological Perspective to the Study of Educational Achievement among Native American Hawaiians.* Honolulu: PhD dissertation, University of Hawai'i at Mānoa.

Meller, Norman (1955). *Hawaii: A Study of Centralization.* Chicago: PhD dissertation, University of Chicago.

Meller, Norman (1958a). "Centralization in Hawaii: Retrospect and Prospect," *American Political Science Review,* 57 (March): 98–107.

Meller, Norman (1958b). "Missionaries to Hawaii: Shapers of the Islands' Government," *Western Political Quarterly,* 11 (December): 788–799.

Meller, Norman (1961/62). "Recent Changes in Composition of Hawaiian Legislatures," *Social Process in Hawaii,* 25: 45–52.

Mendell, David (2007). *Obama: From Promise to Power.* New York: Harper.

Meredith, Gerald (1965). "Observations on the Acculturation of Sansei Japanese-Americans in Hawaii," *Psychologia,* 8 (June): 41–49.

Michener, James A. (1959). *Hawaii.* New York: Random House.

Midkiff, Frank E. (1935). *The Economic Determinants of Education in Hawaii.* New Haven, CT: PhD dissertation, Yale University.

Mills, C. Wright (1956). *The Power Elite.* New York: Oxford University Press.

Mooney, Alexander (2009). "Obama's Inaugural Choice Sparks Outrage," *CNN.com,* December 18.

Moore, Richard A. (1969). *Lanai Management and Development Study.* Honolulu: Richard Moore Associates.

Moreno, Loren (2009a). "Hawaii Schools' Failure to Meet Benchmarks Troubles Officials," *Honolulu Advertiser,* August 3.

Moreno, Loren (2009b). "More than Half of Hawaii High School Grads Head to College," *Honolulu Advertiser,* August 26.

Moreno, Loren (2010a). "Budget Cuts Do Give Hawaii Schools More Say in Spending Funds," *Honolulu Advertiser*, May 9.

Moreno, Loren (2010b). "Hawaii Eases Limit on Number of New Charter Schools," *Honolulu Advertiser*, May 30.

Morgan, Lewis Henry (1870). *Systems of Consanguinity and Affinity*. Washington, DC: Smithsonian Institution.

Morgan, Theodore (1948). *Hawaii: A Century of Economic Change, 1778–1876*. Cambridge, MA: Harvard University Press.

Morris, Aldyth (1955). *Captain James Cook*. Honolulu: University of Hawai'i Press.

Morris, Aldyth (1980). *Damien*. Honolulu: University Press of Hawai'i.

Morris, Nomi (2010). "Analyzing Obama's Bible References," *Los Angeles Times*, August 14.

Morton, J. (2008). "Obama's Background—Impressive Royal and Presidential Connections," *jmortonmusings.blogspot.com/2008/10/obamas-background-impressive-royal-and.html*, October 25.

Morton, N. E., W. T. Stout, and C. Fischer (1976). "Academic Performance in Hawaii," *Social Biology*, 23 (Spring): 13–20.

Moyers, Bill (2009). Program on December 18, 2009, with guests Robert Kuttner and Matt Taibbi.

MSNBC (2008). "Obama Accepts Jesse Jackson's Apology," July 10, *msnbc.msn.com/id/25611808/*.

Muchnic, Suzanne (2009). "Decisive Shift in White House Art," *Los Angeles Times*, October 17.

Murayama, Milton (1975). *All I Asking for Is My Body*. San Francisco: Supa Press.

Myrdal, Gunnar (1944). *An American Dilemma: The Negro Problem and Modern Democracy*. New York: Harper.

Nakaso, Dan (2009). "Lawsuits Could Spur Sweeping Change," *Honolulu Advertiser*, November 9.

Nakata, Bob (1999). "The Struggles of the Waiāhole-Waikāne Community Association," *Social Process in Hawai'i*, 39: 60–73.

National Center for Higher Education Management Systems (1991). *University of Hawaii System Longitudinal Database Project*. Boulder, CO: National Center for Higher Education Management Systems.

National Commission on Excellence in Education. (1983). *A Nation at Risk: The Imperative for Educational Reform*. Washington, DC: U.S. Department of Education.

National Endowment for the Arts (2008). *Artists in the Workforce, 1990–2005*. Washington, DC: National Endowment for the Arts.

National Institute of Education (1978). *Violent Schools—Safe Schools: The Safe School Study Report to the Congress*, 3 vols. Washington, DC: Government Printing Office.

Nelligan, Peter J., and Harry V. Ball (1992). "Ethnic Juries in Hawaii: 1865–1900," *Social Process in Hawaii*, 34: 113–162.

Nemo (1888). "Island Notes," *Pacific Commercial Advertiser*, January 16.

New York Times (2009). "Obama's Judicial Nominations," November 16.

Newman, Katharine (1979). "Hawaiian-American Literature: The Cultivation of Mangoes," *Melus*, 6 (Summer): 44–47.

Newport, Tuck (1991). "What Makes It Tick? The Management of Punahou." In Nelson Foster, ed., *Punahou: The History and Promise of a School of the Islands*, pp. 151–167. Honolulu: Punahou School.

Nicholas, Peter (2009). "Obama's Summer Break Becomes Balancing Act," *Los Angeles Times*, August 14.

Nichols, Hans (2007). "In Hawaii, Media Surfs Obama's Past," *politico.com*, March 14.

Niesse, Mark (2008). "Hawaii and Its Multiracial Society Influenced Obama's View of the World and Politics," *Associated Press*, August 7.

Nihau, Soli Kihei (1999). "Huli: Community Struggles and Ethnic Studies," *Social Process in Hawai'i*, 39: 43–59.

Nordyke, Eleanor C. (1989). *Peopling of Hawai'i*, 2nd ed. Honolulu: University of Hawai'i Press.

O'ahu Filipino Community Council (1975). "Task Force on Education Status Report." Honolulu: Center for Research on Ethnic Relations, University of Hawai'i at Mānoa, *Document Series #9.*

O'Brien, Michael (2010). "Stimulus Has Been 'An Absolute Success,' Says VP Biden," *thehill.com*, June 2.

O'Keefe, Ed (2010). "Sen. Richard Shelby Blocking Obama Nominees," *Washington Post*, February 5.

O'Reilly, Bill (2009). "What President Obama Can Teach America's Kids," *Parade*, August 5.

Obama, Barack (1983). "Breaking the War Mentality," *Sundial*, March 10.

Obama, Barack (1995). *Dreams from My Father: A Story of Race and Inheritance*. New York: Crown.

Obama, Barack (1999). "A Life's Calling to Public Service," *Punahou Bulletin*, Fall: 28–29.

Obama, Barack (2008). *The Audacity of Hope: Thoughts on Reclaiming the American Dream*. New York: Vintage. [The original edition was published in 2006].

Obama, Barack (2009). "We Need Fathers to Step Up," *Parade*, June 21.

Obama, Barack (2010a). *Of Thee I Sing: A Letter to My Daughters*. New York: Knopf.

Obama, Barack (2010b). "To the Class of 2010," *Parade*, May 16.

Obama, Barack (2010c). "Why Haiti Matters," *Newsweek*, January 25.

Odo, Franklin, and Susan Yim (1993). "Ethnicity: Are Race Relations in Hawai'i Getting Better or Worse?," In Randall Roth, ed., *The Price of Paradise*, Ch. 31. Honolulu: Mutual Publishing.

Ogawa, Dennis M., and Evarts C. Fox, Jr. (1986). "Japanese Internment and Relocation: The Hawaii Experience." In Roger Daniels, Sandra C. Taylor, and Harry H. L. Kitano, eds., *Japanese Americans: From Relocation to Redress*, pp. 135–138. Salt Lake City: University of Utah Press.

Oi, Cynthia (2010). "Local Cuts Both Ways in Hawaii Politics," *Honolulu Star-Advertiser*, July 22.

Okamura, Jonathan (1991). "Filipino Educational Status and Achievement at the University of Hawai'i at Manoa," *Social Process in Hawaii*, 33: 107–29.

Okamura, Jonathan (1992). "Filipino Cultural Norms and Values and Higher Education," *Teaching & Learning*, 5 (Spring): 6–8.

Okamura, Jonathan Y. (1994). "Why There Are No Asian Americans in Hawai'i: The Continuing Significance of Local Identity," *Social Process in Hawaii*, 35: 161–178.

Okamura, Jonathan (1998). "The Illusion of Paradise: Privileging Multiculturalism in Hawai'i." In D. C. Gladney, ed., *Making Majorities*, pp. 264–284. Stanford, CA: Stanford University Press.

Okamura, Jonathan (2008). *Ethnicity and Inequality in Hawai'i*. Philadelphia, PA: Temple University Press.

Ong, Vickie (1980). "State's Educators 'Just Want the Feds off Our Back'," *Honolulu Advertiser*, November 29.

Oshima, Harry (1970). "Income Inequality and Economic Growth: The Postwar Experience of Asian Countries," *Malayan Economic Review*, 15 (October): 7–41.

Oshiro, Sandra (1976). "Filipinos Stand up to Be Counted," *Honolulu Advertiser*, November 1.

Pablo, Josephine Dicsen, Belen C. Ongteco, and Stan Koki (2002). *A Historical Perspective on Title VII Bilingual Education Projects in Hawaii*. Honolulu: Pacific Resources for Education and Learning.

Pace, Julie (2010). "Obama Calls Height a Champion of 'Righteous Cause'," *Denver Post*, April 30.

Pace, Julie, and Christine Simmons (2009). "White House Luau: Congressional Picnic Hawaiian Style," *Huffington Post*, July 26.

Pacific Commercial Advertiser (1919). "Territory Should Control Foreign Language Schools," March 17.

Pai, Gregory (1986). "The Evolution of the Hawaiian Economy and Its Relationship to the Social and Economic Status of Women in Hawaii." Paper presented to the Honolulu County Committee on the Status of Women, Honolulu.

Pai, Gregory (1989). "Foreign Investment in Hawaii: An Assessment of Future Prospects." Paper presented to the Honolulu Japanese Chamber of Commerce.

Pak, Gary (1992). *The Watcher of Waipuna and Other Stories*. Honolulu: Bamboo Ridge Press.

Palmer, Anthony J. (1998). "Music." In Michael Haas, ed., *Multicultural Hawai'i: The Fabric of a Multiethnic Society*, Chap. 6. New York: Garland.

Pang, Gordon Y. K. (2004). "Democrats Call Obama Hawai'i's Third Senator," *Honolulu Advertiser*, December 17.

Pang, Gordon Y. K. (2009). "Home Lands Trial Under Way: Class-Action Suit Accuses State of Not Meeting Obligations," *Honolulu Advertiser*, August 5.

Pang, Gordon Y. K. (2010). "66% of Hawaii Residents Favor Recognition for Native Hawaiians," *Honolulu Advertiser*, May 3.

Park, Robert E. (1938). "Introduction." In Andrew Lind, *An Island Community: Ecological Success in Hawaii*, pp. x–xvi. Chicago: University of Chicago Press.

Parker, Kathleen (2010a). "Obama: Our First Female President," *Washington Post*, June 30.

Parker, Kathleen (2010b). "Obama's Missing Sense of Humor," *Washington Post*, October 30.

Parsons, Christi (2009). "In Texas, Obama Honors George W. Bush for Public Service," *Los Angeles Times*, October 17.

Parsons, Christi (2010). "Obama: We Are at War with Terrorists, Not Islam," *Los Angeles Times*, September 11.

Parsons, Christi, and Peter Nicholas (2010). "Obama Talks About Faith," *Los Angeles Times*, September 29.

Parsons, Christi, and David G. Savage (2010). "Wanted: Consensus-Building Justice," *Los Angeles Times*, May 4.

Peery, Nelson (1993). *Entering an Epoch of Social Revolution*. Chicago: Workers Press.

Pennybacker, Mindy (1991). "The 'Haole Rich Kids' School': An Update." In Nelson Foster, ed., *Punahou: The History and Promise of a School of the Islands*, pp. 119–149. Honolulu: Punahou School.

Peterson's Private Secondary Schools 2005 (2004). Princeton, NJ: Thomson/ Peterson's.

Petranek, Li'ana M. (1999). "Ethnic Identity, Identity Politics and the Trouble One Will Have in Constituting an Identity," *Social Process in Hawai'i*, 39:256–274.

Petranek, Li'ana M. (2001). "Will the Task Masters of the New Economy Please Stand Up!," *Social Process in Hawai'i*, 40:1–35.

Pew Research Center (2008). "Hispanics in the 2008 Election: Hawaii." *pewhispanic.org/files/factsheets/vote2008/Hawaii.pdf*

Phoenix Marketing International (2009). *phoenixmi.com/images/uploads/pdf_upload/State%20Rankings%20Millionaires%202006%202007%20 2008%202009.pdf*.

Plant, E. Ashby, Patricia G. Devine, William T. L. Cox, Corey Columb, Saul L. Miller, Joanna Goplen, and B. Michelle Peruche. (2009). The Obama

Effect: Decreasing Implicit Prejudice and Stereotyping, *Journal of Experimental Social Psychology*, 45 (July): 961–964.

Plouffe, David (2009). *The Audacity to Win: The Inside Story and Lessons of Barack Obama's Historic Victory*. New York: Viking.

Pollan, Michael (2010). "The Food Movement, Rising," *New York Review of Books*, June 10.

Port, Richard J. (1979). "The Relationship between the Achievement of Students on the Hawaii State Test of Essential Competencies and Specific Student Background and School Related Variables." Honolulu: Department of Education, State of Hawai'i, unpublished manuscript.

Porteus, Stanley D., and Marjorie E. Babcock (1926). *Temperament and Race*. Boston: Badger.

Prashad, Vijay (2001). *Everybody Was Kung Fu Fighting: Afro-Asian Connections and the Myth of Cultural Purity*. Boston: Beacon.

Pukui, Mary Kawena, and Samuel H. Elbert (1964). *English-Hawaiian Dictionary*. Honolulu: University of Hawai'i Press.

Pukui, Mary Kawena, and Samuel H. Elbert (1965). *Hawaiian-English Dictionary*. Honolulu: University of Hawai'i Press.

Purdum, Todd (2008). "Raising Obama," *Vanity Fair*, March.

Puzzanghera, Joe (2009). "Obama Slams Plan Opponents," *Los Angeles Times*, October 10.

Quindlen, Anna (2009). "Hope Springs Eternal," *Newsweek*, November 2.

Ravitch, Diane (2010). *The Death and Life of the Great American School System: How Testing and Choice Are Undermining Education*. New York: Basic Books.

Reich, Robert B. (1991). *Work of Nations: Preparing Ourselves for 21st Century Capitalism*. New York: Knopf.

Reinecke, John E. (1935). *Language and Dialect in Hawaii*. Honolulu: MA thesis, University of Hawai'i.

Reinecke, John E. (1970). A *History of Local 5: Hotel and Restaurant Employees and Bartenders International Union, AFL-CIO, Honolulu*. Honolulu: Industrial Relations Center, University of Hawai'i at Mānoa.

Reinecke, John E. (1979). *Feigned Necessity: Hawaii's Attempt to Obtain Chinese Contract Labor, 1921–1923*. San Francisco: Chinese Materials Center.

Remnick, David (2010). *The Bridge: The Life and Rise of Barack Obama*. New York: Knopf.

Research Committee on the Study of Honolulu Residents (1986). *The Third Attitudinal Survey of Honolulu Residents, 1983*. Tokyo: Institute of Statistical Mathematics, Monograph #3 [distributed by the University Press of Hawai'i].

Research Information Services (1977). *ESAA Needs Assessment Study*. Honolulu: Research Information Services.

Reyes, Donna (1987). "Switch to English May Mean Talking Pidgin," *Honolulu Advertiser*, September 28.

Rhee, Foon (2008). "Chewing over Obama's 'Mutt' Reference," November 10, *boston.com/news/politics/politicalintelligence/2008/11/chewing_over_ob.html*.

Richter, Paul (2010). "Obama's Ratings Ebb in Muslim World," *Los Angeles Times*, June 18.

Rifkin, Jeremy (1995). *The End of Work: The Decline of the Global Labor Force and the Dawn of the Post-Market Era*. New York: Putnam.

Roberts, Helen H. (1926). *Ancient Hawaiian Music*. New York: Dover.

Roberts, Julian M. (1995a). "Pidgin Hawaiian: A Sociohistorical Study," *Journal of Pidgin and Creole Languages*, 10 (1): 1–56.

Roberts, Julian M. (1995b). "A Structural Sketch of Pidgin Hawaiian," *Amsterdam Creole Studies*, 12 (1): 97–126.

Roberts, Julian M. (1998). "The Role of Diffusion in Creole Genesis," *Language*, 74: 1–39.

Roberts, Sara E. (2000). "Nativization and Genesis of Hawaiian Creole." In John H. McWhorter, ed., *Language Change and Language Contact in Pidgins and Creoles*, pp. 257–300. Philadelphia, PA: Benjamin.

Robinson, Eugene (2007). "'The Moment for This Messenger'," *Washington Post*, March 13.

Rodriguez, Gregory (2007). *Mongrels, Bastards, Orphans, and Vagabonds: Mexican Immigration and the Future of Race in America*. New York: Random House.

Romano, Lois (2009). "Chris Lu, the Son of Chinese Immigrants, Is a Key Advisor in the Obama Administration," October 22, *diversity spectrum.com*.

Rosa, John (2000). "Local Story: The Massie Case and the Cultural Production of Local Identity in Hawai'i," *Amerasia Journal*, 26: 93–115.

Rosenblum, Victor, and A. Didrick Castberg, eds. (1973). *Cases on Constitutional Law*. Homewood, IL: Dorsey.

Ross, Edward A. (1914). *Old World in the New: The Significance of Past and Present Immigration to the American People*. New York: Century.

Rotella, Sebastian (2009). "Obama Calls Troop Decision Difficult," *Los Angeles Times*, December 14.

Roth, Randall W. (2009). "Hawaii's Schools: A Bureaucratic Maze," *Honolulu Star-Bulletin*, August 19.

Rowe, Michael (2009a). "Land of the Free, Home of Hotheads," *Los Angeles Times*, August 17.

Rowe, Michael (2009b). "The New Cuban Revolution," *Advocate*, October.

Rucker, Philip (2009a). "Hawaii's Still Waters Run Deep for the President-Elect," *Washington Post*, January 2.

Rucker, Philip (2009b). "With Obama's Rise, Hawaii School Adds to Its Distinctions," *Washington Post*, January 3.

Ruibai, Sal (2004). "Football Means Community for Hawaiians," *USA Today*, November 9.

Ryan, William (1976). *Blaming the Victim*. New York: Vintage.

Safire, William (1992). "On Language," *New York Times*, February 23.

Sahlins, Marshall D. (1958). *Social Stratification in Polynesia*. Seattle: University of Washington Press.

Saiki, Pat (1994a). "A Pacific Partnership." Honolulu: Saiki for Governor Committee.

Saiki, Pat (1994b). "Pat Saiki Plan for Reform in Hawai'i." Honolulu: Saiki for Governor Committee.

Sakoda, Kent, and Jeff Siegel (2003). *Pidgin Grammar: An Introduction to the Creole Language of Hawai'i*. Honolulu: Bess Press.

Sample, Herbert A. (2009). "Inouye's Earmarks Go to His Donors," *Honolulu Advertiser*, November 9.

Samuelson, Robert J. (2008). "Why It's Not the Economy," *Washington Post*, February 6.

Sananikone, Thanlo (1991). "Project Degree: Report on the Cambodian, Laotian, Vietnamese Students in Hawai'i." Honolulu: Office of Minority Student Affairs & Office of the Chancellor for Community Colleges, University of Hawai'i.

Santa Cruz, Nicole (2010). "Ariz. Ethnic Studies Ban OKd as Law," *Los Angeles Times*, May 12.

Savard, W. G., and C. T. Araki (1965). *The Relationship of Socioeconomic Background to Student Achievement in the Public High Schools of the State of Hawaii*. Honolulu: Department of Education, State of Hawai'i.

Schlesinger, Arthur M., Jr. (1991). *The Disuniting of America: Reflections on a Multicultural Society*. New York: Norton.

Schmitt, Robert C. (1961). "Characteristics of Voters and Non-Voters in Hawaii." Honolulu: Romanzo Adams Social Research Laboratory, University of Hawaii, *Report* #31.

Schmitt, Robert C. (1965). "Demographic Correlates of Interracial Marriage in Hawaii," *Demography*, 2: 463–473.

Schmitt, Robert C. (1977). *Historical Statistics of Hawaii*. Honolulu: University Press of Hawai'i.

Schmitt, Robert C. (1978). "Some Firsts in Island Leisure," *Hawaiian Journal of History*, 12: 99–107.

Schoenberg, Shira (2007). "Law Expert: Obama Will Preserve Constitution," *Concord Monitor*, November 14.

Schooland, Ken (2007). "How Bad is Education in Hawai'i?," *Hawaii Reporter*, November 8.

Scott, Janny (2008a). "A Free-Spirited Wanderer Who Set Obama's Path," *New York Times*, March 14.

Scott, Janny (2008b). "Obama's Mother—An Unconventional Life: Anthropologist Dislikes Ethnic Barriers," *New York Times*, March 14.

Seeto, Margot (2009). "Critical Transformations," *Honolulu Weekly*, April 22.

Segal, Dave (2009). "Central Pacific to Cut West Coast Business," *Honolulu Star-Bulletin*, December 10.

Sendak, Maurice (1963). *Where the Wild Things Are*. New York: HarperCollins, 1991.

Serrano, Richard A. (2007). "Obama's Peers Didn't See His Angst," *Los Angeles Times*, March 11.

Serrano, Richard A. (2010). "Obama Administration Accused of Racial Bias," *Los Angeles Times*, July 31.

Shapiro, Treena (2001). "UH Racial Protest Serves as Final Exam," *Honolulu Star-Bulletin*, December 11.

Shear, Michael D. (2010). "At West Point, Obama Talks of a new 'International Order'," *Washington Post*, May 22.

Shear, Michael D., and Dan Eggen (2009). "Some Obama Donors Are Being Left Out," *Washington Post*, December 4.

Shelley, Percy Bysshe (1840). "A Defense of Poetry." In, Mary Shelley, ed., *Percy Bysshe Shelley Essays, Letters from Abroad, Translations and Fragments*. London: Edward Moxon.

Sherman, Ruth G. (1984). "An Ecological Survey of the College Student Experiences, UHM." Honolulu: University of Hawai'i at Mānoa, unpublished manuscript.

Shoemaker, James H. (1946). "Hawaii Emerges from the War," *Pacific Affairs*, 19 (June): 182–192.

Silva, Mark (2009). "In Media Blitz, Obama Says Vitriol Isn't Racial," *Los Angeles Times*, September 19.

Simonson, Douglas (1981). *Pidgin to Da Max*. Honolulu: Peppovision.

Simonson, Douglas (1992). *Pidgin to Da Max: Hana Hou*. Honolulu: Bess Press.

Simonson, Douglas (2005). *Pidgin to Da Max*. Honolulu: Bess Press.

Sing, David K. (1986). *Raising the Achievement Level of Native Hawaiians in the College Classroom through the Matching of Teaching Strategies with Student Characteristics*. Claremont, CA: PhD dissertation, Claremont Graduate School.

Smith, David James (2008). "The Ascent of Barack Obama, Mr. Charisma," *Sunday Times*, March 23.

Smith, Kit (1995). "Index Shows Hawaii's Economy on Upswing," *Honolulu Advertiser*, April 19.

Sonmez, Felicia (2010). "Neil Abercrombie Wins Democratic Gubernatorial Nod in Hawaii," *Washington Post*, September 19.

Southern Poverty Law Center (2009). "Militia Movement Resurgent, Infused with Racism" *SPLC Report,* 39 (3): 1, 3.

Spear, Rev. William (1856). "The Chinese in the Sandwich Islands," *The Friend,* 13 (August 19): 58–59.

Stannard, David E. (1989). *Before the Horror: The Population of Hawai'i on the Eve of Western Contact.* Honolulu: Social Science Research Institute, University of Hawai'i at Mānoa.

Stannard, David E. (2005). *Honor Killing: How the Infamous "Massie Affair" Transformed Hawai'i.* New York: Viking.

Star-Bulletin & Advertiser (1991). "OHA: A Primer," May 12.

Stauffer, Robert H. (2001). "The University of Hawai'i, Public Policy, and the Process of Globalization," *Social Process in Hawai'i,* 40: 91–200.

Steely Dan (1974). *Pretzel Logic.* MCA record album. [The writers of the song *Barrytown* are Walter Becker and Donald Fagen.]

Steger, Manfred B. (2002). *Globalism: The New Market Ideology.* Lanham, MD.: Rowman & Littlefield.

Steinberg, Danny D., Ronald Johnson, and Robert S. Cahill (1975). "Testimony on Renaming of Porteus Hall—Before the Board of Regents on April 23, 1975." Honolulu: Center for Research on Ethnic Relations, Social Science Research Institute, University of Hawai'i at Mānoa, *Document Series #5.*

Steinhauer, Jennifer (2007). "Charisma and a Search for Self in Obama's Hawaii Childhood," *New York Times,* March 17.

Stephanopoulos, George (2010). "Transcript: George Stephanopoulos' Exclusive Interview with President Obama," *blogs.abcnews.com*

Stern, Bernard (1986). *Labor Relations in the Honolulu Transit Industry.* Honolulu: Center for Labor Education and Research, University of Hawai'i at Mānoa.

Stern, Bernard (1988). *The Aloha Trade: Labor Relations in Hawaii's Hotel Industry, 1941–1987.* Honolulu: Center for Labor Education and Research, University of Hawai'i at Mānoa.

Stevens, Sylvester K. (1945). *American Expansion in Hawaii, 1842–1898.* Harrisburg: Archives Publishing Company of Pennsylvania.

Stolberg, Sheryl Gay (2009). "White House Unbuttons Formal Dress Code," *New York Times,* January 28.

Stolberg, Sheryl Gay, and Marjorie Connelly (2009). "Obama Is Nudging Views on Race, a Survey Finds," *New York Times,* April 28.

Stueber, Ralph (1964). *Hawaii: A Case Study in Development Education, 1778–1960.* Madison: PhD dissertation, University of Wisconsin.

Sue, Newton (1991). *Review of Equal Employment Opportunity and Affirmative Action at the University of Hawaii.* Honolulu: Legislative Auditor.

Sullam, Brian (1976). *Bishop Estate: The Misused Trust.* Honolulu: Hawaii Observer.

Sumida, Stephen (1986). "Waiting for the Big Fish: Recent Research in the Asian American Literature of Hawai'i." In Eric Chock and Darrell H. Y. Lum, eds., *The Best of Bamboo Ridge: The Hawai'i Writers' Quarterly*, pp. 302–321. Honolulu: Bamboo Ridge Press.

Sumida, Stephen (1991). *And the View from the Shore*. Seattle: University of Washington Press.

Sweney, Mark (2008). "Fox News Anchor Taken off Air After Obama 'Terrorist Fist Jab' Gaffe," *Guardian*, June 13.

Takara, Kathryn (1992). "Opele: Report on African Americans at the University of Hawai'i." Honolulu: Center for Studies of Multicultural Higher Education, University of Hawai'i at Mānoa.

Takara, Kathryn Waddell (1999). "Frank Marshall Davis in Hawai'i: Outsider Journalist Looking in," *Social Process in Hawai'i*, 39: 126–144.

Takeuchi, Floyd K. (1986a). "Bunye Charges Job Discrimination in State Government's Hiring Ratio," *Honolulu Advertiser*, August 6.

Takeuchi, Floyd K. (1986b). "Bunye Remark Denounced by Cayetano," *Honolulu Advertiser*.

Talley, Tim (2007). "Obama Draws Enthusiastic Crowd in Okla.," *Associated Press*, March 19.

Tanahara, Kris M. (1993). "KIKI Radio Station's Manager Made Racist Remarks, OHA Said," *Honolulu Advertiser*, June 15.

Tangonan, Shannon (1991). "A Century of History Is Tied up in Ewa Church," *Honolulu Advertiser*, September 23.

Tani, Carlyn (2007). "A Kid Called Barry," *Punahou Bulletin*, spring issue. [She quotes from a *Chicago Tribune* article in 2004.]

Tannersley, Jim (2010). "Summit Was 'No Failure'," *Los Angeles Times*, April 2.

Tatar, Elizabeth (1993). *Hula Pahu: Hawaiian Drum Dances*, vol. 2: *The Pahu-Sounds of Power*. Honolulu: Bishop Museum Press.

Taylor, William (1935). *The Hawaiian Sugar Industry*. Berkeley: PhD dissertation, University of California.

Territorial Surveys (1950). "A Political Analysis, 1950." Honolulu: Hamilton Library, University of Hawai'i at Mānoa, Mimeo.

Thanawala, Sudhin (2008). "Sister: Obama's Success Rooted in Hawaii," *Associated Press*, February 14.

Theroux, Paul (2001). *Hotel Honolulu*. Boston: Houghton Mifflin.

Theroux, Paul (2009). "Happily a State, Forever an Island," *New York Times*, August 20.

Thompson, Edgar (1975). *Plantation Societies, Race Relations and the South: The Regimentation of Populations*. Durham, NC: Duke University Press.

Thompson, Rod (2009). "School Discrimination Probe Results in Deal," *Honolulu Star-Bulletin*, January 18.

Thistlethwaite, Susan Brooks (2009). "Obama's New 'Just War Peace' Policy," *Washington Post*, December 11.

Thomas, Evan, and Katie Connolly (2010). "Learning from LBJ: Obama Is More of a Persuader than a Fighter—But He's Still a Work in Progress," *Newsweek*, April 5.

Thrum, Thos G. (1893). *Hawaiian Almanac and Annual for 1892*. Honolulu: Press Publishing Company.

Tinker, Hugh (1974*)*. *A New System of Slavery: The Export of Indian Labour Overseas, 1830–1920*. Oxford, UK: Oxford University Press.

Tizon, Tomas Alex (2005). "Rebuilding a Hawaiian Kingdom," *Los Angeles Times*, July 21.

Todd, Art (1999). "Hatred of Caucasians Is Encouraged," *Honolulu Star-Bulletin*, May 21.

Todd, Chuck, and Sheldon Gawiser (2009). *How Barack Obama Won*. New York: Vintage.

Tonouchi, Lee A., ed. (2005). *Da Kine Dictionary: Da Hawai'i Community Pidgin Dictionary Projeck*. Honolulu: Bess Press.

Trask, Haunani-Kay (1990). "Caucasians Are Haoles," *Ka Leo o Hawai'i*, September 19.

Trask, Haunani-Kay (1992). "Racism Against Native Hawaiians at the University of Hawai'i: A Personal and Political View," *Amerasia Journal*, 18 (3): 33–50.

Trask, Haunani-Kay (1993). *From a Native Daughter: Colonialism & Sovereignty in Hawai'i*. Monroe, ME: Common Courage Press.

Trimillos, Ricardo (1987). *Na Mele Paniolo: The Songs of Hawaiian Cowboys*. Honolulu: State Foundation on Culture and the Arts.

Tsai, Michael (2009). "Hawaii's Move into Statehood Traumatic for Many Hawaiians," *Honolulu Advertiser*, August 9.

Tsai, Michael (2010). "Sad State of the Arts," *Honolulu Star-Advertiser*, August 15.

Tsai, Stephen (1992). "UH Lauded for Handling Concerns of Black Athletes," *Honolulu Advertiser*, January 18.

Turner, Frederick Jackson (1893). "The Significance of the Frontier in American History," *Proceedings of the State Historical Society of Wisconsin*. [Reprinted in Jackson, *The Frontier in American History*. Tucson: University of Arizona Press, 1896.]

United States, Bureau of the Census (1902). *Twelfth Census of the United States: 1900; Population*. Washington, DC: Government Printing Office.

United States, Bureau of the Census (1913). *Thirteenth Census of the United States, Taken in the Year 1910: Abstract of the Census with Supplement for Hawaii*. Washington, DC: Government Printing Office.

United States, Bureau of the Census (1922). *Fourteenth Census of the United States, Taken in the Year 1920; Vol. 3, Population: Composition and*

Characteristics of the Population by States. Washington, DC: Government Printing Office.

United States, Bureau of the Census (1923). *Fourteenth Census of the United States, Taken in the Year 1920;* Vol. 4, *Population: Occupations*. Washington, DC: Government Printing Office.

United States, Bureau of the Census (1932). *Fifteenth Census of the United States, Taken in the Year 1930; Population: Outlying Territories and Possessions*. Washington, DC: Government Printing Office.

United States, Bureau of the Census (1942). *16th Census of the United States, 1940; Manufactures, 1939*. Washington, DC: Government Printing Office.

United States, Bureau of the Census (1943). *16th Census of the United States, 1940; Census of Business, 1939: Alaska, Hawaii and Puerto Rico*. Washington, DC: Government Printing Office.

United States, Bureau of the Census (1952). *United States Census of Population; Detailed Characteristics: Hawaii*. Washington, DC: Government Printing Office.

United States, Bureau of the Census (1962). *Census of Population, 1960; Characteristics of the Population: Hawaii*. Washington, DC: Government Printing Office.

United States, Bureau of the Census (1972). *1970 Census of Population; Detailed Characteristics: Hawaii*. Washington, DC: Government Printing Office.

United States, Bureau of the Census (1973). *1970 Census of Population; Subject Reports: Japanese, Chinese, and Filipinos in the United States*. Washington, DC: Government Printing Office.

United States, Bureau of the Census (1983). *1980 Census of Population: Characteristics of the Population; General Social and Economic Characteristics: Hawaii*. Washington, DC: Government Printing Office.

United States, Bureau of the Census (1993). *1990 Census of Population: Social and Economic Characteristics, Hawaii*. Washington, DC: Government Printing Office.

United States, Bureau of the Census (2000). *factfinder.census.gov*.

United States, Commission on Civil Rights, Hawai'i Advisory Committee (1983). *Policy vs. Results: Affirmative Action in the Hawaii Department of Education*. Washington, DC: Government Printing Office.

United States, Commission on Civil Rights, Hawai'i Advisory Committee (1991). *A Broken Trust: The Hawaiian Homelands Program; Seventy Years of Failure of the Federal and State Governments to Protect the Civil Rights of Native Hawaiians*. Washington, DC: Government Printing Office.

United States, Congress (1946). *Statehood for Hawaii*. Washington, DC: Subcommittee on the Territories, House of Representatives.

United States, Congress (1993). *Kahoolawe Island: Restoring a Cultural Treasure; Final Report*. Washington, DC: Government Printing Office.

United States, Department of the Interior, Bureau of Education (1920). *A Survey of Education in Hawaii*. Washington, DC: Government Printing Office.

United States, Department of the Interior and Department of Justice (2000). *From Mauka to Makai: The River of Justice Must Flow Freely*. Washington, DC: Report on the Reconciliation Process between the Federal Government and Native Hawaiians, October 23.

United States, Department of Labor (1948). *The Economy of Hawaii in 1947*. Washington, DC: Government Printing Office.

University of Hawai'i (1986a*)*. "Ka'u: University of Hawai'i Hawaiian Studies Task Force Report". Honolulu: Hawaiian Studies Task Force, University of Hawai'i.

University of Hawai'i (1986b). *A Study to Improve Access to Public Higher Education Programs and Support Services for Minority Students: Report to the 1987 Legislature*. Honolulu: University of Hawai'i.

University of Hawai'i (1987–1995). "Graduation and Persistence Rates, University of Hawai'i at Mānoa, Fall 1987–Fall 1995 Cohorts." Honolulu: University of Hawai'i.

University of Hawai'i (1988). "Pamantasan: Report of the University of Hawai'i Task Force on Filipinos." Honolulu: Task Force on Filipinos, University of Hawai'i.

University of Hawai'i (1996–2008). "Fall Enrollment Report." Honolulu: Office of Institutional Research, University of Hawai'i, annually.

University of Hawai'i (2002–2004). "Faculty and Staff Report." Honolulu: University of Hawai'i, annually.

University of Hawai'i (2005). "Romanzo Adams Social Research Laboratory." Honolulu: University of Hawai'i at Mānoa, Library, Archives & Manuscripts Department, unpublished manuscript.

University of Hawai'i (2009a). "Graduation and Retention Rates, Peer and Benchmark Peer Comparisons, University of Hawai'i at Mānoa, Fall 1990–Fall 2006 Cohorts as of 2007." Honolulu: Institutional Research Office, University of Hawai'i at Mānoa.

University of Hawai'i (2009b). "Hawai'i Forecast Update: State Budget Crisis Threatens Recovery," *UHERO Quarterly* [University of Hawai'i, Economic Research Organization], June 12.

Verploegen, Hildegaard (1974). "Students Will Discuss Violence," *Honolulu Star-Bulletin*, October 12.

Verploegen, Hildegaard (1976). "2.5 Million DOE Fund in Jeopardy," *Honolulu Star-Bulletin*, June 25.

Verploegen, Hildegaard (1986). "Low Scores of Hawaiians, Part-Hawaiians Analyzed," *Honolulu Star-Bulletin*, August 27.

Verploegen, Hildegaard (1988). "Critical Study No Surprise to Toguchi: A Survey Pinpointed Some Old Problems," *Honolulu Star-Bulletin*, December 21.

Verploegen, Hildegaard (1989a). "Study: Muscle Needed in Curbing School Violence; A Task Force Says Very Little Has Been Done in 13 Years to Correct the Problems," *Honolulu Star-Bulletin*, September 8.

Verploegen, Hildegaard (1989b). "10 Schools on Waianae Coast to Get Extra Aid: Toguchi Says the Troubled Schools Should Get an Extra $4.2 Million," *Honolulu Star-Bulletin*, May 19.

Viotti, Vicki (1989). "ACLU Asked to Sue State over Quality of Education Offered on Waianae Coast," *Honolulu Advertiser*, February 15.

Vorsino, Mary (2004). "UH Settles Suit Alleging Med School Racial Bias," *Honolulu Star-Bulletin*, May 22.

Vorsino, Mary (2009). "92% in Hawaii Give to Charity Even in Toughest of Times," *Honolulu Advertiser*, November 15.

Vorsino, Mary (2010a). "Hawaii Gets $75 Million in 'Race to the Top' Money," *Honolulu Star-Advertiser*, August 24.

Vorsino, Mary (2010b). "Hawaii Rents, Already Least Affordable in Nation, Get Worse," *Honolulu Advertiser*, April 22.

Vorsino, Mary (2010c). "On Oahu, Crime up," *Honolulu Star-Advertiser*, June 20.

Vorsino, Mary (2010d). "Teacher Dropouts," *Honolulu Star-Advertiser*, September 7.

Vorsino, Mary (2010e). "University of Hawaii's Troubled Manoa Campus Makes Progress," *Honolulu Advertiser*, March 12.

Wallsten, Peter, and Mike Dorning (2009). "President Cheers a 'Teachable Moment'," *Los Angeles Times*, July 31.

Walsh, Bryan (2009). "How Green Is He?," *Time*, June 1.

Walsh, Kenneth T. (2008). "Becoming Barack Obama," *U.S. News & World Report*, May 31.

Walsh, Kenneth T. (2009). "Blazing a New Trail: Obama's Ambitious Proposals Are Redefining the Role of Government," *U.S. News & World Report*, Special Issue, June.

Washington Post (2009). "Obama on Wilson: 'We All Make Mistakes'," September 10.

Washington Post (2010). "Head Count: Tracking Obama's Appointments," April 30.

Watanabe, J., (2001), "Kokua Line," *Honolulu Star-Bulletin*, October 10.

Watanabe, Teresa (2010). "Embracing a Mixed-Race Experience," *Los Angeles Times*, June 16.

Weber, Michael (2004). *Murder in Paradise*. New York: A&E Home Video.

Wegner, Eldon L. (1976). "A Comparison of School Climates and Student Outcomes in Four Public High Schools in Hawaii." Honolulu: Hawai'i Department of Education, unpublished report.

Wegner, Eldon L. (1977). "Misinterpreting the Policy Implications of Social Science Research and Suggestions for a New Direction: The Case of School

Effects." Honolulu: Center for Research on Ethnic Relations, University of Hawai'i at Mānoa, *Working Paper #8*.

Wegner, Eldon L. (1978). "A New Look at Research on School Environments," *integratededucation*, 16 (March-April): 36–39.

Wegner, Eldon Lowell, Gary Kazuo Sakihara, and David Takeo Takeuchi (1976). *The Social Climates of Public High Schools in Hawaii: An Exploration of the Needs and Dissatisfactions of High School Seniors*. Honolulu: Legislative Reference Bureau.

Weisberg, Jacob (2010). "Alone in a Crowd," *Newsweek*, January 22.

Werner, Emmy E., Jessie M. Bierman, and Fern E. French (1971). *The Children of Kauai*. Honolulu: University Press of Hawai'i.

Werner, Emmy E., and Ruth S. Smith (1977). *Kauai's Children Come of Age*. Honolulu: University Press of Hawai'i.

Western Association of Schools and Colleges (1991). *Visiting Team Report*. Oakland, CA: Western Association of Schools and Colleges.

White, Jeremy B. (2009). "GOP Has Big Mauna to Climb in Hawaii," *rolecall. com*, July 7.

Wilcox, Leslie (1974). "Mink Says DOE Lost Millions," *Honolulu Star-Bulletin*, April 9.

Wiles, Greg (2010). "Hawaii Chosen as Manufacturing Site for Electric Mini-Cars," *Honolulu Advertiser*, May 7.

Will.i.am (2008). "Why I Recorded *Yes We Can*," *Huffington Post*, February 3.

Williams, Carole J. (2010). "Political Logjam on Federal Judges," *Los Angeles Times*, August 31.

Wilson, John K. (2008). *Barack Obama: The Improbable Quest*. Boulder, CO: Paradigm.

Wilson, Scott (2009a). "Obama Lists Financial R as 'Most Important Thing' of His First Year," *Washington Post*, December 25.

Wilson, Scott (2009b). "Obama Says Public Schools Must Improve," *Washington Post*, March 11.

Wist, Benjamin O. (1940). *A Century of Public Education in Hawaii*. Honolulu: Hawai'i Educational Review.

Witeck, John (1995). "Working Poor in Hawai'i: The Myth of Hawai'i's Anti-Business Climate and Largesse to Workers." Paper presented to the Ethnic Studies Community Conference, Honolulu, May 20–21.

Wittermans-Pino, Elizabeth (1964). *Inter-Ethnic Relations in a Plural Society*. Groningen, Netherlands: Walters.

Wolffe, Richard (2009). *Renegade: The Making of a President*. New York: Crown.

Wong, Norma (1975). "The Educated Hawaiian." Honolulu: Center for Research on Ethnic Relations, Social Science Research Institute, University of Hawai'i at Mānoa, *Working Paper #4*.

Woo, Douglas (1976). "School Bias Review Sought," *Honolulu Advertiser*, October 21.

Wright, Theon (1966). *Rape in Paradise*. New York: Hawthorn.

Yamamoto, Eric K. (1979). "The Significance of 'Local'," *Social Process in Hawaii*, 27: 38–51.

Yamanaka, Lois-Ann (1993). *Saturday Night at the Pahala Theater*. Honolulu: Bamboo Ridge Press.

Yamanaka, Lois-Ann (1996). *Wild Meat and the Bully Burgers*. New York: Farrar Straus Giroux.

Yaukey, John (2009). "Obama Backs Native Hawaiian Self-Governance Bill," *Honolulu Advertiser*, August 7.

Yoshino, Ryozo, et al. (2002). *A Study of Statistical Science on Acculturation: Hawai'i Resident Survey, 1999–2000*. Tokyo: Ministry of Education, Culture, Sports, Science and Technology, Institute of Statistical Mathematics. [Grant-in-Aid for Scientific Research A2, No.11691111, March.]

Young, Kanalu (2004). "An Interdisciplinary Study of the Word 'Hawaiian'," *Hawaiian Journal of Law and Politics*, 1 (Summer): 23–45.

Yount, David (1996). *Who Runs the University? The Politics of Higher Education in Hawaii, 1985–1992*. Honolulu: University of Hawai'i Press.

Yuen, Mike (1993). "Poll: Saiki Favorite in Governor's Race," *Honolulu Star-Bulletin*, November 4.

Yuen, Mike (1994a). "Saiki's Ahead; Cayetano, Fasi Tangled Second," *Honolulu Star-Bulletin*, June 7.

Yuen, Mike (1994b). "Poll: Cayetano Edges by Saiki, Fasi Is Far Back," *Honolulu Star-Bulletin*, October 8.

Zakaria, Fareed (2009). "Obama, The Anti-Churchill," *Washington Post*, December 7.

Zangwill, Israel (1909). *The Melting Pot: Drama in Four Acts*. New York: Macmillan.

Zeleny, Jeff (2008). "Obama's Zen State, Well, It's Hawaiian," *New York Times*, December 25.

Abbreviations

AFL	American Federation of Labor
AFSCME	American Federation of State, County, and Municipal Employees
BGLT	bisexual, gay, lesbian, and transgendered
BP	British Petroleum
BOE	Hawai'i Board of Education
CIO	Congress of Industrial Organizations
DHHL	Department of Hawaiian Home Lands
DOE	Hawai'i Department of Education
DOH	Hawai'i Department of Health
EEO	equal employment opportunity
EIS	environmental impact statement
ESEA	Elementary and Secondary Education Act
ESS	English Standard School
GPA	grade point average
GSP	gross state product
HCE	Hawai'i Creole English

HERE	Hotel Employees and Restaurant Employees Union
HEW	U.S. Department of Health, Education, and Welfare
HGEA	Hawai'i Government Employees Association
HIFF	Hawai'i International Film Festival
HLAC	Hawai'i Literary Arts Council
HLIP	Hawaiian Language Immersion Program
HOPE	Hawai'i's Opportunity for Probation with Enforcement
HSPA	Hawaiian Sugar Planters' Association
HSTA	Hawai'i State Teacher's Association
ILA	International Longshoremen's Association
ILU	International Longshoremen's Union
ILWU	International Longshore and Warehouse Union
MCH	Media Council Hawai'i
NBC	National Broadcasting Company
NLRB	National Labor Relations Board
NTE	National Teacher Examination
OCR	Office for Civil Rights
OFCC	O'ahu Filipino Community Council
OHA	Office of Hawaiian Affairs
SAT	Scholastic Aptitude Test
SCBM	School/Community-Based Management
SEALs	U.S. Navy's Sea, Air, and Land Teams
SEED	UHM Student Equity, Excellence, and Diversity Office
SHAPS	School of Hawaiian, Asian, and Pacific Studies
SpCt	Supreme Court of the United States
TARP	Troubled Assets Relief Program
UH	University of Hawai'i
UHM	University of Hawai'i at Mānoa

UHPA	University of Hawai'i Professional Assembly
UPW	United Public Workers of Hawai'i
U.S.	United States
USDOL	US Department of Labor
VVV	Varsity Victory Volunteers

About the Editor and Contributors

MICHAEL HAAS (PhD, Stanford) was professor of political science at the University of Hawai'i at Mānoa from 1964 to 1998. After retiring to Los Angeles to become president of the Political Film Society (www.polfilms.com), he has most recently written *International Human Rights: A Comprehensive Introduction* (2008) and *George W. Bush, War Criminal? The Bush Administration's Liability for 269 War Crimes* (2009). A recent Nobel Peace Prize nominee, he is currently a member of the adjunct faculty at California Polytechnic University, Pomona, and a delegate to the California Senior Legislature.

IBRAHIM AOUDÉ, (PhD, University of Hawai'i), a native of Lebanon, chairs the Department of Ethnic Studies at the University of Hawai'i at Mānoa. The author of numerous articles on Hawai'i's political economy and Middle East politics, he has edited *Arab Studies Quarterly*. Among his recent publications are *The Political Economy of Hawai'i* (1994), *The Ethnic Studies Story: Politics and Social Movements in Hawai'i* (1999), and *Public Policy and Globalization in Hawai'i* (2001).

EDWARD D. BEECHERT (PhD, University of California at Berkeley) is Professor Emeritus of History, University of Hawai'i at Mānoa. A labor historian, he has written extensively on organized labor, particularly in the Pacific, and his publications include *Honolulu: Crossroads of the Pacific* (1991) and *Working in Hawai'i: A Labor History* (1985).

DAN BOYLAN (PhD, University of Hawai'i) is emeritus professor of history, University of Hawai'i West O'ahu. He has written and published extensively on political subjects in Hawai'i over more than two decades. In addition to writing a weekly column for *MidWeek*, he coauthored *John A. Burns: The Man and His Times* (2000).

NINA K. BUCHANAN (PhD, Purdue University) is a founder of the first chartered high school in Hawai'i. Now retired from University of Hawai'i at Hilo, she continues to serve as codirector of the UH Charter School Resource Center and is a consulting editor for the *Journal of School Choice* and contributing editor for *Roeper Review*.

A. DIDRICK CASTBERG (PhD, Northwestern University) is professor emeritus of political science, University of Hawai'i at Hilo. He is the author or coauthor of *The Ethnic Factor in Criminal Sentencing* (1966), *Cases on Constitutional Law* (1973), *Japanese Criminal Justice* (1990), and coauthored the script of *Murder in Paradise* (2003).

HELEN GERACIMOS CHAPIN (PhD, Ohio State University) has retired as vice president and dean of Hawai'i Pacific University in Honolulu. She is the author of *Shaping History: The Role of the Newspapers in Hawai'i* (1996), which analyzes the ethnic and Native Hawaiian newspapers as well as the English-language press of Hawai'i. A descendent of Greeks who settled in Hilo, she was named into the Hall of Fame of the Society of Professional Journalists in 2002.

ROBERT A. FOX (PhD, New York University) recently retired as professor and chairman of the Department of Physics and Astronomy at the University of Hawai'i at Hilo, where he continues as co-director of the UH Charter School Resource Center and is deputy director of the Pacific International Space Center for Exploration Systems. A consulting editor for the *Journal of School Choice*, his recent publications focusing on international comparative education systems and the role of religion in public education have been published in American, Colombian, and Irish journals.

YASUMASA KURODA (PhD, University of Oregon) is emeritus professor of political science, University of Hawai'i at Mānoa. Currently a resident of Yokohama, he has written extensively on the comparative politics and international relations of Japan and the Middle East. He has coauthored four monographs and a dozen articles in such journals as *Ethnicity* and *Behaviormetrika* on attitudes of Honolulu voters based on a longitudinal sample survey conducted at five-year intervals from 1971 through 2000.

LĀPAKI is a pseudonym.

RODNEY MORALES is an associate professor in the Department of English, University of Hawai'i at Manoa. He is the editor of *Ho'i Ho'i Hou: A Tribute to George Helm and Kimo Mitchell* (1984), and the author of a collection of short stories entitled *The Speed of Darkness* (1988).

ANTHONY J. PALMER (PhD, University of California at Los Angeles) retired from the University of Hawai'i at Mānoa in 1998 and in 2009 from Boston University, where he remains a visiting scholar at the School of Music. He led the Waltham (Massachusetts) Philharmonic Orchestra from 1999 to 2001 and continues to write about music education, compose music, and add to his extensive list of publications, much of which can be found at orpheusmusicpress.com.

Index

Note: Page numbers followed by *t* denote tables.